Local Government Law

Local Government Law

Keith Davies MA, LLM, JP

of Grays Inn, Barrister
Reader in Law at Reading University

London
Butterworths
1983

England	Butterworth & Co (Publishers) Ltd 88 Kingsway, London WC2B 6AB
Australia	Butterworths Pty Ltd 271–273 Lane Cove Road, North Ryde, NSW 2113 Also at Melbourne, Brisbane, Adelaide and Perth
Canada	Butterworth & Co (Canada) Ltd 2265 Midland Avenue, Scarborough, Ont M1P 4S1
	Butterworth & Co (Western Canada) Ltd 409 Granville Street, Ste 856, Vancouver, BC V6C 1T2
New Zealand	Butterworths of New Zealand Ltd 33–35 Cumberland Place, Wellington
Singapore	Butterworth & Co (Asia) Pte Ltd Crawford Post Office Box 770 Singapore 9119
South Africa	Butterworth Publishers (Pty) Ltd Box No 792 Durban
United States of America	Mason Publishing Company Finch Building, 366 Wacouta Street, St Paul, Minn 55101
	Butterworth (Legal Publishers) Inc 15014 N.E. 40th, Suite 205, Redmond, Washington 98052
	Butterworth (Legal Publishers) Inc 381 Elliot Street, Newton, Upper Falls, Mass 02164

© Butterworth & Co (Publishers) Ltd 1983

Davies, Keith
  Local government law.
  1. Local government—England
  I. Title
344. 202'9   KD4759

ISBN Hardcover 0 406 25266 1
       Softcover 0 406 25267 X

*Front cover photograph: County Hall, London. Reproduced by kind permission
of the Greater London Council Photograph Library.*

Typeset by Phoenix Photosetting, Chatham
Printed by Mackays of Chatham Ltd

Preface

Local Government is something of a Cinderella among legal matters, lying as it does on the boundaries of administrative law, constitutional law, property law and planning law, yet it has human interest as well as topicality. The opportunity has been taken with this book to make something of a fresh approach to the subject, to put it in its historical setting, while at the same time reconsidering the main divisions and sub-divisions into which its details fall and the most appropriate standpoint from which to view them.

Teaching a subject and writing about it constantly provide fresh insights; and discussions with colleagues and students extend these still further, for which I express my appreciation here. In particular I should like to mention Victor Moore and Colin Crawford whose article, 'Local Government: a 2p Rate—in the Interests of the Community' appeared in the New Law Journal of 4 March 1983, and relates to s 137 of the Local Government Act 1972 discussed on p 159 of this book. My thanks are especially due to Miss Alison Cameron, in the Law Department office at Reading University, for typing the ravelled text of my manuscript, and to all my friends who have advised and helped in the project.

University of Reading   KD
February 1983

'We love independent "local authorities" . . .
The degree of local freedom desirable in a country
varies according to many circumstances, and a
Parliamentary government may consist with any
degree of it.'

WALTER BAGEHOT *The English Constitution*
(1872) Chapter V

Contents

Chapter 5. Liability of local authorities in private law   101

Chapter 6. Legal initiatives by local authorities   133

Table of statutes

References in this Table to *Statutes* are to Halsbury's Statutes of England (Third Edition) showing the volume and page at which the annotated text of the Act will be found.

List of cases

Introduction

Local government is a topic which suffers from a 'parish pump' image. It lacks heroic grandeur. The people engaged in it tend to be regarded as prosaic functionaries or pocket grandees—chairmen and clerks, or mayors and bell-ringers. In literature and on the stage various Shakespearean and Dickensian characters spring to mind, such as Dogberry and Mr Bumble, or the small-town worthies in Gogol's 'Government Inspector'. Even a Lord Mayor seems inseparable from show business: processions and turtle soup and declaring the new town hall well and truly open.

Local government law shares this 'Clochemerle' image, so not surprisingly its importance is underestimated. But local government is emphatically government: the exercise of public power. The power is exercised locally because all government must operate in localities. A state cannot consist of a capital city alone, unless perhaps it is a city-state with no ambitions, like San Marino. Central government therefore presupposes local government, and the only question is whether the localities are allowed any measure of autonomy. Whether they are or not, the authority vested in them is not their own. Therefore what gives local government law its importance is the fact that it is part of public and constitutional law in the country as a whole. In England and Wales it is a matter of statutes and statutory instruments, of case law and precedent, not merely of local byelaws and regulations. The status of local government bodies has to be considered by lawyers in the familiar context of the ultra vires doctrine, of constitutional principles, and of the answerability of public and private persons in the courts.

On the whole the general public probably takes more interest in the functional side of local government than the constitutional side. The state of the schools, the roads and the drains is always a source of concern, as are the powers of the police, the planners and the social services. These are local government questions because the national government has made them so. The national government gives, and it also takes away. In the present century planning control has been given, and public utilities and hospitals have been taken away. This book cannot deal with functions in detail, because the bulk of that detail is so great that it would quickly expand one small book into several large volumes. Indeed the various local government functions deserve—and have to some extent received—separate books to themselves, dealing both with their practice and with their law. To place the main emphasis on the functions here would distort a work intended to deal with local government law concisely and comprehensively.

This book, therefore, is meant for a general introduction to local government law, and nothing more. The main emphasis is placed on the principles which are central to this subject—the basic constitutional and legal rules which govern the general question of how people deal with local authorities and how the authorities deal with them. To omit functions would make the book altogether too rarified, because local authorities today exist chiefly to perform those functions. Therefore local government functions are included, but treated panoramically in the final three chapters, and are not allowed to get in the way of the main purpose which is to concentrate on the general principles. Even that discussion has to be limited to an examination in outline. It gives the reader the essential background, together with some signposts to the substance of the law which he can follow up in such detail as his own requirements dictate.

Chapter 1

Evolution of local government in England and Wales

A. Central and local power

1. THE STATE

The concept of local government is a paradox. It presupposes a central authority to which it is to some extent subordinate but from which it is to some extent free and independent. This in turn suggests an equilibrium between dependence and autonomy; but if so there must be an ever-present danger of upsetting that equilibrium by any shift either way. Can any system of local government worthy of the name be compatible with stability?

Many modern and not-so-modern states have taken no chances. Local administration often tends to be not much more than central government's local offices. The French monarchy developed its power by sapping the independence of local authorities; and although the Revolution briefly reversed this process it was soon restored again in a new and modernised form developed resolutely by Napoleon and retained by his successors down to the present day. President Mitterand and his colleagues have re-introduced a policy of decentralisation to offset the long tradition of centralisation in French government.

Some states have resisted centralism by adopting federal constitutions, such as the United States, Canada, Australia and West Germany. Switzerland has a still looser constitutional system, in which separate cantons have come together as a Confederation. But in all these countries the logic of authority has tended to exalt the central power over the local or provincial powers: the central government must ultimately be in control or else it is not a central government and 'the state' will have no international reality. The centripetal forces must prevail if the state is to survive, and the classic illustration of this process is the American Civil War. The problem exists in Canada where the separatist movement in Quebec gives cause for concern to the central government. Separatism took Bangladesh away from Pakistan. Historically more striking still is the mediaeval Holy Roman Empire of the German Nation (so-called, though 'neither Holy nor Roman nor an Empire' in Voltaire's view[1]) in which the central imperial authority steadily lost

1 *Essai sur les moeurs et l'esprit des nations* lxx.

ground from the thirteenth to the nineteenth century and a medley of large and small component states asserted their own independence, some on a federate basis such as Switzerland and the 'United Provinces' of the Netherlands, some on a unitary basis such as Austria and Prussia. The vestigial Holy Roman Empire itself faded away (it ended in 1806) and was replaced by Austro-Hungarian and Prusso-German Empires. In and between them various centripetal and centrifugal tendencies pulled violently against one another with devastating results for modern world history.

At first sight, all this may seem a far cry from English and Welsh local government. Yet the basic problem is the same though the scale is smaller and more domestic. The United Kingdom is emphatically not a federal state but a unitary one, like France and Spain, at any rate in principle. But the absence of a written, British constitution in comprehensive form has made it possible in practice to modify the workings of this principle by introducing a greater element of local self-government than is usual in unitary states. Local self-government is quite distinct from local administration. The latter is merely that part of central administration—a subordinate part—which is situated in localities in order to make the central administration itself more effective. In most organisations branch offices exist solely to further the purposes of their head office.

But if the grip of a central authority weakens, and still more if that authority is willing to allow subordinate local organisations to control their own destiny to some extent, then local administration may develop as a result into local self-government, if what George Borrow calls 'the genuine spirit of localism'[2] is in existence and ready to take advantage of this opportunity. It then becomes a matter of great interest whether an equilibrium is achieved between central and local power-centres which is stable enough to survive, or whether centrifugal forces prevail (as in the Holy Roman Empire) so as to allow the local powers to seize full independence, or whether centripetal forces prevail so as to re-establish full central control. A federal constitution represents an attempt to preserve an equilibrium by casting it in durable form; but this has not been done in the United Kingdom—which, however, may be said to have a quasi-federal character to the extent that Scotland, Northern Ireland and Wales have their separate entities preserved to varying degrees (not to mention the Channel Islands and the Isle of Man). But even a federal state can only survive if in fact the central power succeeds in establishing an ultimate dominance. In the last resort that central power must prevail over the local powers in a crisis, as the American Civil War clearly shows. A federal state which survives is, at bottom, a unitary state; and one which, at bottom, is not a unitary

2 *The Bible in Spain* ch 31.

state does not survive. That is true for any period in history, and is becoming more obviously true with the increasing speed and sophistication of modern communications and modern life, for communications are the lifeblood of government and all society.

It is in the light of these considerations that English and Welsh local government is best understood, both in its present state and in the historical process which led to its present state. In the last 150 years there has been much elaboration of local government; but it is elaboration chiefly of increased obligations, not increased freedom. The central government has called the tune. In the current economic climate it is inclined to call the tune more insistently than before, allegedly because of fears that freedom to raise and spend money may cause local authorities to intensify the dangers of inflation to the national economy. In these circumstances few people are inclined to speak out on behalf of local government autonomy, and those few tend to be in local government anyway and suspected of partiality.

In spite of all this, local democracy has come into its own in modern times, and seems unlikely to be reduced. It may be that the forms of local self-government can be more readily conceded if the substance is restricted; or it may be that public opinion puts more faith in popular election for keeping local government on a tight rein than in non-elective methods of appointing local authorities. If both central and local government are answerable to the voters generally it is perhaps an intelligible view that, at bottom, those voters feel safer if the latter is under strict subordination to the former; but they wish to have the reality of control offset as far as is prudent (but no further) by forms of freedom. The British are politically sophisticated enough to know the value of balance and flexibility; and a counterpoise of form to substance has the advantage, for a subtle and undemonstrative nation, of being not only unobtrusive but adjustable as well. Those who wish to make sense of modern local government will find it easiest to do so bearing that in mind.

2. GOVERNMENT AND LAW

It is also necessary to remember that government and law are inseparable, whatever political entity they are in. Government is vulnerable to dissensions within as well as aggressions without and must enforce some workable system of settling those dissensions in an orderly manner by reference to some intelligible rules, complex or simple. Dissensions over the workings of government itself are not exempt from this, whether central or local. Local government, therefore, is bedded in local government law. The counterpoise of form and substance needs to be viewed in legal terms. Since form is a matter of appearance and substance is a matter of reality it is important to be alert to such differences as may exist between what appears on the surface of the law and what prevails under the service. In the most recent century and a half of English and Welsh local government, the surface appearance of the law shows increasing democracy and increasing activity; but behind that surface central government control can be detected developing its elaborate ramifications. In the century and a half before that the balance had swung the other way round. The Webbs, in their historical survey of English local government,[3] expressed this point vigorously, after describing the law relating to county administration in the period from the Revolution of 1688–89 to the reform legislation of the 1830s. They put the matter as follows:

> 'The foregoing survey of the legal framework of county government might lead the student who confined his reading to statutes and law books to conclusions involving the non-existence of anything that could properly be called local administration. He might infer, first, that the whole internal government of England and Wales was, in 1689, so strictly centralised as to leave no place for local autonomy; and, secondly, that it consisted, not in decisions as to policy and discretional acts, but in a series of judicial awards and sentences as to the obligations of persons, and bodies of persons, according to the law of the land. When, however, we leave the legal constitution, and seek to discover what actually happened in the country, we find ourselves driven to a diametrically opposite conclusion. In spite of all forms and appearances, the Rulers of the English County felt themselves at liberty to administer the local affairs as they thought fit.'[4]

Once this point has been taken it becomes easier to follow the main outlines of the history of English and Welsh local government down to the present day and to appreciate the interplay of legal questions and policy questions, of appearance and reality, of form and substance, of subordination and autonomy, of continuity and innovation. To some extent it is a history of a process of development, but with many cross-currents and much complexity, illogicality and sheer confusion. These elements are more intelligible in the light of the curious balancing process which has been at work in England down the centuries between the countervailing tendencies of central control and local self-assertion.

---

3 S. and B. Webb *The Parish and the County* (repub Frank Cass & Co, 1963).
4 *S. and B. Webb* p 309. See also p 306: 'In the eye of the law the county was not, . . . any more than the parish, an organisation of local self-government. Like the parish, but on a higher plane, it was a unit of obligation.'

B. Evolution of the shires

I. GOVERNMENT DISTINGUISHED FROM SETTLEMENT

It is important not to confound settlement with government. Towns, villages, hamlets and isolated farms are all varying forms of settlement. Depending on the density of settlement and the extent of open land between settlements, whether cultivated or not, it makes sense to differentiate between town and country, or urban and rural land. But government is something separate from all this, imposed on these settlements from above. It shows itself materially in additions to existing settlements or even in wholly new and independent settlements: palaces, castles, public works, government buildings of all kinds. 'God made the country and man made the town', according to the poet Cowper;[5] but if so it was essentially man the settler rather than man the ruler who 'made the town'. Units of government, central or local, are on the other hand the work of man the ruler, who imposes them upon pre-existing settlements and then gives physical expressions to that governmental activity by putting up buildings such as the Tower of London or Westminster Hall or the Mansion House in places convenient for the display and exercise of rule over the community. If a unit of government corresponds with a unit of settlement, well and good, but they are no less distinct for that.

Thus in England the word 'borough' has for centuries meant a town as a legal entity; but it was never applied to all towns, merely to those which had received a charter of incorporation. What is more, the area of a 'borough' did not necessarily coincide with the area of the town itself. In his essay 'Township and Borough', F. W. Maitland[6] quoted the Report of the Royal Commission on Municipal Corporations which made its investigations in 1833 and published them two years later. He said:

> 'You will read that "the local limits of the Borough of Derby contain 1,660 statute acres", that the limits of Northampton comprise 1,520 acres and include "a considerable quantity of agricultural land", that "the Borough of Bedford includes the whole town [that is, the whole house-covered area] which lies nearly in its centre encircled by a broad belt of land; its area being 2,164 statute acres", and, to take one last example, that "the ancient borough" of Nottingham covered no less than 9,610 acres and "included a considerable quantity of forest, meadow and common land without the walls of the town'[7]

5 'The Task', I. 749.
6 *Selected Historical Essays of F. W. Maitland* et H. M. Cam (pub Beacon Press and CUP, 1962.
7 *Selected Historical Essays of F. W. Maitland*, p 8.

Thus a 'town' in its material aspect is a concentration of buildings, but a 'borough' is a legal and governmental entity expressed to exist within boundaries which may be chosen in any location to suit the governmental body which created it. The 'borough' of Nottingham in 1833 comprised a territory nearly 15 square miles in extent, that is to say the best part of an area measuring four miles square, and it may well have been ten times the size of the actual town of Nottingham.

2. THE PATTERN OF AREAS

It becomes obvious from this fact that the borough as a territorial entity existed in a larger pattern of territorial units divided up like a jigsaw puzzle. It is obvious also that this pattern existed, and had been created, primarily for the purposes of government. We are brought back once again to the fundamental realities of central and local authorities. Each local authority exists in respect of a territorial area, but it does not make sense in isolation. Instead it can only presuppose a group of such areas; and in turn the existence of the group presupposes a whole general area, under central or sovereign control, of which they are simply the parts. In addition it becomes apparent that the boundaries between sovereign territories or 'states' represent the current balance of power between respective sovereignties; whereas the boundaries between local authority areas are imposed on them from above by the sovereign power which creates and maintains them. Where subordinate authorities manage to encroach on one another's territories, as in early feudal France or in Germany under the Holy Roman Empire, this is a sign that those subordinate authorities are well on the way to making themselves sovereign states in their own right and casting off the pre-existing sovereign authority above them. Local government bodies cannot do that.

Thus the extent to which the pattern of local governmental areas corresponds to the realities of settlement in the form of towns or cities is largely fortuitous, even illusory. Their effective boundaries are actually dictated by the requirements of the sovereign power over them. A brief historical survey of English local government will show this well enough.

If central authority is both logically and practically prior to local authority, it is reasonable to conclude that larger local units are in turn prior to smaller (or sub-) units. Not surprisingly, therefore, the larger units in England are older and more enduring that the smaller ones, not only in their general pattern but to a striking extent in detail as well. These are the 'counties' or 'shires', which are traceable back in history from today to Anglo- Saxon times a thousand years ago. 'County' is the French 'comté', the area ruled by a 'count' (French 'comte'), the King's powerful subordinate. The term was introduced from France in

1066 by the Normans and applied to the equivalent English area, 'shire' or '*scir*', ruled by the English King's powerful subordinate the 'earl'. Earl and count are interchangeable terms, the earl's lady to this day being called 'countess'. The count's deputy is the vice-count or 'viscount' (French 'vicomte').

This remains a term of rank in England; but the equivalent English term is 'shire-reeve' (Anglo-Saxon '*scir-gerefa*') which became and remained a word not of rank but of office, the 'sheriff', and survived the French incursions of the Norman period as an indispensable English term. What is significant is that the sheriff is not a 'deputy Earl' in name, even though he may have been at first so intended in function, but is as the word suggests an appointee of the King chosen to control of the shire independently of the earl—a King's man, not an Earl's man. Later the King found it necessary in turn to appoint other rulers of each shire independently of the sheriff, to solve the problem that a man strong enough to be effective may be too strong to be safely trusted.

No shire makes sense on its own: it has always been a unit in a system. The shires were the main sub-divisions of the Kingdom. Some—Sussex, Kent, Essex—originated as small independent Kingdoms of the earliest phase of English history in the fifth and sixth centuries. Middlesex and Surrey were parts of another; Norfolk and Suffolk were the two sub-divisions of the East Anglian Kingdom. Hampshire, Berkshire, Wiltshire, Dorset, Somerset, Devon and Cornwall were the main divisions of the Kingdom of Wessex, and so became the earliest actual 'shires'. The word '*scir*' meant an area of authority or control, and these early West Saxon 'shires' began as military commands each ruled by a King's general known as an 'ealdorman' (or 'senior man'). This word became our modern 'alderman', itself a striking illustration of the interrelation of central and local government down the years. In its original significance of ruler of the shire it was superseded by 'earl', which is of Danish rather than strictly English origin.

In the Midlands the pattern of shires was imposed artificially after 900 when English Kings re-established control over land conquered by the Danes. Shires from Derby to Bedford and Lincoln represented separate territories originally ruled by Danish armies based on the towns from which each area took its name; and shires from Stafford to Hertford and Gloucester represented equivalent units set up in territory remaining under English rule. From Cheshire northwards the shire units were fewer, larger, and in fact indeterminate until later centuries had brought about a slow pacification of the wilder regions of the country. But subject to that, the Anglo-Saxon shires had been set in what is largely today's pattern, or at least the pattern until the reorganisation of 1972–74. In course of time anomalies grew up. A de facto division developed in both Suffolk and Sussex, between east and west. Yorkshire and Lincolnshire were each divided into three 'Ridings' (ie 'thirdings'). The 'soke' or separate district of Peterborough led a semi-detached existence linked to Northamptonshire. The relative sizes of shires was accidental rather than rational, and the same is true of relative populousness and wealth. Nevertheless the system of shires has proved to be very durable, and this is because of its usefulness, down the centuries, to the central government.

3. SHIRES AND ROYAL AUTHORITY

That usefulness, however, changed gradually but radically. At first it consisted of the basic requirements of every sovereign state: control and revenue, military and economic survival. The rulers of each shire were answerable directly to the King for the army and taxes. Defence against external enemies was linked to maintenance of order internally. This in turn required administration of law—the settlement of disputes in accordance with workable and acceptable rules. The proper apportionment of revenue and taxation burdens was from the first a part of this system of law and administration, and conversely the imposition of legal penalties in money form became a sizeable part of the public revenue: the 'profits of justice'. The sheriff was supremely responsible for all these matters within his shire. The subordinates he used were his choice, though for the use of resources he was fully answerable. Gradually, however, the King took to imposing separate officials on the shires for particular purposes—judges for legal work, also 'coroners' and specialised financial officers—and this had the effect of producing a gradual distinction between the regular or general government of each shire, under the sheriff, and the intervention of newer officials answering the more specialised up-to-the-minute requirements of central government. The sheriff's government began to take on the appearance of local as against central government.

This state of affairs has nothing to do with local democracy or self-determination. Certainly there existed always a strong tendency towards self-determination; but it took the form of resistance to royal government. It was private self-aggrandisement, often outright rebellion, which had to be suppressed, not encouraged. Yet there was a paradox in this. The only way to make sure of keeping effective governmental control was to impose a regular official procedure. This was achieved by summoning local assemblies, for the sake not of constitutional propriety but of orderliness and efficiency. The leading men of a locality were by this means brought under scrutiny at regular intervals and made to comply collectively with the King's requirements as to the raising and apportionment of taxation, the punishment of crime, the settlement of disputes and the implementation of the sovereign will in other respects. Regular attendance was required from the generality of prominent men in the shire. What was done involved them collectively, and all their dependents and other inhabitants, whether present or not; but the attendance of those men was a duty.

This was how the general business of government was carried out, apart from what was done in the presence of the King or other great men on his behalf. It was regular and static, while the activities of the King and other great men were ever-changing and peripatetic as they went on progress or on campaign. It was local and, from the King's point of view, decentralised; though to the men who had to come from all corners of a shire to meet in an agreed spot it was the opposite of that. Where the King chose to keep his main treasury or to hold his main ceremonies (such as his coronation) also came to be fixed—Winchester under the West Saxons, then Westminster—and gave rise to the practice of having a set place for the enduring functions of central government, that is to say a capital city. But an established routine in the shires was as important for the King as an established routine at Westminster. The great men of the Kingdom would be required at the proper times to attend the King on the move or at his capital, while the great men in each shire would be required at the proper times to attend the King's sheriff.

The regularity of this two-part system established the routine pattern of English government centrally and locally: but all of it was the King's government. By the Laws in Wales Act 1535 the Tudor Henry VIII extended its blessings to his Welsh compatriots.

4. SHIRE MOOTS AND HUNDRED MOOTS

The assemblies in the shires were incidentally, perhaps, deliberative bodies; but first and foremost they were business meetings, all-purpose administrative occasions. Justice was one aspect of administration and not something separate from it. Indeed, down to less than a century ago—the Local Government Act 1888—county government in its latter-day form of Quarter Sessions united both judicial and non-judicial activities in the hands of the same people, the county magistrates. The Anglo-Saxon word for an assembly was a 'moot'—ie a meeting. The Norman-French word was 'court', which in its official or institutional sense is more or less restricted today to law-courts. In this sense there is a continuity between a 'shire moot', a medieval county court and a modern county court, in spite of radical changes in recent times. But 'court' is the equivalent of the Latin 'curia'; and the Curia Regis or King's Court was the generic grouping of the King and his closest adherents or 'courtiers'. 'Court' in a wider meaning of 'governing group' survived long, and in Tudor times it was much in vogue as a word meaning 'government department', as with the Court of Wards and other bodies concerned in royal administration. 'Court' in the physical sense of an open space with buildings round about it is readily associated in everyone's minds with palaces, castles and other public buildings where rulers would find it convenient to assemble and review their adherents en masse, and to speak to them, or for that matter listen to them. The court or moot of the shire is a localised version of all this, just as the modern law-court is the specialised judicial version.

The 'business' or administrative function of the 'moot' presided over by the King's officer in the shire is the germ of modern local government. Its extended development began early. Already by the tenth century the pattern of shires was further elaborated by the introduction of sub-divisions of shires. These were known as 'hundreds' in most of England but alternatively as 'wapentakes' in certain northern and eastern shires where Danish settlers predominated. A 'moot' was held in each 'hundred', at which the leading men of the area were required to attend, and the sheriff appointed a deputy to preside at each. Business in the 'hundred moots' was much the same as in 'shire moots', and the latter were not appeal tribunals in relation to the former. Nevertheless 'shire moots' (or 'county courts') were of more direct importance to the Kingdom because they concerned larger units of government. It was in them that new forms of high-level judicial procedure were introduced when royal judges from the King's Courts of common law came round on circuit to preside over what later became known as 'Assizes' and try the more serious and important cases both civil and criminal. It was in them, between the visits of the judges, that the sheriff disposed of lesser civil cases, and in them that he also controlled the procedure, from the thirteenth century onwards, for electing 'knights of the shire' to sit in the House of Commons.

The hundred courts, being more numerous and less significant, dwindled slowly to the status of local police courts, and were often known as 'courts leet' after transfer to the control of local landowners. Neither shire nor hundred courts were ever officially abolished, in general terms, though various particular hundred courts were terminated by name in the Courts Act 1971. Some hundreds now survive as 'petty sessional' division areas for magistrates' courts; all survive in theory as sub-areas of shires. The pattern of shires and hundreds is an ancient two-tier scheme which has now been superseded in practical terms by a more modern two-tier scheme of counties and districts. It is a striking testimony to continuity in England that the Anglo-Saxon 'hundred' and the up-to- date 'district' are much the same kind of area in terms of system and size, while the national pattern of shires or counties has in general terms not been changed, even though now much changed in detail, since the tenth century.

C. Evolution of the boroughs

1. SEPARATE GOVERNMENT

Shires and hundreds are arbitrary divisions and sub-divisions of the area of the Kingdom as a whole. Each hundred (or district) presupposes the shire, and each shire presupposes the entirety of the Kingdom. The material existence of settlements, large and small, is strictly irrelevant to shires and hundreds since they are areas of control and not types of settlement. Nevertheless each shire and hundred, as an area, was made up of settlements; and in medieval theory each settlement (or 'vill') large or small, was regarded as the centre of a territorial area. There was thus a pattern of 'vills' in each hundred, forming a rough-and-ready third tier in the general system of territorial divisions. They did not have an official 'moot'; though unofficial assemblies must have existed because a collective requirement was at one time placed on all 'vills' that they send representatives to the shire court on certain occasions. Because these assemblies were not official they will not have had any judicial functions, whereas the shire and hundred moots were charged by the King with the duty of dealing with legal matters as well as administrative business.

The inhabitants of each 'vill' or settlement were the people on whom the weight of government ultimately rested: they were the passive subjects of authority, at any rate in theory. But some 'vills' had a strategic significance not possessed by ordinary village settlements. This was partly military, partly economic. Trading towns and cities interested the King's government for the wealth concentrated in them; and fortified settlements (including many walled towns and cities) were essential focal points in the general defence of the Kingdom. As always the attention of the ruler concentrates on power and revenue. Settlements of these kinds were of special importance; and special importance leads to special status.

The Anglo-Saxon word for a fortified stronghold is a *burh*, or in later English: 'borough'. A trading centre of any importance (leaving aside places whose special economic significance depended on the intermittent holding of markets or fairs) must in olden times have been fortified for continuous protection against being plundered, and was virtually by definition a stronghold or *burh* for that reason. Anglo-Saxon London was *Lunden-burh*. But many *burhs* were merely military strong-points without being trading centres, at least in origin. Alfred the Great set in being a policy of national defence against the Danes which involved the systematic creation of *burhs* across southern England: some of these were existing towns or cities, but some were merely defensible places located at or near villages. Yet many *burhs* of the latter sort thrived economically because of the physical security their fortifications offered, such as Oxford and Wallingford. In this way a great many 'boroughs' developed as focal points of the Kingdom in a way which combined wealth and power so as to give them a special value in the eyes of the central government.

The result of this was that by the mid tenth century many 'boroughs'—presumably all those important enough to be part of the national defence scheme referred to above—were required to hold a regular 'borough moot', quite separate from the moots of the shire and hundred in which they were located but of comparable importance. To a notable extent, commented on by Maitland,[8] there is a correlation between important boroughs and shires, so that for many shires there is one borough of special significance—the 'county town' in modern terms—though this is not a universal rule. The special significance is that in terms of ownership the properties in these boroughs seem to have been chiefly distributed among a number of the leading landowners of the shire (including the Church, and the King himself), so that they all shared in responsibility for its upkeep as a stronghold, but that the occupying tenants tended to be largely merchants and traders—though many cultivated adjoining agricultural land as well, or at least drew revenue from it. These 'boroughs' were thus deliberately integrated into the defence and control of their shire as a whole, yet also comprised a community of 'burgesses' whose wealth and power were largely commercial. They were governmental as well as economic entities, and as such stood more or less on an equality with the 'hundreds' in the same shire.

2. SELF GOVERNMENT

From the late twelfth century a new development set in, which was particularly momentous for English local government. Boroughs began to move up from parity with (and independence of) the 'hundreds' in their shire to parity with (and independence of) the shire itself. This was a long and complex process, and it went to differing lengths as far as individual boroughs were concerned. The greatest of them, London, went almost so far as to swallow up its own shire, Middlesex, partly because of its own size and wealth and partly because of the smallness of the shire. The essential factor in all these cases was the freeing of the particular borough from subjection to the sheriff. Clearly no-one could grant this freedom but the King himself. What he did was to issue a charter granting rights to the community of the borough—not just as a group of individuals but as a corporate entity, in attitude and eventually in law, over and above those individuals. The most important practical step at this stage was to allow the borough to account financially to the King's exchequer directly and not through the sheriff; but conceptually the evolution of corporate status is what matters today.

It is necessary to appreciate these two factors justly to understand modern local government in its essence. The first factor made the second possible, but the second factor is the crucial one. The first, the separate treatment of leading boroughs by the King, would have

8 *Domesday Book and Beyond* (pub Collins, Fontana Library, 1960) pp 214, 229.

resulted on its own merely in elevating them to the status of counties alongside the original shires or 'counties at large'; but they would still have been local units of royal government and no more. The second, incorporation, gave them independent legal personality. Shires and hundreds lacked this: all they had was collective liability. This tended to operate in practice as a lever of administrative control applied financially.(local funds would be burdened by penalties, payable to the Crown, on failing to carry out duties such as repairing roads and bridges, or catching criminals). Chartered boroughs, having corporate personality, could pursue policies of benefit to themselves as natural persons can, and with more public effect given their corporate resources. They could buy and sell property, make contracts, sue and be sued, set up trusts; and they could apply these powers in pursuit of public policies for improving their towns, not least by procuring private Acts of Parliament in later days to augment their powers still further. Groups of individual persons could of course always act collectively as partners and co-owners; but corporate personality rises above individual personality and can endure indefinitely. A precedent for it in England existed in the corporate status of the Church, but extending corporate status into the secular sphere of town government was a notable innovation.

3. CONSTITUTIONAL GOVERNMENT

The other aspect of incorporation, equally important for modern local government, can be conveniently termed 'constitutional'. Only by a regular and intelligible constitution can a corporation as a separate legal entity be clearly distinguished from the individual persons involved in it. But the effect of having a constitution is that a measure of self-government is provided as distinct from mere submission to superior authority. Not that every constitution is democratic, but it is capable of becoming so. Shire government was not self-government, still less was it democratic, because it did not comprise corporate bodies and their constitutions. Democratic self-government was only introduced into the counties in 1888 by Parliament as a transplant from the system developed in the boroughs.

This process of local self-government evolution in the towns which achieved corporate status as chartered boroughs was gradual. In King John's time London and a few other towns obtained charters empowering them to elect a leader of their own, commonly named a 'mayor'. The citizens usually took it upon themselves to elect subordinate officials as well, and to hold regular meetings, though these tended often to be oligarchic bodies restricted to leading—ie wealthy—citizens. Thus the City of London acquired a two-tier system of a Court of Aldermen and a Common Council. Some boroughs evolved a system of having their governing council elected or retained a system of meetings at which all freemen could be present; but others evolved exclusive self-perpetuating oligarchies filled by co-option. The old borough 'moots' were left with judicial functions and became 'courts' in the modern sense of tribunals.[9]

Throughout this long period of borough evolution the central government always had the power to take away the rights which had been achieved. In the latter part of Charles II's reign there actually occurred a wholesale revocation of charters, including that of London, and their substitution by charters with greatly watered-down privileges;[10] but the old privileges were restored at the Revolution shortly afterwards. From then on the arbitrary revocation of charters was impossible. But under the common law any assertion of alleged corporate authority could still be challenged and restrained as ultra vires if shown in legal proceedings not to be within the scope of rights lawfully granted by charter; and the Crown in Parliament could legislate to put an end to any such lawful rights. Thus since 1689 constitutional government may have been firmly established in the Kingdom as a whole and also in various chartered boroughs; but the subjection of local to central authority remained unchanged, and this is so today and likely to remain so.

Constitutional government of the Kingdom after 1689 safeguarded (in practice) constitutional government in the chartered boroughs, but did not extend it to the counties. No doubt this was because it seemed that control of the central government by Parliament was effective enough to exclude arbitrary rule at all levels. The government of the counties was now substantially in the hands of the justices of the peace in Quarter Sessions, and this had already been the case for two or three hundred years. It was subject to the retention of the office of sheriff, for purposes of enforcing court judgments and other matters, and the existence (since 1550 in the reign of Edward VI) of the office of lord-lieutenant, who took over the sheriff's military functions as head of the county militia.[11] Lords-lieutenant, sheriffs and magistrates were, however, a largely homogenous group of the leading nobility and gentry in each shire—'the county' in fact—receiving occasional reinforcements from well-to-do yeomen landowners and merchants. This meant that county government was, de facto, collective in nature and to some extent constitutional (or at any rate oligarchical) for that very reason. But all these appointments were in the hands of the Crown, except for the office of sheriff of Middlesex which had, since the twelfth century, been vested in two elective sheriffs of the City of London.

---

9 See Pollock and Maitland *History of English Law* (repub CUP, 1968), Vol I, pp 658–9.
10 D. Ogg *England in the Reign of Charles II* (pub OUP 1972 paperback) pp 634–9.
11 Statute 3 and 4 Edw 6, c 1.

D. Emergence of the modern forms of local government

I. STATUS AND FUNCTIONS DISTINGUISHED

The pattern of local authorities so far described did not change substantially down to the nineteenth century. To understand the changes that then occurred it is important to bear in mind two things in particular. One of these is the distinction between status and function in regard to local authorities. The other is the differentiation between central government functions and local government functions.

As to distinguishing between status and function, the former relates to what an authority is and the latter to what it does. Nowadays function is generally regarded as more important. Local authorities are empowered by a host of statutes to administer highways, housing, environmental health, education, planning control, social welfare and many other things. The public is greatly concerned about what local councils do, even though there may be misgivings about how and when they do them. Status is of less public interest except perhaps for the political complexion of an authority. It is of obvious interest to local councillors and others involved in the workings of local government, because it is to do with the constitution of local authorities: their membership, procedure, resources and control. Nor must the traditional glamour of local ceremonial be forgotten.

The modern emphasis on function in local government dates from the nineteenth century, starting with the cholera epidemics of the 1830s. These caused the central government to fear that unless sanitation problems in the large towns produced by the industrial revolution were to be solved it would be impossible to avoid worse outbreaks. After a series of official investigations and reports, Lord John Russell's government succeeded in passing the Public Health Act 1848, which imposed duties on certain local authorities with regard to drainage and sanitation, water-supply and the control of nuisances affecting health and safety. These local authorities were existing borough councils and, in other areas, a pattern of newly-created district boards of health. In addition a General Board of Health was set up to supervise nationally the exercise of these functions locally. This central body was unpopular, and in 1854 it was abolished. After various expedients an effective new government department was set up by Gladstone's first government in 1871, the Local Government Board; its ultimate successor is the present Department of the Environment. This system of administration, in which public health functions were imposed on local bodies subject to central government supervision, brought about the desired result of preventing further large-scale outbreaks of disease. Its success led to the devising of new administrative functions, notably in regard to education, housing and planning, which were imposed on local authorities in a similar manner, and the modernisation of old ones, notably in regard to highways and police.

The mention of older functions of local government is a reminder that the performance of functions by local authorities is not a new activity but an old activity greatly extended. Police, poor relief and the upkeep of highways were local administrative duties from early times. Borough corporations often undertook other functions such as paving and lighting streets and the regulation of markets, and sometimes took a hand in the provision of education although on the whole this, like the maintenance of hospitals and almshouses, was more usually handled by private charitable bodies. Charity, however, is essentially a matter of carrying out activities for the public benefit; so it is probably fair to say that in part at least the extension of functional activity by local councils represents a transfer of such activity to them from charitable bodies. Indeed for various purposes local authorities are, in legal terms, charitable bodies themselves and have been so for centuries.

2. CENTRAL AND LOCAL FUNCTIONS

As to the differentiation between central and local bodies, it must always be remembered that what local authorities are and do is decided for them in principle—and largely in detail as well—by the central government. Functions such as the collection of taxes are carried out directly by central government agencies, however much these may be subdivided into local areas and branches. Functions entrusted to local authorities are none the less supervised by central government departments; and when the need arises those departments can intervene in local administration by giving instructions or even taking direct charge over what is being done. Yet public opinion counts for much, and where possible it is thought best, in Westminster and Whitehall, to satisfy what is seen as a general public desire to leave administration in local hands and subject to local control of policy. This public desire may on the surface appear to be waning a little; and certainly a determination to keep detailed administration in local hands is less fiercely displayed than it was in the eighteenth and nineteenth centuries. Even so it is still likely that in many matters the role of the central power will continue to be restricted to co-ordination, guidance and supervision on the whole, because this is 'English-style' government.

Local authorities are subject to supervision by the modern Department of the Environment more than by any other part of central government because it has been given the function of general control over local government, as befits the successor to the Ministry of Housing and Local Government (1951–70), The Ministry of Local Government and Planning (1951) and the Local Government Board (1871–1919). But most central departments of state are liable at some point or other to be connected with the activities of local councils, and the relevant functions of the latter will then be subject to supervision accordingly. The Home Office; the Ministry of Agriculture, Fisheries and Food; the Department of Education and Science; the Department of Transport; the Department of Trade and Industry; and the Department of Health and Social Security; all are examples of this.

E. Modes of central government supervision

I. PARLIAMENTARY SOVEREIGNTY

In fact government in England is one and indivisible. The emergence of large central departments of state with separate functions is comparatively recent. Early division of labour came about for the better management of the King's business rather than the service of the governed; and it must be remembered that ministers were the King's servants rather than public administrators until recent times. Admirals and generals commanded his fighting forces; the Exchequer and the Treasury specialised in managing and applying his revenues; judges dealt with the settlement of pleas; Secretaries of State handled his correspondence (especially with foreign powers); the Lord Chancellor supervised internal administration generally. The King's Privy Council embodied his ministers collectively advising him and supervising the work of government either under his direction or on his behalf.

After the Revolution of 1688–89 had subjected the King to Parliamentary control, his leading ministers began to develop as a group of colleagues rather than as subordinates, subject to the authority of the Prime Minister. The King's lesser servants came to be organised departmentally on a wider scale than before, following the pattern of the financial and legal departments which had been developed earlier. In 1782 the two Secretaries of State underwent a transformation of function into Home Secretary and Foreign Secretary respectively; whereupon the Home Office developed a systematic supervisory role over the King's servants at local level. But in spite of this, and of the evolution of a now collective Ministerial responsibility in the Cabinet, the older collective responsibility of the Privy Council persisted, so that modern administrative and judicial functions were developed under the control of Boards and Committees of the Council, such as the Judicial Committee, the Board of Trade, the Board of Education, and also the Local Government Board referred to above. The functional evolution of central government finally emerged into the twentieth century when these and other Boards and assorted Commissioners were converted into ministries in and after the 1914–18 war. The more recent conversion of several ministers into Secretaries of State (of the Environment and so forth) in 1970 does not mark a return to the days before 1914 but a regrouping of the modern bureaucracy.

Local administration comprised the King's servants also, whether sheriffs, lords-lieutenant, or justices of the peace. Even the elected corporations of the boroughs fitted into this pattern. Before 1689 local dignitaries were largely subject to direction and guidance from the Privy Council; but thereafter Parliamentary sovereignty established itself in such a way that the justices of the peace—in whose hands the greater part of local administration had been concentrated—became largely autonomous, despite the fact that they never ceased to be appointed by the Crown. The truth of the matter is that the leading inhabitants of each county were, collectively, the nobility and gentry—ie the landowning class generally who predominated in Parliament. They served the King nationally in Parliament and locally as magistrates in Quarter Sessions. Although placed under the authority of the ministers of the Crown they were at the same time the social equals of those ministers and in turn controlled them in Parliament, where no minister could remain long in office in defiance of majority opinion. Government was at one and the same time unified and decentralised.

2. PREROGATIVE AND COMMON LAW

The one form of effective central control over local administration between the Revolution of 1688–89 and the Reform era of the nineteenth century was judicial. This may seem odd at first sight. But judicial and administrative functions were not separated to any great extent in early times and are not totally separated even today. The doctrine of 'Separation of Powers' (legislative, executive and judicial) can only be fully applied in the abstract. The very word 'court' in early times was an undifferentiated term indicating an assembly of persons summoned by command of the King or some great lord to meet in the 'court' of a palace or castle or other centre of authority. In Henry VIII's reign the new central governmental organisations set up by Thomas Cromwell (the true originator of modern state administration in England) were given names such as the 'Court of Wards', the 'Court of Surveyors', the 'Court of Augmentations'. Parliament itself is the 'High Court of Parliament'. Persons in authority took administrative action or gave legal judgments according to circumstances.

But the overriding governmental need to maintain order carried with it the need to satisfy public opinion by ensuring the just settlement of disputes; and so a sizeable proportion of the King's officials found themselves specialising in this kind of activity, either as 'justices' or judges in the Royal Courts of Common Law or as local 'justices' of the peace. The former were full-time professional specialists in the King's service nationally; the latter were unpaid local landowners. The former served on the King's Council, presided over the King's Courts in West-minster Hall, and administered justice periodically 'on circuit' in the courts of the shires. Their prestige and authority were very great: they stood close to the King in the view of the public. Nevertheless they developed the procedural and substantive principles of the common law independently of Royal intervention on the whole, subject to lapses into subordination from time to time—spectacularly in some instances under the Stuart Kings, which was a factor in the troubles leading to the Civil War and ultimately to the Revolution. The establishment of parliamentary sovereignty after 1689 would not have been effective if it had not carried with it the principal of full independence for the judiciary.

Thus political unity carried with it judicial unity; and it became general practice to give effect to a great deal of administration under legal procedures. Even taxation was administered by the Exchequer in legal forms, and the Court of Exchequer was one of the three central courts of common law, along with King's Bench and Common Pleas. The circuit system carried this down to the shire courts; and the organisation of justices of the peace similarly rested upon a basis of judicial procedure. It is true that the justices in Quarter Sessions were appointed to try criminal cases, and therefore had to act judicially in any case; but they were given administrative tasks as well, and dealt with these largely under judicial forms of procedure in the same quarterly assemblies. This was less irrational than might appear, because fact-finding processes which are a prerequisite of sound judicial decisions are a prerequisite of sound administrative decisions also. Therefore it seemed natural to treat decision-making in much the same way. Administration came to depend on the hearing of factual testimony and argument. The criminal procedure of 'presentment' was used in administrative matters; and just as an individual might be 'presented' to Quarter Sessions on an accusation of theft a parish might be 'presented' for failure to repair a highway. The County Rates Act 1739 ordered that Quarter Sessions must not authorise expenditure of county funds on bridges or gaols without the Grand Jury's presentment. Thus the equivalent procedure to the modern committal for trial by jury, which is a purely criminal proceeding (the Grand Jury has been abolished), was used then as the official mode of *proposing* administrative action. The equivalent procedure to the modern decision as to sentence after a criminal conviction in such a trial was used then in a corresponding way as the official mode of *approving* such administrative action. As a general rule, however, in administrative matters individual magistrates could make 'presentments' which were the equivalent of 'presentment' to and by the Grand Jury. Either way the proceedings could be expected to involve examination and cross-examination of witnesses, legal argument by counsel, and the verdict of a jury.

Administrative control under judicial forms at local level was supplemented by supervision from central authority which was also carried out under judicial forms. This is the more important in that central judicial control continues to exist. As will be seen later, it is the form of control which enforces the observance of the proper limits of legality. Today a strictly administrative supervision exists alongside it of a kind that was very little in evidence between the Revolution of 1688-89 and the Reform era of the nineteenth century.

Until 1688 the King in Council had exercised constant and detailed supervision over the administration carried out by the magistrates; and the King's courts of law did the same in terms of jurisdiction. Then as now persons exercising authority, in their official capacity whether individual ('corporations sole'—eg bishops, parsons, even the King himself) or collective ('corporations aggregate'—for example chartered boroughs and companies) were required to keep within the limits of their jurisdiction. The same was true of judicial tribunals, such as the magistrates—functioning in groups by virtue of the Commissions under which they were (and are) appointed, though not 'corporations aggregate' in the proper sense of that term—and coroners. But in any case executive and judicial functions were not rigidly separated in practice. 'Jurisdiction' was (and is) a term signifying the extent of official capacity however it might be analysed in terms of executive or judicial duty.

3. 'INFERIOR JURISDICTIONS'

Below the King's Courts of Chancery and Common Law, all 'jurisdictions' were 'inferior'. The Courts of Chancery and Common Law, being invested with 'superior jurisdiction', were both empowered and required to control the exercise of official functions in 'inferior jurisdictions'. After 1688-89 the King's Council left the field to them; and this meant that in substance the supervision of local by central government was restricted to supervision by the central courts of law. It was all a matter of 'jurisdiction', whether judicial or administrative. The theory of this system of supervision was that the Crown would institute proceedings, as it does in criminal cases: the defendant was not, however, being proceeded against in a personal capacity, as accused persons are, but in an official capacity. Whereas criminal proceedings normally involved presentment and indictment at Quarter Sessions or Assizes in each county, the proceedings for supervision took the form of a writ from the Court of King's Bench ordering that the subordinate authority or court submit its proceedings for review on the issue of legality—ie compliance with the law. In both cases the issue would lie as a matter of form between the Crown on one hand and the accused or the authority challenged on the other; but the true substantial issue would lie between the prosecutor and the accused, or between the complainant or applicant and the authority challenged. This remains true today.

Thus supervision of local government occurred by the central government acting judicially in the form of the Court of King's Bench. The Court would be responding to an application made to it: no doubt by the King or one of his leading ministers in early times, giving orders for intervention, but after 1689 (and probably before it) by individuals or bodies acting on their own initiative. Nowadays any such person is in effect a civil plaintiff instituting proceedings in a public matter, even though the Crown brings them on his behalf ('ex parte'). In the eighteenth century he would institute them in essentially the same way; but the implication would be that this was the only effective way the national public interest would be served in seeing that illegality by subordinate authorities was restrained.

Three writs were involved for this procedure which are here relevant. *Certiorari* ('investigate') was designed to quash any decision found after trial in the King's Bench to have been arrived at illegally; *prohibition* was designed to declare invalid in advance any such decision not yet made though proposed; *mandamus* was designed conversely to order the taking of a decision evaded or omitted in breach of a positive legal duty. No citizen could ever claim the grant of a prerogative writ 'as of right', only at the Court's discretion if after trial of the issues of fact and law sufficient justification might be shown.

The Court of Chancery could in its equitable jurisdiction also control the decisions of subordinate authorities, the appropriate remedy being an injunction. As with the prerogative writs, the remedy could only be discretionary, like all equitable remedies. At this point it should be noted that the King's officer appointed to uphold the interests of the public was (and is) the Attorney-General. The central government's normal course, therefore, if it wanted to control the workings of local government, would be to institute proceedings by the Attorney-General in the Court of Chancery for an injunction to restrain decisions to commit illegal acts or compel the performance of legal duties. Injunction in equity could thus broadly achieve the same purposes in the public interest as prerogative writs at common law. Unlike the common law, the available remedy in equity was (and still is) the same for public as for private proceedings.

4. REVIVAL OF CENTRAL ADMINISTRATIVE CONTROL

During the nineteenth century statutes reintroduced the practice of central supervision of local government by executive rather than judicial procedures. The result was that the prerogative writs at common law and injunctions in equity largely (though not entirely) lost that official supervisory purpose and today are used instead for the private pursuit of objections to the legality of public decisions. This development was gradual and uncertain at first. During the eighteenth and early nineteenth centuries the collective character of ministerial activity was still strong and the modern apparatus of government departments existed only in embryo in the offices of the clerks assisting the various Boards and Secretaries of State. Even the Home Office in this first period of its existence can hardly be regarded as a department. The Home Secretary was in constant correspondence with authorities locally, especially with magistrates. He might advise or exhort them; but his effective national response to problems was to give advice and recommendations to his Ministerial colleagues, particularly over the need (if any) to promote legislation. Public order was his main concern, and consultation with judges and law officers the normal way of giving it his attention at the level of central government. A very exceptional move, reflecting the unusually difficult problem of controlling London, was the payment of salaries to certain magistrates in Middlesex (notably Henry and Sir John Fielding) to assist them in organising an office at Bow Street to direct the activities of local parish constables. This was the forerunner of the modern police system, but there was no central control apart from a general ministerial decision that there should be some modest continuing financial assistance from the Treasury.

A turning-point came in 1829, when Peel as Home Secretary promoted the Act which set up the Metropolitan Police. That body has never belonged to a pattern of authorities; yet it was the prototype of modern local authorities on the administrative level. Its jurisdiction was (and is) locally limited, and it was made subject to direct permanent supervision by the Home Office. Elsewhere police forces were set up under direct control of local county and borough authorities, with indirect supervision by the Home Office; the latter thus embarked on its modern career as a central supervising and controlling department. Supervision of prisons, factories and mines was soon added; but of these only prisons were for a time subject to local public administration.

Upkeep of highways and poor relief had been the responsibility of local government at least from Tudor times. Legislation to improve the former became the concern of the Home Secretary from the time of the Highway Act 1835 until in 1871 highways, as a subject of central government responsibility, were transferred to the newly-created Local Government Board. The same happened to the central supervision of poor relief; but in the interim it had been placed under the control of an autonomous central body, the Poor Law Commissioners (three in number) whose harsh and rigorous administration between 1834 and 1847 made them intensely unpopular. The Home Secretary then promoted an Act replacing them by a Board which was in its turn superseded by the Local Government Board. When later in the nineteenth century housing functions were conferred on local authorities, the Local

Government Board became responsible for them also, and similarly with town planning from 1909. The poor law administration at local level was for a long time entrusted to special local 'boards of guardians' until the Local Government Act 1929 and the Poor Law Act 1930 transferred it to the regular local government bodies.

Various other administrative functions were developed on local and central government levels in this way, notably education. This too was entrusted to special local authorities, the school boards, and subsequently transferred to the regular local authorities after 1902. It was provided with a central government administration at an earlier date—a Committee of the Privy Council set up in 1839, the task of which was to administer grants made available by the government; these grants were payable to religious organisations (Anglican and Nonconformist schools) down to Gladstone's Elementary Education Act of 1870. An Act of 1899 transformed the central department into a Board of Education with a political president, like the Local Government Board. Another central body was the Board of Agriculture and Fisheries, set up by an Act of 1889 to receive functions transferred to it partly from the Privy Council and partly from certain Special Commissioners. It too supervised administration at local level by local authorities, though it also carried out direct executive tasks of its own.

In this way a pattern of functional administration emerged which now embraced many, though not all, publicly administered services. At local level these were distributed throughout England and Wales among county or district authorities, which became as a result multi-purpose bodies—increasingly so in the present century. At national level the services received supervisory treatment by different government departments according to subject-matter. To some extent most government departments are multi-purpose bodies within functional limits. But the Department of the Environment has become a multi-purpose body for the supervision of local government. This is so partly because it is virtually a Ministry of Local Government in the general sense (like the old Local Government Board), partly because it has been made the residuary beneficiary of the supervisory functions not entrusted for self-evident reasons to other central departments. The main examples are housing, environmental health, town and country planning, recreation and the countryside; but there are others, and the list is not immutable.

F. The local impact of government

1. TOWNSHIPS AND HOUSEHOLDS

In all states there are the rulers and the ruled. The essential one-ness of central and local government comes out in the fact that the incidence of both falls upon broadly the same people: the general body of citizens, the Queen's subjects. The citizen must submit to the exercise of lawful authority—he also gets the benefit of its functional achievements. The agents of government (central or local) have conversely the benefit of power in exercising the authority vested in them but must submit to the disciplines of the service of that authority.

This was so in early times just as it is today, subject to some qualifications. The superstructure of government consisted of institutions already referred to: the Crown and its central agencies (Council, Courts of Common Law, Chancery and other bodies); the shires, hundreds, boroughs and related local authorities and the officials holding sway within them. But the subjects of the Crown lived in settled communities below that level—hamlets, villages and towns—except that the more sizeable of these tended to be at one and the same time both communities (towns, cities) and areas of governmental authority (boroughs).

In earliest English history the King was interested in little more than the taxation and control of his subjects. This was imposed in accordance with the number of peasant households—'hides'—believed to exist (a reckoning which became more artificial as time went on). When in the tenth century England first became a unified Kingdom, the more elaborate governmental organisation which this made necessary was worked out in 'shires' and 'hundreds' as already described; but in addition a system of 'tithings' was instituted. Strictly this meant groups of ten peasant households, the heads of which were made collectively responsible for keeping order and bringing criminals to justice. In southern England at least (ie the old Kingdom of Wessex, the royal family of which had become the royal family of England) 'tithings' were normally the existing villages. The collective responsibility for appointing and paying taxes and maintaining law and order presupposes some kind of regular assembly of the village or township (the word 'town' or *tun* originally meant a stockaded peasant settlement or village); and this is what 'tithing' presumably came to mean in practice. This village 'council of ten' was subject in Norman times—and no doubt before—to a system of control called 'view of frank-pledge', whereby the ten masters of households were collectively responsible but one of their number was made 'chief pledge': in effect a village head-man. In large villages or towns there were probably several 'tithings'; but in any case adult males of peasant status must normally be either 'in frank-pledge and tithing', or in the household of someone else who was, to be produced for justice if accused of crime. Failure to comply with this duty by producing an accused member meant that the 'tithing' collectively would be 'amerced' (ie fined). If the offender should be in a 'tithing' but was not then the township would be 'amerced'—ie fined. The 'view of frankpledge' was a twice-yearly system of inspection held by the sheriff in each hundred-court within the county, at which the 'chief pledge' from each 'tithing' must attend. This sequence of inspections was called the 'sheriff's tourn'.[12]

2. MANORIAL GOVERNMENT

This system became distorted and artificial in course of time, one reason being that the Crown allowed many of the greater landowners to hold a private 'view of frankpledge' within their own manorial estates. This was known as a 'court leet' (from 'laete', an Anglo-Saxon word meaning an estate subject to a lord), and the term came eventually to mean in effect a police court administered by the bailiff of a manorial lord. For general local government purposes a different system of control emerged, based on the local unit of church organisation, the parish.

In a very general way the village ('vill' or township), the parish and the manor tended to coincide. The parish was commonly the village regarded as the jurisdiction of the local church and its parson; and the manor was commonly the village regarded similarly as the jurisdiction of the local secular lord or 'squire'. But a church's parish might comprise more than one village; and a manor might share a village with one or more other manors, or might comprise several villages. If every village had possessed, or been officially required to possess, a definite form of government, that would no doubt have become the basic component of local administration. But in spite of early medieval references to the 'reeve and four men' required to represent each 'vill' at the 'sheriff's tourn', this possibility did not develop. Ecclesiastical and secular authority at village level—parish and manor—made it unnecessary or impossible to develop a separate authority at that same level, even for judicial purposes. Manorial courts applied law for villagers in an immediate sense, and higher up the scale there were the shire and hundred courts and the separate church courts. Any other institutional growth would have been crowded out. What the rulers wanted was submission by local people to higher authority; apart from periodic peasants' revolts, this was achieved.

Mere submission, however, was never enough on its own. Also required were local men who could be relied on to receive orders and see that these were carried out. The peasant farmers had become used to this from the time that they were first required generally to serve as pledges and chief pledges in the 'tithing' and 'frankpledge' system. They were also required to attend at the manorial courts; and depending on seniority and reliability, they were expected to decide disputes and procedures in them in accordance with local custom. In short those of them who had sufficient experience were made answerable for the

12 *Selected Historical Essays of F. W. Maitland* 'Leet and tourn', pp 41 ff.

management of the others. In addition to that many of them will have acquired experience as 'reeves' (ie stewards) administering manorial estates. As far as possible they were kept busy: too busy to get above themselves.

3. PARISH GOVERNMENT

The manorial system was, in effect, local government in the later Middle Ages. But it became too specialised in terms of law and estate management to adapt to new requirements in administration generally, whether the manor coincided with the village or not. The parish organisation was not nearly so specialised and was capable of broad development in unforeseen directions. As a result it became the basis on which the superstructure of modern local government—the county and district authorities—was eventually built.

Authority in a parish was, naturally enough, the authority of the Church, exercised on the spot by the parish priest. But the legal position of the priest and his parish was not merely a matter for the Church and canon law. Since the very earliest time that Christianity came to England it has been placed under the secular protection of the King's law. Under Henry II 'clerks in holy orders' became exempt from criminal penalties in secular courts:[13] this 'benefit of clergy' was slowly reduced during succeeding centuries and disappeared finally in the nineteenth.[14] But the secular courts retained jurisdiction over Church men and Church property in civil cases, most remarkably as regards the appointment of 'clerks' or 'parsons' to Church livings, which was regulated as a feudal property right—an 'incorporeal hereditament'—known as 'advowson' and remains part of the law of landed property to this day. The priest in his parish was subject to the authority of the King's courts no less than to the Church's courts. The former, administering the common law, categorised the priest or parson, like any other official personage (clerical or lay) as the 'corporation sole'. Corporations, 'sole' and 'aggregate' alike, were and are public authorities subject to the ultra vires doctrine which prevails throughout English public law.

4. OFFICIALS OF THE PARISH

During the Middle Ages there came into being other functionaries in the parish—Church 'reeves' or 'wardens'. These were responsible to the Church authorities for the upkeep of the parish church; but it was also considered that a churchwarden was (and no doubt is still) 'a sort of inspector of the morals of the people',[15] and regularly answerable as

---

13 Constitutions of Clarendon 1164.
14 Criminal Law Act 1826.
15 S. and B. Webb *The Parish and the County*, p 21.

such to the bishop. Yet they were not appointed but, by immemorial custom, elected by their fellow parishioners. They were local worthies, like modern councillors. Their official role was remarkably independent and constitutional, sometimes even democratic. This was so not of course because the Church authorities fostered democracy, but because it was a question of imposing responsibilities on local people without pay and therefore politic to let them decide among themselves who should shoulder the burden and for how long.

Yet the free choice was real, even if the electorate was limited. What is more, secular authority came to recognise the status of churchwardens as already a matter of immemorial custom when, from the Reformation onwards, it began to see their usefulness, when the medieval system of manorial local government declined and at the same time religious authority changed. By the seventeenth century the King's judges held that 'the Churchwarden is a temporal officer; he has the property and custody of the parish goods; and as it is at the peril of the parishioners, so they may choose and trust whom they think fit . . .'[16] As a result, the office of churchwarden came to be 'by the common law a special corporation to take goods or personal things to the use of the parish'.[17]

By the fourteenth century a second parish officer had come into existence—the constable. Strictly speaking constables were appointed for the purpose of the courts: the 'hundred' courts already referred to, and the manorial 'court leet'. The 'high constable' of the 'hundred' was superior to the 'petty constable' of the 'vill' or 'tithing'. The manorial 'court leet' jurisdiction existed normally at the latter or lower level, since in a general way there would be an equivalence of manor, village and parish, so that 'petty' constables normally acted as village or parish functionaries and so came to be regarded as 'parish' constables. They were law enforcement officers, whereas churchwardens were property administrators. Like churchwardens constables were unpaid but, unlike them, were not elected, being appointed instead by the nobility and gentry acting as manorial lords or (increasingly) as justices of the peace in quarter sessions. The 'chief pledge' of the 'tithing', otherwise known as the 'headborough' or 'tithingman', although his was an older office, seems usually to have been regarded as the parish constable's deputy (the best known individuals being fictional: Shakespeare's Dogberry and Verges, the constable and headborough in *Much Ado About Nothing*).

The parish rather than the manor had become the accepted unit of general local government by the sixteenth century, when two other officers were created by Parliament: the surveyor of highways in the

16 *S. and B. Webb p 23; Morgan v Archdeacon of Cardigan* (1697) 1 Salk 165.
17 *S. and B. Webb* p 24.

Highways Acts 1555 and 1562 and the overseers of the poor in the Poor Relief Act 1597. Like the churchwardens and constables they were unpaid; yet like them they were required to exercise authority over fellow parishioners (and others). The surveyor's task was to supervise the unpaid work of highway maintenance imposed by statute on local inhabitants generally. The overseers (two, three or four appointed in each parish at the discretion of any two justices of the peace) were required to provide essential financial relief to destitute inhabitants of the parish and set them to work wherever possible. The surveyor was appointed at first by the constables, churchwardens and other substantial parishioners; but the Highways Act 1691 restricted their role to submitting a list of candidates' names for the justices of the peace to make the choice.

These parish officers were at the bottom or receiving end of the chain of command from the Crown and its ministers and judges down through the justices of the peace. Like the latter they were unpaid because they were not full-time professional servants of the Crown, merely general functionaries whose living came from their private patrimony. They were normally landowners, even if only on a local scale, living on the produce or income of their inherited freehold farm property: in a word, the 'yeoman' class. The magistrates were socially above them: the gentry or squirearchy living primarily on the rents received from leasehold or copyhold farm tenants. In one way or another, magistrates and parish officers alike enjoyed settled incomes and managerial status, though at different levels. Accustomed to the management of their family properties, they could be expected to spare some time also for the management of public activities. Only the parish servants under their control—clerk, sexton, beadle and so on—worked for pay, such as it was.

5. MONEY

Lord Macaulay comments on this system as follows:[18]

> 'Of the expense of civil government only a small portion was defrayed by the crown. The great majority of the functionaries whose business was to administer justice and preserve order either gave their services to the public gratuitously, or were remunerated in a manner which caused no drain on the revenue of the state. The sheriffs, mayors and aldermen of the towns, the country gentlemen who were in the commission of the peace, the headboroughs, bailiffs and petty constables, cost the King nothing'.

This is not to say, however, that their activities cost the public nothing, even though (above the level of parish servants) the work was

18 *History of England* (pub Macmillan, 1913 edition) Vol I, Ch III, p 298.

not done for pay. Local administration may have been undertaken at a very modest level, but it did sometimes cost money as distinct from requiring labour. This is the explanation and the origin of rates, a subject for complaint from its beginning until now. When Macaulay says that local government 'cost the King nothing' he meant tax revenue. But this is misleading. Rate income is a form of tax revenue in spite of its peculiar features; and levying rates requires due constitutional authority as much as levying taxes does if it is to be lawful. The King's courts would uphold the raising of public revenue only if the common law recognised the procedure used; and from the Revolution of 1688–89 onwards this was strictly subject to Parliamentary control.

A rate is a levy on occupation of property in accordance with its value, the amount being calculated at a level fixed by persons authorised to do so, at a set 'rate' of a given sum per pound of value. In other words it is a property tax, enforceable by effective political authority like any other tax. English law recognised that each of the four types of parish officer had authority to levy a rate to finance reasonable and necessary expenditure. Local government thus depended on it, and administration from the Crown downwards through the justices of the peace presupposed its existence. The overseers of the poor were statutorily authorised to levy a poor rate, which as Macaulay himself says toward the end of the chapter referred to above: 'was undoubtedly the heaviest tax borne by our ancestors in those days'—ie the seventeenth century. 'It was computed, in the reign of Charles the Second, at near seven hundred thousand pounds a year, much more than the produce either of the excise or of the customs, and little less than half the entire revenue of the Crown'. For this reason it absorbed in course of time the much smaller levy of rates appropriate to the other three officers; nevertheless they were of independent origin. Each surveyor of the highways was empowered to authorise expenditure for which a highway rate was levied as necessary, though the actual order for it was issued by the justices in quarter sessions. The constables were authorised, by an Act of 1662, to levy a parish rate to meet the expenses of putting down vagrancy, on a similar basis to the pre-existing poor rate; but in medieval times constables had by custom levied a rate to cover their general expenses (though in medieval style it was levied on a manorial rather than a parish basis). Independently of these rates the High Constable of each 'hundred' in the county was required to levy a 'county rate' (referred to earlier in this chapter) at the behest of the magistrates in quarter sessions; and this was sub-delegated to parish constables for particular assessment and collection at parish level. Similarly the churchwardens were authorised by legally recognised custom to levy a 'church rate' on parishioners (never authorised by statute except temporarily under the Long Parliament and the Commonwealth). There were other sources of revenue—customary fees and charges of various kinds—yet although rates were at first intended only for making up any shortfall below expenditure of income from such sources, the availability of such taxation inevitably meant that there came to be an ever-increasing reliance on rate revenue.

G. Conclusion: continuity with the past

English and Welsh local government in the twentieth century is set in a pattern created by radical changes made in the nineteenth. But many features are traceable to the system of the earlier centuries, described in this chapter. Administrative functions such as police, highway maintenance and social welfare; the system of rates; the existence of such local government units as the county and the parish (also perhaps, at least indirectly, the district within the county); the system of judicial control; all these play as prominent a part in today's system as they did in the different conditions of those days.

What is different today is the far greater extent of administrative functions. To that must be added the elaborate career-structure of local government staffing by means of paid officers and servants, together with the equally elaborate financial structure in respect both of income (government grants) and borrowing. Above all there is the democratic element of elected councils, which is radically different from the system by which the Crown appointed justices of the peace who in turn appointed parish officers other than the elected churchwardens. Yet the parishioners assembled in vestry meetings used to have some influence over the activities of parish officers in those days, even if it was only to criticise, as local government auditors now do, the accounts they submitted; and it must not be forgotten how the origins of modern features, however tenuously, go back to the earliest times.

Chapter 2

Local authorities today

A. Mid-nineteenth century origins

I. REFORM

The emergence of the modern pattern of local authorities began with the Municipal Corporations Act 1835. This statute put an end to the old system under which each town which had become a chartered borough was governed according to the particular constitution embodied in its charter or charters. Most though not all of these corporate bodies were very restricted in their membership, consisting of a council comprising a small number of the most prominent—ie powerful and wealthy—citizens, usually appointed for life and co-opted rather than elected. In a word these bodies were oligarchical, so that the general run of citizens or 'burgesses' were excluded from any say in the government of the borough. Late in Charles II's reign most boroughs had their charters revoked and reissued in a move to strengthen royal control;[1] and this tended towards increasing the restrictive and oligarchical character of the boroughs, with the intention of making them more amenable. Even so there were exceptions. Maitland reviewed the whole historical process, from the twelfth century to the nineteenth, in the following words:[2]

'The power of acting in the name of the borough passed little by little from a general assembly of burgesses to a council or "select body"; but even until 1835 there were towns, and towns with long histories, in which all the most important business of the corporation had to be brought before a meeting in which every corporator, every burgess or freeman, had a vote: such was the case at Winchester, Maidstone, Cambridge, Ipswich.'

Except in the City of London, where the elaborate medieval constitution with its Lord Mayor, Court of Aldermen and elected Court of Common Council was allowed to continue unchanged (and still does), the Act of 1835 swept all the charter constitutions away, though not the charters themselves and their other contents. In replacement, the bor-

---

1 See ch 1 above, p 14.
2 Pollock and Maitland *History of English Law* (CUP, 1968), Vol I, p 659.

oughs were all given a standardised constitution consisting (like London) of a mayor, aldermen and elected councillors, the number depending on the size of the borough. The area of each borough (again like London) was divided up into constituencies known as 'wards'. This was the decisive step which introduced elective democracy into English local government on a general basis. Equally important, at least in the strict legal sense, is the fact that the corporate body, instead of being confined to the previous small groupings of corporators set up under the charters, was extended to embrace all the 'burgesses' or voting citizens. This was a whig reform, under William IV, to offset the tory restrictions under Charles II.

However, the 1835 reform was constitutional, not functional. Apart from conferring on the reformed corporations a revised standard power to issue bye-laws, levy rates, regulate markets and maintain a police force, and apart from formally separating the borough magistrates from the borough council, the Act did nothing towards producing the local authorities today by conferring administrative functions. The significance of the change was potential rather than actual and immediate. In course of time the reformed boroughs were seen to be the ideal authorities to be used in developing a multi-purpose functional local government system in a democratic age. Then, instead of being under-used and treated with reserve, they were taken up with enthusiasm and worked to full capacity.

The approach to the question of functions was pragmatic and not systematic. Highway maintenance, poor relief and police, being of general importance, were everywhere the responsibility of the parishes, subject to direction and control by the county authorities, that is the magistrates in quarter sessions; except that most sizeable towns, being chartered boroughs, were largely free to carry out those functions in their own way, autonomously. Other functions tended to be optional; and whether they were performed at all depended on local initiative. Thus enterprises of these kinds occurred ad hoc. In this way new main roads were built from time to time, but by groups of local landowners (probably county magistrates more often than not) acting collectively as 'turnpike trustees'. Streets would be paved and lighted, but by groups of prominent citizens acting collectively as 'paving commissioners' or 'improvement commissioners'; these were probably, in most cases, some of the prominent men who served as mayor, aldermen and councillors in the particular borough, and as borough magistrates too, even if as commissioners they were often elected by borough ratepayers.[3] Water and gas supplies would be provided by utility companies, but once again these would usually be created by prominent local citizens.

3 See *Hart's Introduction to the Law of Local Government and Administration* (9th edn, by Hart and Garner, pub Butterworth, 1973) p 23.

2. DEPENDENCE UPON STATUTE

All these collective enterprises depended on statutory authority, so as to give necessary powers to appoint or elect their controlling members and to use land or impose rates or charges. They also depended on it in order to ensure that the personal fortunes of the people involved were excluded from the collective public liabilities to be incurred in carrying out these functions, the varieties of which shaded imperceptibly into trading companies. This was part of the process by which limited liability eventually became the universal principal for enterprises other than those run by individuals or partnerships. The dividing-line was thus not one distinguishing public from private enterprises but one distinguishing statutory (normally with limited liability) from personal enterprises—at any rate as far as the law was concerned.

The statutory powers were mostly obtained by private legislation, the 'promoters' of each body petitioning Parliament, usually at great expense, for leave to introduce the necessary private Bills. Much statutory detail became repetitive and stereotyped; and this eventually led to the passing of *public* legislation in the form of standardised 'Clauses' Acts embodying codes of common-form clauses available for adoption in drafting subsequent *private* Bills (thus reducing the expense, at least to some extent). In turn this opened the way in due course to the passing of substantive public Acts conferring functional powers or duties on a general basis. The coherent policy exemplified by the emergence of this public legislation tended, as a general rule, to be government policy, and the element of private local initiative dwindled.

Thus the scene was set for replacing the ad hoc pattern of functions by a schematic pattern, and not before time, because by the 1880s England was 'a chaos of areas, a chaos of franchises, a chaos of authorities, and a chaos of rates'.[4] The confusion had been made worse by government initiative to bring into operation new administrative functions separately from those already created by ad hoc local initiative. Sanitation led the way; and under the Public Health Acts 1872 and 1875 'sanitary districts' (urban and rural) had been set up, under local Boards of Health, within the counties; though at least they did not duplicate the chartered boroughs which were normally made the sanitary authorities in their own areas. Education policy led to the setting up of a separate group of school board districts. Outside the boroughs the old pattern of poor law and highway administration by parishes was altered by the creation of special parishes or 'unions' of parishes for these purposes, in other words new administrative districts.

The reaction against this disorderly state of affairs eventually produced a new concept—a national pattern of multi-purpose local authorities. The fact that traditional units—counties and boroughs—were

4 *Hart*, p 28.

pressed into service along with a pre-existing (though recent) scheme of urban and rural administrative districts, has in true English style masked the revolutionary character of this reform. The most traditional element in the new system was not so much the administrative units in it as the fact that, although national government policy produced it, local autonomy was its mainstay.

Thus the character of post-Revolution English government, comprising a wide measure of self-determination in counties and boroughs since 1689, was preserved into a new administrative era. There were national administrative functions organised centrally: not only taxation and the armed forces but departments such as the Post Office. But local government received a new lease of life. It ceased to be shapeless and became both comprehensive and democratic.

B. Tiers of multi-purpose councils

1. THE BIRTH OF 'LOCAL GOVERNMENT'

The very term 'local government' comes to us from this period in history. It was apparently coined by a Conservative politician and landowner, C. B. Adderley who was, appropriately enough, a pioneer of town planning, which he began to carry out privately on his estate at Saltley, east of Birmingham, in 1837.[5] He coined the phrase in 1858, when holding ministerial office as President of the Board of Health. That central government department was, as already explained, an unpopular innovation, set up under the fear of cholera; and indeed it was abolished that same year. Its functions were divided between two traditional central government organisations, the Privy Council and the Home Office. Ten years later Disraeli set up a Royal Commission to examine the administration of sanitation and public health, and Adderley presided. The result of its report was that Gladstone's government produced the Local Government Board Act 1871 and the Public Health Act 1872.[6] The latter Act imposed a general pattern of local sanitation authorities over the whole country. These were existing borough corporations, or local boards of health in non-corporate urban areas; and new boards were to be set up for areas not already covered. The former Act was more important still, because it set up the new central government department which would not only supervise local sanitation authorities but local government generally: hence the title Local Government Board. Nevertheless, the only other substantial administrative function it covered was poor relief.

---

5 Ensor *England 1870–1914* (OUP, 1949) p 124.
6 *Ensor* p 126.

Other functions continued on traditional lines or were developed ad hoc by local initiative under private legislation, the co-ordination of which was procedural rather than substantive, under the Local Act Branch of the Home Office. The Local Act Branch and the Public Health Department of the Privy Council were detached from their parent bodies and united in the new Board with the other recently created central government functional department, the Poor Law Board (1847–1871), whose ministerial president in Gladstone's cabinet, J. Stansfeld, became the first President of the Local Government Board. The Act of 1872 which followed was his major legislative achievement, and by it he made the existing rural poor law authorities, the rural boards of guardians, do double duty as new rural sanitary authorities. This reform was in turn taken up into the major consolidating statute passed by Disraeli's government, the Public Health Act 1875.

Despite the notoriously restrictive attitude of mind of the government's poor law administration (the original three Poor Law Commissioners of 1834–1847 having been dubbed the 'Pashas of Somerset House' or the 'pinch-pauper triumvirate') which not surprisingly, since the same minister remained in charge, dominated the new Board, it was the first central government body to be designed to look after local administration as a whole. This co-ordinated approach was gradually developed and strengthened. The idea of proper answerability to the electorate added another dimension in coherence. Adderley's timely phrase 'local government' neatly labelled this new compound idea of local administration under central supervision which was at the same time systematic and constitutional. Whitehall's appreciation of this was, however, tepid. The expression 'local government' as part of the title of the central government department responsible for its supervision was dropped in 1919, taken up again in 1951, and dropped once more in 1970.

The first fruits of the new approach to local administration came with the Municipal Corporations Acts, 1882 and 1883.[7] The latter abolished a number of small borough corporations which had not been reformed by the Act of 1835, so that they were left to the ordinary parochial organisation within their counties. The former re-enacted and consolidated the 1835 Act and intervening amending legislation. In the result the 1882 Act remained the principal statute regulating the general powers and workings of boroughs down to 1933. It had, however, little to do with particular administrative functions, being concerned with the legal details of borough status.

2. REFORM IN THE COUNTIES

In 1888 came the most fundamental change of all. The Local Government Act of that year, introduced by C. T. Ritchie, President of the

7 *Hart* p 35.

Local Government Board under Lord Salisbury, set up elected county councils to replace the magistrates in quarter sessions as rulers of the counties.[8] The magistrates retained their judicial functions together with one or two administrative tasks such as licensing public houses; and indeed a great many individual magistrates (prominent local land-owners for the most part, and thus members of 'county society'—or more briefly 'the county', in social terms) reappeared as elected county councillors. This does not alter the fact that the reform was radical. It did not change the county authorities' functions, but their status for the purpose of administering most of those functions was dramatically altered by turning them into elected councils on the same pattern as the boroughs under the Municipal Corporations Acts 1835 and 1882. The head of a county council was to be its chairman, in the same way as the head of quarter sessions but in contrast to the head of a borough, who was a mayor; but chairmen and mayors alike were elected from among the members (including aldermen). The legal corporate body, however, in a county was confined to the council whereas in a borough it was the mayor, aldermen and burgesses (ie citizens), although a borough cor-poration could only act through the agency of its council.[9]

The Act of 1888 applied the general pattern of a borough council to each county but did not directly affect the boroughs themselves. It did, however, affect boroughs in another way. It took the larger boroughs (normally those with 50,000 or more inhabitants) out of their respective counties and made them autonomous under the title of 'county bor-oughs'. Others were set up by later Acts. Not only did this make the major provincial cities such as Birmingham, Manchester, Liverpool, Sheffield, Leeds, Newcastle-on-Tyne and Bristol, and certain smaller towns down to Reading and Northampton and others of a like size, independent of the shires in which they had been administratively, and were still geographically, located.[10] It had the further effect of creating two quite different functional systems, a 'one-tier' and a 'two-tier' sys-tem. The 'county boroughs' operated in a 'one-tier' system because each of them administered at one and the same time the functions pre-viously allotted to county authorities and those previously allotted to all boroughs and to poor law and health authorities outside the boroughs. On the other hand 'non-county boroughs' (often confusingly called 'municipal boroughs' regardless of the fact that all boroughs were municipal corporations) operated in a 'two-tier' system as before, because they did not in their areas administer the functions allotted to the county authorities.

Not that the Act of 1888 was much concerned with functions, which

8 *Hart* p 30; *Ensor* p 203.
9 *Hart* pp 35–6, 282.
10 *Ensor* p 203.

continued in the counties more or less as they were before it had been passed: county bridges; county hospitals and lunatic asylums; and the county police (the control of the latter being exercised thenceforward by 'standing joint committees' composed equally of county councillors and magistrates). Main roads in rural areas, to which quarter sessions had previously contributed half the cost of upkeep, were now transferred completely to the county councils; and the latter were also given functions concerning diseases of animals. Licensing of public houses was, by accident, not transferred, because of disagreements in Parliament over a proposed scheme for suppression of licences and consequent compensation; instead, money earmarked in the Budget of 1890 for such compensation was made available for county and county borough councils to provide technical education.[11] Poor law and general highway administration, though exercised in earlier times by county magistrates in quarter sessions in the usual manner through supervision of the parish overseers and surveyors, had already been withdrawn from them in favour of the new district authorities referred to earlier (boards of guardians, acting also as boards of health and highway boards, together with boroughs exercising those same functions). It should be added that certain of the traditional counties had already been divided for administrative reasons: the three 'ridings' of Yorkshire and Lincolnshire, the eastern and western divisions of Sussex and Suffolk. These were all given separate county councils in 1888.

3. REFORM IN LONDON

The other important change made by the Act of 1888 concerned London.[12] The City Corporation's constitution had been left untouched by the Act of 1835 (and other Acts since), including the right which it had bought from the Crown in the twelfth century to appoint the sheriff of the county of Middlesex, in which London lay, that office being held jointly by the City's own two sheriffs. The Metropolis Management Act 1855 set up the Metroplitan Board of Works to administer health and sanitation, bridges, and a few other functions in an area now approximately represented by 'inner London'—ie stretching from Hammersmith to Woolwich and from Hampstead to Streatham—and including the City. This area covered segments of three counties: Middlesex, Kent and Surrey. Subsequent public and private Acts gave this Board other functions, including major public works such as the construction of the Victoria Embankment and Queen Victoria Street and the creation and maintenance of parks and the London Fire Brigade. Its members were elected by the various constituent local bodies—parish

11 Technical Instruction Act 1889; Finance Act 1890. See *Ensor* pp 203–4.
12 See *Hart* p 279.

authorities in the London area ('vestries') and local boards of works, concerned with upkeep of highways—which were themselves reorganised by the Act of 1855.

The Act of 1888 swept away the Metropolitan Board of Works and converted its area into a new county, the County of London, which was given a county council on the same pattern as those elsewhere. The members of the London County Council were—unlike the Metropolitan Board but like county and borough councils generally—directly elected, including members from a double-sized electoral district comprising the City of London itself. The new council took over the administrative functions of the Metropolitan Board and in addition received those of the other county councils. The County of London, moreover, as distinct from its council, was immediately equipped like the old-established traditional counties with a lord-lieutenant, a high sheriff, and quarter sessions of its own. But although the functions of the London County Council were exercised within the City as well as in the rest of the County of London, the City Corporation continued as before. Middlesex, Kent and Surrey, as administrative counties, were deprived permanently of the segments of territory embodied in this new county.

4. REFORM OF THE 'SECOND-TIER' AUTHORITIES

Six years later local government outside the 'one-tier' county boroughs was simplified by the substitution of general-purpose district councils for the medley of urban and rural health and highway authorities—the 'local boards'.[13] H. H. Fowler, President of the Local Government Board in Gladstone's fourth cabinet, introduced the Local Government Act 1894, which introduced the new local authorities, termed urban and rural district councils.[14] These, together with the non-county boroughs, together made up the lower tier of a new multi-functional 'two tier' system of which the upper tier was composed of the county councils. Their main functions were public health and sanitation, housing, highway and street lighting and upkeep, refuse disposal, parks and open spaces and other services. These included in many cases the provision of gas, water and electricity under various private Acts, though they have now of course been transferred to nationalised industries and water authorities. At no time, then or since, have all public administrative functions been provided by local authorities: some were added later, some were subtracted later, some have never been included in local government at all. But from 1894 onwards the 'one-tier' and 'two-tier' systems of county, county borough, non-county borough and

13 *Hart* p 31.
14 *Ensor* pp 213–4.

urban and rural district councils operated a general and comprehensive system of local administrative authorities which were neither ad hoc nor single-purpose bodies but bodies to which any or all public administrative duties might be entrusted if for other reasons it should become convenient to do so.

The Act of 1894 made two other important changes.[15] First, it made a general extension of the right to vote in local elections, and the right to stand for election, to women, on a similar footing to men. (Single women had already been given the right to vote, but not stand for election, for county and borough councils; married women had not been given any such rights.) Second, it set up a system of elected parish councils. These were established in rural parishes only, to the number of nearly 7,000, and created in those areas a third tier of local government. But so strict a limit was placed on their spending powers that they were prevented from playing any but a minor part in local administration then and thereafter. Even in rural areas, therefore, local government effectively remained a 'two-tier' system in substance even though it was a 'three-tier' system in form.

In the County of London a similar reform took place when the London Government Act 1899 abolished the existing vestries and boards and replaced them by a uniform system of 28 metropolitan borough councils with mayors and elected councillors. Although these were vastly inferior to the City Corporation in terms of status the City was made roughly comparable with them in terms of functions. They were in fact multi-functional local authorities much like the councils of non-county boroughs and urban and rural districts outside the County of London, and with some exceptions their functions were broadly the same. Thus by 1900 the simplified 'two-tier' system had been extended to London as well as to the country as a whole outside the county boroughs.[16]

C. Evolution in the twentieth century

1. THE FIRST SEVENTY YEARS

The local government pattern endured with little fundamental change for more than 70 years. The Education Act 1902 abolished the separate system of school boards and made county and county borough councils education authorities; save that some of the larger non-county borough and urban district councils, though 'second-tier' authorities were made elementary (as distinct from secondary and technical) education author-

---

15 *Ensor* p 214.
16 See *Hart* p 279.

ities for their areas. The Local Government Act 1929 abolished the 'boards of guardians' which administered poor relief and transferred their functions to county and county borough councils. The Local Government Act 1933 then proceeded to consolidate the general law of local government outside London; that is to say the main provisions as to constitution, finance and procedure contained in the Municipal Corporations Act 1882 and the Local Government Acts 1888 and 1894 were restated coherently in one act.

There were some far-reaching functional changes. The National Health Service Act 1946 and The National Assistance Act 1948 transferred hospitals and poor relief from local to central government. The Electricity Act 1947 and the Gas Act 1948 transferred electricity and gas undertakings, some of which had been set up by local authorities, to nationalised industry corporations. Water supply and conservation, sewerage, land drainage and protection of fisheries, which had to some extent been local authority functions, were transferred to regional bodies known as water authorities by the Water Act 1973. On the other hand the Fire Brigades Act 1938 imposed on borough and district councils the duty of maintaining a fire service, which duty was transferred to county and county borough councils by the Fire Services Act 1947; and a long series of Acts conferred and extended functions relating to planning control upon county, borough and district councils.

The Local Government Acts 1948, 1958 and 1966 largely dealt with finance; though the 1958 Act set up Local Government Commissions for England and Wales which were concerned with the reviews of boundaries of local government areas but were terminated in 1967.[17] A general review of local government was put in hand when a Royal Commission chaired by Lord Redcliffe-Maud was set up for the purpose in 1966. It reported in 1969, and recommended a revision and simplification of local government by creating a new pattern of unitary areas, in other words the 'one-tier' system of the county boroughs applied to the country as a whole (except in certain 'conurbations'—ie heavily built-up areas). This would incidentally achieve another desired effect, which was to obliterate what was thought to be the out-of-date distinction between rural and urban local authorities.

The Labour government of the day broadly accepted these proposals and embodied them, with modifications, in a White Paper published early in 1970.[18] But it was replaced by a Conservative government which rejected the idea of a wider application of the 'one-tier' system and instead published another White Paper early in 1971[19] proposing a total application of the 'two-tier' system (once again with a variation for

17 Local Government (Termination of Reviews) Act 1967.
18 Cmnd 4276/1970.
19 Cmnd 4584/1971.

the 'conurbations'). The pattern of counties would in essence be retained, though with a great many detailed changes, as the 'upper tier'; but the 'lower tier' would be radically simplified by having a single rank of 'district' authorities much larger in size and fewer in number than the existing urban and rural districts and non-county boroughs. County boroughs would be swallowed up by the revised counties and their areas down-graded to districts. Boroughs in fact would disappear. The system of parish councils would, in a general way, continue as before. The new county and district councils, or 'principal councils', were to have a chairman and elected councillors, but no aldermen.

This major rearrangement, as will be discussed below, duly went ahead and was enacted in the Local Government Act 1972 (see s 270 as to 'principal councils'). The changes in question were brought generally into effect in April 1974, with some superficial modifications.

2. GREATER LONDON

The Act of 1972, however, did not extend to London. The London Government Act 1963 had already radically altered local government in London in a way which broadly foreshadowed the pattern embodied in the Act of 1972, being a revised 'two-tier' system. The County of London and the London County Council were abolished, as were the 28 metropolitan borough councils set up in 1899. A new and much larger area was created, called Greater London, extending from Uxbridge to Romford and Barnet to Croydon. That is to say its boundaries were drawn more or less at the edge of the existing built-up area of the London 'conurbation'. This meant taking in more territory from Surrey and Kent, together with a great deal of territory from Essex which had not been affected by the creation of the County of London in 1889, together with some slight boundary modifications affecting Buckinghamshire and Hertfordshire. Middlesex was swallowed up and disappeared altogether as an administrative county.[20] A great many borough and district councils (including three county boroughs) were swept away in this accretion of new territory. The only local authority left unscathed by this upheaval was—once again—the Corporation of the City of London. The changes took effect on 1 April 1965.

Greater London was given a single 'upper-tier' authority, the Greater London Council, which took over County Hall in London from the defunct London County Council as its headquarters. It was constituted with a chairman and councillors, but no aldermen. So were the new 'lower-tier' authorities, called London Borough councils. These were classed in two groups: 12 'inner' London and 20 'outer' London boroughs, totalling 32.[1] The former were created within the area of the old

20 London Government Act 1963, s 3.
1 Ibid, ss 1, 2. (See also the Local Government Act 1972, Sch 2.)

County of London; while the latter were created in the new accretion of territory previously belonging to the surrounding administrative counties. So much for status. The distribution of functions was made on the lines that most matters involving detailed routine administration were given to the London borough councils and matters of most general 'strategic' significance were given to the Greater London Council.[2] A broadly similar principle was applied in the 1972 Act to the authorities in the 'conurbations'. Neither in Greater London nor outside it, however, is this principle pushed to its furthest length. One striking qualification is that the 'outer' London boroughs are all separate education authorities, whereas there is one single, unified education authority for all the 'inner' London boroughs, the Inner London Education Authority, which is to all intents and purposes a perpetuation of the London County Council solely in the sphere of education.[3] It consists of the Greater London councillors representing 'inner' London plus one representative of each of the 'inner' London boroughs and of the City Corporation. In terms of functions generally (apart from education) the work of the latter authority is closely comparable with the detailed routine administration of the London boroughs. The broad 'strategic' administrative functions of the Greater London Council include planning and transport policies, the upkeep of principal ('metropolitan') roads, sewerage, refuse disposal, housing, fire and ambulance services, and control of some of the larger parks and open spaces.

3. THE LOCAL GOVERNMENT ACT 1972

With the system of authorities in Greater London in their minds, the framers of the Act of 1972 picked out six provincial conurbations for special treatment, and confusingly called them 'metropolitan' areas. All the previous 'metropolitan' authorities were so called because they had been set up in the Metropolis, the Capital City (and its environs), ie London. In this generally accepted sense of the word the name is quite inappropriate and therefore confusing when applied elsewhere. In any case the whole idea of these special areas, and indeed Greater London itself, is difficult to reconcile with the principle supposedly embodied in all the recent reform of local government that authorities should not be specially set up for urban or rural areas as such. Be that as it may, six new English administrative counties were created by the 1972 Act, to be 'metropolitan' counties: Tyne and Wear, West Yorkshire, South Yorkshire, Greater Manchester, Merseyside, and the West Midlands.[4] The required territory was carved out of the pre-existing county areas of Northumberland, Durham, the West Riding of Yorkshire, Lan-

2 Ibid, s 4. All are 'principal councils' (Local Government Act 1972, s 270).
3 Ibid, s 30.
4 Local Government Act 1972, Sch 1.

cashire, Cheshire, Staffordshire and Warwickshire. Other new administrative counties were created, such as Cumbria, Cleveland, Humberside and Avon (out of the pre-existing county areas of Cumberland, Westmorland, Lancashire, Durham, the North and East Ridings of Yorkshire, Lincolnshire, Gloucestershire and Somerset), but as ordinary and not as 'metropolitan' counties. Of the 'non-metropolitan' (or 'shire') counties generally, few escaped boundary changes and rearrangements of some kind. The most notable alterations are perhaps the combination of Hereford and Worcester into one county, and the absorption of Rutland into Leicestershire and of Huntingdonshire and the Soke of Peterborough into Cambridgeshire. Yorkshire North Riding, enlarged, is now North Yorkshire, while the East Riding has disappeared. Lancashire and Berkshire are truncated. Wales has had most of its old counties demoted to districts within the boundaries of four new large counties bearing the archaic names: Gwynedd, Clwyd, Powys and Dyfed; but Glamorgan, like Gaul, is divided into three parts (Mid, West and South) and Gwent replaces Monmouthshire.

Part IX, and Schedules 14 to 26, of the Local Government Act 1972 set out in detail the distribution of functions between the upper and lower tier authorities, in other words, between the 'metropolitan' county and district councils and similarly between the 'non-metropolitan' county and district councils. The effect of these detailed provisions was summarised in Circular No 121/72 issued by the Department of the Environment. The essence of the distinction between the six 'metropolitan' counties and all the others is functional, in that because of the densely populated nature of those six, a group of functions has been allotted not to the 'metropolitan' county councils but to their district councils; whereas those same functions have been allotted to the county councils and not to the district councils elsewhere. The functions in question are, first and foremost, education, together with libraries, youth employment and personal social services. Of the remaining functions, county councils generally administer highways and transport planning, police, fire services, consumer protection (including food and drugs, and weights and measures), refuse disposal, diseases of animals, and smallholdings; while district councils in general administer housing, environmental or public health (including building regulations, clean air, factories, slaughterhouses, refuse collection, food safety and hygiene, home safety, and communicable diseases), cemeteries and crematoria, markets and fairs, coast protection, allotments, and local licensing. Planning control was made a function of both county and district councils, though the latter are chiefly concerned with routine detailed administration while the former deal with broad 'strategic' policies for the most part. Concurrent powers are given over a variety of functions, such as airports, swimming baths and recreation, parks, footpaths, and museums and art galleries. Parish councils continue much as before (converted into community councils in Wales), with minor functions such as allotments, parking, footpaths, open spaces, recreation and cemeteries; and they must be consulted over planning matters.

The multitudinous provisions of the Act of 1972 will be considered in detail in the chapters which follow.

D. Latest developments

It would not be reasonable to contemplate another major reform of local government within a short space after the Act of 1972. It is true that considerable political dissatisfaction had been caused, not surprisingly, by the government's ruthless demotion of the 'one-tier' authorities, the county boroughs—at any rate in the major provincial cities—for the greater exaltation of the counties and their rulers. But resentment and disagreement are not of themselves a sufficient basis for justifying further upheaval. The modern age is not, however, a period of stability, and the local government system has been undergoing some change since 1972.

The Local Government Act 1974 introduced changes even before the 1972 had come into effect on 1 April 1974. Part III extended to local authorities and certain similar bodies the 'ombudsman' procedure enacted for central government by the Parliamentary Commissioner Act 1967. As under that earlier Act, the purpose of the Commissions for Local Administration in England and in Wales set up by the 1974 Act is to investigate and publicise 'maladministration', that is to say wrongful conduct by local authorities which for formal or practical reasons is not capable of redress in legal proceedings. Apart from this creation of 'local ombudsmen', slightly modified by the Local Government Act 1978, the 1974 Act is almost entirely concerned with finance. It amended both the grant system[5] and the rating system[6]; but that was merely a foretaste of things to come. The most important specific grants to local authorities are those made for housing, and these tend to be radically changed with each political change of government. The Housing Rents and Subsidies Act 1975 and the Housing Act 1980 duly recast the system of housing subsidies twice in succession.

A number of changes were made by the Local Government (Miscellaneous Provisions) Act 1976.[7] But the greatest upheaval occurred in the Local Government, Planning and Land Act 1980. Leaving aside

---

5 Part I of the Act, modifying both general and specific grants.
6 Part II of the Act, dealing with rating of unoccupied premises and other matters.
7 This and other Acts referred to will be mentioned where appropriate in the chapters which follow.

Parts IX to XVII of that Act, which made various changes in the law relating to planning control and the use and acquisition of land by local authorities, as well as creating urban development corporations as a sort of inner-city equivalent of new town development corporations, a concentration on Parts I to VIII reveals a many-sided initiative to change the face of local government. The first aspect shows a relaxation of central government control over local administration; but this is a case of *reculer pour mieux sauter*. Part II empowers the Secretary of State for the Environment to issue a code of practice directing local authorities as to what matters they shall publish. Part III imposes a system of central control over 'direct labour' work. Part IV broadens the system of financial allowances payable to local councillors. Part V makes the rating system more flexible in some respects and broadens the scope of intervention by the Secretary of State. Part VI, which is especially far-reaching, drastically alters the rate support grant system in order to tighten the hold of the Secretary of State over local authorities' expenditure and revenue. Part VII touches on one or two special aspects of the grant system; and Part VIII tightens central control over local authorities' capital expenditure. Whether these changes are or are not desirable is a political question, a matter for individual judgment. What is scarcely in dispute is that they amount to a notable increase in control of local authorities by the central government.

It is perhaps too early to say whether this Act represents an important stage in a process whereby the development of autonomous local government is put into reverse; but it is consistent with such a view. The Acts of 1835 to 1894 which introduced a democratically controlled system of local government, and made it available for the public administration of all kinds of governmental functions at local level, have now to some extent been neutralised by the central power in the state. It is not a new departure, because the steady increase in the proportion of local authority revenue which comes from the central government by way of grants in aid of expenditure has, throughout the twentieth century, increased commensurately the leverage exercisable over local councils by the central government. One reason for thinking this is that, in general, these grants are payable at ministerial discretion and are thus capable of being reduced or withheld as a punishment for the pursuance of local government policies which the central government dislikes. Where there are central and local power centres the question 'who is master?' cannot help but arise. The steady increase in grant revenue, and the passing of such a statute as the Act of 1980, underline the fact that it is the state which is master, and is moreover determined to strengthen that mastery for financial reasons even if for no other. This is likely to continue.

Gone are the days when county and borough authorities suffered little in the way of central control except by the courts exercising their jurisdiction to grant prerogative writs to restrain ultra vires policies. It is true that those days, from the Revolution of 1688–89 to the Municipal Corporations Act 1835, were before the days of local democracy in multi-purpose local councils; but they were not before the days of the sovereignty of Parliament. Admittedly the supervision of the courts was not necessarily exercised entirely for the state's benefit in practice, even if it was so exercised in theory. A pamphlet published in 1736 pointed this out, with particular reference to licensing of public houses by magistrates:[8]

> 'When a Justice of the Peace, inspired with a true public spirit, meets with inferior officers of courage and intrepidity, and sets about a reformation of the unlicensed houses, he finds himself surrounded with numbers of pettifogging attorneys and solicitors, who watch his steps, and if there happens to be the least flaw in the method of drawing up and managing the proceedings, he finds himself obliged to attend a certiorari in the King's Bench, where, failing in some circumstances, the whole proceedings are quashed, and the magistrate, who has been at great expense, has the mortification to see the impudent fellow triumph over him and increase his iniquitous trade.'

The pressure by central on local authorities, it seems, will never let up for long, for money talks with one accent or another and it cannot be assumed that 'impudent fellows', 'pettifogging attorneys' and 'iniquitous trades' are entirely a thing of the past.

By 1982 the central government was far from satisfied that it had sufficiently brought local government to heel. Grants might be tightened up, but rates could still be levied in such a way as to enable elected local authorities to pay for the policies they wished to follow. Indeed rates were intended from the earliest days for that purpose, ie to put local authorities' financial destinies under their own control and make the discretion conferred on them—freedom of action in regard to policies within these fields of administration appointed to them—a reality. The Local Government Finance Act 1982 has now intensified existing restrictions on local authorities' powers to levy rates: this and the Act's other provisions will be discussed in the appropriate places in a later chapter.[9] It looks as if the future path of local government will be strait and narrow, and stony into the bargain, whether there is any additional reorganisation or not.

---

8 *S. and B. Webb* p 336.
9 Chapter 7 (see below, p 178). There is also new law in the Local Government (Miscellaneous Provisions) Act 1982 which will be touched on in various later chapters.

Chapter 3

Local authorities as corporations

A. Corporate personality

I. 'OFFICIAL CAPACITY'

The Local Government Act 1972, ss 2 and 21, provides that every English and Welsh county and district council 'shall be a body corporate'. The same Act, s 14, provides that in England a parish council 'shall be a body corporate', and s 33 makes similar provision in Wales for a community council. These provisions substantially re-enact earlier legislation to the same effect.

The concept of a body corporate, or corporation, and of the nature of 'incorporation', is a more difficult matter of law than perhaps appears at first sight; and because of its fundamental importance it needs to be examined at the outset. It is derived from the Latin *corpus*, a body. A corporation is something treated by the law as a 'body'; and to be 'incorporated' means to be recognised in law as requiring to be so treated thenceforward. Under the common law only the Crown, subject to the sanction of Parliament, can confer this artificial status. It is capable of being conferred on any number of persons; therefore the essence of the matter is corporate *personality* in law.

Speaking incidentally of the borough of Cambridge, F. W. Maitland wrote as follows in his historical essay 'Township and Borough' (Lecture I):[1] 'The invention of 'fictitious personality', as it is sometimes called, is put before us as a feat of skill, an ingenious artifice of jurisprudence.' He went on to speak of the 'moral and economic achievement accomplished in the medieval boroughs, the differentiation of "its" from "ours". This was a moral and economic, not primarily a legal achievement . . . Nowadays it is difficult to get the corporation out of our heads . . . We are not content with what the law does for us. Morally, *though not legally*, some at least of our multitudinous societies and clubs are persons . . . I say this because we ought to notice that if there is anything that should be called fiction in this matter—and I doubt it—we must not regard that fiction as the work of lawyers . . . It is not the lawyer but the man of business who makes the mercantile firm', ie a business partnership, 'into a person distinct from the sum of

---

1 *Selected Essays of F. W. Maitland* ed H. M. Cam (pub Beacon Press and CUP, 1962), p 11.

the partners' and . . . 'the layman who complains' when his sports club needs trustees because it is unfortunately not a legal fictitious person or corporate body.[2] In short, it is the general run of ordinary people who instinctively favour the concept of corporate personality. The law is prepared to recognise this, but not for institutions generally, only for some of them. Laymen tend to regard 'institution' and 'corporation' as virtually interchangeable terms, which the law will not do. The law was for a long time not even prepared to confer corporate status on local authorities, except in the royal charters granted to the boroughs, until the statutes of recent times created the comprehensive modern system of local authorities.

It is also important to realise that corporate status is not fundamentally a question of numbers, but of 'official capacity'. This is recognised by the law in the public interest, as and when appropriate. When a group of people are recognised in law as a 'body corporate', this is meant not to emphasise or reinforce their numerousness, but to counteract it. They are then to be treated artificially as *a* 'person', singular. This is because, being plural in actuality, they are in their natural personal capacities difficult to deal with effectively at any rate over an appreciable period of time, however important it may be to do so for various practical and public reasons. Groups are fluid: their membership is continually changing. The groups endure, after a fashion; but it is hard to say from one moment to the next who actually composes them, for the purpose of getting to grips with them as groups.

Therefore, in their 'official capacity', persons in a group are artificially regarded as one 'person'. And this is something which appeals even more to individuals themselves, who recognise the importance of groups as institutions—clubs, schools, firms, administrations—in regard not only to the convenience of getting things done but also to the inconvenience of being subjected to unlimited responsibility (as individual persons) for the things which do get done. In the event, 'official capacity' is recognised by the law only to the extent which suits the public interest in the eyes of the state, not to the wider extent which would suit the private interest of all individuals up and down the land, as Maitland recognised.

2. CORPORATIONS 'AGGREGATE' AND 'SOLE'

The fact that 'official capacity' and not numerousness is the essence of the matter can be seen from the terminology 'corporation aggregate' and 'corporation sole'. The former signifies a plurality of natural persons artificially treated as one 'person' for official purposes in the public interest. The latter signifies *one* natural person treated for such pur-

2 *Selected Essays of F. W. Maitland*, pp 12–14.

poses as *one* artificial 'person'. Each minister of the Crown, and indeed the monarch, is thus a 'corporation sole'. This concept, and corporate status generally, seems ̀ first to have achieved legal clarification, as distinct from practical significance, in the field of religion. The medieval common law was the more readily able to apply corporate status to boroughs for having had to recognise it already for the Church as a whole, for institutions within the Church, and for particular Church functionaries. Canon law showed common law the way. A modern illustration of this is unexpectedly furnished by the remarkable case of *Hayward v Chaloner*.[3]

This was a dispute over a claim by the rector of Bilsthorpe in Nottinghamshire to title by adverse possession—'squatter's rights'—in respect of a small piece of garden land. The plaintiffs had paper title to the freehold. The land had been leased orally at a yearly rent to a former rector, in whom the normal church property in the village was already vested in the customary way (ie the church, the rectory and the glebe land). A subsequent rector discontinued payment of rent for the garden land in 1942. A series of rectors then allowed local cottagers to use the land. In 1966 the plaintiffs claimed to determine the lease, whereupon the current rector (apparently at the bidding of the diocesan authorities) claimed title by adverse possession of more than twelve years, in accordance with the Limitation Act 1939.

Lord Denning MR thought that all the rectors in turn had possessed the land purely in their private capacity, for a series of short discontinued periods; but Davies and Russell LJJ regretfully decided instead that there had been continuous possession by each rector for the time being in an official capacity throughout. Russell LJ said:

> 'I do not consider that it is open to us . . . to hold . . . that the tenancy was other than one to the rector as corporation sole. The whole object was to make available to the rectory or the glebe cottages this piece of land: and the notion of a tenancy the personal property of the incumbent is not consistent with that object. There was, moreover, no suggestion of any assignment of the tenancy to a new incumbent, or of any new tenancy being granted to a new incumbent.'

Thus the nature of corporate status lay at the heart of this matter without there being any question of a group of persons constituting the corporate body. It is true of a 'corporation sole' and a 'corporation aggregate' alike that each is a single artificial person recognised at law for the purposes of acting in an official as distinct from a private capacity.

Maitland makes some penetrating comments on corporate status. He

3 [1968] 1 QB 107, [1967] 3 All ER 122.

observes:[4] 'It is not easily that lawyers come to think of one man as two persons, or to talk of "official capacities" and "corporations sole".' But he is of course talking of medieval law. Later he has much more to say, including the following remarks.[5]

'We have become so familiar with the idea of "a corporation aggregate of many" that we have ceased to wonder at it . . . Little enough in common have the divers of corporations known' (in the 1890s, much as in the 1980s, except for some differences of detail), 'to English law: for example, the Ecclesiastical Commissioners for England; the Dean and Chapter of Ely; the Chancellor, Masters and Scholars of the University of Oxford; the Mayor, Aldermen and Burgesses of the Borough of Cambridge; the Governor and Company of the Bank of England; the Great Northern Railway Company; Styles, Nokes and Company (Limited)'. But, 'we can hardly call one corporation more normal than another and modern legislation is constantly supplying us with new kinds. Thus we are not likely to find the essence of a corporation in any one rule of law'. Now, this is true enough as far as the detailed rules go. Yet it can hardly be true as far as the basic principle is concerned, otherwise the word 'corporation' as a generic legal term would be meaningless, which it manifestly is not.

Maitland goes on to say that we cannot in law point exclusively to common law or to statute as the source of incorporation. But this is a truism, because in any case common law and statute do not operate in isolation from one another: statute always presupposes common law in principle while enjoying an unrestricted freedom to modify it in detail at any time. Maitland continues:[6] 'to come to a more vital point, shall we demand that an individual corporator'—eg one individual shareholder or councillor—'shall not be liable for the debts of the corporation?'; and he points to statutory exceptions to this apparent rule. Yet once again it is a truism that the Crown in Parliament can make any changes in the laws within the bounds of intellect; but for all that, the legal concept of corporate status—one artificial 'person' inhering in a sole natural person or in a fluctuating aggregate of natural persons—remains valid. It is a rational abstraction, as well as a useful one.

3. CORPORATIONS AND THEIR CORPORATORS

A layman would probably distinguish between a corporation sole and a corporation aggregate by regarding the one as a 'functionary' and the other as an 'institution'; but a lawyer at least will remember that a corporation of whatever kind is a singular 'person' for legal purposes how-

---

4 Pollock and Maitland *History of English Law* Book II, Chapter II, Section 4 (Vol I, p 438).
5 In section 12 of that chapter (*Pollock and Maitland* pp 486–487).
6 *Pollock and Maitland* p 487.

ever few or many persons are the 'corporators'. He will also remember
that corporations, being abstract, cannot act in any material sense.
Their decisions are taken in practical terms by their 'corporators', or at
least a significant number of them, and are ultimately carried into effect
by personal agents—whether servants, officers or some or all of the
'corporators' themselves. This is not in any way affected by the fact
that institutional bodies—'corporations aggregate'—usually have a
'head', whether a president, chairman, mayor, chancellor, governor,
principal or other such personage. To have a 'head' is desirable in order
to ensure the orderly conduct of business, focus public attention and
enhance dignity; it has nothing to do with corporate abstraction.

This concept took a while to clarify in the history of English legal
development. Maitland[7] discusses a case argued in the reign of Edward
IV, in 1481, when the 'Mayor, Sheriffs and Commonalty of
Norwich'—ie the Corporation of the Borough of Norwich—resisted an
action to enforce a bond and relied on the defence that the plaintiff (a
powerful local Abbot) had imprisoned the mayor and 'extorted the
bond by duress'. Counsel argued:[8]

> 'In this case there is an alleged imprisonment of one of the distinct
> members named in the title of the corporation, to wit, the mayor,
> who is the head and (as in a body natural) the principal
> member . . . and if one member of the body natural be restrained
> or beaten, that is a restraint or battery of the whole body.'

In these words the aggregation of the persons who were the individual
'corporators' of the 'corporation aggregate', as duly constituted, was
being regarded as the 'corporation' itself. A plurality of natural persons
was being confounded with the single abstract person, by regarding the
'head' man of that group of natural persons as the 'head' of the abstract
'person'. Maitland comments: 'This idea . . . that every act of the corporation requires the assent of its head, that, if for a while it is headless,
it is capable of no act save that of electing a new head . . . is perhaps
capable of giving trouble even at the present day.' He gave another
striking example from Edward IV's reign: ' . . . the Mayor and Commonalty of Newcastle gave a bond to the person who happened to be
mayor, naming him by his personal name. It was held void, for a man
cannot be bound to himself. So long as such a decision for such a reason
is possible, the modern idea of a corporation is not secure . . .'

Maitland also refers[9] to an interesting earlier case, in Henry VI's
reign in 1429, when 'an action of trespass was brought against the

7 *Pollock and Maitland* p 491.
8 *Pollock and Maitland* p 492.
9 *Pollock and Maitland* p 493.

Mayor, Bailiffs and Commonalty of Ipswich and one J. Jabe. The defendants pleaded the marvellous plea that Jabe was one of the commonalty and therefore was named twice over. If the defendants are found guilty, then (it was urged) Jabe will be charged twice over; besides he may be found not guilty and the commonalty guilty: that is to say, he may be found guilty and not guilty.' The outcome of the case is unknown, but its argument shows a total confusion between the concept of a corporation as an abstract 'person' and the concept of it as an aggregate of many natural persons.

There was also discussion about the fundamental question whether, in the event of judgment being given against the corporation, execution could be levied against the goods of the individual 'corporators'. Maitland comments that the uncertainty over this as being an open question was 'remarkable'; but he expresses his own view that perhaps 'the non-liability of individual corporators for the debts of the corporation can not be regarded as of the essence of a corporation. Still unless such non-liability had been common, the modern idea of a corporation would hardly have been formed'. Yet that non-liability is virtually taken for granted in modern law, to say nothing of the reliance put on it by untold numbers of business men. Parliament may of course decide at any time to provide that individual members of a modern corporation aggregate (or even the individual who becomes a corporation sole) will be made personally liable for the corporation's debts. The result could be startling.

4. SEALS AND CHARTERS

The essential symbol of personality which the common law recognises is a seal. Even today, when documents are authenticated by the signature of the person executing them, or his mark if he cannot write, the application of a seal has a special formal significance which signature lacks. It authenticates conveyances of property and other deeds. Its contractual effect at common law (although not in equity) is to dispense with the need for 'consideration'. A sealed document is thus significantly different from an unsealed one, and because of its special nature an obligation contained in it is known as a 'specialty'. A natural person can therefore carry out most of his legal business by means of signed documents, contractual or otherwise; but he must use a seal where the common law and statute so require, which they do for particular cases demanding a display of solemn formality. When he does so he says, or is supposed to say, 'I deliver this as my act and deed' (which is why 'deed' is the generic term for instruments under seal) and this expresses the idea that the formality of sealing constitutes an individual's solemn and formal 'act' or 'deed', *par excellence.* As far as the law is concerned the seal embodies or expresses the individual's personality. It is fundamental in a way in which signatures or assertions or even oaths are not, no matter how much more satisfactory these may be for a variety of practical purposes.

For most people nowadays the existence of a personal seal is a legal fiction. Any document they execute is 'sealed' if it carries 'wax or wafer or other indication of a seal', as the Court of Appeal said in *First National Securities v Jones*[10] and this requirement is satisfactorily met by the use of standard-form paper supplied with an embossed mark, printed circle or similarly acceptable indication already on it. Clearly the 'sealing' of a document has a purely formal significance under this practice, though no less important for that. The question here is, how does this affect corporations?

There is no reason why artificial persons, like natural persons, should not 'seal' documents in this way; and indeed many of them, such as commercial limited liability companies, do so. A deed will often bear a printed circle with words next to it stating that 'the common seal of (the company) was hereunto affixed in the presence of' named persons, authorised so to act on the company's behalf. But in fact corporate bodies continue to do what any person (natural or artificial) is always entitled to do, which is to use an actual and not a notional seal. A seal is a carved or engraved or similarly produced device comprising a recognised emblematic design which can be stamped into hot wax, or onto the paper or parchment substance of the document itself. It is as individual and recognisable as a signature, and perhaps more imaginative. It can be affixed by someone else in the presence or absence of the person to whom it belongs; but this is of importance in practice rather than principle, because an agent can sign a document on the signatory's behalf. An actual seal, as distinct from a notional one, has an impressive or ceremonial function, analogous to the heraldic function of a coat of arms; and indeed the emblem used on a person's seal and coat of arms (if he has one) may well be the same, at least in essentials. The point is to express an individual personality in pictorial terms, so as to promote instant recognition and minimise any danger of confusion with other personages. Even now the law gives recognition to rights in heraldry; and amusingly it was a local authority which showed this by bringing proceedings in the High Court of Chivalry in 1954 to restrain another institution from making free with the municipal coat of arms: *Manchester Corp v Manchester Palace of Varieties*.[11] But this is a side issue. The common law came to recognise the seal, not the coat of arms, as the essential symbol of personality. Corporate bodies like natural persons are entitled to a seal and a coat of arms; but the latter's legal significance is purely ceremonial, like robes and procession and other pageantry.

10 [1978] Ch 109, [1978] 2 All ER 221.
11 [1955] p 133, [1955] 1 All ER 387. See below, p 220.

Maitland discusses how the adoption of the custom of using a seal crystallised the concept of artificial personality, corporate status, as against the mere aggregation of natural persons in a particular community. For contrast, he quotes a case[12] showing 'how the men of Toddington . . . by their unanimous consent' granted some land to the Priory of Dunstable; but afterwards, in proceedings brought against them by the Prior in 1293, 'they asserted that the transaction did not bind them because some of them were infants when the grant was made. This is not the way in which corporators behave; it is the way in which co-owners behave.' Yet it is important to note that it is not the receipt of a charter which was the determining factor in acquiring corporation status. Some charters gave property rights to the individual inhabitants of a town, in severalty: Maitland quotes by way of example a grant by the Abbot of Malmesbury to the men of Pilton near Barnstaple, 'declaring that the burgesses and their heirs shall hold their tenements in free burgage'.[13] The same could be done to individuals as coowners. At the other extreme, some charters were not grants to individuals at all, whether natural or incorporated, but legislation as distinct from donation: Magna Carta itself is an example, and Maitland also quotes[14] a charter of King John to 'the men of Cornwall', shires and sub-divisions of shires being portions of England as a whole, as far as the common law is concerned.

The borough communities which procured the grant of charters were the authors of their own corporate status, not the King who granted them those charters. Maitland says:[15] 'When in 1200 the community of Ipswich received its charter from King John, one of their first acts was to obtain a common seal and commit it to the care of the two bailiffs and one other of the chief portmen . . .' He goes on to describe this as 'a step towards the co-ordination of the boroughs with the religious houses, which in their turn were being co-ordinated with individual men'. He points out that although individuals may have seals, co-owners never have a collective seal (it is 'a formality which is never used by co-owners'). 'The community at Ipswich . . . seems to feel . . . that some new degree or even kind of unity has been attained: it must have a seal that is its, for it may now come before the law as pure unit and live as a person among persons. Rules as to when and by whom this seal may be affixed will be developed in course of time . . .' Chartered boroughs, having obtained privileges of self-government (including justice and finance) from the Crown as commercial communities, are thenceforth under the representative government of a group of promin-

---

12 *Pollock and Maitland* Book II, Chapter III, Section 7 (Vol 1, p 684).
13 *Pollock and Maitland* p 675.
14 *Pollock and Maitland* pp 673–674.
15 *Pollock and Maitland* pp 683–684.

ent and powerful citizens acting in council, who strengthen their collective resolve by taking a leaf out of the book of religious communities. Quite apart from their individual personal seals (if any) they equip themselves with a 'common' seal which, though meant in substance to bind them in the aggregate, gives them in form a single personality which the King's courts of common law duly and readily recognise because of its familiar nature.

The possession of a charter, then, was not the prerequisite for obtaining a seal; and Maitland quotes evidence that at one period shires, which were communities without charters, could have a seal.[16] But a charter, because it conferred a special status, seems to have been the prerequisite for the common law going on to recognise a seal as the official indication of incorporation. So the King's courts came to recognise corporate personality whenever a chartered community had taken it upon itself after receiving the charter to have a seal. It comes to this: (i) the royal charter if genuine was legally unchallengeable; (ii) the whole point of granting that charter was to give privileged status to the recipient community; (iii) a separate *personality* expressed by a common seal fitly marked that status. The common law accepted this the more readily because it suited the Crown to deal with borough communities on such a footing. It was a gradual process but a momentous one.

5. MUNICIPAL CORPORATIONS STANDARDISED

The Municipal Corporations Act 1835 reformed and standardised the constitutional machinery of the chartered boroughs apart from the City of London. But it was concerned with their councils, and how those councils were elected. Admittedly it incorporated the 'mayor, aldermen and burgesses (ie enfranchised citizens)' regardless of what the various charters had previously provided; but it did not alter the basic common law principle recognising the boroughs' corporate status as artificial persons. The changed constitutional pattern and the unchanged corporate status were later extended to county, district and parish councils by the Local Government Acts 1888–1933.

It follows from these common law and statutory principles that the provisions of the Local Government Act 1972,[17] referred to at the beginning of this chapter, by re-enacting that these local authorities are bodies corporate, impliedly recognises that each shall have a common seal. Section 14(3), however, provides: 'Notwithstanding anything in any rule of law, a parish council need not have a common seal . . .', though in that event 'any act of theirs which is required to be signified by an instrument under seal', eg a conveyance of land, 'may be signified

16 *Pollock and Maitland* p 535.
17 See ss 2, 14, 21 and 33.

by an instrument signed and sealed by two members of the council.'
Parish meetings, however, as distinct from parish councils, are not
bodies corporate. For them s 13 provides that any such act may be
sealed for them by the parish council, if the parish has its own parish
council because it is not a subordinate part of a larger parish council
area. If not, the two 'parish trustees', who are a body corporate comprising the chairman of the parish meeting and a specially appointed
officer of the district council, may seal it. If the parish council or the
parish trustees (as the case may be) have no common seal then the person presiding at the meeting and two local government electors also
present may make use of their personal seals (and must in any case sign
the relevant documents). The implication of s 13 is that, whereas individual persons may seal documents in the modern notional way, a local
authority as corporate body can only have a common seal of the ortho-
dox, specific kind. Parallel provisions apply to community councils and
meetings in Wales, except that there are no 'community trustees'.[18]

A crucial distinction has to be observed between how corporate
bodies *reach* a decision and how they give *effect* to it; and local authorities are no exception. The use of the common seal applies not to the
former but to the latter point, ie giving effect to decisions. In *Ludlow
Corp v Charlton*,[19] Rolfe B said: 'The seal is the only authentic evidence
of what the corporation has done, or agreed to do'. This expresses the
definitive common law rule. The words 'agreed to do' refer essentially
to contracts, and their effect in modern law has been relaxed very
greatly by the Corporate Bodies' Contracts Act 1960, which will be
referred to in a later chapter.[20]

The above judgment continues: 'The resolution of a meeting, however numerously attended, is, after all, not the act of the whole body.
Every member knows he is bound by what is done under the corporate
seal, and by nothing else'. Leaving aside the point that strictly it is the
corporation that is bound, not the individual members, the important
matter to note here is that this pronouncement does not in any way
impugn the validity of resolutions passed by majority vote as distinct
from those passed unanimously. The words 'act of the whole body' refer
to the giving of effect to decisions and not to the process of arriving at
those decisions. The passing of a resolution is indeed the only way in
which a body of persons can arrive at them. It may be that such a body
can be said to 'arrive at' a decision only as a unit; but if so, that is a question
of form rather than substance. In terms of practical business procedure
there must be votes on decisions, actual or tacit, despite the frequent
assertion nowadays that decisions are reached by 'consensus'. Majority

18 Act of 1972, ss 32, 33.
19 (1840) 6 M & W 815.
20 See below, ch 5, p 103.

decisions are authorised by the Local Government Act 1972, s 99 and Sch 12, para 39: ' . . . all questions coming or arising before a local authority shall be decided by a majority of the members of the authority present and voting thereon at a meeting of the authority'.

B. The ultra vires doctrine

1. PERSONALITY, POLICY AND POWER

Given that the law of England recognises the existence of artificial or 'corporate' personality for the more convenient pursuit of activities in the public interest, the question arises of practical interpretation of the law. It is established that an artificial person can exist in principle; but what does that mean in detail? How close is the analogy with a natural person? We know that a natural person is a human being and that what he or she is physically capable of doing is a pure question of fact: only the rights and wrongs of such conduct raise questions of law. Is this also true of artificial persons?

Clearly it cannot be true. The very concept of an artificial person exists purely as a matter of law: it follows logically that its attributes must therefore be a question of law as well. First, an artificial person being abstract, can do nothing physical in a direct sense; this however does not prevent natural persons doing or purporting to do physical acts on its behalf, just as they do on one another's behalf. The rights and wrongs of this in law raise the all-important question of agency, which rests on the principle that one person can incur benefits and liabilities through the actions of another (whether servant or otherwise): *qui facit per alium facit per se*. A considerable body of law has evolved round the question of when and how a person incurs them. In general, the law of agency applies to artificial as well as natural persons, subject to the obvious qualification that the material activities which give rise to any assertion of agency can only be the actions of natural persons.

Facts which are to be explained on the basis of agency cannot depend solely on the conduct of the alleged agent, otherwise no-one would ever be able to avoid the imposition of unwanted or unwelcome liabilities. Therefore the conduct of the alleged agent's principal and also the rights and wrongs of that conduct are also relevant. What the principal has instructed the agent to do is important in deciding whether the latter has acted on the former's behalf; but what the principal did not tell the agent, and what he *impliedly* told him, are equally important. In legal terms this is usually established by reasonable inference from all the facts, including decisions as well as the physical actions occurring as a consequence of those decisions. The importance of this for artificial persons is that decisions are a matter of policy, not inherently a matter of fact even though they involve many matters of fact. The significance of artificial persons is that the law deems them to exist for the purposes of policy, and recognises them so that policies may be carried out more effectively in the public interest. Natural persons, singly or in the aggregate, act in an 'official capacity' to this end.

'Policy' is nowhere defined in law. Some might say it is not a legal term at all; but if so 'discretion' is its equivalent. 'Policy' or 'discretion' is central to the law relating to public authorities. The essential question is to decide what policy decisions, taken by natural persons either singly or in the aggregate in an official capacity, the law imputes to the artificial persons whom those natural persons are deemed, in that capacity, to constitute.

The doctrine of vires (Latin for 'powers') exists in law to answer this question. Because policy decisions purport to be taken in the name of an artificial person it has to be decided whether these are intra vires or ultra vires: ie 'within' or 'beyond' the legal 'powers' of the artificial person in each particular case. Whenever this question is in issue it is a clear matter of law, to be decided judicially in the light of the relevant facts in the same way as any other judicial decision. The court charged with the task of making this judicial decision has to know where to look in order to discover the basis of these legal 'powers'. The question is, from what source does each corporation sole or corporation aggregate derive its 'powers'? The fundamental answer is that all 'powers' are derived immediately or ultimately from the central authority of the state, acting legislatively, in other words the Crown in Parliament, either by statute or by exercise of royal prerogative not overruled by statute. The basic principles derive from the common law and any grant or enactment has to be interpreted in the light of them.

Thus all corporations have either been expressly set up by Parliament, or impliedly sanctioned by Parliament with or without later statutory modification. If they have been impliedly sanctioned by Parliament this means that they were created by royal charter. Alternatively, in the case of religious corporations, such as bishops or cathedral chapters, and of secular functionaries such as sheriffs or coroners, they were appointed or recognised by the Crown from very early times, whether or not there have been later statutory refinements such as the Sheriffs Act 1887 or the Coroners (Amendment) Act 1926.

2. CORPORATIONS UNDER CHARTER AND STATUTE

Essentially a corporation created by charter is treated as possessing vires on a more liberal scale than one created by statute. A statutory corporation, in the words of Danckwerts LJ, in *Bell Houses Ltd v City Wall Properties Ltd*,[1] 'is not thereby created a corporation with inherent

1 [1966] 2 All ER 674 at 681.

common law powers'. Its powers are more restricted—in principle. Yet since they are expressly or impliedly restricted by the statute it may well be that the wording of the relevant statute is wide and generous.

In the *Bell Houses* case the corporate body was a commercial company set up with limited liability under the Companies Acts. Its memorandum of association thereunder empowered it to 'carry on the trade or business of civil and engineering contractors' and 'any other trade or business whatsoever which can, in the opinion of the board of directors, be advantageously carried on . . . in connection with . . .' that business. The judge said that on the authorities such a clause 'is able to make the bona fide opinion of the directors sufficient to decide whether an activity of the . . . company is intra vires'. Though in theory a policy discretion in such terms is less than if the company were 'a corporation with inherent common law powers', it is hard to see that it can be much less for practical purposes. A memorandum of association so worded virtually confers common law powers on the directors. If the company had been set up by royal charter and thus been created a 'common law corporation' its directors would, subject to the charter, have had all the freedom of decision-making that natural persons have. In this case the memorandum itself virtually gave them this freedom anyway.

It is probably true to say that the only surviving local authority in England to have enjoyed this measure of freedom is the Corporation of the City of London, whose existence derives from a series of royal charters and not from the various statutes which have constituted other local authorities on a very carefully circumscribed basis. Now even the City of London has had its functions regulated by statute.[2] However, it all comes down to interpretation at common law. The leading case for statutory corporations generally is *Ashbury Rly Carriage and Iron Co Ltd v Riche*,[3] The limited liability company in that case was set up under wording empowering it to manufacture railway rolling-stock but not to construct railways: a purported policy decision to embark on railway construction was thus ultra vires or, in the words of Lord Cairns LC, 'beyond the objects in the memorandum of association . . .'.

The common law principle is that wording must be reasonably interpreted. Harman LJ remarked somewhat jocularly upon corporate status in *Re Introductions Ltd, Introductions v National Provincial Bank Ltd*:[4] 'As Lord Davey said, the little man starting a grocery business usually combined groceries with power to bridge the mighty Zambesi;

---

2 In Chapters 10–12 below it will be seen broadly what functions are now statutorily conferred on the City Corporation.
3 (1875) LR 7 HL 653.
4 [1969] 1 All ER 887 at 888.

but still one cannot have an object to do every mortal thing one wants, because that is to have no object at all'. Natural persons are of course privileged to have no object at all; but artificial persons, even the little man's grocery company, and certainly all local authorities, must be content with the objects which the law prescribes (as reasonably interpreted): no more and no less.

Thus in *Tynemouth Corp v A–G*[5] Lord Macnaghten said that an interpretation of a statutory provision 'founded on the letter, of a subsection in an Act could not be sustained if it were 'contrary to the spirit and intention of the Act . . .' The Municipal Corporations Act 1882, s 140(3) (b), allowed certain local authorities to make payments only when empowered to do so by a statute *or* a court *or* 'by order of the council (of an authority)'; and it was asserted that this enabled a borough to 'order' a payment even if it were not a payment authorised by statute. The House of Lords rejected this, and held that a borough council could only authorise payments which were intra vires some relevant Act—ie made under statutory authority— notwithstanding the borough's chartered status.

Since the passing of the Local Government Act 1972, the part played by royal charters in conferring corporate status on local authorities has all but vanished. Yet, for the sake of understanding the general principle, it should perhaps be emphasised here that long before 1972 the chartered boroughs were largely regulated by statute in the same way as other local councils. The leading authority on the general question of the supersession by statute of the royal prerogative—under which the charters were issued until 1835—is the decision of the House of Lords in *A–G v De Keyser's Royal Hotel Ltd*,[6] which dealt with government requisitioning of property under prerogative and statute respectively. Lord Parmoor said that ' . . . where a matter has been directly regulated by statute there is a necessary implication . . . that as far as such regulation is inconsistent with the claim of a Royal Prerogative right, such right can no longer be enforced'. This does not mean that the entire prerogative is obsolete, merely that it survives to the extent that Parliament, in W. S. Gilbert's phrase, 'withholds its legislative hand'.

Royal charters could only be issued to boroughs after 1835 in accordance with the Municipal Corporations Act 1835 and subsequent Acts, not by independent exercise of the prerogative. This makes it hard to believe that the decision in *A–G v Leicester Corp*[7] was not made per incuriam. The defendant corporation were held to be as freely entitled as a natural person to buy and run a bus service without regard to any statutory authority because they had been granted a royal charter by exercise of the prerogative before 1835. This is hardly consistent with the *Tynemouth Corp* case.

5   [1899] AC 293 at 302.
6   [1920] AC 508.
7   [1943] Ch 86, [1943] 1 All ER 146.

3. EXTENT OF STATUTORY POWERS

Now that common law corporations set up under the prerogative (except the City of London) have in effect come to an end, the ultra vires rule is to be met with in local government virtually only in regard to statutory corporations. These are empowered only to pursue policies authorised by statute. The authorisation may be by express statutory words; but in the nature of things this can cover little more than the basic principles of their allotted functions.

Within those express statements of broad principle the statutory authorisation extends to implication of whatever is reasonable by way of detail. Lord Selborne LC said in *A–G v Great Eastern Rly Co*[8] 'whatever may fairly be regarded as incidental to, or consequential upon, those things which the legislature has authorised ought not (unless expressly prohibited) to be held by judicial construction to be ultra vires'. Lord Watson, in *Wenlock (Baroness) v River Dee Co*,[9] said that every statutory corporation's policies or 'objects . . . must be ascertained from [each relevant] Act itself [and also] that the powers which the corporation may lawfully use in furtherance of these objects must either be expressly conferred or derived by reasonable implication from its provisions'.

This principle is now expressed in statute. The Local Government Act 1972, s 111(1), states that ' . . . subject to the provisions of this Act and any other enactment passed before or after this Act, a local authority shall have power to do any thing (whether or not involving the expenditure, borrowing or lending of money or the acquisition or disposal of any property or rights) which is calculated to facilitate, or is conducive or incidental to, the discharge of any of their functions'.

The detailed application of this principle can be seen from various leading cases. In *A–G v Fulham Corp*,[10] a statutory power to provide baths and wash-houses was held not to imply a power to run a laundry service: the provision of the latter was thus ultra vires. In *A–G v Manchester Corp*,[11] it was held similarly that a statutory power to carry parcels on the corporation's trams did not imply a power to carry on a general delivery service for parcels. But in *A–G v Smethwick Corp*,[12] the corporation succeeded in claiming that the setting up of their own printing, bookbinding and stationery department was intra vires by being incidental to the performance of their functions generally; and in *A–G v Crayford UDC*,[13] it was held that the provision of a group insur-

---

8 (1880) 5 App Cas 473.
9 (1885) 10 App Cas 354.
10 [1921] 1 Ch 440.
11 [1906] 1 Ch 643.
12 [1932] 1 Ch 562.
13 [1962] Ch 246, [1961] 3 All ER 1002; affd. [1962] Ch 575, [1962] 2 All ER 147, CA.

ance policy for council house tenants was intra vires, in relation to the general powers of management of council houses enjoyed under Part V of the Housing Act 1957. The engagement of a consultant rating surveyor to advise on the effects of new statutory rating provisions was held to be intra vires the rating authority in *Grainger v Liverpool Corp.*[14]

C. The legal limits of policy discretion

I. JUDICIAL INTERPRETATION

The main question in modern public law, including local government law, is how the ultra vires principle should be applied from case to case. If the application becomes too lax, local authorities will enjoy a wider power than Parliament intended they should have; and if it were relaxed altogether their freedom of action would become absolute and their exercise of power would be quite arbitrary—however well-meaning the authorities' policy-makers might be. In the well-known words of Lord Acton: 'Power tends to corrupt, and absolute power corrupts absolutely'.

If on the other hand the application becomes too strict, local authorities will enjoy a narrower power than Parliament intended they should have, and ultimately they would exercise no independent power at all. Then local government would be transformed into the local arm of central government administration, if it did not wither away completely.

The courts' attempt to maintain a proper balance may not escape, or perhaps even deserve to escape, criticism; but there is no question of their not attempting to maintain it. In contested cases, when the legality of authorities' policy decisions is challenged, the courts consider each decision in relation to the relevant statutory powers, decide upon the extent of those powers, and reach a conclusion whether the particular decision falls within the boundary or outside it—whether it is intra vires and valid, or ultra vires and invalid. The result of a judgment that a policy decision is intra vires is that it remains undisturbed. The possible consequences of a judgment that it is ultra vires are various and will be discussed in the next chapter.

The clearest kind of case is the direct challenge on a point of detail in interpreting the statutes. In *Moore v Minister of Housing and Local Government*,[15] a local housing authority compulsorily purchased four existing houses in private ownership for use as council housing. This was alleged to be ultra vires; but the challenge failed because the relevant enactment, s 91 of the Housing Act 1957, refers to 'the provision

---

14 [1954] 1 QB 351, [1954] 1 All ER 333. For committees, see below, p 212.
15 [1966] 2 QB 602, [1965] 2 All ER 367.

of further housing accommodation', and since the four houses had been left empty for a long period there would be 'further housing accommodation' if the authority acquired and used them for council housing. The decision to acquire was thus intra vires.

General questions of function are less likely to give rise to disputes because it is usually clear enough from the express statutory provisions being interpreted whether particular authorities can carry out a given function or not. Whether by implication they enjoy a power to do something on the basis that it is 'incidental' to the discharge of any of their functions is more likely to be disputed; and the cases discussed earlier in this chapter on such matters as laundry services, parcels delivery services, setting up a local authority printing department, and insuring on behalf of tenants are examples of such disputes.

2. REASONABLENESS: THE WEDNESBURY PRINCIPLE

More problematical and interesting is the question of the *mode* in which authorities carry out policies, if those policies are inherently proper and therefore clearly intra vires in principle. Here the important factors are the common law concept of reasonableness and the equitable concept of fairness or good faith. They have been applied in countless cases since early times, dating back long before 1873 in the days of the separate courts of common law as well as the Court of Chancery in which the rules of equity emerged. They are now summed up in the *Wednesbury* principle.

In *Associated Provincial Picture Houses Ltd v Wednesbury Corp*,[16] the defendant authority's decision to impose certain restrictions on the Sunday opening of cinemas was challenged (unsuccessfully) as being ultra vires the relevant statute. In the Court of Appeal Lord Greene MR said: 'the Court is entitled to investigate the action of the local authority with a view to seeing whether it has taken into account matters which it ought not to take into account, or conversely, has refused to take into account matters which it ought to take into account'. This refers to the direct interpretation of the relevant statutes in principle or in detail. He then went on: 'once that question is answered in favour of the local authority, it may still be possible to say that, although the local authority have kept within the four corners of the matters which they ought to consider, they have nevertheless come to a conclusion so unreasonable that no reasonable authority could ever have come to it. In such a case, again, I think the Court can interfere. The power of the court to interfere in each case is not that of an appellate authority . . . but is that of a judicial authority . . . concerned only to see whether the local authority have contravened the law by acting in excess of the powers which Parliament has confided in it'—ie by making a policy decision which was ultra vires.

16 [1948] 1 KB 223, [1947] 2 All ER 680.

It is essential therefore to distinguish between being 'unreasonable' (i) subjectively and (ii) objectively. Subjective reasonableness is a policy matter: one person would consider it reasonable to follow a given policy but another would not. The judges are concerned only with objective reasonableness and must confine their attentions to deciding objectively whether a given policy is of such a nature that no reasonable person acting in furtherance of the relevant statute would follow it. In the *Wednesbury* case they decided that, regardless of what their subjective reactions to the council's policy might be, that policy was not objectively 'unreasonable'.

In recent years the crucial significance of this judgment has come to be recognised; and the test of objective reasonableness is increasingly referred to as 'the *Wednesbury* principle'. It would be hard to disagree with it without opening the door to arbitrary rule, even though the application of the principle to particular factual situations is itself a matter of judgment. Thus in *Congreve v Home Office*,[17] the authority in question exercised its undoubted discretion to revoke television licences purely in order to inflict reprisals on people who had surrendered licences and taken out new ones just before the date when increased charges took effect. This decision was held to be ultra vires because, though doubtless an understandable reaction on the part of the officials concerned, it was arbitrary and therefore, in objective terms, unreasonable.

Another leading case on the same point is *Roberts v Hopwood*.[18] A local authority resolved to pay employees wages which were found as a fact to be far higher than wages for comparable employment: the House of Lords held that this was an objectively unreasonable exercise of policy discretion and thus ultra vires. It should be noted that no principle was being laid down that local authority wages must not exceed the level in comparable employment, merely that on the facts of this case the wages paid were so high as to be unreasonable. This point is underlined by a contrasting case, *Re Walker's Decision*,[19] in which the payment of children's allowances by a local authority to their employees was upheld because the court considered it to be on a reasonable scale.

Reasonableness in this objective sense may have to be considered by another public body; and if that other body comes to a conclusion which is in turn unreasonable in the objective sense that conclusion will, by the same token, itself be ultra vires. In *Secretary of State for Education and Science v Tameside Metropolitan Borough Council*,[20] there was a dispute over the effect of the Education Act 1944, s 68, which

17 [1976] QB 629, [1976] 1 All ER 697.
18 [1925] AC 578. Contrast *Pickwell v Camden LBC* (1982) 80 LGR 798.
19 [1944] 1 KB 644 [1944] 1 All ER 614.
20 [1977] AC 1014, [1976] 3 All ER 665.

enables the Secretary of State to overrule the decision of a local education authority which is 'unreasonable'. The local authority in this case
made a policy decision to reverse a previous scheme for secondary education in their area. The Secretary of State concluded that this reversal
of policy was 'unreasonable'; but the House of Lords held that although
such a conclusion could well be arrived at as a matter of subjective judgment it was not legally sustainable as an objective judgment on the
facts, and s 68 must be interpreted as using the term 'unreasonable' in
the objective sense. Furthermore, although the fact that a policy decision is arrived at as part of a political programme has no relevance to the
question of the *legality* of that decision, yet it has great relevance to the
subordinate question of the objective *reasonableness* of the decision.
That is so because reasonableness is in itself a matter of proper inference from the facts, even though in its turn it will have an important
bearing on the ultimate question of legality. This is a distinction upon
which Lord Wilberforce laid great emphasis in relating the Tameside
case to the GLC fares case which will be discussed below.

Another leading case which throws light on this matter, notwithstanding that it involved the central government and not a local
authority, is *Padfield v Minister of Agriculture Fisheries and Food.*[1] The
claimants applied for a dispute to be referred under s 19 of the Agricultural Marketing Act 1958 to a committee of investigation set up under
that Act. The Minister, claiming that he had a discretion to do so,
refused. The House of Lords declared his decision to be invalid,
because a policy discretion is subject to reasonable limits and is not
'unfettered'. It must not be used to frustrate the objects of the statute
conferring it, including in this case the investigation of complaints
which were genuine and not trivial.

3. FAIRNESS AND GOOD FAITH

Fairness and good faith are also relevant to the validity of official decisions. In *Cannock Chase District Council v Kelly,*[2] a local housing
authority served notice to quit on the tenant of a council house in Ruge-
ley and then, the tenant having refused to leave, began proceedings in
the county court claiming an order for possession. The tenant raised the
issue of ultra vires by way of defence and, the council having succeeded in the county court, raised it again in the Court of Appeal.
Megaw LJ said: 'The argument for the tenant . . . is that, because it
was accepted that she was a good tenant . . . there was thus, without
more, established a prima facie case that the local authority must have
abused its powers'—ie acted ultra vires in its public capacity when ser-

1 [1968] AC 997, [1968] 1 All ER 694.
2 [1978] 1 All ER 152, [1978] 1 WLR 1.

ving the notice to quit—'by having taken into account some consideration which it ought not to have taken into account or, negatively, by
having failed to take into account some consideration which it ought to
have taken into account'. This of course is how the matter was put in
the *Wednesbury* case, referred to above.

Megaw LJ went on: 'One of the grounds on which a challenge can be
made, and, if established, should certainly succeed, is bad faith'. As
Lord Greene MR says:[3] 'Bad faith, dishonesty—those, of course, stand
by themselves'. But bad faith, or 'lack of good faith' must not be used
merely 'as a synonym for an honest, though mistaken, taking into consideration of a factor which is in law irrelevant'. In this case, the
tenant's counsel 'disclaimed any charge of dishonesty on the part of the
local authority or its officials. Lack of good faith goes'. But had it been
established, the council's decision would undoubtedly have been ultra
vires, which in this case it was not.

Yet even if they do not act dishonestly and in 'bad faith', public
bodies may still be held to have acted ultra vires if they have acted
unfairly. In *R v Liverpool Corp, ex p Liverpool Taxi Fleet Operators'
Association*,[4] the local authority made a policy decision on the number of licences to be issued for taxi-cabs, without considering representations on the matter made by the applicants. The Court of Appeal held
that although the courts should not interfere with policy decisions as
such, yet they 'could and should intervene to ensure that the council
acted fairly in deciding that policy after due regard to conflicting interests'. Lord Denning MR said that 'when the corporation consider
applications for licences . . . they are under a duty to act fairly. This
means that they should be ready to hear not only the particular applicant but also any other persons or bodies whose interests are
affected . . . and the court will see that they do so'.

4. QUASI-JUDICIAL AND ADMINISTRATIVE ASPECTS OF POWER

But this requirement of fairness, unlike 'good faith', applies only when
a public body's policy decision involves a 'quasi-judicial' element and is
not 'purely administrative'. In *Franklin v Minister of Town and Country
Planning*,[5] the Minister made an order designating the New Town at
Stevenage. The House of Lords held this to be, in the words of Lord
Thankerton, 'purely administrative'. In *Re City of Plymouth (City Centre) Declaratory Order, 1946, Robinson v Minister of Town and Country
Planning*,[6] a decision of the Minister to designate a 'declaratory area'
for redevelopment after extensive war damage was similarly regarded,

3 [1947] 2 All ER at 682.
4 [1972] 2 QB 299, [1972] 2 All ER 589.
5 [1948] AC 87, [1947] 2 All ER 289.
6 [1947] KB 702, [1947] 1 All ER 851.

as was a decision by the Minister of Transport to approve a draft compulsory purchase order for a new trunk road, in *Re London–Portsmouth Trunk Road (Surrey) Compulsory Purchase Order (No 2) 1938.*[7] Many procedures of this kind involve the holding of a public local inquiry by an inspector from the central government department involved. The purpose of these inquiries is for the authority involved in each case to hear what other interested authorities have to say (particularly the authority, if any, whose order or scheme is being considered for approval or rejection) and what objectors have to say, before a final official decision is taken. It is not to conduct a trial at which any of those authorities or objectors can 'win' or 'lose' their case, even though the inspector appears superficially to be acting as a judge by controlling the proceedings and inviting counsel to examine and cross-examine witnesses on behalf of one party or another.

The House of Lords has recently summed up this matter in *Bushell v Secretary of State for the Environment.*[8] In that case an attempt to hold up a scheme to construct a motorway by claiming that the decision to proceed was ultra vires, because of a failure to allow objectors to cross-examine at a public enquiry, was rejected. Lord Diplock said that in 'the common case in which a minister's functions are to confirm, modify or reject a scheme prepared and promoted by a local authority . . . the minister's ultimate decision is a purely administrative one'. That 'ultimate decision' is of course the essential factor in the whole procedure, the act of policy to which everything else relates. When a minister makes it, 'what he does bears little resemblance to adjudicating on a *lis*'—ie an action in a court of law—'between the parties . . . There is a third party who was not represented at the inquiry, the general public as a whole whose interests it is the minister's duty to treat as paramount'. This must be true generally of policy decisions taken by public bodies, whether local authorities, government departments, or others. It is equally true whether a government department is deciding to approve or reject another body's policy scheme or whether a public body is making an ultimate decision on a policy scheme of its own. There can be 'no obligation to disclose to objectors and give them an opportunity of commenting on advice, expert or otherwise . . .'

So, at least in so far as there is a matter where the interest of 'the general public as a whole' is the prime concern, the policy decision of the relevant authority is 'purely administrative'. A distinction must, however, be drawn—in the light of circumstances as a whole—between that kind of decision and other kinds of decision, whether independent or subordinate, where the interests of individuals (singly or in groups) as distinct from the general public interest come to the fore. The proper

7 [1939] 2 KB 515, [1939] 2 All ER 464.
8 [1981] AC 75, [1980] 2 All ER 608.

making of this distinction involves a careful judgment based upon a skilful and genuine analysis of all the factors. The principle is wide, and must be applied accordingly. Where the interest of individuals comes to the fore in accordance with this analysis, they must be treated fairly, within the limits which are appropriate.

The courts have tended to express this by saying that in the appropriate part of an official decision-making process there is a 'quasi-judicial' element. This is recognised in regard to the conduct of public inquiries, among other things. It does not apply to the eventual policy decision itself, for the reasons stated above. But, where it does apply, the courts will consider whether the conduct of the 'quasi-judicial' element of decision-making is vitiated by unfairness. If so, the ultimate 'purely administrative' decision itself is liable to be quashed as a result. But this kind of judgment, like the awarding of equitable remedies in private causes of action, is governed by the courts' discretion. This is to be applied, since the courts recognise that they, like all other public bodies, are required to keep within their proper jurisdiction and not behave arbitrarily, objectively and with judicial propriety. Such discretion is given further definition in many cases by Parliament, which frequently states that application to the courts to quash various administrative decisions must be made within a stated time: customarily six weeks. This should be distinguished from statutory provisions which state that certain administrative decisions are 'final' because that ought to be regarded as meaning something rather different—ie that those decisions are final 'on the merits' but not as regards whether they are or are not ultra vires. The latter in principle can only be a question for the courts, time-limit or no time-limit. To put it another way, a time-limit on application to the courts is appropriate always provided that it helps simply to guide them in deciding when an ultra vires decision should be quashed and does not prevent them from deciding the ultra vires question at all.

5. THE CONCEPT OF NATURAL JUSTICE

The proper recognition by the courts of a 'quasi-judicial' element in any administrative procedure, by reason of the fact that in the circumstances the interests of individuals have rightly come to the fore, as against the general public interest, lets in the consideration of 'fairness' to those individuals, when they seek redress from the courts. Fairness is often referred to as 'natural justice'. This does not mean 'justice' in the developed sense of the correct judicial procedure appropriate to proceedings in court (a lis inter partes). That point has been made above. It may be clinched here by reference to the speech of Lord Loreburn LC in *Board of Education v Rice*,[9] when he said that a public

9 [1911] AC 179.

authority 'must act in good faith and listen fairly to both sides . . . But I do not think they are bound to treat such a question as though it were a trial . . .' An objector is not necessarily entitled even to an oral hearing at an inquiry, public or private; but he must be allowed to state his views by letter at least, and have them considered.

Natural justice comes down to two basic propositions. The 'quasi-judicial' proceedings must be conducted (i) without bias, and (ii) in such a way that each party involved must be given an adequate hearing on each contested issue. Bias is seldom alleged directly these days, but the danger is always present. As Lord Hewart CJ said in *R v Sussex Justices, ex p McCarthy*:[10] 'justice should not only be done but should manifestly and undoubtedly be seen to be done'. In *R v Hendon RDC, ex p Chorley*,[11] the decision of a local authority on a town planning scheme was quashed for bias because a councillor voting for it was the professional adviser of a landowner involved.

As to affording an adequate hearing (the Latin phrase for this is audi alteram partem), the leading case is *Errington v Minister of Health*,[12] in which a public inquiry into a slum clearance scheme was properly conducted in itself, but the inspector subsequently had further private discussions with the local authority without the objectors being involved; the Court of Appeal quashed the minister's decision approving the scheme. In *Fairmount Investments v Secretary of State for the Environment*,[13] a compulsory purchase order for slum clearance was confirmed as a result of the report made by the inspector who had duly held a public inquiry but based his recommendation on a factor (settlement of the foundations of the houses involved) which was neither relied on by the local authority nor dealt with at the inquiry. The order was quashed because, as Lord Russell put it, 'Fairmount has not had . . . a fair crack of the whip'.

As far as public inquiries are concerned, at least in regard to planning and compulsory purchase, 'natural justice' is now supplemented by subordinate legislation, in the form of Inquiries Procedure Rules, of which probably the most important requirement is that the authority involved must supply in advance a written statement of its case. Failure to comply sufficiently with these rules will make the ultimate official decision liable to be quashed.

The House of Lords gave particularly thorough attention to natural justice in *Ridge v Baldwin*,[14] in which they declared the decision of a police authority to dismiss a chief constable to be null and void

10 [1924] 1 KB 256.
11 [1933] 2 KB 696.
12 [1935] 1 KB 249, [1934] All ER Rep 154.
13 [1976] 2 All ER 865, [1976] 1 WLR 1255.
14 [1964] AC 40, [1963] 2 All ER 66.

because (i) the appropriate procedure laid down by statute had not been followed and (ii) there had been a failure of natural justice by not telling the appellant what the charges against him were and not giving him an opportunity of being heard. The first ground was simply a matter of applying detailed statutory provisions to facts; but the ground of natural justice required a deeper analysis of principle. It should be noted that this case did not take the form of a private cause of action for breach of contract by way of wrongful dismissal of an employee, but of a public cause of action for removing a person from a public office in a manner which involved an ultra vires decision. Had the office been held 'at pleasure', the appointing and removing authority could remove the officer without stating any reason and still be acting intra vires; but here the relevant legislation clearly restricted removal to cases of unfitness for the post.

The principle of natural justice infringed in this case was audi alteram partem, as it was in the *Errington* and *Fairmount* cases. The appellant's solicitor was allowed to appear before the relevant committee, being 'received with courtesy but in silence'. Lord Reid, who described this as 'a very inadequate substitute' for proper hearing, discussed the main issue as follows: 'The principle audi alteram partem goes back many centuries in our law and appears in a multitude of judgments of judges of the highest authority'. Accusations that it is 'vague' are 'tainted by the perennial fallacy that because something cannot be cut and dried or nicely weighed or measured therefore it does not exist'. But negligence is an accepted legal concept, 'and natural justice as it has been interpreted in the courts is much more definite than that'. It is a common law concept, applied in early cases such as *Bagg's Case*,[15] which arose from the deprivation of the privilege of being a burgess of Plymouth, and *R v Cambridge University*,[16] which arose from the deprivation of the eminent but recalcitrant scholar, Dr. Bentley, of his university degrees.

6. THE AMBIT OF NATURAL JUSTICE

It has been said in the past that natural justice only applies to a 'judicial act' or a body 'having the duty to act judicially'. The cases make it clear, however, that its operation is in no sense restricted by this to courts of law. The phrase 'quasi-judicial' has been brought into use precisely to show that the concept is widely applied. Governmental bodies and public authorities generally have policy, or at least executive, functions; the courts must not interfere with the mode of performing these in so far as those functions affect the public interest generally, if there is

---

15 (1615) 11 Co Rep 936. The plaintiff had insulted the mayor.
16 (1723) 1 Stra 557. The plaintiff had insulted his colleagues.

no independent ground of challenge. But in so far as they affect subjects individually, in regard to person or property, there must be fairness, ie such bodies are to that extent acting 'quasi-judicially' and 'natural justice' must be observed. This being an aspect of the limited nature of their functions—the boundary of their 'jurisdiction'—it is for the courts to decide, when a challenge is made, whether they have been acting intra or ultra vires.

In *R v Electricity Comrs, ex p London Electricity Joint Committee Co (1920) Ltd*,[17] Atkin LJ said that this supervision by the courts 'has extended to control the proceedings of bodies which do not claim to be, and would not be recognised as, courts of justice. Whenever any body of persons having legal authority to determine questions affecting the rights of subjects, and having the duty to act judicially, act in excess of their legal authority, they are subject to the controlling jurisdiction' of the High Court. Lord Reid's comment on the case is that Bankes LJ and Atkin LJ 'inferred the judicial element from the nature of the power,' which was 'to make schemes with regard to electricity districts and to hold local inquiries before making them'.

But although the holding of inquiries is one of the best known procedures imparting a 'quasi judicial' flavour to administration, it is not essential. In *Cooper v Wandsworth Board of Works*,[18] the defendant authority made a demolition order for an unauthorised building, in accordance with statutory powers conferred on them by the Metropolis Management Act 1855, and carried it out themselves. The plaintiff sued successfully in the Court of Common Pleas in trespass for damages. Erle CJ said: 'I fully agree that the legislature intended to give the district board very large powers indeed: but the qualification I speak of', ie that the board 'should hear the party before they inflict upon him such a heavy loss', happens to be 'one which has been recognised to the full extent. It has been said that the principle . . . is limited to a judicial proceeding, and that a district board ordering a house to be pulled down cannot be said to be doing a judicial act . . . I do not quite agree with that . . . I think . . . that many exercises of the power of a district board would be in the nature of judicial proceedings'. This statement of the law is emphatically vindicated by the House of Lords in *Ridge v Baldwin*. All that has to be done to bring it up to date is to substitute 'quasi-judicial' for 'judicial'.

7. FIDUCIARY DUTY IN RESPECT OF FINANCE

One final aspect of the ultra vires doctrine which should be noted is financial. In the political *cause célèbre* of the Greater London Council's

17 [1924] 1 KB 171.
18 (1863) 14 CBNS 180.

policy to reduce fares on London Transport trains and buses, *Bromley London Borough Council v Greater London Council*,[19] the House of Lords referred to a principle 'that a local authority owes a fiduciary duty to the ratepayers from whom it obtains moneys needed to carry out its statutory functions, and that this includes a duty not to expend those moneys thriftlessly but to deploy the full financial resources available to it to the best advantage'.[20] The concept of a fiduciary duty is derived from equity, not common law.

Any general principle can be modified in particular cases; but the alleged modification in this case was held to be ineffective. The Transport (London) Act 1969 confers a general duty on London Transport Executive to provide public transport for Greater London, subject to guiding principles of policy laid down by the GLC, and also to aim for 'efficiency, economy and safety of operation' (s 5(1)). The GLC may 'take such action' as is necessary to enable the LTE to balance its accounts (s 7(6)). The GLC may make grants to the LTE 'for any purpose' (s 3(1)). Knowing that the government would withhold part of the rate support grant if fares were reduced in a manner not approved, the GLC on making that reduction issued a supplementary rate precept to cover the consequent loss of income in addition to the grant they themselves made to LTE under s 3(1) for meeting the reduction in fares. These statutory provisions were held by the House of Lords not to authorise the GLC's policy in this matter because the 'purpose' (s 3(1)) must be consistent with the application of business principles; and the power to 'take such action' (s 7(6)) must be confined to financing operations on a 'break-even' basis, so that only unavoidable losses can be covered by a GLC grant to LTE.

These points of interpretation depend on the particular wording of the relevant enactment. In *Prescott v Birmingham Corp*,[1] fare concessions to old-age pensioners were struck down on the same general principle of the fiduciary duty to the ratepayers. Though statutory authority for such concessions was shortly afterwards conferred by the Public Service Vehicles (Travel Concessions) Act 1955, *Prescott's* case is nevertheless authority for that general principle, and the House of Lords in the GLC fares case endorsed it. The House also said that, even though statutes may authorise a modification of or departure from this principle, no election manifesto can do so. Electoral support may be relevant to the question of reasonableness and thus a 'weighty factor', as in *Secretary of State for Education and Science v Tameside Metropolitan Borough Council*,[2] but it is irrelevant to the overriding question of legality.

19 [1982] 1 All ER 129, [1982] 2 WLR 62.
20 Ibid, at 165, per Lord Diplock. For subsequent compliance with this duty by the GLC, see *R v London Transport Executive, ex p GLC* (1983) Times, 28 January.
1 [1955] Ch 210, [1954] 3 All ER 698.
2 [1977] AC 1014, [1976] 3 All ER 665.

Chapter 4

Liability of local authorities in public law

A. Legal challenges and appeals

I. OBJECTING TO OFFICIAL DECISIONS

Natural persons may incur legal liability in various ways, whether at common law (contract or tort) in equity or by statute, whether civilly or criminally. Corporations, being artificial persons, may equally well incur such liability, subject to special qualifications as to detail; but because they are artificial persons they may also incur liability of a different kind which derives from their artificiality and which therefore natural persons cannot incur. Since this second, special kind of liability relates to the 'official capacity' which gives them their corporate status it depends on the operation of the ultra vires doctrine described in the last chapter.

It can be said that civil proceedings against a corporate body are either founded on a private cause of action, because that body is a 'person', or founded on a public cause of action under the ultra vires doctrine, because that body's personality is artificial. Much turns on this distinction, which is not merely technical but one of substance. The procedures followed when these public causes of action are litigated therefore differ markedly from those followed in pursuance of private causes of action. They are covered today by the generic heading of 'judicial review'.

One major cause of difficulty in this part of the law arises from the distinction between legal proceedings respectively at first instance and on appeal. This distinction is recognisable without trouble in private causes of action: the allegation of a tort, or a breach of contract or of trust, is tried at first instance in the County Court or High Court, and subsequent proceedings by way of appeal go to the Court of Appeal or House of Lords. But it is not so clear-cut in public causes of action. To challenge the legality of the actions of any public body proceedings may be brought at first instance in the High Court; and appeal lies in the Court of Appeal and House of Lords. But what appear to be first-instance proceedings in the High Court are themselves sometimes referred to as 'appeals'. The law here is confusing because the raising of these issues in the High Court is often referred to by words such as 'apply', 'challenge' 'complain of' or 'question', instead of 'appeal'.

Thus the Supreme Court Act 1981, s 31, speaks of: 'An *application* to the High Court for . . . relief, namely . . . an order of mandamus, prohibition or certiorari . . . a declaration or injunction . . .' Section 28, concerning decisions of the Crown Court, provides that they 'may be *questioned* by *applying* to the Crown Court to have a case stated by that court for the opinion of the High Court . . .' The point here is that this refers to Crown Court proceedings which, not being related to a criminal trial on indictment, therefore involve that court in its capacity as an 'inferior' court, so that in consequence it can be controlled by the High Court in the same way that public bodies generally, other than the High Court itself and the other 'superior' courts, can be so controlled. Section 111 of the Magistrates' Courts Act 1980 speaks similarly of applications to *question* a 'proceeding' of a magistrates' court by way of 'case stated'. The heading of s 111 of the 1980 Act simply says: 'Statement of case . . .'; but the heading of s 28 of the 1981 Act says: 'Appeals . . .'

2. 'APPEALS' AND 'APPLICATIONS'

This leads to the point that the word 'appeal' itself is ambiguous, or at any rate has more than one meaning. 'Appeal' for the purposes of s 28 of the 1981 Act means a challenge purely on an issue of law; whereas an appeal to the Court of Appeal commonly involves a rehearing of legal argument and reconsideration of the inferences to be drawn from the facts proved at the trial at first instance.[1] But 'appeal' is also commonly used in a wider sense. If a local planning authority, for example, decide to refuse an application for a grant of planning permission, the applicant may 'appeal' to the Secretary of State for the Environment, under the Town and Country Planning Act 1971, s 36. Lord Widgery CJ referred to this in *R v Hillingdon London Borough Council, ex p Royco Homes Ltd*,[2] ' . . . there is now . . . a comprehensive system of appeals from decisions of local planning authorities. In the instant case the applicant could . . . have gone to the Secretary of State for the Environment in the form of a statutory appeal . . . There would . . . have been open to them a further appeal to this court on a point of law following on the decision of the Secretary of State.'

But this 'further appeal' is not so described in the relevant statutory provision, namely s 245 of the Act of 1971, which states instead that a person who 'desires to question the validity' of the Secretary of State's decision on an appeal under s 36 may 'make an application to the High Court' which, 'if satisfied that the . . . action in question'—ie the Secretary of State's decision—'is not within the powers of this Act, or that the interests of the applicant have been substantially prejudiced by a

---

1 This does not apply to an appeal by way of 'case stated' from the Lands Tribunal to the Court of Appeal, which is purely a point of law (Lands Tribunal Act 1949, s 3).
2 [1974] 2 All ER 643 at 648.

failure to comply with any of the relevant requirements in relation thereto, may quash that . . . action'. Yet s 246, dealing with a parallel procedure relating to decisions of the Secretary of State in appeals against enforcement notices in planning, states that 'the appellant . . . may . . . appeal to the High Court against the decision on a point of law . . .' The 'application' under s 245 and the 'appeal' under s 246 are both by originating notice of motion under Order 55 of the Rules of the Supreme Court 1965;[3] though the time-limit for the former is six weeks (as stated in s 245 itself) but under the latter is only 28 days ('as rules of court may provide': s 246(1)).

An example of an 'application' under s 245 is the decision in *French Kier Developments Ltd v Secretary of State for the Environment*[4] when Willis J who described the proceedings as 'an appeal under s 245', quashed a decision by the Secretary of State dismissing the appeal of the applicants under s 36 against a refusal of planning permission by the local planning authority, Thurrock Borough Council. The applicants were held to have been 'substantially prejudiced by not being given a clear and intelligible statement of the reasons for the decision' of the Secretary of State—a point concerning the construction of a document, and thus a point of law. On the other hand, in an 'appeal' under s 246 (or rather the corresponding provision in an earlier Act), *Green v Minister of Housing and Local Government,*[5] the Queen's Bench Divisional Court denied emphatically that the proceedings could be treated as an 'appeal on fact involving a re-hearing with fresh evidence'. This 'blatant' contention by the applicant (or appellant), although plausibly based on Order 55 rule 7 of the Rules of the Supreme Court, was rejected because it is clearly at variance with the statement that such proceedings are 'an appeal on a point of law'.

It may be noted that Order 55, which includes procedure under s 245 as well as 246, is expressed in wide and general terms to 'apply to every appeal which by or under any enactment lies to the High Court from any court, tribunal or person'. This use of 'appeal' covers the spectrum of expressions, referred to above, of 'applications' to 'question' or to 'challenge' or otherwise to attack decisions of inferior courts, tribunals or other public bodies.

3. NATURE OF ADMINISTRATIVE APPEALS

These government departments and other public authorities are executive and not judicial bodies. The appeals they consider, in planning or other matters, are therefore administrative and not judicial appeals. This involves two substantial differences. First administrative as distinct from judicial appeals concentrate on issues of policy rather than

3 SI 1965/1776.
4 [1977] 1 All ER 296.
5 [1967] 2 QB 606, [1966] 3 All ER 942.

issues of law. Second, they lack a 'respondent'—or it may be truer to say that the body appealed from is also the 'respondent' to the 'appeal'.

Thus an appeal to the Secretary of State for the Environment against a refusal of planning permission by the local planning authority is conducted against that authority by the appellant before the Secretary of State. The Secretary of State must ascertain the relevant facts and comply with the relevant law; but his chief concern throughout, and that of the appellant and the local planning authority, is policy. The authorities—not the courts—are the experts on planning policy, and the appellant is concerned with them on that footing. Even when the law is eventually invoked for the purposes of proceedings under ss 245 or 246, the questions of policy are in truth untouched by that, though it no doubt often happens in fact that a successful challenge on a point of law may induce the planning authorities to change their minds on the issue or issues of policy.

In these planning disputes, therefore, and many other comparable administrative matters, there will be administrative 'appeals' from a lower to a higher executive body—commonly from local to central government—then legal 'appeals' in the sense of 'challenges' on issues of law from the higher executive body to a judicial body (the High Court), then perhaps further legal 'appeals' on issues of law to the Court of Appeal and House of Lords. In this scheme of things the second and third level of 'appeals' constitute appeals in the legal sense, while those at the first level do not—except in so far as the legal maxim *ignorantia legis neminem excusat* applies ('ignorance of the law excuses no man').

A variant of this progression can be seen where tribunals are involved. For example, in a dispute over compulsory purchase compensation a claimant who will not accept the amount as assessed and offered by the acquiring authority can refer the matter to the Lands Tribunal, which will make an adjudication on the disputed valuation, and also on disputed issues of law, if necessary. Appeal then lies, by way of case stated on an issue of law only, to the Court of Appeal and the House of Lords.[6] At every stage the individual concerned will think of himself as lodging an 'appeal'; but it will not be the same kind of appeal at each stage, and the first stage will in most cases not involve an 'appeal' in the true legal sense.

4. ADMINISTRATIVE APPEALS AND THE COURTS

Often the legal issues will not fully emerge until the dispute first reaches the High Court or possibly, as in compensation cases, the Court of Appeal. From a strictly legal standpoint that stage will be the equiva-

6 See above, p 74, note 1.

lent of a case at first instance, at any rate if it is heard in the High Court. The fact that it is described as an 'appeal' from an administrative tribunal or an executive authority makes no material difference to this, even though it will be a dispute of law and not—except incidentally— one of fact. In terms of the regular courts it will be a proceeding at first instance on a point of law seeking a prohibitory or a declaratory judgment.

Parliament has put much reliance on these administrative appeals to the courts. The origins of this tendency are quite remote, and show how artificial the doctrine of 'separation of powers' is. Judicial and executive functions were—and still are—considerably interlinked. In the law of highways, for example, the common law rule that a highway, once created, endures perpetually was modified by the operation of a procedure for stopping up highways under a writ ad quod damnum,[7] now long obsolete. An executive purpose, the termination of a highway, was achieved by judicial means, the empanelling of a jury by the sheriff, as directed by the writ, to deliver a verdict on whether or not injury to the public interest would result if the Crown were to licence the claimant to 'stop up' the particular highway. The 'public interest' has always meant primarily the collective public interest and only secondarily the interest of individual members of the public. The collective public interest is represented, first and foremost, by the needs and wishes of the Crown.

The Highway Act 1697 granted an appeal to quarter sessions against the jury's verdict in such cases. This would be an appeal in the sense of a legal challenge to a quasi-judicial proceeding, not the re-hearing of a case at first instance. The taking of an inquisition before a jury, the sheriff presiding, though judicial in form and procedure, was not a trial before a judge but the settlement of an issue of fact on examination and cross-examination of witnesses. In early procedures for compulsory purchase of land it was adopted for the ascertaining of compensation, as an alternative to arbitration. This choice was made available because the testimony might comprise either ordinary or expert evidence, or both. Whichever was the case, the issue was nevertheless a limited question of fact. An 'appeal' from such a proceeding would be akin to the statement of a case by an arbitrator to the High Court or an appeal by case stated from the Lands Tribunal to the Court of Appeal; except that an 'appeal', even from a tribunal or other public body, is not necessarily restricted solely to issues of law unless the relevant statute clearly so provides. An 'appeal' may be strictly judicial, or administrative with a 'quasi-judicial' aspect; but whether it is being used to decide an issue which is ultimately one of law or one of policy is an independent question.

7 See *Ex p Vennor* (1754) 3 Atk 766.

5. STATUTORY DEVELOPMENT OF THE APPEALS SYSTEM

The statutory appeal against an administrative or quasi-judicial decision to a court of law became an established concept in the eighteenth
century. It was given a wide and general application in a consolidating
statute for highways, the Highway Act 1773. Section 80 of that Act provided 'that if any person shall think himself or herself aggrieved by anything done by any justice of the peace or other person in the execution
of any of the powers given by this Act, and for which no particular
method of relief hath been already appointed, every such person may
appeal to the justices of the peace at any general quarter sessions of the
peace . . . giving . . . notice in writing . . . to the justice or other person or persons against whom such complaint shall be made, within six
days after the cause of such complaint arose . . .'
   As if to emphasise to modern lawyers that the justices of the peace
against whom such complaint was made would be acting not in a judicial but in an administrative or quasi-judicial capacity, that section
went on to require the return of 'all proceedings . . . touching the matter of such appeal' to quarter sessions, ' . . . on pain of forfeiting five
pounds . . .' Penalties for default are imposed on persons or bodies
failing to carry out an executive duty, not on courts of first instance
whose decisions are appealed against. Another example of this comes
from s 44 of the Lands Clauses Consolidation Act 1845, under which
any default by a sheriff or juryman in proceedings for assessing compulsory purchase compensation was penalised by forfeiture of a sum not
exceeding £50 or £10 respectively, 'applied in satisfaction of the costs of
the inquiry'.
   Even the court of quarter sessions, to whom the highway appeals lay
in accordance with the Acts of 1697 and 1773, should not be regarded
as hearing them in a purely judicial capacity. This can be seen from a
later statute, the Highway Act 1835, s 85 of which empowered two justices of the peace to certify that a highway should be 'turned, diverted
or stopped up' at the request of the local surveyor of the highways after
an inspection and the publication of official notices. Section 88 gave any
person 'injured or aggrieved' a right of appeal to quarter sessions, and
s 89 provided that the issue should be decided by a jury of 'twelve dis-
interested men' who, 'after hearing the evidence produced before
them', should return a verdict either for or against the proposed
change. Quarter sessions should accordingly either 'allow such appeal'
and make no order, or 'dismiss such appeal'. In the event of there being
no appeal, or of any appeal being dismissed, quarter sessions should,
under s 91, make an order for the proposed change in the highway;
'and the proceedings thereupon shall be binding and conclusive on all
persons whomsoever'. This order must clearly have been an administrative no less than a judicial order—all the more so as quarter sessions

could include wording giving power 'to purchase the ground and soil' for the site of a new highway.

Orders stopping up highways, other than trunk roads and motorways, are still made by justices of the peace, but in a magistrates' court on an application (not an 'appeal') by the highway authority under s 116 of the Highways Act 1980, no longer in quarter sessions (or rather the Crown Court which has replaced quarter sessions). A judicial hearing has to be given to the highway authority and to any other public body, or any landowner or member of the public, expressing a desire to be heard. Yet the administrative quality of the decision is underlined by the fact that alternative procedures are provided in which the orders are made not by any court but by administrative authorities, for example the Secretary of State for the Environment under s 209 of the Town and Country Planning Act 1971.

6. APPEALS TO THE COUNTY COURT

During the last century or so statutory 'appeals' have greatly increased. 'Appeals ' and 'applications' to the High Court were referred to above.[8] In housing law, the tribunal most favoured for this purpose by Parliament seems to be the county court. Under s 11 of the Housing Act 1957 persons aggrieved by various specified decisions of local housing authorities relating to repair notices or demolition or closing orders for unfit houses have 21 days in which to appeal to that court, which is empowered to confirm, quash or vary the official decision appealed against or to accept an undertaking to carry out works.

A similar right of appeal lies against notices to demolish 'obstructive buildings', under s 72 of the same Act, and against notices restricting the number of occupants of houses 'in multiple occupation' under s 90. The Housing Act 1964, ss 82–83, gives a right of appeal to the county court within six weeks against the making, by local housing authorities, of 'control orders' or schemes of capital expenditure for houses 'in multiple occupation'. The Housing Act 1974, s 91 gives a similar right of appeal against the service of an 'improvement notice' to carry out works for the provision of 'standard amenities' for water-supply and sanitation, normally in general improvement areas or housing action areas, in houses where they are lacking. See also pages 194–195 below.

7. APPEALS TO THE MAGISTRATES' COURT

Statutory appeals to magistrates' courts are also provided in regard to various matters. Under the National Assistance Act 1948, as amended by the Mental Health Act 1959, homes for old or physically or mentally disabled persons are subject to a system of registration by certain local

8 See p 74.

authorities, against whose decisions a right of appeal lies to the magistrates. Under the Town and Country Planning Act 1974, s 105, a similar right of appeal lies against the service of notices by local planning authorities ordering landowners to remedy the condition of any waste land detrimental to amenity. Rejection by local public health authorities of plans for building construction submitted in accordance with the Building Regulations gives a right of appeal to the magistrates under the Public Health Act 1961 ss 31–33. A similar right, relating to works for the construction of new streets in accordance with new street bye laws made by local highway authorities is given by s 191 of the Highways Act 1980.

In housing law appeal lies to the magistrates against notices by local housing authorities requiring proper standards of management to be complied with in regard to houses 'in multiple occupation', under s 14 of the Housing Act 1961; though under s 17 appeal against similar notices requiring works to be carried out to remedy defective conditions in such premises lies instead to the county court (the same time-limit, 21 days, applies in each case).

8. APPEALS TO THE CROWN COURT

Decisions by the magistrates are normally subject to an appeal in turn to the Crown Court, in civil as well as in criminal cases. For example the Highways Act 1980, s 317, makes a general provision to this effect under that Act. The Town and Country Planning Act 1971, s 106, provides for appeals to the Crown Court against the decisions of magistrates' courts in appeals against waste land notices under s 105, referred to above. Section 106 expressly gives this right of appeal only to 'the appellant or . . . the local planning authority'; but it is perhaps more usual (as in s 317 of the 1980 Act, above) to give it to a 'person aggrieved'. This latter phrase means not only the person who appealed to the magistrates against the local authority (if that appeal has been dismissed) but also (if that appeal has been successful) the local authority themselves, provided that they are 'left with a legal burden' which they otherwise 'would have discharged', as it was put by Parker J (as he then was) in *R v Nottingham Quarter Sessions, ex p Harlow*.[9] In that case the 'burden' was the provision of dustbins, for which either the landowners or the authority would be liable. But the same judge, as Lord Parker CJ, held in *Ealing Borough Council v Jones*[10] that mere dissatisfaction with an adverse decision is not enough, saying: 'a person is not aggrieved when that person being a public body has been frustrated in the performance[11] of one of its public duties . . .' Nor is an order to pay

9   [1952] 2 QB 601, [1952] 2 All ER 78.
10   [1959] 1 QB 384, [1959] 1 All ER 286.
11   Failure of a prosecution in this case.

the costs of an appeal enough to make the authority concerned a 'person aggrieved': *R v Dorset Quarter Sessions Appeals Committee, ex p Weymouth Corp.*[12] But this does not necessarily mean that the authority may not have some other right of recourse to the courts.

Sometimes, however, a statute gives a direct right of appeal to the Crown Court. The Highways Act 1980 has a leaning in this direction. Section 195 gives such a right of appeal to anyone 'aggrieved' at a refusal by the relevant local highway authority to approve plans for building 'a bridge to carry a new street'. Section 177 gives a similar right of appeal (subject to important exceptions) against a refusal to grant a licence to construct a building over a highway. Sections 188 and 196 provide similarly in regard to orders declaring existing highways to be 'new streets'.

A further complication is that these 'appeals' shade off into 'applications' ('application' and 'appeal' may sometimes appear almost as synonymous, as they are in regard to statutory procedures for challenging planning decisions in the High Court, referred to earlier in this chapter). Here the flavour is partly judicial and partly administrative. The Highways Act 1980, s 56, allows any person, if certain requirements are met, to 'apply to the Crown Court for an order' requiring the local highway authority to repair a neglected highway or bridge if the authority do not admit liability; and it allows an application to the magistrates for a similar order if liability is admitted yet upkeep is neglected. Here the judicial element is predominant, and bears some resemblance to an action in the High Court for a mandatory injunction. Procedure under s 116 of the same Act to 'stop up' highways other than trunk or special roads, as described earlier in this chapter, has a stronger administrative flavour in spite of being brought in the magistrates' court for an order to the required effect. There is provision for a hearing, because any member of the public can oppose the order. Yet it is only the relevant local authority which can apply, and they will do so obviously for administrative reasons. Moreover the procedure is paralleled by strictly administrative procedures to 'stop up' highways under the Town and Country Planning Act 1971 in which the decision is a ministerial one, made by the Secretary of State for the Environment.

9. PROCEEDINGS BY LOCAL AUTHORITIES THEMSELVES

The function of local authorities themselves to bring legal proceedings against others, as distinct from meeting legal proceedings brought against them, will be dealt with generally in a later chapter.[13] What should be pointed out here is that many special statutory provisions

---

12 [1960] 2 QB 230, [1960] 2 All ER 410.
13 Chapter 6 below.

envisage the making of applications by local authorities to magistrates' and other courts. The essential purpose of so doing is administrative, to secure the proper discharge of their appointed functions; but the procedure involved is sometimes mainly administrative, sometimes mainly judicial.

Thus in regard to 'statutory nuisances' under the Public Health Act 1936, if premises are in a sufficiently insanitary or unhealthy condition as to be 'prejudicial to health or a nuisance', the local public health authority 'shall serve . . . an abatement notice', under s 93, on the person responsible ordering him to carry out works to put the premises into a satisfactory state. If this is not properly complied with, 'the authority shall cause a complaint to be made' under s 94 to the magistrates' court, which leads to a judicial hearing and, if the complaint is proved, to the making by the magistrates of a 'nuisance order' to enforce the abatement notice. Appeal lies to the Crown Court. Alternatively the local authority may, under s 100, bring proceedings in the High Court. Under s 99 persons other than the local authority may bring a complaint if 'aggrieved'—which is particularly useful if it is the local authority themselves who are alleged to be liable for the statutory nuisance, as in *Salford City Council v McNally*.[14] Prosecutions may be instituted as well (ss 94–95).

In these proceedings the combination of judicial and administrative elements is remarkable. The latter can be stressed by drawing a comparison with procedures under the Town and Country Planning Act 1971, where a variety of notices may be served to compel landowners to remedy the state of land (uses or works) which is contrary to planning control or amenity (ss 65, 87, 96, 103, 108, 109). These are made administratively by local planning authorities and not the courts; though, as with statutory nuisances, prosecutions may be instituted in the event of failure to comply. The authority can carry out the specified works themselves, and recover the cost from the person in default. This can also be done in respect of 'statutory nuisances' under the Public Health Act 1961, s 26—but as a speedier alternative to nuisance order procedure and not at the stage of default. The person receiving the notice under s 26 of the 1961 Act is given the right to do the work himself provided that he takes action within a specified period. This in turn may be compared with administrative procedures under the Housing Acts 1957 and 1974 whereby owners of unfit or unsatisfactory houses can give undertakings to do works in lieu of having to comply with a demolition or closing order or an improvement notice.

Yet another combination of judicial and administrative elements can be seen in Part XI of the Highways Act 1980, which deals with the compulsory 'making up' of private streets at the cost of the frontagers by

14 [1976] AC 379, [1975] 2 All ER 860.

the instigation of the local highway authority. Under s 208 frontagers are given the right to object to the proposed works, on certain specified grounds but no others. At that stage the proceedings are purely administrative. It is for the authority, not the objectors, to make them judicial thereafter by applying to the magistrates under s 209 to 'hear and determine the objections in the same manner as nearly as may be as if the authority were proceeding summarily against the objectors to enforce payment of a sum of money summarily recoverable'. This in essence assimilates the procedure to a civil cause of action at law for debt: yet the magistrates may quash or amend the relevant resolution of the authority or the details of its proposed administrative action in furtherance of the proposed street works.

10. APPEALS CONFINED TO ISSUES OF LAW

Apart from other forms of legal challenge or appeal, the Magistrates' Courts Act 1980, s 111, and the Supreme Court Act 1981, s 28, as referred to earlier in this chapter,[15] give a general power to appeal to the High Court by way of case stated. This applies respectively to proceedings generally in the magistrates' courts and to proceedings in the Crown Court other than criminal trials on indictment (and certain matters relating to betting and gaming). The magistrates or the Crown Court are 'required to state a case' for the High Court on any relevant points of law which are in dispute; and it is for the Queen's Bench Divisional Court to decide them, subject to further appeal to the Court of Appeal and House of Lords.

Appeals by 'case stated' do not challenge findings of fact. Appeals by way of rehearing from the magistrates to the Crown Court, on the other hand, are general in scope, so that evidence of fact can be reheard as well as arguments on law. As for other legal proceedings by way of statutory appeals or applications, their scope varies according to the wording of the particular statutory provisions in each case, wide or narrow as the case may be. For example, objections to private street works which the local highway authority may bring before the magistrates by an application under s 209 of the Highways Act 1980, referred to above, can only be made under s 208 which lists six grounds of objection. The magistrates, therefore, cannot consider other grounds.

Yet it is the case that, in statutory appeals, courts which are empowered to hear these against the decisions of administrative authorities have jurisdiction to substitute their own decisions for those which are being appealed against,[16] to the extent that they find the case for each appeal to be made out and taking into account law, fact and policy matters as appropriate. In this they resemble ministers.

15 See above, p 74.
16 See *Pocklington v Melksham UDC*, below. For ministerial power to substitute, see *Norwich City Council v Secretary of State for the Environment* [1982] 1 All ER 737.

Any further appeal to the High Court or Court of Appeal can, however, only be made on legal grounds; though it must always be remembered that it is itself a question of *law* whether an inferior tribunal or other public authority has reached a decision reasonably or arbitrarily. Thus in *Pocklington v Melksham UDC*,[17] a local housing authority made a demolition order for an unfit house under s 16 of the Housing Act 1957, specifying 28 days for vacating the house and six weeks thereafter for the demolition. These were the minimum periods they were allowed to impose by s 21 of that Act. The county court, to which an appeal was made under s 11, considered the order to be justified in principle but wrong in detail, and the judge substituted for the two periods a single period requiring demolition within seven years. The local authority appealed to the Court of Appeal, the required legal grounds being, first, that the variation was unreasonable in principle and, second, that the replacement of the two specified periods by a single one was an infringement in detail of the requirements of s 21. The Court of Appeal upheld the appeal on the basis of these arguments and restored the demolition order in its original terms.

B. Prerogative orders and relator actions

1. COMMON LAW, EQUITY AND STATUTE

All the foregoing procedures are today based on statute, whatever forerunners they may have had at common law. They have been produced for a variety of particular purposes, and this explains their wide variations without necessarily justifying them. There is, however, another set of procedures for challenging official decisions at law, which are of general, though by no means universal, application. These occupy a central position in the scheme of legal remedies in the public sector as against the specialised positions of the ones discussed so far. They possess an underlying unity or coherence which has been obscured by superficial confusions until recently. Fortunately the Rules of the Supreme Court, Order 53, were revised in 1977 in such a way as largely to simplify and clarify this area of the law; and the Supreme Court Act 1981, s 31, has given full statutory endorsement to this reform. The term 'judicial review', having evolved as a convenient term among English lawyers, has now been adopted as the official description of the procedures governed by s 31 and Order 53. Not all sources of confusion, however, have yet been entirely eliminated, as will be seen; but they are much reduced.

The oldest stratum of judicial review comes from the common law,

17 [1964] 2 QB 673, [1964] 2 All ER 862.

though equity and statute have intervened subsequently. Common law recognised a fundamental distinction between public and private causes of actions. In private causes, ie contract and tort and analogous cases, the available remedy was and is compensatory, in the form of damages, apart from orders or writs of possession for successful claimants to legal estates in land. But in public causes, ie ultra vires proceedings, originally the remedies were the 'prerogative writs' of habeas corpus, quo warranto, certiorari, prohibition and mandamus. Of these the first remains a writ in order to mark its special significance for safeguarding the liberty of the subject; the second has been abolished as obsolete; and the other three were restyled 'prerogative orders' with a simplified procedure by the Administration of Justice (Miscellaneous Provisions) Act 1938.

These prerogative orders are central to the whole legal apparatus of making provisions for the judicial control of public authorities, in other words for ensuring compliance with the ultra vires doctrine described in the previous chapter. Under the original common law the issue of original writs in private causes—which means private by subject-matter, even if public authorities, up to the Crown itself, were parties to them—compelled defendants to do right to plaintiffs or else answer for their refusal, successfully or unsuccessfully, in the appropriate common law court. But the issue of original 'prerogative' writs in public causes operated to bring the official proceedings under the scrutiny of the appropriate common law court, King's Bench, to test their validity.

Of the three writs in question, certiorari would result in ultra vires proceedings being quashed if they had already taken place; prohibition would pronounce them invalid in advance if they had not yet taken place; and mandamus would order that official action must occur, in the event of an ultra vires decision having resulted in an omission to act. The original form of proceeding lay between the Crown and the challenged authority. But in course of time private subjects, including other public authorities, were allowed to apply of their own volition, ex parte, to the Crown, provided that they could satisfy the fundamental requirement of locus standi which will be discussed below. The proceedings then became in substance, but not in form, a legal dispute between subjects in the Court of King's Bench to determine an issue between the applicant and the defendant authority whether the latter had made a valid or an invalid decision; though in form they appeared to determine an issue between the Crown and the defendant authority. In spite of reforms and simplifications this is still the case today.

The clear-cut distinction between private and public causes of action at common law was not observed in equity, as far as remedies were concerned. The Court of Chancery was prepared to grant redress in public causes, and so invalidate ultra vires decisions, by awarding injunctions just as it did in private causes. When the Judicature Acts 1873–75 authorised the granting of declarations, the same applied to that remedy. This made for simplicity, by contrast with the complex spread of remedies at common law; but it also tended to produce potential confusion by obscuring the distinction which the difference of procedure and remedies made obvious at common law.

Remedies

	Private causes	*Public causes*
Common Law	Damages	Prerogative orders
Equity	Injunctions	Injunctions
Statute	Declarations	Declarations

2. 'RELATOR' ACTIONS AND THE ATTORNEY-GENERAL

The Attorney-General in particular found it convenient to seek injunctions and, in due course, declarations. He represents the Crown, which protects the public interest, and so by virtue of his office, being a public authority in his own right,[18] he has long been recognised as having a special and indeed unique role in bringing or defending proceedings in the public interest. He has therefore commonly become, ex officio, a party to innumerable public causes of action. The Crown acting of its own volition to restrain ultra vires decisions realised that it need not initiate proceedings by prerogative writ in the King's Bench when it was more convenient for proceedings to be brought in Chancery by the Attorney-General for an injunction.

Then in turn these proceedings became attractive to private subjects, including public authorities, wishing to challenge other public authorities' decisions. As an alternative to moving ex parte for a prerogative writ they would apply to the Attorney-General to bring proceedings for an injunction on their behalf, it being understood that they and not he would meet the costs of the litigation. If the Attorney-General agreed[19] he would bring proceedings 'at the relation' of the private citizen; and these have in consequence become known as 'relator' actions or proceedings. In spite of the similarity in form there is therefore a radical difference in substance between public causes of action brought by the Attorney-General on his own initiative in the public interest, as the result of an official policy decision to that effect, and 'relator' actions.

In *Gouriet v Union of Post Office Workers*,[20] Lord Wilberforce said: 'But the Attorney-General's role has never been fictional. His position in relator actions is the same as it is in actions brought without a relator,

---

18 Presumably he is a 'corporation sole'.
19 His decision is not subject to review by the courts: see *LCC v A–G* [1902] AC 165 per the Earl of Halsbury LC.
20 [1978] AC 435, [1977] 3 All ER 70.

with the sole exception that the relator is liable for costs . . . He is entitled to see and approve the statement of claim, and any amendments in the pleadings; he is entitled to be consulted on discovery; the suit cannot be compromised without his approval; if the relator dies the suit does not abate. For the proposition that his only concern is to "filter out" vexatious and frivolous proceedings there is no authority—indeed there is no need for the Attorney-General to do what is well within the power of the court. On the contrary he has the right, and the duty, to consider the public interest generally and widely.' Thus the relator seeks to bring the proceedings in the public interest, as viewed from his own standpoint; but the Attorney-General's necessary co-operation is given, or withheld, in the public interest as viewed from his ex officio standpoint as a Minister of the Crown.

In the *Gouriet* case Lord Fraser of Tullybelton observed:[1] 'The only case in which jurisdiction has been asserted to entertain an action for injunction or declaration in the public interest by a private person without the concurrence of the Attorney-General seems to be *A–G (on the relation of McWhirter) v Independent Broadcasting Authority.*[2] In my opinion there was no jurisdiction to grant the temporary injunction in that case, because at the stage when the temporary injunction was granted the Attorney-General had not given his consent to relator proceedings.'

The principle upheld by the House of Lords, therefore is, that no private person can sue for an injunction or declaration in a public as distinct from a private cause of action without obtaining the Attorney-General's collaboration in relator proceedings. This establishes in regard to proceedings for injunctions and declarations the same difference between private and public causes of action as that which independently exists at common law between private causes of action founded in contract, tort and analogous proceedings and public causes of action founded on the prerogative orders. There is however a circumstance in which private proceedings in public causes of action can be brought without involving the Attorney-General. This, as stated by Buckley J in *Boyce v Paddington Borough Council,*[3] is where ultra vires activity by a public body causes loss or damage that is special to an individual, whether natural or corporate, or infringes a property right belonging to him. In *London Passenger Transport Board v Mosscrop,*[4] Viscount Maugham in the House of Lords expressed this as 'interference with any private right . . . [or] special damage peculiar to [an individual] from the alleged breach . . .'

---

1 Ibid at 117.
2 [1973] QB 629, [1973] 1 All ER 689.
3 [1903] 1 Ch 109 at 114.
4 [1942] AC 332, [1942] 1 All ER 97.

But the exception is more apparent than real. Such interference or damage is essentially a private cause of action anyway: the ultra vires activity is merely its setting. In *Boyce's* case it was an alleged obstruction of a private right of light. In *Clowes v Staffordshire Potteries Waterworks Co*,[5] it was the fouling of a stream. In *Manchester Corp v Farnworth*,[6] it was the emission of poisonous fumes from a power station, thus causing damage to crops. Yet, in these cases the courts tend to consider whether there is a prima facie case of private liability, and then if the damage appears to be reasonably avoidable they stigmatise it as 'negligent' and say that this factor is itself a sufficient reason for holding the activity in question to be ultra vires. This seems to confound liability in public law with liability in private law.

3. FIDUCIARY DUTY TO INDIVIDUALS—PRIVATE OR PUBLIC?

A more problematical exception emerges from certain recent cases where private plaintiffs have in fact been allowed to sue for an injunction or declaration in regard to ultra vires conduct without involving the Attorney-General in a relator action; though it has not necessarily followed that they were successful on the substantive claim. A notable example is *Prescott v Birmingham Corp*,[7] in which the plaintiff claimed that a decision of the defendants to remit fares on their buses was ultra vires. Apparently no objection was made to the plaintiff suing on his own account. It was a public cause of action and yet the Attorney-General was not a party either in relator proceedings or ex officio on behalf of the public at his own official cost. The only justification in these circumstances seems to be that the plaintiff suffered interference with a private right or special damage particular to himself. Yet there was no cause of action here in contract or tort or any analogous field.

It seems that the justification may lie in equity. The Court of Appeal said in *Prescott's* case[8] that local authorities owe a 'fiduciary duty to their ratepayers in relation to the application of funds contributed by the latter'. At first instance in *Cumings v Birkenhead Corp*,[9] Ungoed-Thomas J said that this fiduciary duty is 'analogous to a trust and is owed to the ratepayers. This appears to me to summarise, so far as relevant for present purposes, the effect of *Board of Education v Rice*,[10] *Roberts v Hopwood*,[11] and *Prescott v Birmingham Corp*.' In *Bromley London Borough Council v Greater London Council*,[12] Lords Wilberforce, Diplock,

---

5 (1872) 8 Ch App 125.
6 [1930] AC 171.
7 [1955] Ch 210, [1954] 3 All ER 689.
8 Ibid at 706 per Jenkins LJ.
9 [1970] 3 All ER 302 at 312.
10 [1911] AC 179.
11 [1925] AC 578.
12 [1982] 1 All ER 129, [1982] 2 WLR 62.

Keith and Scarman all endorsed this principle of a fiduciary duty to the ratepayers. It must, however, mean that only conduct which has a financial effect detrimental to the ratepayers as such can possibly count as an infringement of this rule, as indeed Ungoed-Thomas J pointed out in *Cumings'* case; and also that the duty, though at first sight public in nature, must in fact be private and personal if it is to enable an individual to sue in his own name without applying to the Attorney-General.

Comparison may be made with *Dyson v A–G*,[13] in which the plaintiff obtained a declaration that because various demands by the Commissioners of Inland Revenue that he should submit detailed returns, subject to penalties on default, were illegal he was not under an obligation to comply with them. Lord Fraser of Tullybelton commented on this in *Gouriet's* case:[14] 'Other taxpayers could have made the same claim but the plaintiff was merely asserting his own right, and he did not purport to be acting on behalf of the public'; and Lord Edmund Davies in the same case,[15] described Dyson as having acted 'to institute what were, in effect, quia timet proceedings to protect his private rights and this nonetheless because the different private rights of many others were similarly threatened'. Thus a claim for a quia timet injunction was being regarded as equivalent to a claim for a declaration, in so far as both were intended to forestall future harm or loss.

Yet the harm or loss in such proceedings, though regarded as affecting the private rights of individual taxpayers such as Dyson or ratepayers such as Prescott, undoubtedly stems in these cases from ultra vires activities of public bodies. Nevertheless the courts say there is no need to invoke the Attorney-General's aid. Not that there is any guarantee that the action will succeed even though the plaintiff is allowed to bring it on his own initiative. For instance in *Smith v Cardiff Corp (No 2)*,[16] an action was brought for a declaration that a differential rent scheme for council houses was illegal, but it failed. In this case the plaintiffs were treated as suing on a personal basis, though aggrieved by a council decision alleged to be ultra vires. They must surely have been aggrieved in their capacity as rent-payers rather than ratepayers, however. Presumably a fiduciary duty is owed to taxpayers or rent-payers in the same way as it is to ratepayers, which gives each of them the right to bring proceedings in his or her own name to safeguard his private interest. It may in fact be necessary now to formulate a general fiduciary duty resting on all public authorities towards all members of the public

13 [1911] 1 KB 410.
14 [1977] 3 All ER 70 at 119.
15 Ibid at 111. Presumably the "rights" relate to money and other private assets.
16 [1955] Ch 159, [1955] 1 All ER 113. See also *Belcher v Reading Corp* [1950] Ch 380, [1949] 2 All ER 969, and *Summerfield v Hampstead Borough Council* [1957] 1 All ER 221, [1957] 1 WLR 167.

whose rights of property are affected by the policies of those authorities.

In the present state of the law, however, it is doubtful whether any such general fiduciary duty can be authoritatively formulated, despite *Smith v Cardiff Corp (No 2)* or even *Dyson v A–G*. In *Heywood v Hull Prison Board of Visitors*,[17] Goulding J pointed out that an applicant for 'judicial review' must 'obtain preliminary leave ex parte from a Divisional Court of the Queen's Bench Division or in vacation from a judge in chambers. There are very good reasons (among them an economy of public time and the avoidance of injustice to persons whom it is desired to make respondents) for that requirement of preliminary leave. If an action by writ or originating summons is used instead . . . that requirement of leave is circumvented'. In *Barrs v Bethell*,[18] Warner J refused to allow the plaintiff's action against councillors of the London Borough of Camden and the Borough itself to proceed for this very reason, the action having been begun by a writ of summons as in an ordinary private civil case though the cause of action was public. He said that it is necessary for there to be 'a filter in the form of a requirement that either the consent of the Attorney-General to a relator action or the leave of the Court for an application for judicial review should be obtained.'[19] The 'fiduciary duty' may vanish and leave claimants to choose, as appropriate, between pursuing a private cause of action and seeking judicial review.

C. Judicial review

1. RULES OF THE SUPREME COURT, ORDER 53

The Supreme Court Act 1981, s 31, which gives statutory reinforcement for the revised Order 53 of the Rules of the Supreme Court dating from 1977, states that 'application for judicial review' shall be the procedure whenever application is made for one of the prerogative orders of mandamus, prohibition or certiorari or for an injunction or declaration in lieu of a prerogative order. Application must be made to the High Court, which must consider 'all the circumstances of the case' as well as the availability of the prerogative orders before deciding which 'form of relief' to grant. Thus there is a unified procedure, 'application for judicial review', which is to be followed by any person seeking 'one or more' of those 'forms of relief'. Damages are also obtainable, but only on an ancillary claim where the circumstances are such that it would have been appropriate to award damages independently in an ordinary civil action (see below, p 132).

The general effect seems to be that the established law on the prerogative orders continues to apply, and that injunctions and declarations are

17 [1980] 3 All ER 594 at 598.
18 [1982] Ch 294, [1982] 1 All ER 106.
19 Ibid at 120.

to be available on the same basis as the prerogative orders. Since those orders have always been available at the discretion of the High Court and not as of right, the choice to be made between all these 'forms of relief' must itself be part of that exercise of discretion. Nothing here is available 'as of right', except the first hearing which is itself dependent on the prescribed procedure. Order 53 imposes a time-limit of three months from the occurrence of the decision complained about; but within that period any 'undue delay' will be a factor weighing against the grant of relief if substantial hardship or prejudice is likely to result against the person or if it 'would be detrimental to good administration'. This last phrase confirms, if that were necessary, that public bodies generally, and not inferior tribunals merely, are subject to judicial review.

2. LEAVE TO PROCEED: 'SUFFICIENT INTEREST' OR 'LOCUS STANDI'

Two other important requirements must be met. They are really two aspects of the same thing. As a question of form and procedure, the leave of the High Court must first be obtained before an application for judicial review can proceed. Thus, if the above-mentioned decisions in *Barrs v Bethell* and *Heywood v Hull Prison Board of Visitors* are right, as it is to be hoped they are, no proceedings for injunctions or declarations will be entertained in future which are begun by writ or originating summons if the cause of action in each case is not private but public—ie founded on some aspect of the ultra vires doctrine in relation to a public body—and if no private rights have been infringed or particular private loss suffered, unless the Attorney-General allows himself to be made a party by relator proceedings. Thus a truly public cause of action requires proceedings to be brought either (i) by judicial review for a prerogative order or an injunction or declaration, or (ii) by the Attorney-General in a relator action for an injunction or declaration.

As a question of substance, the High Court 'shall not grant leave'[20] to apply for judicial review 'unless it considers that the applicant has a sufficient interest in the matter to which the application relates'. This requirement of 'sufficient interest' is a modernised version of a long-established Latin expression, locus standi. The applicant, in brief, must be more than a 'mere busybody'. As Warner J put it in *Barrs v Bethell*,[1] public bodies including local authorities 'are particularly vulnerable to actions by busybodies and cranks' and so are their members.

So an applicant must satisfy the High Court first that he is not one of these in order to be granted leave to proceed. The substantial issue is another matter, and is the public cause of action which, in the circum-

20 Supreme Court Act 1981, 31(3).
1 [1982] 1 All ER 106 at 120.

stances, makes judicial review or relator proceedings appropriate instead of a private civil action. The grant of relief depends on the High Court's judgment on this substantive issue, and is still discretionary even then. It will be a decision based solely on one or more points of law, not on any general issue involving disputed facts.

At one time it was thought that locus standi required some property right of the applicant to be at risk. This is much the same as the interpretation of the words 'person aggrieved' in statutory appeals. In *Buxton v Minister of Housing and Local Government*,[2] neighbouring landowners who objected to the grant of planning permission to a company to work a chalk-pit were held not to be 'persons aggrieved'. Similarly, in *Gregory v Camdem London Borough Council*,[3] a neighbouring landowner was held to have no locus standi to claim that planning permission to change a convent into a school was invalid by reason of an ultra vires departure from the prescribed planning procedure.

But now the requirements of locus standi, or 'sufficient interest', have been relaxed. In *R v Greater London Council, ex p Blackburn*,[4] the applicants were a man and wife who sought an order of prohibition to prevent the local authority from granting certificates to show indecent films, the authority's decision being ultra vires because a wrong test had been used. They were held to have locus standi because the wife was a ratepayer and also, according to Lord Denning MR because they had children who were liable to be harmed by being exposed to such films. The latter justification is attractive but tenuous. The former seems hardly relevant to a case where the applicants' pocket was not at risk. In *R v Hereford Corp, ex p Harrower*,[5] contractors who claimed that the authority had infringed their own standing orders (which have the effect of law) on the submission of tenders were held to have locus standi, but only on the ground that they were ratepayers. The financial angle here was genuine but only indirectly relevant: ie they claimed as ratepayers but suffered as contractors. But this distinction may no longer be important.

The definitive treatment of locus standi in its new formulation of 'sufficient interest' was given by the House of Lords in *IRC v National Federation of Self-Employed and Small Businesses Ltd*.[6] There was an application for judicial review, for a prerogative order of mandamus and a declaration. The applicants succeeded in the Court of Appeal; but the Commissioners appealed successfully to the House of Lords. Their Lordships held that the total confidentiality of assessments and negotia-

---

2 [1961] 1 QB 278, [1960] 3 All ER 408.
3 [1966] 2 All ER 196, [1966] 1 WLR 899.
4 [1976] 3 All ER 184, [1976] 1 WLR 550.
5 [1970] 3 All ER 460, [1970] 1 WLR 1424.
6 [1982] AC 617, [1981] 2 All ER 93.

tions relating to income tax, unlike the publicity given to rates and rateable values, meant that the applicant federation as taxpayers had no 'sufficient interest' to concern themselves with the tax position of other taxpayers. These were the so-called 'Fleet Street Casuals', who were being subjected to more stringent inquiry for the tax years 1977–78 and after, in return for receiving an undertaking not to pursue questions of unpaid tax in previous years. Leave to proceed in the application for judicial review was thus refused. Lord Diplock added that on the substantive issue the applicants would fail anyway, because the Commissioners' methods could not be regarded as ultra vires. Lord Wilberforce expressed the view that the requirements of 'sufficient interest' may be 'stricter', or at least 'different', as between one remedy and another in judicial review (with particular reference to mandamus) because 'we should be unwise in our enthusiasm for liberation from procedural fetters to discard reasoned authorities which illustrate this'.

The question whether 'sufficient interest' is shown by an applicant only becomes relevant after it has become clear that an application for judicial review is appropriate; it is therefore quite separate from the question discussed earlier in this chapter whether the applicant can sue in his own name because it is a private cause of action or on the contrary should proceed by a relator action or judicial review because it is purely a public cause of action. *Prescott v Birmingham Corp* is a difficult authority to rely on because neither of these questions was dealt with, and it is all too easy as a result to assume that the court took either or both for granted. Perhaps it is best to say that in *Prescott's* case the Court of Appeal took locus standi for granted—after all, the applicant was a ratepayer—but ignored altogether the prior question whether it was open to the applicant to bring the proceedings in his own name anyway.

The House of Lords has recently attempted to clarify this matter by dealing with its central problem, namely the fact that injunctions and declarations are obtainable in both private and public causes of action. Now that the procedure for 'judicial review' has been overhauled there is no justification left for instituting civil proceedings against a public authority by a writ or originating summons except in a private cause (ie one arising in contract, tort, trusts or anything analogous to them.) Cases in which the proper exercise of an authority's policy discretion is in issue are essentially public and not private causes, and 'judicial review' with all its safeguards must be used, whether the remedy (if granted) is to be an injunction, a declaration or a prerogative order. In *O'Reilly v Mackman*[7] the appellants were prisoners who had sought declarations that procedures carried out by the prison authorities were void for breaches of statutory rules and of natural justice. The House of

---

7 [1982] 3 All ER 1124. See also *Cocks v Thanet District Council* below, p 128.

Lords dismissed their appeals because their actions had been instituted by writ and originating summons. Lord Diplock said 'to allow the actions to proceed would be an abuse of the process of the court. They were blatant attempts to avoid the protection for the respondents for which Order 53 provided'. All that was in issue was the alleged 'nullity of the decisions of a statutory tribunal'; and so unless 'none of the parties objected to the adoption of the procedure by writ or originating summons', or unless the claim was 'a collateral issue in a claim for infringement of a right of the plaintiff arising under private law', procedure must be by judicial review.

3. JUDICIAL REVIEW EXEMPLIFIED BY 'CERTIORARI'

The nature of judicial review, as it has evolved down to the present day, can best be understood from a consideration of the chief remedy in practice, the order of certiorari. Its significance is that it lies to quash invalid decisions. As a result the principal point at issue, which is whether an inferior tribunal or other public authority has acted ultra vires, comes most clearly into focus. Prohibition is less commonly required because it relates to future activities, and the time element in legal proceedings is such that any challenged decision of a public body usually lies in the past by the time the dispute reaches court. Mandamus is also less common because its purpose is to cure unlawful omissions, which is harder than curing unlawful actions. These two remedies together with injunctions and declarations are, so to speak, variations on the main theme expressed by certiorari.

In *R v West Sussex Quarter Sessions, ex p Albert and Maud Johnson Trust*,[8] Lawton LJ sketched in the background of certiorari. 'The origins of certiorari are medieval; as a remedy it developed out of the medieval concept that the King through his curia regis was entitled to and, because he was the fountain of justice, should supervise and discipline all inferior . . . courts. By the second half of the 17th century this remedy had begun to take its modern form and the Court of King's Bench began to exercise supervision over many of the so-called "quasi-judicial" activities, largely administrative, of quarter sessions which, under the Tudors, had become one of the organs of government.' He referred to the judgment of Lord Mansfield CJ, in *R v Moreley*,[9] who said: 'A certiorari does not go, to try the merits of the question . . . but to see whether the limited jurisdiction have exceeded their bounds'. He referred also to the judgment of Lord Denman CJ in *R v Bolton*,[10] who said that '. . . the legislature has trusted the . . . jurisdiction in the merits to the [tribunal] below. . . . All that we can then do, when their

8 [1973] 3 All ER 289 at 299.
9 (1760) 2 Burr 1040 at 1042.
10 (1841) 1 QB 66 at 72.

decision is complained of, is to see that the case was one within their jurisdiction . . .'

4. ERRORS OF LAW, EVIDENCE AND DISCRETION

The wording of the old common law writ of certiorari can be seen by reading the judgment of Denning LJ (as he then was) in *R v Northumberland Compensation Appeal Tribunal, ex p Shaw.*[11] He went on to deal with the distinction between 'excess of jurisdiction' and 'errors of law', to make clear that *certiorari* applied to both. It is probably best to say that the former means ultra vires in principle (if for example a tribunal or authority set up to deal with one matter decides to deal with a different one) and the latter with ultra vires in detail. The latter cannot be investigated in the absence of evidence as to that detail, known as 'the record' of the lower tribunal or other public authority. Certiorari required 'the record' to be sent up to the Court of King's Bench. In civil matters 'the record' meant documents establishing the jurisdiction (ie function) conferred on the body in question and the decision arrived at. But the 'error of law' had to 'appear on the face of the record'; and since the evidence and the reasons for the decision need not be sent up, any error residing in them could not be checked. If the evidence found was in fact submitted for consideration this was known as a 'case stated', which has in modern times been turned into a separate appeal procedure, distinct from certiorari as described earlier in this chapter.

If an alleged error of law did not appear 'on the face of the record', evidence could not be produced to the King's Bench. But evidence could be produced for the purpose of proving that the record was not complete: see *R v Anon.*[12] Evidence could in any case only be presented in documentary form, by affidavits. This is consistent with the fact that, as Denning LJ said:[13] 'the King's Bench does not substitute its own views for those of the tribunal, as a court of appeal would do'. It acts 'not in an appellate capacity, but in a supervisory capacity'. The point of law being settled one way or the other, the inferior tribunal or other public authority is free to consider the matter again in the light of the clarification of the law, and may indeed be commanded to do so. As for the giving of reasons, many statutes now require this to be done in various circumstances, notably the Tribunals and Inquiries Act 1971, s 12, which requires ministers to do so in cases in which public inquiries are or could be held.

The current of opinion now favours the abandonment of the distinction between (i) 'error of jurisdiction' and (ii) 'error of law within jurisdiction' whether on or not on the face of the record. In *Pearlman v*

---

11 [1952] 1 All ER 122.
12 (1816) 2 Chit 137.
13 [1952] 1 All ER 122 at 127.

Keepers and Governors of Harrow School,[14] Lord Denning MR said:
'The way to get things right is to hold thus: no court or tribunal has any
jurisdiction to make an error of law on which the decision of the case
depends. If it makes such an error, it goes outside its jurisdiction and
certiorari will lie to correct it'.

This does not apply to the judgment of a court of law when statute
declares that there is no appeal from it, as the House of Lords stressed in
Re Racal Communications Ltd.[15] But in that case Lord Diplock also said
that 'the old distinction between errors of law that went to jurisdiction
and errors of law that did not was for practical purposes abolished'[16] by
the decision of the House of Lords in *Anisminic v Foreign Compensation
Commission*.[17] He added: 'Any error of law that could be shown to have
been made by [inferior tribunals or other public authorities] in the
course of reaching their decision on matters of fact, or of administrative
policy, would result in their having asked themselves the wrong question with the result that the decision they reached would be a nullity.
The Tribunals and Inquiries Act 1971 [referred to above] . . . now
supplemented by the provision for discovery in applications for judicial
review under RSC Ord 53, facilitates the detection of errors of law by
those tribunals and by administrative authorities generally'.

On the question of evidence, in *R v Secretary of State for the Environment, ex p Powis*,[18] Dunn LJ said: 'What are the principles on which
fresh evidence should be admitted on judicial review? They are:
(1) . . . to show what material was before the minister or inferior tribunal . . .; (2) where the jurisdiction . . . depends on a question of fact,
or . . . whether essential procedural requirements were observed, the
court may receive and consider additional evidence to determine the
jurisdictional fact or procedural error . . .; (3) where the proceedings
are tainted by misconduct . . . (such as) bias by the decision-making
body, or fraud or perjury by a party . . .' But the courts take care to
stress the discretionary nature of judicial review. Shaw LJ said in *R v
Herrod, ex p Leeds City District Council*:[19] 'An applicant for a prerogative order . . . is . . . a suppliant who seeks to invoke those remedial
measures on the ground that the High Court would wish to correct
some irregularity . . . which has caused him to be aggrieved, so that
justice may be done. Whether the order sought will be granted or
refused is a matter wholly within the court's discretion: prerogative
orders are not to be claimed as of right. . . . If there has been unreasonable delay, then even though the application for leave is made within

14 [1979] 1 All ER 365 at 372.
15 [1980] 2 All ER 634 at 638–639.
16 Ibid.
17 [1969] 2 AC 147, [1969] 1 All ER 208.
18 [1981] 1 All ER 788 at 797.
19 [1976] 1 All ER 273 at 292.

[the proper time], resulting hardship to an opposing party may well be a reason for refusing the order sought'. In the same case Lord Denning MR said:[20] 'If a person comes to the High Court seeking certiorari to quash the decision [of an inferior tribunal or other public authority] . . . he should act promptly and before the other party has taken any step on the faith of the decision. Else he may find that the High Court will refuse him a remedy'.

5. CONVENIENCE OF REMEDY

What if a statutory right of appeal or challenge exists apart from judicial review? It has been thought that judicial review only applies when there is no other remedy. As Lord Widgery CJ said in *R v Hillingdon London Borough Council, ex p Royco Homes:*[1] '. . . it has always been a principle that certiorari will go only where there is no other equally effective and convenient remedy. In the planning field there are very often . . . equally effective and convenient remedies'. Often 'the statutory system of appeals is more effective and more convenient than an application for certiorari, and the principal reason . . . is that an appeal to the Secretary of State on all issues arising between the parties can be disposed of at one hearing. Whether the issue between them is a matter of law or fact, or policy or opinion, or a combination . . . [he] has jurisdiction to deal with them all, whereas of course an application for certiorari is limited to cases where the issue is a matter of law . . . Furthermore . . . in some instances . . . an action for a declaration is more appropriate and more convenient . . . But an application for certiorari has this advantage that it is speedier and cheaper than the other methods, and in a proper case, therefore, it may well be right to allow it to be used in preference to them.'

The exercise of this choice in an appropriate matter is clearly part of the discretion which the High Court will exercise when application is made for judicial review. An interesting example of this is *Chief Constable of the North Wales Police v Evans,*[2] in which the House of Lords held that a declaration, and not mandamus, was the appropriate remedy for an ultra vires dismissal of a probationary constable, since mandamus 'might border on an assumption of the powers of the chief constable.'

6. SUBSTANTIVE ISSUES

In all this procedural complexity it is hard not to lose sight of the substantive issues which may lead to the award of a remedy by way of judicial

---

20 Ibid at 278. Lord Denning stressed that 'certiorari is not an appeal at all. It is an exercise by the High Court in its power to supervise inferior tribunals . . . The timelimit . . . is not an entitlement. It is a maximum . . . [and] there is the overriding rule that the remedy by certiorari is discretionary.'

1 [1974] 2 All ER 643 at 648–649.

2 [1982] 3 All ER 141, [1982] 1 WLR 1155.

review. An example of an appropriate case for certiorari is *R v Barnsley Metropolitan Borough Council, ex p Hook*.[3] A market trader had his licence as a stallholder in Barnsley market revoked for life after he had undergone 'an urgent call of nature' and relieved himself in an adjoining street. The local authority in question was held to have acted in breach of the rules of natural justice by the arbitrary manner in which the affair was handled. There was bias, and the trader was not given a proper hearing; and the penalty imposed was altogether—and thus unreasonably—disproportionate to the offence. Certiorari was granted to quash the decision.

An example of an application for an order of prohibition can be seen in *R v Greater London Council, ex p Blackburn*,[4] discussed above. An example of an application for an order of mandamus can be seen in *R v Bristol Corp, ex p Hendy*,[5] in which the claimant had been displaced from an unfit house and the local authority had rehoused him temporarily. His claim was that he should be given a council house; but the application for an order of mandamus was refused on the ground that it would force the authority to let him 'jump the queue' of persons on their waiting list, which would be quite unreasonable. More successful was the application in *R v Poplar Borough Council (No 2)*,[6] where a rating authority rejected a county council precept for rates without any legal justification, and it was held that mandamus was the appropriate remedy to compel them to comply with the precept.

As for injunctions and declarations, *Barrs v Bethell* and s 31 of the Supreme Court Act 1981, as discussed above,[7] seem to suggest that those remedies are appropriate in a purely public cause of action so long as the procedure for seeking judicial review is properly followed. But Lord Denning MR, in *Heywood v Hull Prison Board of Visitors*,[8] in the Court of Appeal, has suggested that injunctions and declarations are unnecessary in these cases now that the prerogative orders operate under the revised Ord 53 of RSC by way of 'judicial review'.

D. Preclusive clauses

Many Acts of Parliament state that the decision of inferior tribunals and other public authorities are 'final', or 'shall not be questioned'. Sometimes this is expressed unconditionally; sometimes it is said that they shall not be questioned *except* under some prescribed procedure or

3 [1976] 3 All ER 452, [1976] 1 WLR 1052.
4 [1976] 3 All ER 184, [1976] 1 WLR 550.
5 [1974] 1 All ER 1047, [1974] 1 WLR 498.
6 [1922] 1 KB 95.
7 See p 90.
8 (1982) Times, 30 June.

within a limited time or both. Lord Wilberforce, in *Anisminic v Foreign Compensation Commission*,[9] refers to these as 'preclusive clauses'. The 'preclusive clause' in the *Anisminic* case said that the relevant decisions of the defendant body 'shall not be called in question in any court of law'. The House of Lords, by a majority of three to two, held that this restriction could not apply to a decision which was a nullity. In the words of Lord Reid:[10] 'It is one thing to question a determination which does exist; it is quite another thing to say that there is nothing to be questioned'. In the latter case the supposed decision is a nullity, and a superior court is entitled to say so, in proceedings for judicial review. If the law were otherwise, according to Lord Pearce,[11] 'the court . . . could not even enquire whether a purported determination was a forged or inaccurate order'.

In *R v Secretary of State for the Environment, ex p Ostler*,[12] however, the Court of Appeal refused to apply the *Anisminic* decision to a compulsory purchase order which was alleged to have been protected from challenge by prevention of relevant information from being made public. It was pointed out that the decision to confirm the order was subject to challenge in the High Court whereas the 'preclusive clause' in *Anisminic* was unconditional; though the period of challenge was limited to six weeks, as is common in these statutory provisions. The question of time is of course relevant in any case to the way in which the discretion of the High Court is exercised, as Lord Denning's remarks in the *Herrod* case (discussed above[13]) indicate. But the question of 'nullity' is important independently of this.

The essential distinction seems to be the familiar one between the ultra vires principle and challenge 'on the merits'. The latter is not appropriate for judicial review while the former is. In *Graddage v Haringey London Borough Council*.[14] Walton J held that certain notices purportedly issued under s 9 of the Housing Act 1957 by a local housing authority were clearly invalid on their face because they were signed by the council treasurer whereas the Act required them to be signed by the clerk. There was thus no need to appeal against them and they could be ignored. Similarly in *West Ham Corp v Charles Benabo & Sons*[15] an invalid demand for reimbursement of expenses could be ignored, not having been signed by the correct council officer; whereas in *Benabo v Wood Green Corp*,[16] a notice could not be challenged out of time because

9 [1969] 1 All ER 208 at 244.
10 Ibid at 212.
11 Ibid at 237.
12 [1977] QB 122, [1976] 3 All ER 90. See also *Smith v East Elloe RDC* [1956] AC 736, [1956] 1 All ER 855, and *Routh v Reading Corp* (1970) 217 Estates Gazette 1337.
13 See p 97.
14 [1975] 1 All ER 224 [1975] 1 WLR 241.
15 [1934] 2 KB 253.
16 [1946] KB 38, [1945] 2 All ER 162.

the objection was made on the merits, and not on the ground that it was a nullity.

In *London and Clydeside Estates v Aberdeen District Council*,[17] however, Lord Hailsham LC gave warning that 'language like "mandatory", "directory", "void", "voidable", "nullity" and so forth . . . may be misleading'. An individual may not always be justified in ignoring a decision as a 'nullity'; and 'it may be necessary for a subject, in order to safeguard himself, to go to the court for a declaration of his rights, the grant of which may well be discretionary', ie judicial review. He quoted the words of Lord Wilberforce in *Calvin v Carr*:[18] 'Their Lordships' opinion would be . . . that a decision made contrary to natural justice is void, but that, until it is so declared by a competent body or court, it may have some effect, or existence, in law. This condition might be better expressed by saying that the decision is invalid or vitiated'.

There are some cases where the 'nullity' of an official decision is so obvious that it can be disregarded, but many others where it needs to be established in appropriate legal proceedings. In the latter it may, when so established, none the less be a 'nullity' within the meaning of the *Anisminic* principle. But legal validity or invalidity remains the underlying question.

---

17 [1979] 3 All ER 876 at 883.
18 [1974] 2 All ER 440 at 445–446.

Chapter 5

Liability of local authorities in private law

A. Restrictions on liability

I. CORPORATE PERSONALITY AND AGENCY

The legal liability of local authorities in private causes of action has the same basis as that of natural individuals. To sue (or prosecute) the local council requires the same procedure as to sue (or prosecute) the man next door. Even so there are some important divergencies of detail. These stem from the fact that the liability of public bodies in private causes is conditioned by the same special factor as their liability in public causes: artificial personality. For the local council to be liable (or guilty) is not quite the same thing as for the man next door to be liable (or guilty), because of the difference in personality.

As a matter of principle this does not depend on the ultra vires doctrine, except where trusts are concerned, but on agency. Regrettably, the ultra vires doctrine has intruded into this area of law, and in the law of contract at least it has retained a foothold, as will be seen.

Qui facit per alium facit per se is lawyers' Latin for the legal concept of agency. It is a concept that needs to be expressly kept in mind where natural persons are concerned, because in the truly literal sense no natural person acts 'through' another person, he merely 'acts' or does not 'act'. What the phrase means is that one person is to be regarded in law as 'acting' when in sober fact it is another person who is doing so, if the circumstances are such as to justify this view of the matter. But where artificial persons are concerned we can say that the concept never needs to be expressly stated, because an artificial person can never 'act' in any other way except 'through' one or more natural persons. 'Action' is of course natural and not artificial. Yet if artificial personality is to be of any use at all in law, 'action' must be attributable to it. In other words, all 'activity' by artificial persons is vicarious activity, performed in fact by natural persons but attributed to the artificial ones for the sake of legal effectiveness.

Vicarious *liability* is different from vicarious *activity*, though they may co-exist. As will be seen, a great deal of the legal liability of local authorities is indeed vicarious for the same reason that the activities themselves must be; but 'liability' is more abstract than 'activity' and there is often legal justification for imposing liability directly even upon artificial persons.

The mysteries of artificial personality have at times led to vicarious activity and liability in tort becoming entangled with the ultra vires doctrine. In 1866 the House of Lords was faced with this in *Mersey Docks and Harbour Board Trustees v Gibbs*,[1] in which an action was brought in tort for negligence against the public authority when a ship was damaged by going aground on a mudbank while in harbour, as a result of a failure by the authority's servants to dredge out the harbour. It was urged by the authority as a defence that there could be no liability because no statutory body is authorised to commit a tort—in other words all tortious conduct is, for such a body, ultra vires and so that body has no power to commit it. This contention involves a confusion of thought between the meaning of power in the normal sense of that word, ie 'ability,' and its meaning in the more special and very different sense of 'statutory authority'. The ultra vires doctrine relates to *authority*; but that is usually irrelevant in tort, where the power to do acts is a question of *ability*. The artificial personality of the public body means that its 'ability' has to be demonstrated by the activity of natural persons attributed vicariously to the artificial person; whereas its 'authority' is not normally in question. If it were otherwise, no statutory body could ever be liable in tort, because the commission of all torts is ultra vires that body. Such a rule would no doubt be workable, but quite unacceptable on grounds of public policy. It would prevent the imposition of vicarious liability on a corporate employer without preventing its imposition on a natural individual employer, and so work most unfairly.

Since 1866 actions in tort, for negligence or otherwise, have been brought constantly against public bodies; though in *Campbell v Paddington Corp*,[2] another attempt seems to have been made to use the *ultra vires* doctrine as a defence. The defendants built a temporary stand in the highway to accommodate spectators of King Edward VII's funeral procession. In so doing they blocked the view from the plaintiff's windows so that she could not hire out rooms to spectators. In defence to her claim in tort for damages in respect of loss special to herself arising from the public nuisance of obstructing the highway, it was argued that whatever might be the liability of the council's servants individually the council as such could not be liable because the commission of a tort was ultra vires. Avory J gave this short shrift: ' . . . that . . . is to say that no corporation can ever be sued for any tort . . . That would be absurd'. By saying this he very effectively and properly put paid to the intrusion of the ultra vires doctrine into the law of tort. A principle purely applicable to public law is out of place in private law.

1 (1866) LR 1 HL 93.
2 [1911] 1 KB 869.

2. LOCAL AUTHORITIES' CONTRACTS

The ultra vires doctrine has put in an appearance in relation to author-ities' liability in contract. If a public body enters into a contract which is not within the ambit of its statutory powers that contract is void. It follows from this that neither party to the contract can enforce it. Even if the other party is unaware of that fact this makes no difference. In *Rhyl UDC v Rhyl Amusements Ltd*,[3] the local authority granted a lease which required Ministerial consent under the Public Health Act 1875, s 177; but that consent had not been obtained. As the House of Lords has emphatically confirmed in *National Carriers Ltd v Panalpina Northern Ltd*,[4] a lease is normally none the less a contract for being also an estate in land. Therefore the failure to obtain the necessary consent in the *Rhyl* case in accordance with the requirement imposed in the statutory power conferred on the local authority made the grant of the lease, in as much as they entered into a contract thereby, an ultra vires contract. The company could not therefore enforce it but claimed that, even so, the council were estopped from denying the validity of the lease that they had themselves made. It was held that the ultra vires principle overrode this. The general principle of the unenforceability of ultra vires contracts was laid down by the House of Lords in *Ashbury Rly Carriage and Iron Co Ltd v Riche*.[5]

In general, public bodies are empowered to enter into contracts and be bound by them just as natural persons are. They *act*, in these as in other matters, vicariously through their servants, who are their agents. But their *liability* is not vicarious: it rests upon them directly. When agents negotiate contracts for their principals it is for the purpose of binding the principals and not themselves by the contractual obliga-tion; though there may be circumstances which, operating indepen-dently, make the agents liable intentionally or unintentionally.

Two other principles also apply to exclude the contractual liability of local authorities. The first is largely formal. There is a long-established rule of common law that corporations in general cannot bind them-selves by a contract unless it is 'under seal', that is to say embodied in a deed. Whatever the original justification for this rule, it is obviously quite out of place in modern life when contracts large and small are being entered into by everyone, day in and day out. The Corporate Bodies' Contracts Act 1960 belatedly modified this by providing that corporate bodies may bind themselves in contract by the same formali-ties, or lack of them, as private individuals can. Thus the general run of contracts entered into by corporate bodies will be enforceable if made orally. Provisions such as the Law of Property Act 1925, s 40, which

3 [1959] 1 All ER 257, [1959] 1 WLR 465.
4 [1981] AC 675, [1981] 1 All ER 161.
5 (1875) LR 7 HL 653. See above, chapter 3, p 59.

makes land contracts unenforceable (though valid in themselves) in the absence of sufficient written evidence signed by or on behalf of the 'party to be charged', duly apply. Since corporations are artificial each contract, made verbally or in writing, must be entered into by the corporation vicariously by someone acting with due authority to do so, express or implied, as the corporate body's agent—though as stated above the corporation's liability will normally be direct, not vicarious. Corporations can still of course make contracts in writing, for purposes of record and evidence, and under seal, for purposes of solemnity, where there is reasonable desire to do so.

3. 'FETTERING' THE EXERCISE OF DISCRETION

The other principle of exclusion is more of a question of substance. The courts say that corporate bodies cannot 'fetter their discretion' improperly. This is because to fail unjustifiably to exercise powers within the scope of statutory authority is as much an ultra vires policy as to purport to exercise powers beyond it. This principle applies generally and is not confined to contract, though it most commonly arises in relation to contracts. In *British Transport Commission v Westmorland County Council*,[6] for instance, it arose in relation not to contracts, but to property, specifically the power of a landowner to dedicate a highway over his land.

The true rule appears to be that a corporate body is forbidden to 'fetter' the exercise of 'discretion', or of 'future executive action', but only where to do so would be 'incompatible' with the due exercise of the functions conferred upon it. Any wider prohibition could presumably prevent an authority from committing itself to any course of action at all, and would of course hamper it in its continual day-to-day dealings with other parties by way of contract. Indeed there might be no contracts. The principle, though important where it takes effect, is thus a restricted one and applies only as far as is necessary to ensure the proper performance of the authority's functions. It was applied to the Crown in the leading case of *Rederiaktiebolaget Amphitrite v R.*[7]

In *William Cory & Son Ltd v City of London Corp*,[8] the plaintiff company contracted with the defendant council to transport disposable refuse in barges. The council later made by-laws, in furtherance of its functions under the Public Health Act 1936, which had the effect of causing the company's existing barges to contravene the new rules. The company would therefore be put to great expense to alter or replace the barges required for performing its contract, and claimed that the contract must impliedly include a term preventing the council from mak-

6 [1958] AC 126, [1957] 2 All ER 353.
7 [1921] 3 KB 500.
8 [1951] 2 KB 476, [1951] 2 All ER 85.

ing the bye laws in question. It was held that no such term could be applied: it would 'fetter the exercise of discretion' incompatibly with the due performance of the council's public health functions. Had there been an express term in the contract, it would have been void, for the same reason.

There might well be an argument here for distinguishing between the private law and public law elements in such a case. The contractual term (express or implied) could be held to be valid in personam, so as to render the council liable in damages, while the validity of the exercise of the statutory function would stand or fall independently of the contract. Failure duly to exercise that function for fear of incurring contractual liability in damages would render the authority liable in public law to judicial review by mandamus or otherwise, or to a relator action. But this does not appear to be the law at present.

The House of Lords upheld the principle forbidding the 'fettering of discretion' in *Ayr Harbour Trustees v Oswald*,[9] in which the authority concerned acquired land for harbour construction but covenanted not to build on part of that land so that the landowner would have unimpeded access to the waterfront from his adjoining land. This clearly enabled them to obtain the land at less cost. But it was held to be an unenforceable restriction obliging the authority to fetter the exercise of a discretion—ie whether or not to construct the harbour works on the relevant piece of land—conferred by Parliament. Thus the landowner paid (by adjustment of the price for the land) in good faith for a right he was prevented from enforcing. This seems to strengthen the case for separating the contractual liability from the statutory duty in the way referred to above.

On the whole however the 'fettering' of discretion usually turns out to be quite compatible with the due exercise of statutory functions. In the *Westmorland* case referred to above it was held that to dedicate a highway over railway property (a private bridge used by the public on foot for several years) was inherently compatible with the due exercise of the transport authority's functions. In *Dowty Boulton Paul v Wolverhampton Corp*,[10] Pennycuick V–C said that 'where a power is exercised . . . to create a right extending over a term of years, the existence of that right pro tanto excludes the exercise of other statutory powers in respect of the same subject-matter, but there is no authority and I can see no principle upon which that sort of exercise could be held to be invalid as a fetter upon the future exercise of powers.' In *Dowty Boulton Paul v Wolverhampton Corp (No 2)*,[11] the corporation were held to be free to infringe a covenant they had earlier entered into over land constituting a municipal airport, the reason for the proposed infringe-

9 (1883) 8 App Cas 623.
10 [1971] 2 All ER 227, [1971] 1 WLR 204.
11 [1973] Ch 94, [1972] 2 All ER 1073; affd [1976] Ch 13, [1973] 2 All ER 491, CA.

ment being a policy decision to appropriate the airport land to development for council housing (of which the area was much in need) with the result that the plaintiff company would be unable to exercise their rights under the covenant to use the airport as a landing-ground for company planes. The court held that the plaintiffs' rights would have to be satisfied by compensation for loss of the benefit of the covenant and not an injunction to prevent its infringement. This approach could well be adopted with advantage in disputes such as the *Cory* and *Ayr* cases referred to above. The covenant was overridden, not because it 'fettered the exercise of discretion' by the authority, but because statutory provisions empowered the authority to override it.

A particularly instructive type of case occurs in planning. An example from New Zealand, where the relevant law is sufficiently close to English law, can be seen in *Devonport Borough Council v Robbins*.[12] A local council contracted with a developer that if he put forward an acceptable scheme for recreational development of certain coastal land they would lease the land to him and grant planning permission for the development. A new council was elected containing a majority of members pledged to prevent this development altogether on the ground that it would harm the flora and fauna of the hitherto unspoiled coastal land, and told the developer that therefore no scheme would be accepted. His claim that this was a breach of contract was met by the argument that the contract could not be enforced because it would 'fetter the exercise of discretion' enjoyed by the council in carrying out lawful policies which they were elected to put into effect. The court rejected this. It would have meant that any public authority could repudiate contractual obligations with impunity on the ground that they were fully changing their policies. On the contrary they must be regarded as lawfully 'fettering' their freedom to do this, just as any natural person must do on entering into a contract or other lawful obligation.

Therefore some independent reason has to be produced for saying that on the facts an authority must not 'fetter the exercise of discretion' by adhering to some policy decision because it is incompatible with the proper exercise of statutory functions. In *Royal Borough of Windsor and Maidenhead v Brandrose Investments Ltd*,[13] a planning agreement with a developer was overridden by 'listed building' control because the agreement was not compatible with that control.

Freedom of action in making contracts is part of a wider freedom conferred on local authorities by the Local Government Act 1972, s 111, which empowers them to do anything 'calculated to facilitate, or is conducive or incidental to' the carrying out of any of their functions. There are some more specific provisions, such as Fire Services Act

12 [1979] 1 NZ 1.
13 (1983) Times, 3 February. But the independent reason is elusive.

1947, s 3, which prohibits fire authorities from making a charge for their fire-fighting services to members of the public who benefit from them. Section 135 of the 1972 Act requires all authority contracts to comply with the standing orders made by the authority. Standing orders are purely internal to the workings of local authorities, but are none the less law for that—internal bye laws, in effect; though, unlike bye laws, they require no ministerial approval for being made or unmade (Act of 1972, Sch 12). In *R v Hereford Corp, ex p Harrower*[14] the local authority excluded various contractors from tendering for certain contracts. This contravened standing orders. It was held the council's decision so to act was ultra vires and thus illegal, so that it was subject to judificial review by an order of mandamus. It is likely now that an aggrieved contractor would, in that capacity, be held to have 'sufficient interest' or locus standi for the purposes of judicial review; but at the time it was held that a contractor could enjoy locus standi only by the fact (which was so in this case) of being a ratepayer. The court suspended the issue of the order of mandamus in order that the council could themselves suspend or alter their standing orders, which they were entitled to do at any time.

4. FIDUCIARY RESPONSIBILITY AND TRUSTS

The special position of ratepayers in local government law was touched on in the previous chapter.[15] All local authorities owe a fiduciary duty to the ratepayers in their area to manage their finances in a proper manner. As Du Parcq LJ said in *Kent v East Suffolk Rivers Catchment Board*,[16] public authorities 'have to strike a balance between the claims of efficiency and thrift'; and presumably a sufficient compliance with this requirement is a sufficient compliance with their fiduciary duty to their ratepayers.

This duty, being fiduciary, is equitable, as is the liability of trustees to beneficiaries. Now, trusts are either private or public, and valid public trusts must always be 'charitable' within the meaning of that term as interpreted by the House of Lords in *Income Tax Special Purposes Comrs v Pemsel*.[17] The fiduciary duty owed to ratepayers is undoubtedly private in nature because it can be invoked by any individual ratepayer suing by writ or originating summons for a declaration or an injunction without bringing in the Attorney-General by way of a relator action, as for example in *Prescott v Birmingham Corp*.[18] This duty is universally imposed by law, not expressly or impliedly entered into by any decision of a particular local authority.

14 [1970] 3 All ER 460, [1970] 1 WLR 1424.
15 See above, pp 88–93.
16 [1939] 4 All ER 174 at 184.
17 [1891] AC 531.
18 [1955] Ch 210, [1954] 3 All ER 698.

A trust, on the other hand, is as a matter of choice undertaken or accepted by each trustee either expressly by clear statement or impliedly by behaviour which is interpreted as appropriate in equity. No public authority can lawfully exercise any sort of choice, which involves a policy matter, if it is ultra vires the purposes for which such authorities were set up. They can therefore only undertake a trusteeship in the field of public law, not private, since this is a question of policy; even though their corporate personality (whilst conceived artificially) is a private matter and in general involves the capacity to bring and defend actions in contract and tort.[19] The only valid trusts in the public field being charitable trusts, these are the only trusts which local authorities can undertake, except in those cases where equity implies otherwise—as it does, for example, by making any vendor under a land contract a trustee to the extent of holding the property for the purchaser's benefit until the title is ultimately conveyed; though this form of implied trust is termed an 'estate contract'.

On this footing local authorities, especially the historic towns and cities which have enjoyed corporate status for a long time under ancient charters, have over the years received a great deal of property not (in form) beneficially for the purpose of carrying out their statutory functions but to hold on trust for various charitable purposes. In borderline cases there may be uncertainty whether the purposes for which local authorities acquire particular land or other property are those of their statutory functions or are independent of them and charitable.

In *Hauxwell v Barton-on-Humber UDC*,[20] the private owner of a mansion and park conveyed them in 1930 to the defendant district council 'for the purposes and upon the trusts hereinafter mentioned'. But the conveyance also specifically authorised the use of the mansion for offices, or for a hospital, 'or for any other purpose within their powers and under the Public Health Acts 1875 to 1925 . . .', and of the park 'as a Public Park or Pleasure Ground'. In 1970 the district council decided to sever part of the park and sell it to the county council for road-widening, and denied that the land was held on any trust. Local residents issued an originating summons for declarations and an injunction to establish that the park was held on a charitable trust, including the part earmarked for road-widening, and to prevent the severance and sale. Brightman J (as he then was) decided that, prima facie, the conveyance intended a charitable trust of the park. But he decided also that the local residents had no locus standi to bring proceedings, though for-

---

19 This distinction was expressed by Lord Diplock in *Swain v Law Society* [1982] 2 All ER 827, [1982] 3 WLR 261, when he said of the Law Society that it 'acts in two distinct capacities: a private capacity as [a body] incorporated by royal charter . . . and a public capacity as the authority on whom . . . various statutory duties are imposed'.
20 [1974] Ch 432, [1973] 2 All ER 1022.

tunately for them the Attorney-General agreed to be substituted as plaintiff. Only he, it was held, is entitled to enforce a charitable trust against the person in whom the property is vested, if the existence of the charitable trust is denied; and only he or the relevant charitable trustees can sue to recover charity property from a third party.

The Charities Act 1960[1] empowers local residents to enforce a 'local charity' in 'charity proceedings'. But it was held in *Re Belling, Enfield London Borough Council v Public Trustee*,[2] that this applies 'exclusively to administration' of an admitted charity, not to cases in which the very existence of the charity is in dispute.

B. Vicarious and direct liability in tort and crime

1. JUSTIFICATION OF VICARIOUS LIABILITY

Local authorities, like all persons whether artificial or natural, are subject generally to liability in tort. Unlike liability in contract their tortious liability is mostly vicarious, though if the tort is 'breach of statutory duty' the liability may well be direct if the statutory duty rests only on authorities and not on their members, officers, servants or other agents. Any member of a local authority, that is to say a chairman or councillor, may as an individual act as an authority's agent. But, in general, members as such merely have the function of conducting official business collectively by participating in council or committee or similar meetings and settling the authority's policies by passing resolutions to that end in a lawful manner.[3] Officers are persons filling specified offices created for the purpose of carrying out the functions conferred upon local authorities, such as the clerk or treasurer (more usually these days termed the 'chief executive' or 'director of finance', or something similar).

The general rule in the English law of tort is that a 'master' (employer) is liable, jointly and severally (collectively and individually), with any one or more of his 'servants' (employees) for any tort committed by the latter in the scope of the employment. If the master is a natural person, this means that he has not done the wrongful act but his servant has, yet the master is none the less liable as well as the servant provided that, and because, the servant was acting as a servant at the time. If the master is an artificial person, being a corporate body, there is no possibility of any act whatever being carried out by that master; but there will normally be liability on the same footing and for the same reasons as when the master is a natural person. The master's actions are vicariously incurred through the servant.

1 S 28.
2 [1967] Ch 425, [1967] 1 All ER 105.
3 See chapter 8, below, p 200.

The reason for this has been forcefully expressed by various judges. Sir John Holt CJ said: 'Seeing somebody must be the loser by this [wrongdoing] it is more reason that he that employs, and puts a trust and confidence in the [wrongdoer] should be a loser than a stranger': *Hern v Nichols*[4]. And Lord Brougham said: 'The reason that I am liable is this, that by employing him I set the whole thing in motion; and what he does, being done for my benefit and under my direction, I am responsible for the consequences of doing it': *Duncan v Finlater*.[5] If the master and servants together are regarded institutionally as 'the firm' or 'the authority', a victim as plaintiff is entitled to get redress from 'the firm' or 'the authority' for wrongful damage inflicted on him in circumstances such that he can reasonably regard the firm or authority as the wrongdoer irrespective of the actual individuals whose behaviour materially caused the harm. This does not normally make those actual individuals any less liable; while the master (whether natural or corporate) is liable in such cases not as a personal wrongdoer in his employing capacity, which is what vicarious liability means.

Holt and Brougham and other judges have of course been saying in effect that it is public policy which dictates a need for vicarious liability, not strict reason and logic. If servants cause damage by their wrongdoing they can be sued in accordance with the general principles of the law of tort; and if the servant has more money than the master a judgment against him is of more use anyway, though of course servants are seldom in that position particularly when employed by large bodies corporate enjoying vast incomes.

2. SCOPE OF EMPLOYMENT

The local authority as master will be vicariously liable for the torts perpetrated 'in the course (or scope) or employment' of any servant. This goes wider than tortious conduct which has been expressly authorised, and may even include such conduct which contravenes strict instructions from the employer provided that the conduct is 'within the sphere of the employment' and not outside it. Thus in *Smith v Martin and Kingston-upon-Hull Corp*[6] the council were liable for negligent conduct by a school teacher which they had expressly forbidden, ie relying on a child to tend a fire. In *Rose v Plenty*,[7] the first defendant was a milk roundsman employed by the second defendant, Cooperative Retail Services Ltd. There were notices displayed at the depot informing roundsmen as follows: 'Children and young persons must not in any circumstances be employed by you in the performance of your duties'. As

---

4 (1701) Holt KB 462, 1 Salk 289.
5 (1839) 6 Cl & Fin 894.
6 [1911] 2 KB 775.
7 [1976] 1 All ER 97, [1976] 1 WLR 141.

Lord Denning MR said: 'Both employers and trade union did their utmost to stop it . . . But in spite of all these warnings the practice still persisted. Boys used to hang about the depot waiting to be taken on: and some of the roundsmen used to take them'. The plaintiff was a boy of 13 who did this. By a combination of his and the first defendant's negligence he was injured. The Court of Appeal held (by a majority) that in the circumstances the second defendant, as employer, was vicariously liable because the roundsman's conduct in employing the plaintiff to help him deliver milk and collect 'empties' was within the scope of his employment as a roundsman, despite being prohibited. It was a case where, in Lord Denning's words, 'the prohibition affects only the conduct within the sphere of the employment and did not take the conduct outside the sphere altogether'. Whereas in *Twine v Bean's Express Ltd*[8] the prohibited conduct during which the injury had been caused consisted of giving a lift, and this was not only 'contrary to a prohibition' but 'not for the purposes of the employers'. The latter point was the crucial one and meant that the employers were not vicariously liable for their employee's negligence in that case.

A comparable case to *Rose v Plenty* involving a local authority, on this occasion as plaintiff, is *LCC v Cattermoles (Garages) Ltd.*[9] The defendant company employed a man to move vehicles inside a garage though he was forbidden expressly to drive them. He drove one for the purpose of moving it and negligently damaged one of the plaintiff's vans. His employers were liable vicariously for this because what he did was within the scope of his employment even though the manner of his doing it was both wrongful and prohibited. The distinction in these cases, though difficult at the borderline, is well established. Lord Dunedin in the House of Lords, in *Plumb v Cobden Flour Mills Co Ltd*,[10] expressed it by saying: 'there are prohibitions which limit the sphere of employment, and prohibitions which only deal with conduct within the sphere of employment'. The former rule out vicarious liability in cases where their infringement leads to the commission of a tort; the latter, as in *Rose v Plenty*, do not. In cases such as *Twine v Bean's Express Ltd* the servant is commonly described as being 'on a frolic of his own', a phrase which has caught the fancy of lawyers in general but was uttered first by Baron Parke in *Joel v Morison.*[11]

The general principle does not depend on any particular prohibitions but on the facts as a whole. In *Hilton v Thomas Burton (Rhodes) Ltd*,[12] the employers were held not to be vicariously liable, even though they

8 [1946] 1 All ER 202.
9 [1953] 2 All ER 582, [1953] 1 WLR 997.
10 [1914] AC 62 at 67.
11 (1834) 6 C & P 501 at 503.
12 [1961] 1 All ER 74, [1961] 1 WLR 705.

had actually permitted their servant to drive their van on the journey in which the servant caused death by negligent driving, because that journey had not been undertaken for the employer's benefit. But in *Century Insurance Co Ltd v Northern Ireland Road Transport Board*,[13] the employers were vicariously liable for damage caused by the negligence of one of their petrol tanker drivers who lit a cigarette and threw down the match while petrol was being transferred out of his lorry to a tank for storage, thus causing a fire which led to an explosion.

There are a great many torts besides negligence, and vicarious liability may be established in regard to any of them. In *Lloyd v Grace, Smith & Co*,[14] the tort was fraud, committed by a solicitors' managing clerk who in his employers' offices tricked the plaintiff into parting with the ownership of some property. The solicitors were held liable because their fraudulent clerk was acting within the scope of his employment: he had ostensible authority to induce the plaintiff 'widow woman' to sign documents supposedly for her benefit. The employer is liable in such circumstances whether the fraud is carried out for the employer's or the employee's own benefit. In *Morris v C. W. Martin & Sons*[15] the plaintiff's mink coat was sent to the defendant to clean and their servant, employed to clean it, stole it. They were liable vicariously for his 'conversion'—ie tortious interference with goods. But Salmon LJ (as he then was) said that when goods are handed over ('bailed'), 'a theft by any servant who is not employed to do anything in relation to the goods bailed is entirely outside the scope of his employment and cannot make the master liable'.

3. FELLOW EMPLOYEES

It makes no difference in principle if the plaintiff is a fellow employee. But, since the master and servant are jointly and severally liable, the master can in any of these cases of vicarious liability obtain an indemnity from the latter, or perhaps only a contribution if the master himself is partly to blame, under the Civil Liability (Contributions) Act 1978. In the case of an individual employer this could mean, and in the case of a corporate employer must mean, being to blame by reason of the fault of another employee. In *Lister v Romford Ice and Cold Storage Co Ltd*,[16] the plaintiff was injured by the negligence of his son, both father and son being fellow-employees of the defendant company. The company was held vicariously liable for the negligence. The House of Lords held that an insurance firm, having met the company's claim to be reimbursed for the award of damages, was thereby entitled, under the equit-

13 [1942] AC 509, [1942] 1 All ER 491.
14 [1912] AC 716.
15 [1966] 1 QB 716, [1965] 2 All ER 725.
16 [1957] AC 555, [1957] 1 All ER 125.

able doctrine of 'subrogation', to stand in the company's place in order to recover under the right of indemnity against the son, for whose negligence the company as employer was vicariously liable, the amount of damages and costs successfully claimed by the father.

4. INDEPENDENT CONTRACTORS

The principles established through these leading cases apply to local authorities in the same way as they do to any employer, more precisely any corporate employer. The sort of cases which have tended to actually occur in regard to local authorities themselves have arisen not so much over the concept of 'the scope of the servant's employment' as over the question whether an individual is a 'servant' at all. The effective distinction is between a 'servant' and an 'independent contractor'. This applies generally in the law of tort, but the number of cases involving local authorities is considerable.

The reason for the distinction is that there are many persons who perform work for other persons for reward, but the circumstances in which this is done vary so widely that all cases cannot be treated in the same way. The law therefore differentiates between those whose work for the persons engaging them is such that they can reasonably be said to be in the 'employment' of the latter and those who cannot. The former group can, within the scope of their employment, be reasonably regarded as having a general power to saddle the persons engaging them with vicarious liability; but this cannot be said of the latter group. The test is control. Employers exercise a right of control, supervision or direction over servants, but not over independent contractors. A servant is employed under a contract for service, an independent contractor under a contract for services. In the latter case the employer 'can order or require what is to be done', while in the former case 'he can not only order or require what is to be done but how itself it shall be done'. This was how Hilbery J put it in *Collins v Hertfordshire County Council.*[17]

Essentially the law is this, that whereas employers are vicariously liable for the torts of their servants to the extent discussed above, they are not vicariously liable for the torts of independent contractors as such. There may be vicarious liability if the conduct of some particular independent contractor has made him an authority's agent; but, if so, the vicarious liability arises from the activities of that person in the capacity of agent. More important here is the fact that an employer is frequently liable as a result of the acts of an independent contractor, yet *not* vicariously. In such cases the circumstances given rise to an independent and direct liability resting on the employer.

Hardaker v Idle District Council,[18] the defendant local authority

17 [1947] KB 598, [1947] 1 All ER 633.
18 [1896] 1 QB 335.

engaged an independent contractor to construct a sewer. The contractor, by negligence, damaged a gas-main, causing an explosion which damaged the plaintiff's house. It was held that the decision to construct the sewer was the authority's, and therefore they themselves were under an independent duty to take care in carrying out the work. Delegation of the work to the contractor did not absolve them of this liability. The negligent physical activity was vicariously executed by the contractor; but the misguided choice of contractor was made by the authority's own members and officers. Therefore liability rested directly and not vicariously on the local authority. In view of the tendency of works contractors to become insolvent from time to time, this separate liability of public authorities is a great blessing to plaintiffs. Such independent duties may be inferred from circumstances or imposed by statute. However, 'collateral' negligence, or other wrongdoing by a contractor outside the scope of the contract does not impose such liability on the employer. In *Padbury v Holliday and Greenwood Ltd*,[19] a metal tool had been negligently left on a window-ledge by an independent contractor's workman, and it was knocked over and fell and injured the plaintiff. This was held to be 'collateral' negligence; in other words it was not a consequence of an ill-judged choice of contractor, and so no liability rested on the contractor's employer. The original authority for this distinction was the case of *Quarman v Burnett*.[20]

Apart from this, where the cause of action arises in fact on premises in the occupation of the employer of an independent contractor, and takes the form of negligent harm inflicted on a visitor to those premises as a result of danger caused by faulty work of construction, maintenance or repair carried out by the independent contractor, the occupier will not be liable on these facts alone if his choice and supervision of the contractor can be regarded as reasonable in the circumstances. This is provided by the Occupiers' Liability Act 1957.[1]

5. SPECIALISTS

This difference between servants and independent contractors does not turn on the ability of a master to give detailed instructions. A man can be a skilled expert—craftsman, practitioner, adviser—such that the master is quite incapable of telling him how to do his job, yet the relationship can none the less be that of master and servant. An ignorant master can employ a clever servant in fact no less than in fiction. Control and supervision are the governing factors. In other words the employer is the servant's 'boss' however specialist the latter's working skills may be, but is not the independent contractor's 'boss'. The ser-

---

19 (1912) 28 TLR 494.
20 (1840) 6 M & W 499.
  1 S 2(4).

vant's duty of service includes a duty to conform with control and supervision, except in so far as these impair his skills; he is 'under orders'. The independent contractor's duty is simply to do what he has contracted to do; he is not 'under orders'.

In *Collins v Hertfordshire County Council*[2] referred to above, the plaintiff sued in respect of negligent acts by a resident surgeon employed under a contract of service by the defendant council. The latter were vicariously liable on a master-and-servant basis, despite the surgeon's specialist professional standing. In *Roe v Minister of Health*,[3] vicarious liability was also held to apply in respect of a part-time appointee, an anaesthetist, for negligent acts. In *Gold v Essex County Council*,[4] there was similar liability in respect of a full-time radiographer. The essential question seems to be whether the individual concerned is 'on the staff' of the firm or the authority, full-time or part-time, in which case he is a servant and not an independent contractor.

One peculiarity of this part of the law which should be noted here is that payment of salary or wages does not conclusively show that the payee is a 'servant'. In *Fisher v Oldham Corp*,[5] it was held that although a police officer was paid by the local authority he was not their 'servant' and they were not therefore vicariously liable on such ground for his tortious conduct. A police officer is a public officer (in line of descent from the parish constable of medieval times) and not even a 'servant' of the Crown.[6] The Police Act 1964[7] now makes the chief officer of a police force civilly liable for the tortious acts of those police officers who are subject to his authority. Much the same approach can be seen in *Stanbury v Exeter Corp*[8] where the 'public officer', though paid by a local authority, was required also to carry out instructions from the central government: he was an agricultural inspector concerned with the diseases of animals. Unlike the *Fisher* case, however, it seems to be implied that there may well have been vicarious liability upon the local authority in regard to services performed by the inspector in the course of his work for them.

6. CRIMINAL LIABILITY

Local authorities are also criminally liable, although in practice such liability is much less often met with because prosecution does not usually serve any useful purpose against corporate bodies compared

2 [1947] KB 598, [1947] 1 All ER 633.
3 [1954] 2 QB 66, [1954] 2 All ER 131.
4 [1942] 2 KB 293, [1942] 2 All ER 237.
5 [1930] 2 KB 364.
6 See below, chapter 10.
7 S 48.
8 [1905] 2 KB 838.

with civil actions for damages. The same basic problem is raised, but answered in quite different ways. 'Did you ever expect a corporation to have a conscience, when it has no soul to be damned nor body to be kicked?' is a rhetorical question attributed to Lord Chancellor Lord Thurlow in the eighteenth century. Vicarious liability in the law of tort is one reaction to this; but vicarious liability does not have such a place in criminal law, where the purpose is to punish persons in respect of their misdeeds and not (as in civil actions) to find a source of redress for their victims. Since artificial persons can only *act* vicariously, and vicarious *liability* is not in question, the important concept in criminal law in this connection arises from a choice between two approaches. The first is that there are individual persons whose position vis-a-vis the corporate body so as to make it criminally liable for their misdeeds. The second is that the corporate body is not to be regarded as criminally liable at all, but those individual persons just referred to where appropriate, are to be regarded as criminally liable if they have participated in some way in a criminal offence. Lord Thurlow would probably have preferred the latter alternative; but the law accepts the former.

The leading case which clarifies this matter, *Tesco Supermarkets Ltd v Nattrass*,[9] relates to a commercial company but its ratio decidendi applies to corporate bodies generally including local authorities. A local manager of one of the company's stores was responsible for a criminal infringement of a statute, and the company itself was prosecuted. The company succeeded in its defence by proving that the crime was caused by 'the act or default of another person' and that the company 'had taken all reasonable precautions and exercised all due diligence to avoid the commission of the offence.'

At common law a criminal conviction requires proof of mens rea (a guilty mind) as well as actus reus (criminal activity), meaning that the accused person must be shown beyond all reasonable doubt to have intended the harm as well the activity that caused the harm. But by statute many offences have been created in recent times which are said to be 'absolute', so that proof of the actus reus is sufficient to convict the accused. This has sometimes been applied specially to employers. Lord Reading CJ said in *Mousell Bros v London and North Western Rly Co*:[10] 'Prima facie . . . a master is not to be made criminally responsible for the acts of his servant to which the master is not a party. But it may be the intention of the legislature . . . to impose a liability upon a principal even though he does not know of, and is not a party to, the forbidden act done by his servant. Many statutes are passed with this object . . . In those cases the Legislature absolutely forbids the act and makes the principal liable without a mens rea.' This may look like vica-

9 [1972] AC 153, [1971] 2 All ER 127.
10 [1917] 2 KB 836 at 844.

rious criminal liability but it is not. It is absolute direct criminal liability, which a great many statutes impose generally on all perpetrators. But some statutes impose it specially on persons in their capacity as employers in connection with criminal acts of their employees, irrespective of whether the latter are subject to proof of mens rea or to absolute liability.

7. 'DIRECTING MIND AND WILL' OF A CORPORATE BODY

Where the accused is an artificial instead of a natural person, 'the question of criminal liability must be considered (i) generally and (ii) in relation to the special liability of employers just referred to. In the *Tesco* case Lord Morris put the question:[11] 'How . . . does a company take all reasonable precautions and exercise all due diligence? . . . When is some act the act of the company, as opposed to the act of a servant or agent of the company (for which, if done within the scope of employment, the company will be civilly liable)?' This puts the difference between civil and criminal liability of corporate bodies in a nutshell. Lord Morris went on to quote the words of Lord Haldane LC in *Lennard's Carrying Co Ltd v Asiatic Petroleum Co Ltd*[12] who said: '. . . a corporation is an abstraction. It has no mind of its own any more than it has a body of its own; its active and directing will must consequently be sought in the person of somebody who for some purposes may be called an agent, but who is really the directing mind and will of the corporation, the very ego and centre of the personality of the corporation'.

For criminal liability, and presumably for every kind of direct legal liability as distinct from the vicarious sort, the law thus treats a corporate body as having a 'directing mind and will', a 'very ego and centre', where the corporate personality for practical purposes (notwithstanding the abstract nature of corporate personality in strict logic) resides. Lord Reid, in the *Tesco* case, said:[13] 'Normally the board of directors, the managing director, and perhaps other superior officers of a company, carry out the functions of management and speak and act as the company. Their subordinates do not. They carry out orders from above, and it can make no difference that they are given some measure of discretion'. So the crucial point is this, that any member of an organisation who 'carries out orders from above' is *not* part of the 'directing mind and will'; conversely anyone who is part of the 'directing mind and will' does not 'carry out orders from above'. Lord Reid also said that the 'functions of management' can, in part at least, be delegated. If so, the normal 'directing minds' will have 'put such a delegate in their place so that within the scope of the delegation he can act as the company.'

11 [1971] 2 All ER 127 at 139.
12 [1915] AC 705 at 713.
13 [1971] 2 All ER 127 at 132.

Where public authorities are concerned, presumably the councillors or other members of the authority are equivalent to the directors of a company, the chairman or leader of the council is equivalent to the managing director, and the chief officers can be equated with the 'other superior officers' mentioned by Lord Reid. Committees, and particularly their chairmen, will count as the 'delegates' referred to. So much for the direct liability of corporate bodies generally.

As for the special liability of corporate employers for the purposes of criminal law, it is clear from the *Tesco* judgments that the people with the 'directing mind and will' may not only be liable as natural persons but also saddle the corporate body with liability; though in the latter case they must presumably be shown not only to have participated in the actus reus but to have done so in their capacity as 'directing mind and will' or part thereof. Whether they must in the same way be shown to have had mens rea depends simply on whether the offence so requires, or is 'absolute' and does not.

The decision in the *Tesco* case came to this: that the company had to be regarded as distinguishable from the delinquent local manager (who was 'another person' for the purposes of the company's corporate defence); that as a question of particular statutory interpretation the company came within the special 'absolute' criminal liability of a master in the manner referred to by Lord Reading CJ;[14] but that the company had successfully made out the relevant defence to the criminal charge because the facts showed that the 'directing mind and will' of Tesco had put into effect a supervisory system such that the requirement of 'all reasonable precautions' and 'all due diligence' was satisfied. Tesco fell into the pit of 'absolute' liability, but was delivered from it by good and prudent conduct. Similar adventures can befall local authorities, depending on the qualities of each one's 'directing mind and will', the 'very ego and centre' of corporate personality.

C. Fault and strict liability in tort

I. GENERAL TORTIOUS LIABILITY

In general the substance of liability in tort is the same for local authorities as for other defendants. This extends to defamation. In *De Buse v McCarthy and Stepney Borough Council*,[15] a report on losses of petrol from the council's depots included a reference to the plaintiff which amounted to a libel. The report was discussed at a council meeting, where privilege covered the proceedings. Unfortunately it was also cir-

---

14 In the *Mousell* case; see above, p 116.
15 [1942] 1 KB 56, [1942] 1 All ER 19.

culated with other council papers to public libraries and reading rooms; this was held to be publication which went well outside the scope of the privilege, and the local authority shared in the resulting liability for the libel contained in the report.

In nuisance, local authorities are liable vicariously as other employers and occupiers are for indirect harm to the enjoyment of nearby land or rights over land, caused by the faulty use of their own land whether deliberate or negligent. Thus in *Pride of Derby and Derbyshire Angling Association v British Celanese and Derby Corp*[16] the defendant local authority were held liable because of the discharge of sewage into a river where the plaintiffs had fishing rights, with consequent damage to the fishing. Their plea that the sewerage system had originally been adequate, before recent increases in the number of local inhabitants and buildings, was held to provide no defence. Yet in *Smeaton v Ilford Corp*[17] the authority were held not liable for an irruption of sewage into the plaintiffs premises from an overloaded sewer, on the ground that although an increase in inhabitants and buildings had caused an originally adequate sewerage system to become inadequate, the authority lacked the power to construct larger sewers of their own volition because central government sanction was required. The *Derby* case differed at this point, because there it did lie within the authority's power to improve the mode of treatment and discharge of sewage; they were to blame, by acting negligently even though not deliberately, whereas in the *Ilford* case the authority were held not even to be negligent. The negligent (or deliberate) harmful use of land may arise not merely from the acts of the authority's servants and agents but from the acts of other persons permitted by them to be on the land, as in *Hall v Beckenham Corp*,[18] where nuisance was inflicted on nearby residents from the noise of power-driven model aircraft in the defendants' park.

Negligence is the tort most frequently met with. This is negligence in its own right as distinct from being an element of fault in nuisance or other torts. The existence of the duty of care owed by defendants to plaintiffs, the breach of that duty and the consequent damage may be established by facts of endlessly varied kinds. In *Owens v Liverpool Corp*[19] the actionable damage was nervous shock caused to relatives on their way to a funeral who witnessed the deceased's coffin tipped out of its hearse in a collision caused by a wildly-driven tramcar. In *Sayers v Harlow UDC*[20] it was injury caused to a lady who was left locked in a lavatory through the carelessness of the council's employees, which

16 [1953] Ch 149, [1953] 1 All ER 179.
17 [1954] Ch 450, [1954] 1 All ER 923.
18 [1949] 1 KB 716, [1949] 1 All ER 423.
19 [1939] 1 KB 394, [1938] 4 All ER 727.
20 [1958] 2 All ER 342, [1958] 1 WLR 623.

befell her when she tried to climb out of it. In *Morrison v Sheffield Corp*,[1] it was injury caused by unguarded spiked railings in an unlit street. In *Refell v Surrey County Council*,[2] it was injury caused to a child at school which was attributable to insufficiently safe premises and supervision.

2. DANGEROUS PREMISES AND HIGHWAYS

Dangerous premises give rise to the form of negligence known as occupiers' liability under the 'common duty of care' now regulated by the Occupier's Liability Act 1957 for the benefit of 'visitors' to premises. Reasonable care must be taken by the occupier to ensure that any visitor is reasonably safe in using the premises for the purposes for which he is allowed to be there. This duty weighs heavily on local authorities because of the great number of premises belonging to them. Admittedly it is not owed to trespassers; but the House of Lords in *Herrington v British Railways Board*,[3] held that occupiers do owe a duty to trespassers though a more restricted one, which is to take care 'in common sense and common humanity' to guard them against dangers of which it may reasonably be foreseen that they are unaware. This duty is obviously going to apply to children more widely than to adults: in *Herrington's* case it was a question of providing a fence between an open space and an electrified railway.

But the occupier of land does not owe a duty of care, even of this restricted kind, to persons on his land as of right. In *Greenhalgh v British Railways Board*,[4] a public right of way on foot had come into existence, by implied dedication from long use, over a railway bridge that had originally been intended for private use. The plaintiff, who tripped and was injured while crossing the bridge because of a pot-hole, failed in a claim for damages because the duty of care to 'visitors' was held not to apply to persons on premises exercising a *right* to be there. That this applies to private as well as public rights appears from *Holden v White*.[5] In this case the access to a house was by a private right—easement—of way along a path over intervening land. The plaintiff, delivering milk to the house, was injured when stepping on a defective manhole-cover in the path. The Court of Appeal, applying the principle of its decision in *Greenhalgh's* case to these facts, said that the duty of care relating to dangerous premises, being owed only to 'visitors' within the meaning of the 1957 Act, could not apply because the plaintiff had been exercising the private right of way enjoyed by the owner of the house. Logically it

1 [1917] 2 KB 866.
2 [1964] 1 All ER 743, [1964] 1 WLR 358.
3 [1972] AC 877, [1972] 1 All ER 749.
4 [1969] 2 QB 286, [1969] 2 All ER 114.
5 [1982] QB 679, [1982] 2 All ER 328.

ought to follow from this that the plaintiff was, and should be entitled to redress as, the 'visitor' of the actual house-owner. The fact that persons on other people's land as of right are altogether at the mercy of dangerous premises, when lawful visitors and even some trespassers are not, seems quite anomalous.

There is an important exception to this rule about persons present on land 'as of right' which affects local councils as highway authorities. The common law principle, which lies behind the cases just discussed and behind the 1957 Act, recognised no civil liability for damage suffered by members of the public using a highway as a result of negligent upkeep;[6] though the duty of 'the inhabitants at large' to repair highways was enforceable at the suit of the Crown in proceedings which were criminal in form. After the Highway Act 1835 local highway authorities were set up, and these unlike 'the inhabitants at large'—ie the parish—were corporate bodies. Civil liability for highways in a dangerous state came to be recognised in cases where the authorities had interfered with the substance of a highway ('misfeasance'), though the common law exemption was retained where they merely failed to act ('non-feasance'). Plaintiffs thus succeeded in cases such as *Skilton v Epsom and Ewell UDC*,[7] in which the local highway authority fixed metal studs in the surface of a road but failed to maintain them, with the result that one became loose and caused an accident. But they did not succeed in cases where mere neglect caused road surfaces to crumble and form pot-holes.

This survival of the common law rule for 'non-feasance' caused much resentment (except among highway authorities). The Highways (Miscellaneous Provisions) Act 1961, s 1, finally abolished it, with effect from 1 August 1964. But the civil liability which now rests on local highway authorities at the suit of plaintiffs who are injured because of the defective condition of highways depends on the 'adoption' of the highway by the authority concerned. This means that at some date since 1835 for roadways, and since 1959 for footpaths and bridleways (Highways Act 1959, s 39), a formal decision has been taken by that authority, or a predecessor, to assume liability. Dedication as a highway (express or implied) is not enough on its own. With some rare exceptions the landowner as such is not civilly liable, on the common law principle referred to above; and the highway authority is not civilly liable unless the highway is 'adopted'.

Where the liability does exist, by virtue of 'adoption', as a result of the 1961 Act (above), it is founded on negligence and is not strict, as the Court of Appeal made clear in *Meggs v Liverpool Corp*.[8] The public

6 *Russell v Men of Devon* (1788) 2 Term Rep 667.
7 [1937] 1 KB 112, [1936] 2 All ER 50.
8 [1968] 1 All ER 1137, [1968] 1 WLR 689.

must take reasonable care for their own safety and not expect to obtain damages for every upset, regardless of circumstances. The liability is distinct from liability in nuisance for obstruction of or dangers in the highway whether caused by the highway authority or any other person. The latter is public nuisance, actionable solely at the suit of the Attorney-General at common law, or of the local highway authority by virtue of the Local Government Act 1972, s 222,[9] which empowers local authorities to bring proceedings 'in their own name' in such cases, the remedy being a declaration or injunction. But it was held in *Winter-bottom v Lord Derby*,[10] that no member of the public as such can sue; though if anyone suffers loss or damage peculiar to himself and not merely as a member of the public the case is then one of public nuisance privately actionable on the same footing as ordinary private nuisance. Examples are the cases of *Castle v St Augustine's Links Ltd*,[11] where a taxi-driver was struck and injured by a golf-ball; *Halsey v Esso Petroleum Co Ltd*[12] where chemical fumes damaged paintwork on a car parked on the highway; and *Barber v Penley*,[13] in which performances of 'Charley's Aunt' at a London theatre caused crowds of people seeking admission to queue up in the street to such an extent that access to the plaintiff's premises was substantially obstructed.

3. PUBLIC AUTHORITIES AND THEIR 'DUTY OF CARE'

The ambit of the tort of negligence has been made more effective and extensive in the last fifty years by what Lord Wilberforce, speaking in the House of Lords in *Anns v Merton London Borough Council*,[14] called 'the trilogy of cases decided in this House, *Donoghue v Stevenson*,[15] *Hedley Byrne & Co Ltd v Heller & Partners Ltd*,[16] and *Home Office v Dorset Yacht Co Ltd*.[17] So now, 'in order to establish that a duty of care arises in a particular situation, it is not necessary to bring the facts of that situation within those of previous situations in which a duty of care has been held to exist.' In short, the 'duty of care' in the tort of negligence is founded on a broad principle; it is not dependent on a laborious and pedestrian exercise in which precedent merely takes the law on from case to case according to the chance events of litigation.

---

 9 See below, chapter 6, p 145. The Highways Act 1980, Part IX, makes provision for a
    number of criminal offences comprising highway obstructions and dangers of spe-
    cified kinds.
10 (1867) LR 2 Exgh 316.
11 (1922) 38 TLR 615.
12 [1961] 2 All ER 145, [1961] 1 WLR 683.
13 [1893] 2 Ch 447.
14 [1977] 2 All ER 492 at 498.
15 [1932] AC 562.
16 [1964] AC 465, [1963] 2 All ER 575.
17 [1970] AC 1004, [1970] 2 All ER 294.

The result of this is that activities which, unlike most other persons, local authorities are statutorily required to carry out may if not properly performed involve them in liability for negligence in circumstances of an unprecedented kind. This has arisen in regard to their duty of inspection. Local and central government bodies are required to carry out many forms of inspection. One of these is building inspection, a duty imposed on district councils by the Public Health Acts 1936 and 1961 and the Building Regulations made under the latter Act. In *Dutton v Bognor Regis UDC*,[18] approval was given to plans for building a new house after the building inspector had failed to raise objection to the fact that the ground was unstable and the foundations insecure as a result. Serious subsidence became apparent after some years. The Court of Appeal held that the building inspector had been negligent and the council that employed him became vicariously liable as a result. This liability was separate from the liability of the builders.

In *Anns v Merton London Borough Council*, the same issue arose and was taken by the local authority concerned on further appeal to the House of Lords. A two-storey block of maisonettes was built by a private development company, the plans having been approved by Mitcham Borough Council in 1962. Cracks, subsidence and sloping of floors became apparent during 1970. The occupants of the flats, who held them on long leases, sued the builders for breach of contract and Merton London Borough Council—successor to Mitcham Borough Council in consequence of reorganisation under the London Government Act 1963—in negligence. The cause of the damage and loss suffered by the plaintiffs was, as in the *Dutton* case, the faulty foundations.

The House of Lords upheld the claim against the local authority. The issue turned on the function of inspection, because the authority argued that the nature of inspection was such that it was quite inappropriate to impose liability in negligence in relation to it. Lord Wilberforce formulated the gist of that argument thus:[19]

'the local authority is under no duty to inspect, and . . . if it need not inspect at all, it cannot be liable for negligent inspection: if it were to be held so liable . . . councils would simply decide against inspections. I think that this is too crude an argument . . . local authorities are public bodies . . . with a clear responsibility for public health in their area. They must, and in fact do, make their discretionary decisions responsibly . . . If they do not exercise their discretion in this way they can be challenged in the courts. *Thus to say that councils are under no duty to inspect, is not a sufficient*

18 [1972] 1 QB 373, [1972] 1 All ER 462.
19 [1977] 2 All ER 492 at 501.

*statement of the position. They are under a duty to give proper consider-
ation to the question whether they should inspect or not . . .'*

Lords Diplock, Simon of Glaisdale and Russell of Killowen agreed.
Lord Salmon, however, expressed a minority view[20] that failure to
inspect at all would be 'an improper exercise of discretion which . . .
might be corrected by certiorari or mandamus. I doubt however
whether this would confer a right on any individual to sue the council
for damages . . .'

Lord Wilberforce stated:[1] 'The duty is to take reasonable care, no
more no less, to secure that the builder does not cover in foundations
which do not comply with [building regulations] requirements'. Presumably this might be re-formulated more widely thus: '. . . to secure
that the builder does not in any material particular fail to comply with
(etc)'. The duty is owed to owners or occupiers of the property, in that
capacity, but 'not of course to a negligent building owner, the source of
his own loss. A right of action can only be conferred on an owner or
occuper, who is such when the damage occurs. . . .'

Whether an inspector's report that building work has been carried
out in compliance with building regulations can, if incorrect, itself
found an action on the footing of a negligent mis-statement, under the
principles laid down in the *Hedley Byrne* case, is uncertain. But it is
worthy of note that in *Ministry of Housing and Local Government v
Sharp*[2] a local authority was held liable in damages for negligence to the
plaintiff Ministry for inexcusably failing to disclose to a purchaser of
land, who applied for a search of the local land charges registry maintained by that local authority, that a planning compensation notice had
been registered which entitled the Ministry to recover a refund of compensation when eventually the land in question was developed. This
failure exempted the purchaser from the duty to repay the money to the
ministry, to whom damages were therefore payable by the local authority to make good that loss. The negligence of their staff in the registry
made them liable vicariously. The inaccuracy in the certificate of search
would seem to be a negligent mis-statement.

4. STRICT LIABILITY AND BREACH OF STATUTORY DUTY

Again, local authorities are in general subject to torts of strict liability
just as other persons are. Libel has been referred to earlier.[3] An example of trespass to land is *Tunbridge Wells Corp v Baird*,[4] where the

20 Ibid at 507.
1 Ibid at 504. Also see *Acrecrest v Hattrell* [1983] 1 All ER 17.
2 [1970] 2 QB 223, [1970] 1 All ER 1009.
3 See above, p 118.
4 [1896] AC 434.

appellants, in whom the area of the Pantiles was vested as local highway authority, committed a trespass there against the landowner by building a subterranean public lavatory. There is also liability under the rule in *Rylands v Fletcher*,[5] which is imposed, irrespective of negligence, on an occupier of land for all the direct consequences of the 'escape' of anything he has brought and kept there by way of 'non-natural user' which is likely to do damage if it 'escapes'. In *Midwood & Co Ltd v Manchester Corp*[6] the defendant corporation was held liable under the rule, for damage done to premises adjoining a public street in an explosion caused by an escape of inflammable gas.

But the kind of strict liability which seems to be increasingly affecting local authorities occurs in the tort known as breach of statutory duty. Practically all the functional duties which public authorities in general and local authorities in particular are required to perform are statutory in origin, for reasons discussed in an earlier chapter.[7] They are so multitudinous that it is not surprising that local authorities resist as far as they can any suggestion that such duties are enforceable in private civil actions. Are not statutory duties part of public rather than private law?

There have been cases which support a principle that no private action can be brought if there is some other mode of enforcement laid down in the authorising statute itself. In *Atkinson v Newcastle and Gateshead Waterworks Co*,[8] the plaintiff's premises were not saved during a fire because there was insufficient water-pressure in the fire-hydrants, which was a contravention of the Waterworks Clauses Act 1847, s 42. But that default was, under the Act, expressly made punishable by a fine of £10, which according to Lord Cairns LC must be taken to exclude an alternative sanction by way of a civil action for damages. Failure to provide adequate sewerage was similarly held, by the House of Lords in *Pasmore v Oswaldtwistle UDC*,[9] not to give a cause of action to a civil plaintiff, on the ground that there was a statutory right of appeal—essentially administrative—to the relevant central government department, which was the Local Government Board.

There have been many cases to the contrary effect in more recent times. The principle upon which the courts will allow an action for breach of statutory duty was expressed as follows by Lord Normand in *Cutler v Wandsworth Stadium*:[10]

'If there is no penalty and no other special means of enforcement provided by the statute, it may be presumed that those who have

5 (1868) LR 3 HL 330.
6 [1905] 2 KB 597.
7 Chapter 3.
8 (1877) 2 Ex D 441.
9 [1898] AC 387.
10 [1949] 1 All ER 544 at 551.

an interest to enforce one of the statutory duties have an individual right of action. Otherwise the duty might never be performed, but, if there is a penalty clause, the right to a civil action must be established by a consideration of the scope and purpose of the statute as a whole. The inference that there is a concurrent right of civil action is easily drawn when the predominant purpose is manifestly the protection of a class of workmen by imposing on their employers the duty of taking special measures to secure their safety'. The inference may be drawn wherever the circumstances warrant it.

Thus a decision whether a civil action will lie depends on 'the scope and purpose of the statute as a whole'. In *Thornton v Kirklees Metropolitan Borough Council*[11] the Court of Appeal held that an action would lie to compel local housing authorities to carry out their duties under the Housing (Homeless Persons) Act 1977, s 3. No specific remedy was given in the Act itself; but the main point is that a specified category of persons was clearly indicated as being meant to benefit. Megaw LJ commented that the fear of the local authority 'that there would be a multiplicity of actions, many of them small, many of them without substance or merit, many of them incapable of succeeding', though based on 'practical' arguments, could not 'provide a valid answer to what appears to me to be the fair intent of Parliament to be gathered from this Act . . . on the true construction [of which] . . . there should be a cause of action for damages'. But this was qualified by a warning that though the plaintiff's contention was sound in principle, proof of the necessary matters in detail might well be very difficult.

5. NEGLIGENCE AND BREACH OF STATUTORY DUTY

These considerations make the civil liability of local authorities for breach of statutory duty a tort whose boundaries are hard to establish. It is a form of liability which is not confined to local authorities, or even public authorities or corporate bodies generally. In the *Anns* case, Lord Wilberforce said:[12] '. . . since it is the duty of the builder (owner or not) to comply with [building regulations] I would be of opinion that an action could be brought against him, in effect, for breach of statutory duty by any person for whose benefit or protection the [regulations were] made'—in other words owners and occupiers of buildings—in the event of his failure to comply.

Other cases in which local authorities have been made liable for breach of statutory duty may be noted. In *Reffell v Surrey County Coun-*

---

11 [1979] QB 626, [1979] 2 All ER 349. But see below, p 128.
12 [1977] 2 All ER at 504–5.

cil,[13] in addition to being liable for negligence at common law for injury to a child who fell through a glass door, the defendant authority was held to be in breach of statutory duty by failing to comply with statutory regulations prescribing the minimum thickness of glass to be used in such doors, and consequently liable in damages on that ground.

In *Read v Croydon Corp*[14] the defendant council were held liable to an action for damages when a girl was infected with typhoid fever from a contaminated public water supply. They were liable to her at common law in tort for negligence. They were also liable to her father for breach of statutory duty under the Waterworks Clauses Act 1847—the same Act as was in issue in the *Atkinson* case, referred to above[15]—because s 35 imposed a duty on the council as water-supply authority to provide 'pure and wholesome water' in their area. The duty was owed to 'persons entitled to demand and receive a sufficient supply of water for domestic purposes, having paid or tendered the water rate' as stated in s 53 of the Act; and the girl's father, as a ratepayer, qualified under this head. His damages reflected the expense to which he had been put, whereas his daughter's damages related to her own pain and suffering. But the liability for breach of statutory duty here, it should be noted, was not strict; it was founded on negligence or fault. Stable J said: 'I do not think that, on the true construction of the Act, the corporation can be held to be liable for the consequences of the presence in the water supplied by it at the point where it reaches the consumer of some impurity which no care or skill could have prevented'. Since the standard of liability for breach of statutory duty was in this case held to be not strict but co-incident with negligence at common law, the reason for making such a claim in these proceedings lay in the fact that the duty was not owed to the victim who was infected but to the victim's father as a ratepayer. Thus there had been negligence at common law in regard to the daughter and negligence comprising breach of statutory duty in regard to the father.

6. EXCLUSION OF STATUTORY DUTY TO INDIVIDUALS

None of this alters the fact that the main principle of exclusion still stands. As stated in *Doe d Bishop of Rochester v Bridges*,[16] the principle is that 'where an Act creates an obligation, and enforces the performance in a specified manner, we take it to be a general rule that performance cannot be enforced in any other manner'. It was applied in *Southwark London Borough v Williams*,[17] where the statutory duty was that

13 [1964] 1 All ER 743, [1964] 1 WLR 358.
14 [1938] 4 All ER 631.
15 See p 125.
16 (1831) 1 B & Ad 847 at 859.
17 [1971] Ch 734, [1971] 2 All ER 175.

stated in the National Assistance Act 1948, s 21(1), to be imposed on
'every local authority', namely to provide '. . . temporary accommodation for persons who are in urgent need thereof . . .' The procedure for
enforcing this duty is, under s 36(1) of the Act, that if the Secretary of
State for Social Services hears representations which convince him that
'a local authority have failed to discharge any of their functions under
this part of this Act', he must proceed administratively on the basis that
the authority are in default. Lord Denning MR said: 'It cannot have
been intended by Parliament that every person who was in need of temporary accommodation should be able to sue the local authority for
it . . .'

The contrast between the court's interpretation of the National Assistance Act 1948 and the Housing (Homeless Persons) Act 1977 is as
instructive as it is remarkable. In the upshot, therefore, the existence of
a right to sue can only be determined on a general construction of the
relevant statute. Though the appearance in the statute of a 'specified
manner' of enforcement does not rule out a personal right to sue, it
makes the task of successfully asserting the existence of any such right
much harder.

This matter has recently been further clarified by the House of Lords
in *Cocks v Thanet District Council*[18] when it allowed an appeal by the
local authority claiming that the plaintiff was not entitled to sue for a
declaration and damages in tort for 'breach of statutory duty' under the
Housing (Homeless Persons) Act 1977. Lord Bridge of Harwich said
that public authorities have 'a dichotomy of functions'. Thus: 'On the
one hand the council were charged with decision-making functions . . .' These were public law 'functions', and subject to challenge
by 'judicial review' alone. But: 'On the other hand, the council were
charged with executive functions'; so that once the relevant 'decision-
making' (ie policy) procedures had been carried out, 'rights and obligations were immediately created in the field of private law . . . But it was
inherent in the scheme of the Act that an appropriate public law decision of the council was a condition precedent to the establishment of
the private law duty'. Unlike *Thornton v Kirlees MBC* referred to earlier, the appellants in this case claimed that they were exercising their
'decision-making' and not their 'executive' functions when resisting the
plaintiff's claim under the 1977 Act, and the House of Lords upheld
this contention. 'The plaintiff was not entitled to continue his proceedings otherwise than by an application for judicial review'. (It may be
noted that under the Supreme Court Act 1981, s 31, a successful application for judicial review may lead also to an award for damages if a private law duty has been infringed *incidentally* to the breach of the public
law duty which gave rise to the proceedings).

---

18 [1982] 3 All ER 1135. See also *O'Reilly v Mackman*, above, p 93.

D. Statutory authority

1. IMMUNITY IN NUISANCE

One beneficial characteristic of the law of tort in the eyes of local authorities and public bodies generally, is the defence of 'statutory authority', which is unlikely to be available as a general rule to private defendants. In the House of Lords, deciding the case of *Allen v Gulf Oil Refining Ltd*[19] Lord Roskill expressed the relevant legal principle as follows:

> 'My Lords, for a period of over one hundred and fifty years the principles on which statutes such as [the Gulf Oil Refining Act 1965] have to be construed have been considered and authoritatively determined by your Lordships' House. Where Parliament by express words or necessary implication authorises the construction or use of an undertaking, that authorisation is necessarily accompanied by immunity from any action based on nuisance. The underlying philosophy plainly is that the greater public interest arising from the construction and use of undertakings such as railways must take precedence over the private rights of owners and occupiers of neighbouring lands not to have their common law rights infringed by what would otherwise be actionable nuisance. In short, the lesser private right must yield to the greater public interest . . . But the immunity to which I have just referred is not unqualified or unlimited. The statutory undertaker must in return for the rights and privileges which he has thus obtained exercise his powers without negligence, a word which has been interpreted as meaning reasonable regard for the interests of others.'

This principle of excluding liability on the ground of statutory authority for the defendant's activities is said to apply to the tort of nuisance. Trespass is not mentioned, nor is the tort of negligence itself—not surprisingly since 'negligence', though defined as a factor in an authority's conduct rather than a tort in its own right, is emphatically said to negative the right to exemption based on statutory authority. Strict liability under the rule in *Rylands v Fletcher* is not mentioned either; yet there is independent authority from the Court of Appeal, in *Dunne v North Western Gas Board*,[20] that such liability does not arise where statute imposes a mandatory obligation to supply a service: gas, electricity, water, and so on. No statutory undertaker can reasonably be

---

19 [1981] 1 All ER 353 at 364.
20 [1964] 2 QB 806, [1963] 3 All ER 916.

said to 'collect' such things on any land for its 'own purposes'. Yet this is scarcely consistent with earlier cases in which statutory undertakers, including local authorities have been held liable strictly under this rule—ie without proof of negligence—for damage caused by escapes of gas, electricity etc, such as *Midwood & Co v Manchester Corp*, referred to above,[1] or *Charing Cross Electricity Supply Co v Hydraulic Power Co*.[2]

To make confusion worse confounded it has become customary for statutes to impose on public authorities acting as statutory undertakers—today, mostly nationalised industry corporations—a 'nuisance clause'. This proclaims that the authority in carrying out the prescribed functions shall *not* be exempted from liability in nuisance. Yet this is subordinate to the rule upheld by the House of Lords in the *Gulf Oil* case. Therefore, only in the event of 'negligent' nuisance will an action lie. Yet there seems to be no ground for thinking that in the absence of a 'nuisance clause' the liability of a statutory undertaker would be any less; and indeed this was said to be the case on the facts in *Dunne v North Western Gas Board*.

2. DENIAL OF COMPENSATION

The words 'reasonable regard for the interests of others' in Lord Ros-kill's speech in the *Gulf Oil* case sounds like an impressive quid pro quo for the exemption referred to. Yet they do not requite a plaintiff in the one way in which he ought to be requited—ie by a payment of compensation by way of an award of damages. The words 'common law rights' and 'actionable nuisance' in Lord Roskill's speech presuppose the normal common law right to damages. But in the *Gulf Oil* decision, and the earlier authorities on which it rests, the only remedy considered was equitable: an injunction. It has been pointed out again and again that to award injunctions would prevent the carrying out of the very activity that Parliament has authorised in each case, which would be a reductio ad absurdum of the law in this area. This is perfectly true. Yet injunctions, being equitable, are a discretionary remedy. There would be little logical difficulty in the way of the courts laying down a rule that an injunction is not to be available where the intentions of Parliament will be frustrated thereby, and leaving the successful plaintiff to his remedy in damages. This already happens in cases like *Ough v King*.[3] In that case a suburban house-owner sued her neighbour in private nuisance for building an extension on to his house in such a way as to infringe her easement of light. It was held that her action succeeded, but that because she did not sue until after the building work was put in hand it

1 See p 125.
2 [1914] 3 KB 772.
3 [1967] 3 All ER 859, [1967] 1 WLR 1547.

would be inequitable to award an injunction and she must take her remedy at common law by way of damages. These were assessed on the basis of the depreciation in the capital value of her property. It would have been just if the *Gulf Oil* case could have been decided in a similar way.

The facts of the *Gulf Oil* case were, briefly, that the company obtained powers under a private Act[4] to purchase compulsorily land near Milford Haven and build a very large oil refinery together with ancillary works such as access roads, railway lines and dock installations. Not surprisingly, owners of nearby houses saw the amenities and the market value of their properties fall drastically. They brought their action, claiming an injunction to make the company forthwith desist from the acts of nuisance and negligence which caused noxious odours, vibration, offensive noise-levels, excessive flames from burning waste gas, and consequent ill-health and fear of an explosion. The legal position was argued on a preliminary point of law, a course which the House of Lords disapproved of. The plaintiffs had succeeded in the Court of Appeal, but failed in the House of Lords because of the statutory immunity referred to by Lord Roskill.

Authority for the proposition that the claim against Gulf Oil in nuisance would have succeeded had there been 'negligence' in the carrying out of the works is to be found in the decisions of the House of Lords in *Manchester Corp v Farnworth*,[5] which related to the building and operation of a power station, *Metropolitan Asylum District Managers v Hill*,[6] which related to the siting of a small-pox hospital, and *Geddis v Proprietors of the Bann Reservoir*.[7] But there was little likelihood of establishing 'negligence' in the *Gulf Oil* case, merely the grievous harm by way of nuisance which was actually suffered by the plaintiffs.

Authority for the main proposition that absence of negligence rules out liability in nuisance, which the *Gulf Oil* decision upheld, is to be found in the decision of the House of Lords in *Hammersmith and City Rly Co v Brand*,[8] affirming the correctness of decisions of lower courts in *Vaughan v Taff Vale Rly Co*,[9] and *R v Pease*.[10] Lord Edmund-Davies did comment on the regrettable fact that the private Act imposed no requirement for Gulf Oil to compensate adjoining owners. He said: 'The general legal approach unquestionably is that the absence of compensation clauses from an Act conferring powers affords an important indication that the Act was not intended to authorise inter-

4 The Gulf Oil Refining Act 1965.
5 [1930] AC 171.
6 (1881) 6 App Cas 193.
7 (1878) 3 App Cas 430.
8 (1869) LR 4 HL 171.
9 (1860) 5 H & N 679.
10 (1832) 4 B & Ad 30.

ference with private rights'; and he referred to the *Metropolitan Asylum District* case. But he conceded that 'the indication is not conclusive.' As can be seen from a study of the public Acts governing the general law of compulsory purchase compensation, this qualifying statement is in fact a considerable understatement. 'Nuisance clauses' are cynical and futile in the light of this.

In truth, the concept of the defence of 'statutory authority', like the ultra vires doctrine which is another aspect of the same matter, is an unwelcome intrusion into the area of private law. It were better excluded and confined to the area of public law, for the purpose of determinging the legality or illegality of the policy decisions of local and other public authorities, by judicial review or relator actions. Proceedings in private law should be dealt with on the established principles involving damages at common law available as of right, and remedies in equity, or declarations, available in accordance with the exercise of proper judicial discretion. At the very least it should be enacted that in all cases where projects are carried out in compliance with statutory authority compensation should be paid to those who, through no fault of their own, suffer loss.

NOTE—The House of Lords, as shown by its decision in *Cocks v Thanet District Council*[11], is now trying hard to compel observance of the distinction between causes of action in public and private law respectively. The Court of Appeal is responding to the call. In *Davy v Spelthorne Borough Council* the defendants, as local planning authority, had agreed with the plaintiff that if he did not appeal against an enforcement notice they would not act on it for three years. His claim for damages in this case, on the ground that they had misled him by negligence, was held to be one which—unlike the claim in the *Cocks* case—could begin by writ, because even though a claim for damages can be included in judicial review the claimant in such proceedings 'would at the mercy of the exercise of discretion of the Queen's Bench Division' (per Cumming-Bruce LJ).[12]

11 See above, p 128.
12 (1983) Times, 10 February. See ch 4, p 90.

Chapter 6

Legal initiatives by local authorities

A. Legislative procedures

I. EARLY LEGISLATION AFFECTING LOCAL GOVERNMENT

Local authorities are almost entirely creatures of statute, and have been created in their present form to carry out functions conferred on them by statute. Since this has been done nationally it is not surprising that the general pattern of statutory authorisation appears in public general Acts, above all in the Local Government Act 1972. But public Acts do not make up the whole of the pattern. There are also local and private Acts; and there is a great deal of subordinate legislation as well. In settling the legal disputes which arise on every side the courts have to give due weight to all this mass of legislative material.

Local and private Acts have long played a part in local affairs. Ever since medieval times subjects of the Crown have petitioned Parliament to amend the law for their particular benefit and corporate bodies have participated in this process. In local government unincorporated bodies also took part. From the seventeenth century onward prominent local inhabitants took to promoting private Acts to set up new ecclesiastical parishes, usually carved out of large populous existing parishes, such as those on the outskirts of London. Thus an Ordinance of the Long Parliament in 1645, confirmed at the Restoration by an Act of 1660,[1] created the new separate parish of St Paul's Covent Garden out of the existing parish of St Martin-in-the-Fields. In this way a new local government unit came into being, since the present divorce of the church organisation from the secular organisation of parishes was then still far in the future. The many private Acts of this kind that were passed normally took care to set up a restricted or 'close' vestry of local parishioners to whom the parish officers should be accountable in so far as they were accountable to anybody other than the magistrates in quarter sessions, who commonly appointed them, and the Court of King's Bench.

This was a step deliberately taken to supersede the turbulent unrestricted or 'open' vestries, where all the local parishioners might have a say, in favour of local oligarchies of prominent inhabitants usually few in number but substantially well-to-do and influential. This introduced

---

1 12 Car 2, c xxxvii.

a differentiation, increasingly emphasised by the authorities, between the general run of ratepaying local inhabitants and the 'vestrymen'. The latter in due course, at any rate in London, evolved into the elected councillors of the secular parishes or 'vestries' produced by nineteenth- century reforms as part of a counter-current then moving back from oligarchy to democracy in local affairs. At one point, under Queen Anne, a general Act was passed, the Church Building Act 1711,[2] to get new parishes set up in this way, and new churches built, through a systematic programme to be carried out by a statutory body of Church Building Commissioners. But it seems that this initiative achieved only eleven new parishes before it faded away and the system of promoting separate private Acts was resumed whenever and wherever local interests saw fit to do so.[3]

These Acts altered the composition of local authorities at parish level without changing such local government functions as existed in those days. But other Acts did change or extend those functions. Some were public general statutes, such as the Acts of 1706 and 1708,[4] under Queen Anne, concerning parish provision of fire-engines, the Acts of 1738 and 1753,[5] under George II, for controlling the sale of gin and licensing public houses, the Act of 1762,[6] under George III, for collecting taxes and for recruiting and billeting for the army and navy, and the Act of 1786,[7] also under George III, for inspecting slaughter-houses. But mostly the initiative to improve and extend the administration of existing functions or to embark on new ones took the form of local and private legislation promoted for particular parishes by interested local notables. An Act of 1756,[8] under George II, was obtained by the Vestry at Kensington, Middlesex, to secure additional powers of levying rates for highway maintenance and poor relief; and an Act of 1790,[9] under George III, was obtained by the Vestry at Manchester—which in those days had not yet been granted corporate status as a borough—empowering it to build a workhouse, to appoint certain paid officers and servants, and to bring into effect a differential assessment system for distinguishing between different kinds of rateable property.

2. GROWTH OF PRIVATE LEGISLATION

But it became increasingly common in the eighteenth century for local notables to promote private legislation which conferred administrative

---

2 10 and 11 Anne, c 11.
3 S and B Webb *The Parish and the County*, ch 5 section (c).
4 6 Anne, c 58, and 7 Anne, c 17.
5 11 Geo, 2., c. 26, and 26 Geo, 2, c. 31.
6 3 Geo, 3 c. 7.
7 26 Geo, 3, c. 71.
8 29 Geo, 2, c. lxii.
9 30 Geo, 3 c. lxxxx.

functions—new ones, or existing ones with or without changes in detail—upon separately created authorities rather than the vestries of existing parishes. Bodies of inclosure commissioners were set up in this way in hundreds of localities to redistribute agricultural land in order to replace medieval by modern farming methods. Bodies of turnpike trustees were set up similarly to improve the maintenance of existing rural main roads and provide new ones, with the help of tolls levied on highway-users; while in the towns a corresponding movement to improve the paving, lighting and cleansing of streets (financed by rates rather than tolls) resulted in the setting up of bodies of street commissioners or paving commissioners. These were genuine local authorities, though specialised in their function; but they were not normally corporate bodies in themselves, in that their legal effectiveness took the form either of groups of commissioners acting under the authority conferred on them by the Crown in Parliament or of bodies of trustees answerable as such to the Court of Chancery. But existing municipal corporations might well be entrusted with these functions. As far as poor relief is concerned it is interesting to note that a fashion developed in the eighteenth century for passing local Acts to establish in a number of places new corporate bodies termed Incorporated Guardians of the Poor.

As Sidney and Beatrice Webb put it:[10]

'If the principal inhabitants were sufficiently energetic and sufficiently influential, they would succeed in getting a private Act of Parliament to set up new authorities for local affairs—to relieve the poor, cleanse the streets or maintain a turnpike road—exactly in the same way as a great landowner would get an Act to settle his estate or divorce his wife'.

In the nineteenth century it became customary for groups of interested persons to seek local and private Acts to set up utility undertakings in their area, notably gas and water supply companies, and later on electricity supply, telegraph and telephone companies. Canal, rail and road transport undertakings were set up. Again, many municipal borough corporations took some part in this process. In due course a number of these undertakings amalgamated; certain of them eventually became the nationalised industry corporations of today, while others developed into analogous specialised public bodies such as water authorities. Yet others found themselves, or at any rate their functions, included in the workings of local authorities. The statutes creating these bodies were mainly private Acts in earlier years, then tended to become public Acts as the twentieth century succeeded the nineteenth. Generally these various public bodies were able to seek further private

10 Op cit, pp 151–152.

legislation, though it often happens today that the central government promotes legislative changes for them before they wish to do it for themselves.

3. PRIVATE SUBORDINATE LEGISLATION

There are certain matters in regard to which public general Acts are less suitable than local and private Acts. These are matters relating to particular projects, including acquisition of land. Yet for Parliament to pass an Act, of whatever sort, to sanction any and every particular project would be impossible without either slowing down the processes of authorisation in a way which would be quite unacceptable in regard to the purposes of modern administration, or else reducing Parliament to a 'rubber-stamping' agency which, at least on the scale required, would be equally unacceptable. Abdication of central control is still more abhorrent. A two-tier process has therefore been evolved during the last century or so. Although local and private legislation is still very much alive, it is now more common to confer functions on local and other public bodies in wide and general terms by public Acts, and at the same time to state in those Acts that their implementation in the form of specific projects requires central approval by means of subordinate legislation instead of full primary legislation.

This subordinate legislation is made at ministerial level, and at first sight looks like straightforward administrative action. An example is the procedure under the Coast Protection Act 1949 in accordance with which district councils are empowered in general terms to provide or improve sea-walls along coastal sites in their respective areas. But they cannot do this purely of their own volition. Each project of this kind requires a particular 'scheme' to be made by the authority concerned. The details of the scheme must be published; and the scheme itself will be of no legal effect until the relevant minister, that is the Secretary of State for the Environment, has approved it after first following a procedure laid down in the Act itself, which involves publicity and the hearing of objections.

This is typical, not special. It is not confined to local authorities' projects. If the Secretary of State for Transport wishes to have a new motorway ('special road') built, the Highways Act 1980[11] requires him to prepare and publish a draft scheme to that effect, and not to 'make' it until the procedure prescribed in the Act has been duly complied with. 'Orders' or 'schemes' made, or confirmed, by a minister may be treated as public rather than private subordinate legislation; if so they are embodied in 'statutory instruments' and given a consecutive reference number in accordance with the Statutory Instruments Act 1946.[12]

---

11 S 16. See below, ch 11.
12 The Acts under which they are made will state if they are to be embodied in 'statutory instruments'. For an example of this, see the Highways Act 1980, s 325.

4. COMPULSORY PURCHASE ORDERS

This is not the end of the matter. Usually the carrying out of such projects requires capital expenditure (which in itself normally needs Ministerial approval) and depends on the acquisition of land. No statutory body can lawfully do anything unless that action is expressly or by clear implication authorised by statute, in accordance with the ultra vires doctrine discussed in an earlier chapter. Should the relevant authority be empowered in this way to acquire land for the project in hand, then they can buy the land they require, by agreement on the open market. But often power to acquire land compulsorily is necessary. Acquisition is one thing, compulsion is another. There are a number of statutory purposes for which authorities are empowered to acquire land but are not empowered to do so compulsorily. With a few special exceptions, no authorising Act confers the power to purchase land compulsorily on any authority for any purpose by purely administrative action. Subordinate legislation is required here, in the shape of a compulsory purchase order expressly specifying the acquiring authority, and the purpose, and the statutory authorisation, and the particular land.

Like the 'schemes' referred to above, compulsory purchase orders must be made in draft, published, and approved or confirmed by the relevant minister after due consideration of objections.[13] Such an order, when finally effective, makes it lawful for the compulsory purchase to take place but does not in any sense implement that purchase. The acquiring authority must decide to implement the purchase and do so within a stated time-limit, which is normally three years. The necessary step to this end is the service of a 'notice to treat' (ie to negotiate) or the execution of a 'vesting declaration' in relation to each and every property interest, freehold or leasehold, to be acquired, in other words a step in conveyancing. It is this subsequent procedure which amounts to executive action as distinct from the legislative step of making the compulsory purchase order. Further details may be studied in works dealing separately with compulsory purchase; they are too complex to be pursued here.

The fact that compulsory purchase orders are legislative in nature appears from their history as well as their present nature and that of the procedure for making them. Until 1845 each separate compulsory purchase required a separate Act, namely a local and private Act obtained by the local authority or other body of 'promoters' initiating it. Because this involved endless repetition of standard-form clauses and other wording from one private Act to the next, a public general Act was passed, the Lands Clauses Consolidation Act 1845, which set

---

13 Acquisition of Land Act 1981. A minster may also be empowered to draft and 'make' his own orders, if an authorising Act so provides. CPOs are not required to be embodied in 'statutory instruments'.

out standard-form clauses once and for all which were to be incorporated by reference into every subsequent private Act for the compulsory purchase of land, unless otherwise specified. These clauses dealt with the conveyancing and the compensation; but private Acts were still necessary for the authorisation and the choice of specific land.

Soon afterwards a trend set in of authorising compulsory purchase in general terms by public Acts such as the Public Health Act 1875. This made it possible to avoid having separate private Acts for each separate land acquisition, which instead was to be done at ministerial level. At first, a half-way procedure was laid down in the public general authorising Acts whereby a minister could make a 'provisional order' for each acquisition but such orders still needed to be approved in batches by Provisional Order Confirmation Acts, a procedure almost as time-consuming and expensive as having separate private Acts. But from 1909 onwards 'compulsory purchase orders' were devised, so that each authorising Act will now normally allow particular land to be earmarked for compulsory acquisition by the appropriate body or bodies for the appropriate purpose or purposes by one of these orders which requires ministerial confirmation, not parliamentary enactment. Yet for many years thereafter each compulsory purchase order together with the appropriate provisions of the 1845 Act incorporated into it by reference, was officially termed 'the Special Act', thus underlining both its descent from private legislation in the full sense and its continuing legislative nature.

5. CHALLENGING SUBORDINATE LEGISLATION

Local authorities, like other public bodies, are in this way constantly procuring new legislation in furtherance of their functions. They can go to the trouble, if necessary, of promoting local and private Acts; or they can make compulsory purchase orders, or schemes and orders for particular projects, which normally require ministerial approval only and not separate parliamentary enactment. Some of these are subject to 'special parliamentary procedure',[14] which means that they have to be laid before both Houses of Parliament and therefore, if they do not meet with approval, will be prevented from taking effect. The former type of conferment of power is full legislation; the latter type is 'subordinate' or 'delegated' legislation.

Subordinate or delegated legislation is more precarious than full legislation. In principle it is subject to the ultra vires doctrine because it is made under powers conferred by an Act and must be within the ambit of those powers if it is to be valid. The courts can therefore quash what purports to be subordinate legislation if on challenge it is shown to

14 Statutory Orders (Special Procedure) Acts 1945 and 1965.

be ultra vires, just as they can quash purely administrative decisions for the same reason. An example is *Re Ripon (Highfield) Housing Order 1938, White and Collins's Application,*[15] in which there was a dispute over a compulsory purchase order made under the Housing Act 1936. That Act stated that land included in a 'park' could not be the subject of a compulsory purchase order; the minister confirmed an order which included a park (this was a 'jurisdictional fact') and that order was duly quashed.[16] But it is common nowadays for statutes to provide that various ministerial decisions cannot be 'questioned' in any legal proceedings except within a stated time—usually six weeks—on stated grounds and by a stated procedure. This whole question has been discussed in an earlier chapter.[17]

Compulsory purchase orders, and other orders and schemes made by local authorities which require confirmation by a minister, are in effect subordinate legislation corresponding to local and private Acts; just as ministerial regulations, rules and orders are subordinate legislation corresponding to public general Acts. But whereas functional powers which local and other public authorities procure for themselves by subordinate legislation in this way can be challenged in the courts, local and private Acts themselves cannot be so challenged because they are legislation in the full sense and not subordinate. The fact that such Acts are procured by subjects of the Crown makes no difference to this. Since the Revolution of 1688–89 the courts will not question Acts purporting to have been passed by Lords and Commons given the Royal Assent in due form. This rule has recently been challenged and reaffirmed in the House of Lords. The case is clearly relevant to local authorities, though on the facts it involved a nationalised industry: *British Railways Board v Pickin.*[18]

In this case a private Act, the British Railways Act 1968, provided that land being the site of any abandoned railway-line would vest in the Board notwithstanding the provisions of previous legislation stating that it should vest in adjoining owners. The respondent bought from the owner of a plot of land adjoining a disused railway line for 50p 'ALL THAT his estate and interest' in the railway line 'together with the fixtures and appurtenances attached thereto including the metal rails the sleepers and the ballast laid on the said track TO HOLD the same unto the Purchaser in fee simple'. He then brought an action claiming against the Board, and also against the contractors then being employed by the Board to dismantle the track, a declaration than he owned the land, plus damages and other redress. He alleged that the Board had

15 [1939] 2 KB 838, [1939] 3 All ER 548.
16 See also ch 9, pp 230–231.
17 Ch 4, pp 98–100.
18 [1974] AC 765, [1974] 1 All ER 609.

procured the Act of 1968 by fraudulently concealing various relevant facts from Parliament, and that the relevant provision of the Act of 1968 was therefore inoperative.

The House of Lords unhesitatingly rejected the contention that any Act of Parliament, public or private, can be questioned in the courts. Lord Wilberforce said that 'whether the attention of Parliament . . . was called to the provision in question, or what decisions . . . were taken, are not matters into which the courts can inquire. Private Acts, such as the 1968 Act, as the authorities . . . show, are as fully Acts of Parliament as public Acts, and compel acceptance by the courts'. As Lord Campbell said in *Edinburgh and Dalkeith Rly Co v Wauchope*,[19] '. . . all that a court of justice can look to is the parliamentary roll; they see that an Act has passed both Houses of Parliament, and that it has received the royal assent, and no court of justice can inquire into the manner in which it was introduced into parliament, what was done previously to its being introduced, or what passed in parliament during the various stages of its progress through both Houses . . .' Apparent authority to the contrary, in the early House of Lords decision in the Scots case of *M'Kenzie v Stewart*,[20] was disposed of by showing that the decision turned on the true construction of the relevant private Act[1] in that case and not any denial of its validity.

6. PRACTICAL DIFFERENCES BETWEEN PUBLIC AND PRIVATE LEGISLATION

But although there is no formal legal difference between public and private legislation the practical difference is real enough. Public legislation, whether in the shape of Acts which are not subject to the supervisory jurisdiction of the courts, or of regulations, rules and orders which are, normally emanates from the central government and is thus imposed on local authorities from above (though they are often consulted first). Private local legislation, whether in the form of Acts or orders, normally emanates from local authorities themselves, if it relates to them at all; though of course locally-promoted orders of this kind are usually though not necessarily made under authority of some public Act—ie the relevant legislation is public in principle and local only in detail. This is normally true of compulsory purchase orders, and of the various functional schemes embodied in orders for new roads, seawalls and the like. Local subordinate legislation of this kind is no doubt more frequently met with today than local and private Acts because the central government commonly wishes local government policies to be worked out within a national framework.

But local and private Acts are still met with also, and new ones may

---

19 (1842) I Bell SC App 252 at 279.
20 (1754) I Pat App 578.
 I 12 Geo 2 c vii.

still be passed. The larger the local authority the wider the scope of the authority's administrative functions and the more likely there is to be a desire to promote private Acts. Thus the Greater London Council, and its predecessor (before 1965) the London County Council, have promoted a long series of private 'General Powers' Acts over many years; and other major city and county authorities do so from time to time. Perhaps the most important of modern private Acts obtained by local authorities are the London Building Act 1930 and the London Building Act (Amendment) Act 1939, also promoted by the London County Council. These enact for London an extensive code of building control for the inner London boroughs. This code, with some differences, serves the same general purpose as do the Building Regulations—made under ss 4–11 of the Public Health Act 1961, a public general Act—for the outer London boroughs and local government areas elsewhere in England and Wales.[2]

It is fairly uncommon for leading cases under private Acts to reach the superior courts; but when they do they are interpreted in the same way as public Acts. Indeed a private Act may well incorporate provisions in a public Act. In *Argyle Motors (Birkenhead) Ltd v Birkenhead Corp*,[3] a compensation dispute in a compulsory purchase, a private local Act, the Birkenhead Corporation (Mersey Tunnel Approaches) Act 1965, expressly incorporated s 68 of the Lands Clauses Consolidation Act 1845, which was a public general act. Section 68 is now replaced by s 10 of the Compulsory Purchase Act 1965. As a result the decision of the House of Lords in *Ricket v Metropolitan Rly Co*[4] given on the interpretation of s 68 of the 1845 Act was held to be directly applicable to the current case.

A case in which a private local Act had to be interpreted on its own account is *Gyle-Thompson v Wall Street (Properties) Ltd*.[5] The London Building Acts (Amendment) Act 1939[6] s 46, concerning the right of an owner to demolish and rebuild a 'party fence wall' without the consent of the neighbouring owner (the boundary being situated in mid-wall) was in issue. Brightman J said that it was 'important that the steps laid down by the Act should be scrupulously followed throughout, and short cuts are not desirable'. This strict approach is essential because the rights of an owner can be interfered with compulsorily under s 46; there would be no difference in approach if the provision were contained in a public general Act.

7. BYELAWS: NATURE AND ENACTMENT

Other legislation, of a subordinate kind, in the field of local government consists of byelaws. This phrase is of medieval origin and originally meant

2 On this, see ch 11, pp 280–281.
3 [1975] AC 99, [1974] 1 All ER 201.
4 (1867) LR 2 HL 175.
5 [1974] 1 All ER 295.
6 2 and 3 Geo 6, c xcvii.

'town laws' or 'village laws'. Village and town communities seem to have been recognised at common law as having power by immemorial custom[7] to make byelaws for ensuring the proper regulation of the life of the particular community. This came to be summed up in the phrase 'for good rule and government' and 'for the prevention and suppression of nuisances'. Statutory bodies can only make such byelaws today if some Act gives clear statutory authorisation for doing so. The Local Government Act 1972, s 235, gives such authorisation to the councils of districts and London boroughs, but only in so far as the subject-matter of the byelaws is not covered by any other enactment.

Byelaws are primarily part of the criminal law of the land, and are therefore enforced by way of prosecution, normally for punishment by a fine, by the authority which made them and which as a result must be recognised as having an interest in seeing that they are complied with. Especially frequent are byelaws regulating the behaviour of the users of public parks and open spaces. In *Newman v Francis*,[8] the plaintiff brought a civil action for damages for injury suffered by being knocked down by a dog in a public open space where a byelaw was in force making it an offence for anyone to permit his dog to cause annoyance or injury. It was held that the byelaw imposed no civil liability on a dog-owner or the local authority concerned.

There are also, however, regulatory byelaws, for example new street byelaws under Part X of the Highways Act 1980. These require persons intending to construct new streets to deposit plans and sections for prior inspection by the local highway authority, which must approve them unless they contravene the byelaws or are otherwise defective or unsuitable for various special reasons. Contravention of byelaw control is liable to be met by the authority requiring work to be done to remedy the breach, failing which they may do the remedial work themselves at the defaulter's expense, much as in planning law; but byelaws can include provision for prosecution and fines as a punishment for contravention. There used to be building byelaws as well as new street byelaws, enforceable in much the same way. The purpose of these byelaws, which is the control of new building construction in the interests of public safety and health, was in 1961 thought to be better served by replacing them with a set of Building Regulations in force nationally (except in inner London) as described above,[9] in order to achieve general uniformity and consistency. But the system of byelaws has been retained for new streets, which means that a different set of rules can obtain in each separate local highway authority area.

Nevertheless some possibility of harmonisation of different sets of

7 S. and B. Webb, op cit, p 39.
8 [1953] 1 WLR 402.
9 See p 141.

byelaws does exist. Since the power to make byelaws is dependent on statute, except for the common law powers of parishes to make byelaws for the parishioners and chartered corporations to make them for their members—which are now virtually obsolete—the relevant statutory requirements must be strictly observed. It is now unthinkable that any statute would confer on any public authority the power to make byelaws of any kind free of a requirement that they must first be confirmed by some central government department.

As far as local authorities are concerned, the Local Government Act 1972, s 236 states that all byelaws, and not only those relating to 'good rule and government' and 'the prevention and suppression of nuisances', must be made in accordance with a standard procedure except where some statute clearly provides otherwise. The procedure is that the byelaws shall be made under seal and must first be submitted in draft to the 'confirming authority'—ie the Secretary of State for the Environment unless some other minister is specified in the relevant authorising Act—and given local publicity with the opportunity for public inspection. The 'confirming authority' then decides whether or not to confirm the byelaws, which take effect one month after being confirmed unless some other date is specified. It is customary for central government departments to have available a set of 'model byelaws', drawn up in the light of past experience, to give authorities an idea of suitable detailed wording.

In so far as byelaws are regulatory, such as new street byelaws or (in the past) building byelaws, the authority that made them cannot relax or waive them, unless the relevant statute allows this or (which is less likely) the 'confirming authority' approves the inclusion of a provision to that effect in the byelaws themselves. This was made clear in *Yabbicom v King*.[10] But enforcement by way of criminal prosecution is a matter of policy discretion for the byelaw authority as such, or for any other potential prosecutor, to decide. In *R v Stewart*[11] it was held that anyone can prosecute unless statute clearly provides otherwise.

8. BYELAWS: CHALLENGE PROCEDURE

Because byelaws, unlike private Acts, are subordinate private legislation, they are subject to the general supervisory jurisdiction of the superior courts, which can therefore quash them if they are ultra vires the Act under which they purport to be made or are contrary to law for any other reason. In *Nash v Finlay*[12] a byelaw that: 'No person shall wilfully annoy passengers in the streets' was held void for uncertainty.

10 [1899] 1 QB 444.
11 [1896] 1 QB 300. See also the Local Government (Miscellaneous Provisions) Act 1982, s 12, as to enforcement by constables.
12 (1901) 85 LT 682.

In *Powell v May*[13] a Glamorgan County Council byelaw prohibited betting 'in a public place' despite the fact that two public general Acts permitted it in certain circumstances. The byelaw was held to be 'repugnant' to the general law of the land under those statutes and therefore void. In *Scott v Pilliner*[14] a Staffordshire County Council byelaw on the same subject was held void on the different ground that it was unreasonably wide and uncertain in its wording. This spoke of 'written or printed matter devoted wholly or mainly to giving information as to the probable result of races, steeplechases or other competitions', which may or may not have referred to betting-slips. In *Galer v Morrisey*[15] a byelaw against any 'nuisance' caused by animals kept on particular premises was interpreted in terms of statutory nuisances 'prejudicial to health' under the Public Health Act 1936. As a result it was held not to be applicable in regard to animals which were noisy (constantly barking greyhounds) as distinct from insanitary.

The basic test of reasonableness and consistency with the general law has always been applied. 'The jurisdiction of testing byelaws by their reasonableness was originally applied in such cases as those of manorial bodies, towns or corporations having inherent powers or general powers conferred by charter of making such laws', according to the House of Lords in *Slattery v Naylor*[16] (per Lord Hobhouse). But this is 'reasonableness' in the strictly objective sense required by the common law, as expressed by Lord Greene MR in the *Wednesbury* case described in an earlier chapter.[17] As Lord Russell of Killowen CJ said in *Kruse v Johnson*:[18] 'A byelaw is not unreasonable merely because particular judges may think that it goes further than is prudent or necessary or convenient'. 'Reasonableness' as a subjective question of policy is a matter for the authorities making the byelaws, not of the courts adjudicating on them. In this particular case a Kent County Council byelaw prohibiting anyone from 'playing music or singing in any place within fifty yards of any dwelling-house after being requested to desist' was upheld. It was not ambiguous, uncertain, repugnant to the general law, arbitrary or tainted with bad faith; nor did it involve 'such oppressive or gratuitous interference with the rights of those subject to [it] as could find no justification in the minds of reasonable men'. But any byelaw, 'if validly made . . . has the force of law within the sphere of its legitimate operation'. And since local authorities at least are democratically elected representative bodies, the fact that they are entrusted by Parliament with the task of making byelaws means that these should be upheld where possible.

13 [1946] KB 330, [1946] 1 All ER 444.
14 [1904] 2 KB 855.
15 [1955] 1 All ER 380, [1955] 1 WLR 110.
16 (1888) 13 App Cas 446 at 452.
17 Ch 3. See above, p 63.
18 [1898] 2 QB 91.

9. STANDING ORDERS

The last kind of subordinate legislation in the local government field, which requires a brief mention here, is that known as 'standing orders'. Statutory authority for making these is conferred on local authorities generally by the Local Government Act 1972.[19] These are rules intended to have purely internal effect, which govern the way business is carried on in councils and their committees[20] and the relations between them, and how council officers carry out their duties. Standing orders in force have the effect of law, and must be complied with; but since the local authority that made them can change them at any time no aggrieved person is likely to be able to enforce them to any practical extent. In *R v Hereford Corp, ex p Harrower*[1] the local authority disregarded its standing orders governing the procedure for submitting tenders for council contracts. An aggrieved contractor applied to the High Court for judicial review, and it was held that this should on principle be granted; but since standing orders can be changed at any time the action was suspended to allow the local authority to do this if they so wished.

B. Legal proceedings by local authorities

1. POWER TO LITIGATE 'IN THEIR OWN NAME'

The Local Government Act 1972, s 222, provides as follows:

> '(1) Where a local authority consider it expedient for the promotion or protection of the interests of the inhabitants of their area—(a) they may prosecute or defend or appear in any legal proceedings and, in the case of civil proceedings, may institute them in their own name, and (b) they may, in their own name, make representations in the interests of the inhabitants at any public inquiry held by or on behalf of any Minister or public body under any enactment.'

A 'local authority' is defined for the general purposes of the Act, by s 270, as meaning any county, district, parish or community council or any London borough council or the Greater London Council; and s 222(2) adds, for the purposes of the above provision, the Common Council of the City of London.

---

19 S 99 and Sch 12, Part VI, para 42 (and also Part III, para 20: parish meetings).
20 S 106; this includes joint committees set up by more than one council.
  1 [1970] 3 All ER 460, [1970] 1 WLR 1424.

The power of local authorities to bring civil actions to uphold their rights as corporate persons in tort, contract or trusts has not in a general way given rise to much difficulty or controversy. It is so obvious that any legal person, artificial as well as natural, must have the power to assert such rights that there is seldom likely to be any incentive to try and persuade a court otherwise. An attempt has been made to deny that a local authority has any cause of action in defamation. In *Bognor Regis UDC v Campion*[2] the defendant published leaflets containing some colourful statements about the alleged behaviour of the plaintiff council and various members of it, purporting to do so 'on behalf of the Save Bognor Group'. It was urged as a matter of law that only the individual councillors and officers could have a cause of action for damage to their reputation. The answer is that admittedly only they can sue if their individual reputation is damaged. But it is also the case that a corporate body, notwithstanding the fact that it is only an artificial 'person', is still an entity in its own right. That being so, it has a reputation which may well be damaged independently of what happens to the reputations of the individual people who belong to it or work for it. Browne J quoted Spencer Bower on *Actionable Defamation*[3] who 'submitted that a "body of persons" has a collective character independently of the question whether it is a mercantile body or not, which the law is bound to protect; in other words that any such body can sue in respect of an imputation of *any conduct whatsoever* of which its agents, and, therefore, itself *by its agents* can be guilty'. He gave judgment for the council and awarded £2,000 damages. It should be pointed out that there is no question of smothering public or private criticism of the council. The statements complained of included genuine and proper criticisms but, to put it mildly, did not stop at these; and the judge held that on the facts defences of justification, fair comment and privilege failed.

Local authorities can therefore stand up for themselves as 'persons' in private law. The difficult question is, how far can they stand up for the general public. This is not the same as the question whether public authorities should have their ultra vires acts or omissions invalidated by the High Court, which was discussed in an earlier chapter;[4] though the two questions may well be linked from time to time in practice. In regard to the *ultra vires* issue, a public body will be a defendant in a public cause of action. Here the question is whether it can be a plaintiff in a public cause of action.

If the cause of action is an allegation of *ultra vires* conduct, then the defendant will in any case be a public authority of some kind. A local authority or other public body can be a plaintiff in such a case if they

2 [1972] 2 QB 169, [1972] 2 All ER 61.
3 (1908) pp 278–279.
4 Ch 4, pp 84–88.

have *locus standi* or 'sufficient interest' on the same footing as any private person. An example is *R v Minister of Housing and Local Government, ex p Chichester RDC*.[5] The defendant minister was successfully challenged for ultra vires conduct, proceedings for certiorari being brought by a plaintiff which happened to be a local authority and which had locus standi because the minister was trying to force the authority to buy certain land which they did not want. Another is the London fares case: *Bromley London Borough Council v Greater London Council*.[6]

The Local Government Act 1972, s 222, which has been referred to above, clearly covers proceedings of that kind as it does civil proceedings in private causes of action. In general terms s 222 re-enacts earlier legislation, namely s 276 of the Local Government Act 1933. There is one significant difference. In s 222 of the 1972 Act the words are that local authorities may institute proceedings 'in their own name'. This all-important phrase was absent from s 276 of the 1933 Act. Its presence or absence obviously makes no difference in respect of the private or public (ultra vires) causes of action so far discussed. But that is not the case where proceedings are brought for infringement of public rights or 'the public interest'.

A case of this kind is a public cause of action in a rather different sense from proceedings to challenge ultra vires conduct by a public authority. The defendant may be a public authority, but may not; whereas of course the whole point of ultra vires proceedings is that in them the defendant is a public authority of some kind. The essence of the matter, however, is that in proceedings to uphold 'the public interest', as distinct from proceedings to challenge ultra vires acts, it is the public in general who have suffered a wrong, and not any particular person whether natural or artificial, private or corporate.

2. ASSISTANCE TO LOCAL AUTHORITIES BY THE ATTORNEY-GENERAL

Yet there is a unifying principle between these cases and ultra vires cases. Either way the cause of action is public and not private. Therefore the general common law rule applies that no private person, neither individual nor corporate, can bring proceedings. Only the Attorney-General can do so as the upholder, for the Crown, of the public interest. In ultra vires cases the exceptions to this are widespread, as has been seen in chapter 4, because private persons and corporations frequently wish to attack the policy decisions of official bodies and can bring proceedings to do so provided that they can demonstrate the necessary locus standi for judicial review, which is easier now than it used to be, or persuade the Attorney-General to agree to the bringing of relator proceedings.

---

5 [1960] 2 All ER 407, [1960] 1 WLR 587.
6 [1982] 1 All ER 129, [1982] 2 WLR 62. See ch 3, p 72.

Locus standi or 'sufficient interest', however, has no relevance to proceedings to be brought to uphold the public interest. It makes no difference whether the wrongdoer is a public authority or a private person. Only if the facts which give rise to the contravention also give rise to a separate and distinct private cause of action can a subject sue, and even then of course only for the private cause of action, as when circumstances of a public nuisance cause particular loss or damage to an individual clearly distinguishable from the public nuisance. The classic example of this is a public nuisance by obstructing a highway if it not only incommodes the public generally in using that highway but causes particular harm by obstructing access to premises with frontages on that highway. In *Lyons Sons & Co v Gulliver*,[7] the defendants were held responsible for the obstruction of a street caused by theatre queues at their premises, which was a public nuisance in the highway, and were in consequence liable on a private law basis for the particular loss resulting from the fact that the queues blocked the access to the plaintiff's premises. But no-one can sue merely in the capacity of a member of the public for any contravention of the public interest.

Clear statutory authority alone can enable some party other than the Attorney-General to bring proceedings against a defendant in respect of activity contravening the public interest. The Local Government Act 1933, s 276, was thought to confer such authority on local councils by empowering them to bring proceedings which they considered 'expedient for the promotion or protection of the interests of the inhabitants of their area'; but in a public nuisance case, *Prestatyn UDC v Prestatyn Raceway Ltd*,[8] this was rejected. It continued therefore to be necessary to make use of relator proceedings involving the Attorney-General. In *Hampshire County Council v Shonleigh Nominees Ltd*,[9] the question of public interest arose when the continued existence of a highway was alleged over land acquired by the defendant property company after ceasing to be the site of a war-time airfield. Hampshire County Council wished to enforce the alleged public right of way against the company's denial; but the point was taken and decided against them and the action was only able to proceed because the Attorney-General agreed to take charge of it in relator proceedings.[10]

It was because of this state of affairs that when s 276 of the 1933 Act was re-enacted in s 222 of the 1972 Act the words 'in their own name' were added. The long line of cases in which proceedings have been brought to counteract contraventions of the public interest or of public rights have as a result been marked, since 1972, by the successful

7 [1914] 1 Ch 631.
8 [1969] 3 All ER 1573, [1970] 1 WLR 33.
9 [1970] 2 All ER 144, [1970] 1 WLR 865.
10 [1971] 3 All ER 473, [1971] 1 WLR 1723.

appearance of local authorities in their own right as plaintiffs. The substantive law is of course unchanged by this, both as to the nature of the wrongdoing and the remedies to be sought. These are injunctions and declarations, the effect of which is obviously no different whether it is the Attorney-General or local authority who seek them.

3. UPHOLDING THE PUBLIC INTEREST

In *Kent County Council v Batchelor*,[11] the defendant cut down trees on his land in defiance of certain tree preservation orders. The plaintiff council sought and obtained an interlocutory injunction against him. They later alleged that he disregarded the injunction and applied to have him committed to prison, this of course being the ultimate sanction for enforcing injunctions. The defendant claimed that the injunction should be discharged. Admitting that the plaintiff council enjoyed a power to bring proceedings in their own name under s 222, he argued that they and the Attorney-General alike could only proceed, as Talbot J put it: 'where there are commissions of criminal acts, the penalties for which are wholly inadequate, or where there is some great urgency to take action'. But Talbot J said:

> 'It is not just a case of taking action to prevent a criminal offence. It is a case of preventing interference with the areas of natural beauty which [the plaintiff council] have sought by their tree preservation orders to preserve . . . As counsel for the plaintiff has pointed out, the limitation which lies on a local authority in using their powers under s 222 is that it must be for the promotion or protection of the interests of the inhabitants of their area. In my judgment the wording of that section is wide enough to give these plaintiffs the power to take proceedings in the interest of the inhabitants of their area to prevent infringements of the tree preservation orders that they have made.'

The supposed emphasis on criminal law was misconceived: whether criminal sanctions are applicable to a particular wrongdoing or not is merely one issue among several. In any case, 'counsel for the plaintiffs says with some force it is not only justice to the defendant that must be considered, but justice to the plaintiffs and those for whom they are bringing these proceedings. The plaintiffs have a duty to protect public amenities'.

This puts the relevant law on a reasonably stable footing. From the point of view of local authorities the change is quite considerable, in spite of the fact that the law in this area is as stated by Lord Dilhorne as follows in *Gouriet v Union of Post Office Workers*:[12]

---

11 [1978] 3 ALL ER 980, [1979] 1 WLR 213. See ch 11, p 297.
12 [1977] 3 All ER 70 at 94.

'The conclusion to which I have come in the light of the many authorities . . . is that it is the law, and long-established law, that *save and in so far as the Local Government Act 1972, s 222, gives local authorities a limited power to do so,* only the Attorney-General can sue on behalf of the public for the purpose of preventing public wrongs and that a private individual cannot do so on behalf of the public though he may be able to do so if he will sustain injury as a result of a public wrong. In my opinion the cases establish that the courts have no jurisdiction to entertain such claims by a private individual who has not suffered and will not suffer damage.'

The effectiveness of s 222 of the Local Government Act 1972 was also tested in *Solihull Metropolitan Borough Council v Maxfern,*[13] in which the council sought and obtained an injunction to prevent the wrongful use of premises as a Sunday market. The defendant's argument amounted to this, that s 222 of the 1972 Act was to be regarded merely as having the same effect as s 276 of the 1933 Act. The supposed justification for this argument was that the Public Health Act 1936, s 100, which empowers local authorities to take proceedings in regard to premises in an insanitary or dangerous condition amounting to a statutory nuisance, and to do so 'in their own name', is worded in some respects differently from s 222 of the 1972 Act. Oliver J in the Chancery Division of the High Court was not impressed by this non sequitur; and in any case the 1936 Act is a specialised Act whereas the 1972 Act is general. But the defendant's argument was little more than an attempt to make superficial comparisons so as to divert attention from any serious substantive interpretation of the actual words of s 222.

It can therefore now be accepted that s 222 has been demonstrated as giving local authorities co-equal jurisdiction with the Attorney-General to bring proceedings to deal with contraventions of public rights in the public interest in so far as these are prejudicial to the people in their area. The next step is to consider the main line of cases in this branch of the law.

4. LEADING CASES BEFORE 1972

In the appropriately named *A–G v Sharp,*[14] the facts were that Manchester Corporation enjoyed statutory powers of licensing buses and other public conveyances operating in their area. The defendant did not dispute this; he ignored it. Breach of that licensing control was an offence punishable by fines. The defendant ran unlicensed bus services

---

13 [1977] 2 All ER 177, [1977] 1 WLR 127. But in contrast see *Wolverhampton Borough Council v B & Q (Retail),* (1983), Times, 19 January, for a more restrictive decision on this subject.
14 [1931] 1 Ch 121.

and was repeatedly fined, no doubt treating the fines as an operating cost. The Court of Appeal upheld the claim of the Attorney-General, brought at the relation of the local authority, to an injunction. Lawrence LJ said:

'. . . the court has jurisdiction to retrain an illegal act of a public nature at the instance of the Attorney-General suing on behalf of the public, although the illegal act does not constitute an invasion of any right of property and although the Act imposing . . . liability prescribes the remedy for its breach.'

In other words, administrative or regulatory control is imposed on individuals on behalf, and for the benefit, of the public as a whole. Even if criminal sanctions are applied, they are not of the essence of enforcement for breach. Where it is reasonably necessary to do so in the public interest—not arbitrarily, nor on the other hand in blind subordination to some technical rule like the unavailability of alternative enforcement procedures—the courts can apply the equitable remedy of injunction, with its sanction of imprisonment, at the suit of the Attorney-General or appropriate local authority. In the words of Lawrence LJ where 'the defendant is wilfully persisting in an illegal course of conduct which . . . if no injunction be granted will continue to be a permanent habit . . . the only appropriate remedy is by way of an injunction at the instance of the Attorney-General'.

In that case and others the regulatory control happened to be a function conferred on a local authority, which of course had the incentive to attempt to enforce it. Sec 222 of the 1972 Act has merely enacted that any local authority can sue without involving the Attorney-General. It might have been better in principle to enact that all authorities entrusted with regulatory functions, and not merely local authorities, should be able to sue independently of the Attorney-General. But no doubt in practice most of these functions belong to local authorities and there is little urgency to extend the power to other public bodies.

Another case of this kind is *A–G v Premier Line*,[15] where the defendants ran unlicensed coaches. In *A-G v Harris*,[16] the defendants were habitually selling flowers in an unauthorised place; and Pearce LJ observed that proceedings in these cases might be brought 'whether the breaches be an invasion of public rights of property or merely an invasion of the community's general right to have the laws of the land obeyed'. In *A-G v Bastow*,[17] the injunction applied for was a mandatory injunction to remove caravans from an unauthorised site, not merely a

15 [1932] 1 Ch 303.
16 [1961] 1 QB 74, [1960] 3 All ER 207.
17 [1957] 1 QB 514, [1957] 1 All ER 497.

prohibitory injunction to cease doing unlawful acts; and Devlin J said that if the Attorney-General, 'having surveyed the different ways . . . for seeing that the law . . . is not defied, has come to the conclusion that the most effective way is to ask . . . for a mandatory injunction—and I am satisfied that the very nature of a relator action means that he has surveyed those ways and has come to that conclusion—then I think that [the High Court], once a clear breach . . . has been shown, should only refuse the application in exceptional circumstances'.

In *A-G v Melville Construction Co Ltd*,[18] the wrongful act, as in the *Batchelor* case, was the cutting down of protected trees with a declared intention to go on doing so. Prosecution is an available sanction in such cases; but Megarry J rejected a defence argument that no injunction could be awarded unless criminal proceedings had first been brought. He said that 'it cannot be right that the defendant company should remain free to injure and cut down trees while it is being prosecuted for breach of the tree preservation order and thus be allowed to commit such irreparable harm. The court should . . . intervene by injunction to prevent irremediable injury . . .'

In *A-G v Chaudry*,[19] the injunction sought was to prevent a London hotel from being occupied, or let for occupation, until adequate provision had been made for escape in the event of a fire and a certificate to that effect had been issued by the relevant local authority. The council's officer who gave evidence said: 'I have had some experience of fire risks in London buildings and while I have no wish to be alarmist, it is my considered opinion that in the event of a fire on the ground floor of [the premises] taking hold, there would, if the premises were occupied, be loss of life'. The defendants based themselves on the plural word 'breaches' in the judgment of Pearce LJ in the *Harris* case, referred to above, and claimed that only persistent breaches of the law would justify an injunction and that their conduct did not amount to persistent breaches. But Plowman J did not accept this quibble. He pointed out 'that at least for one month, which is the minimum period of time it is going to take to satisfy [the local authority] in regard to fire precautions, the defendants will be free to subject hotel guests to the risk of losing their lives as a result of fire in the premises . . . and in my judgment the court is not so powerless as to be unable to prevent that state of affairs existing'. The Court of Appeal, in which Phillimore LJ spoke pointedly of conduct amounting to 'deliberately flouting the law in order to make money', which is what these cases come down to, unanimously agreed.

5. LEADING CASES SINCE 1972

As a result of the passing of s 222 of the 1972 Act, local authorities can now be seen bringing further proceedings of this kind in their own name. In *Stafford*

---

18 (1968) 67 LGR 309. See above, p 149.
19 [1971] 3 All ER 938, [1971] 1 WLR 1614.

Borough Council v Elkenford Ltd,[20] the defendants used land for the site of a Sunday market, much as in the *Maxfern* case referred to above, in contravention of the Shops Act 1950 and the Town and Country Planning Act 1971, undeterred by fines. As in the *Chaudry* case, an injunction was granted in the High Court, and the grant was upheld by the Court of Appeal. Oliver J, at first instance, said: 'I really cannot accept that anyone can plead that the enforcement, in accordance with its spirit, of the provisions of an Act of Parliament can constitute a hardship justifying the withholding of injunctive relief'.

In *Hammersmith Borough Council v Magnum Automated Forecourts Ltd*,[1] the cause of dispute was the relentless use of a converted petrol filling-station as a 'taxi care centre', 24 hours a day, by a fully automated system of oil-dispensing equipment, washing hoses, vending machines and the like. In the words of Lord Denning MR: 'The noise was particularly bad in the early hours of the morning . . . Taxis came in every five or six minutes. No other vehicles came at that hour. The people living nearby could not sleep'. The local authority decided to take action against the owners, as being responsible for 'pollution by noise', under the Control of Pollution Act 1974. Sec 58(1) of that Act, in Lord Denning's words, 'imposes a positive duty on the local authority' to serve a notice requiring appropriate steps to be taken to deal with the nuisance. In this case, cessation between 11pm and 7am of the offending use was ordered. The company exercised their statutory right under s 58(3) to appeal to the magistrates' court, and continued to use the premises all night long. The local authority brought proceedings in their own name in the High Court for an injunction to stop this. The magistrates adjourned the company's appeal because of the High Court proceedings; while the judge refused an injunction because of the appeal to the magistrates. The authority then appealed to the Court of Appeal and succeeded. Lord Denning pointed out that the authority were entitled to seek the injunction both under the 'inherent power' of the High Court displayed in the cases referred to already and under an express provision in s 58(8) of the Control of Pollution Act 1974 itself. He pointed out also that, since in these cases an interlocutory injunction may well be granted, pending the trial and final decision of the substantive dispute, the normal practice in the High Court would take effect requiring the plaintiffs to give an undertaking in damages to the defendants in the event of the claim failing on the eventual decision.

6. SPECIFIC STATUTORY AUTHORISATION

The statutory power, given to local authorities by s 222 of the 1972 Act, to share in the Attorney-General's function of applying to the High

20 [1977] 2 All ER 519, [1977] 1 WLR 324.
1 [1978] 1 All ER 401, [1978] 1 WLR 50.

Court to grant injunctions under its 'inherent power' in order to uphold the public interest, shades into more specific types of statutory power conferred on local authorities. They may seek injunctions similarly, in order to restrain particular wrongdoings, under provisions such as s 100 of the Public Health Act 1936, or s 58(8) of the Control of Pollution Act 1974. These are powers rather than duties. In this context the duty of local authorities is to exercise their discretion properly in respect of applying these powers by taking care to do so only when reasonable and only within such limits as are specified. To go beyond this is to exceed jurisdiction and thus act in a manner which is ultra vires. In the *Hammersmith* case[2] discussed above, Shaw LJ pointed out that the power to seek an injunction under s 58(8) of the Control of Pollution Act 1974 is conditional, under s 58(4), upon the authority having first properly formed the opinion that proceedings by way of prosecution under that subsection in the magistrates' court would not provide an adequate or effectual remedy, as in fact was done in that case.

In other types of case they may well have a duty rather than a mere power to act. Under s 58(1) of the Control of Pollution Act 1974 there is a duty to serve a notice, though only where the local authority are 'satisfied that noise amounting to a nuisance exists'. This sort of duty is paradoxical, since it is totally within the authority's power whether or not to disclose that they are 'satisfied'; but countless statutes make provision of this kind in regard to all manner of public authorities, including ministers. A similar function,[3] but only in the form of a power, is conferred on local authorities to apply to a magistrates' court for a nuisance order under the Public Health Act 1936, s 94.

Again, local authorities have various duties in respect of children in need of care;[4] and this may involve them in proceedings for supervision orders or care orders in juvenile courts, or in adoption proceedings in juvenile courts, county courts or the Family Division of the High Court. Local Authorities undoubtedly exercise discretionary powers in regard to these proceedings; but they are under a duty to exercise that discretion in a proper lawful manner, that is to say reasonably.

Then there is the criminal law. Numerous statutes empower local authorities to prosecute for particular kinds of offence. It is improbable that the courts would hold it to be intra vires for local authorities, as distinct from individuals, to bring prosecutions in any types of case where some statute does not clearly authorise them to do so. Where they are empowered to prosecute it is sometimes to the exclusion of any other prosecutor, sometimes not. Prosecutions under the Weights and

2 [1978] 1 All ER 401 at 406.
3 See ch 11, pp 281–282.
4 See ch 12, pp 307–311.

Measures Act 1963, s 51, may only be brought by the local authority for the area or the police. Prosecutions under the Food and Drugs Act 1955, s 87, are entrusted to the local authority for the area;[5] but it was held that individuals may prosecute also, in *British Fermentation Products Ltd v British Italian Trading Co.*[6] Prosecutions are common in the field of planning, notably for disregarding enforcement notices. Two fairly recent prosecutions by local planning authorities for breach of tree preservation orders led to unsuccessful appeals by way of case stated in the Queen's Bench Divisional Court: *Barnet London Borough Council v Eastern Electricity Board*,[7] and *Maidstone Borough Council v Mortimer*.[8] The scope of all these prosecutions depends on the wording of the relevant Acts, and generalisations are difficult.

One generalisation which can, however, be confidently made is that authorities should not use their power to engage in litigation for unsuitable ends. On this, see *R v Greater London Council, ex p Royal Borough of Kensington and Chelsea*,[9] in which McNeill J deplored 'the tendency to use the court for political purposes by dressing up what was really a matter of politics as a point of law . . .' The courts are not a substitute for the ballot-box.

5 See ch 12, pp 323–325.
6 [1942] 2 KB 145, [1942] 2 All ER 256.
7 [1973] 2 All ER 319, [1973] 1 WLR 430.
8 [1980] 3 All ER 552.
9 (1982) Times, 7 April.

Chapter 7

Local government finance

A. Financial management

I. GENERAL POWERS AND DUTIES

The stringent requirements of the ultra vires doctrine apply with no less force to local authorities' financial affairs than to anything else they do. The provisions of Part III[1] of the Local Government Act 1972, supplemented by decided cases, regulate local authorities' finances as a whole, subject to particular provisions in other Acts which qualify them in regard to various specific matters.

The ultra vires doctrine, being part of the common law and of equity (which 'follows the law'), takes account of any general common law or equitable principles relevant to these affairs, such as the observance of reasonableness and good faith. Most importantly there is the principle, already touched on in an earlier chapter, that local authorities are subject to a general *fiduciary* duty in regard to the proper management of their finances. This is owed to the general public and is enforceable by the Attorney-General, acting for the Crown, on their behalf, as laid down in *A–G v Aspinall*.[2] This applies particularly as regards local authority rates and all who pay them, as expressed in *A–G v Lichfield Corp*.[3] Indeed this fiduciary duty extends to anyone dealing with local authority funds, unless in good faith and without notice of its breach, as held in *A–G v Wilson*.[4]

The Local Government Act 1972, s 111, lays down a general rule that 'a local authority shall have power to do any thing (whether or not involving the expenditure, borrowing or lending of money or the acquisition or disposal of any property or rights) which is calculated to facilitate, or is conducive or incidental to, the discharge of any of their functions', but 'shall not by virtue of this section raise money, whether by means of rates, precepts or borrowing, or lend money except in accordance with the enactments relating to those matters respectively'. The general rule is in any case subject to particular qualifications enac-

1 Ss 147–178.
2 (1837) 2 My & Cr 613. See ch 3, pp 71–72.
3 (1848) 11 Beav 120. Ratepayers' rights are private, not public.
4 (1840) Cr & Ph 1.

156

ted in the 1972 Act or any other statute. The 1972 Act, s 151, further provides that 'every local authority shall make arrangements for the proper administration of their financial affairs and shall secure that one of their officers has responsibility for the administration of those affairs'. Whether this officer is known as the 'treasurer' or 'director of finance', or by any other title, he 'is not a mere servant of the council: he owes a duty and stands in a fiduciary relation' to anyone to whom the authority owe their own financial duty and stand in their own fiduciary relation. Therefore 'although he holds office during the pleasure of the council only'—or otherwise—'this does not enable him to plead the orders of the council as an excuse for an unlawful act' in the course of carrying out his duties, as stated by Farwell J in *A–G v DeWinton*,[5] one of the facts in this case being that moneys belonging to a municipal corporation were paid into a private bank account. Similarly observations had been made by Erle J concerning county treasurers and funds in *R v Saunders*.[6] The Attorney-General can seek a declaration or injunction against individual members or officers acting in breach of this duty, or persons receiving money with notice of any such breach (*A–G v Wilson*, referred to above), or sue to recover money improperly so paid, as well as proceeding against the local authority themselves: *A–G v Newcastle-upon-Tyne Corp and North-Eastern Rly Co*.[7]

This is all quite distinct from the question whether ratepayers, or anyone else with locus standi, can bring proceedings for judicial review in respect of ultra vires policy decisions, as discussed in an earlier chapter. It is also quite distinct from the separate question whether proceedings can be taken in respect of such decisions and other financial wrongdoings in consequence of the findings of a district auditor, as discussed below.[8]

2. STATUTORY REQUIREMENTS

Subject to eventual replacement by the Local Government Finance Act 1982, Part III,[9] which will be brought into effect at a later date, ss 154–168 of the 1972 Act currently make provision for the submission of financial statistics and for the auditing of local authorities' accounts. The latter are as a general rule to be made up yearly to 31 March of each year, subject to any direction to a different effect from the Secretary of State[10] and to such detailed regulations governing accounting administration as he may make.[11] Audit is discussed later in this chapter.[12]

5 [1906] 2 Ch 106.
6 (1854) 3 E & B 763.
7 [1892] AC 568.
8 See p 185.
9 Ss 11–36 and Schs 3 and 4.
10 S 155.
11 S 166.
12 See p 182.

Section 148 of the 1972 Act requires district and London Borough councils to keep a 'general rate fund', county councils to keep a 'county fund', and the Greater London Council to keep a 'general fund'. All receipts and liabilities of each council must respectively be carried to and discharged out of that fund, and accounts are to be kept of these receipts and liabilities, to be called 'general' accounts for 'general' expenses and 'special' accounts for 'special' expenses. Section 147 deals with these expenses, for which the liabilities are incurred, and provides that all expenses are to be 'general expenses', chargeable on the whole of each council's area, except those which some enactment declares to be 'special expenses' chargeable only on part of their area. Section 147(3) itself gives district councils a power in general terms to declare any expenses to be 'special'. On the other hand, all councils may treat as 'general' expenses such part of their 'special' expenses as appears reasonable to them.[13] The expenses of the parish meetings in England and community meetings in Wales are charged on the parish or community as a whole; the same is true for parish and community councils, though where any such council covers a group of parishes or communities the expenses are charged on the group as a whole.[14] These meetings and councils too must keep accounts.

To obtain sums necessary to meet their expenses parish and community authorities are empowered to issue 'precepts' to the district council for their area for the purpose of raising the money by way of rates. County councils and the Greater London Council also are empowered by s 149 of the Act of 1972 to issue precepts. These go to the district or London borough councils in their area to levy rates in order 'to meet all liabilities falling to be discharged by the [precepting] council for which provision is not otherwise made',[15] including supplementary precepts. For 'general expenses' the precepts must require rates to be levied throughout their area; while for 'special expenses' the levy must be restricted to 'the area chargeable therewith'.[16] As regards the actual rates themselves, the corresponding distinction must be observed by district and London borough councils.[17] The general question of rates is dealt with later in this chapter.[18]

Expenditure, or 'expenses', must of course not only be duly charged and accounted for in the manner stated, but duly authorised by law. There must always be some statute which can be shown to do this expressly or by clear implication, as required by the ultra vires doctrine described in an earlier chapter.[19] There are innumerable statutes which

13 S 147(5).
14 S 150.
15 S 149(1).
16 S 149(2).
17 S 149(3).
18 See p 174.
19 Ch 3.

confer functions of greater or lesser importance on local authorities and authorise expenditure accordingly. The Local Government Act 1972 itself contains provisions to this effect. The general freedom of action conferred (within reasonable limits) by s 111 has been mentioned already. It would appear to include appointment of staff and acquisition of premises required. Section 112 empowers local authorities to appoint such *officers* as they think necessary, at such remuneration as they think fit (subject to exceptions relating to certain officers who, under other statutes, have to be appointed).

Section 120 empowers local authorities to buy or lease land by agreement for their authorised functions, or for 'the benefit, improvement or development of their area', including acquisition on behalf of themselves acting together with other local authorities; and s 121 empowers them to buy land compulsorily for their functions, subject to certain exceptions, if authorised to do so by the appropriate minister (depending on the function). The procedural statutes governing compulsory purchase, including compensation, apply; the relevant law is too detailed to be considered here, but it should be noticed that, where an acquisition occurs by agreement under s 120, it carries with it the power to override any particular rights of other persons in the land acquired (on payment of compensation) as if the acquisition were compulsory.

3. AUTHORISED EXPENDITURE ON SPECIFIED MATTERS

Section 137 empowers local authorities to 'incur expenditure which in their opinion is in the interests of their area or any part of it or all or some of its inhabitants', up to a limit which 'in any financial year shall not exceed the produce of a rate of 2p in the pound' (or such other figure as the Secretary of State may by order substitute), including contributions to charitable or similar funds to be applied in the United Kingdom and also to expenditure by other local authorities in connection with their functions; but there must be no overlap with purposes covered by other statutes.[20]

Section 138 empowers them to 'incur such expenditure as they consider necessary in taking action themselves (either alone or jointly with any other person or body and either in their area or elsewhere in or outside the United Kingdom)' including making grants or loans, which is 'calculated to avert, alleviate or eradicate in their area or among its inhabitants the effects or potential effects' of any 'emergency or disaster

---

20 This celebrated statutory provision appears to give local authorities total freedom, within reason and the prescribed 2p rate limit, to choose the objects of their expenditure. The phrase 'in their opinion' appears to allow purely subjective judgments to be made; but it is likely that the courts will subject it to the overriding test of objective reasonableness. See ch 3, p 63.

involving destruction of or danger to life or property', provided that such an event 'occurs' or is imminent or there is reasonable ground for apprehending' that it will occur; but they must notify the Secretary of State as soon as practicable, and comply with his directions thereafter. Expenditure on certain flood works is excluded from this provision to avoid overlap with the responsibilities of land drainage authorities.[1]

Certain items of local authority expenditure have attracted legislation since 1972, for example payment of allowances to members. No salary can be paid to members for service on their council; and s 116 of the 1972 Act prohibits any member from being given 'paid office' by his local authority up to a year after ceasing to be a member. This does not apply to 'employment' which is not paid. Pay is not in law an absolute prerequisite of employment: *A–G v Ulverston UDC*.[2]

Sections 3 and 5 of the Local Government Act 1972 empower authorities to pay 'allowances' to their chairman and vice-chairman to enable each 'to meet the expenses of his office' (in the GLC this also applies to the deputy-chairman who represents the opposition). Sections 173–178 authorise payment to members of attendance and financial loss allowances, travelling and subsistence allowances, and also allowances for attending conferences, or making official and courtesy visits, all of which are to be subject to regulations made by the Secretary of State. In *Hopson v Devon County Council*,[3] it was held that the wording of s 173 excludes from entitlement to attendance allowances anyone appointed to a council committee from outside, even if a councillor from another authority. Part IV[4] of the Local Government, Planning and Land Act 1980 amends the law by allowing elected members to opt for a financial loss allowance, hitherto restricted to co-opted members, instead of an attendance allowance,[5] and by modifying the rules for subsistence allowances and attendance at conferences.[6] An additional 'special responsibility' allowance has been introduced.[7]

4. DIRECT LABOUR WORK

A branch of expenditure which has received more elaborate statutory attention is 'direct labour' work, dealt with by Part III[8] of the Local Government, Planning and Land Act 1980. 'Direct labour organisations' are departments maintained by local authorities for carrying out building and engineering work of construction, repair and maintenance

1 On these, see ch 11, pp 279–280.
2 [1944] Ch 242, [1944] 1 All ER 475.
3 [1978] 1 All ER 1205, [1978] 1 WLR 553.
4 Ss 24–27.
5 S 24.
6 S 25.
7 S 26.
8 Ss 5–23.

required for their functions (housing, highways, education, health and so on). It is these 'DLO's', except small ones below a prescribed limit,[9] which are subject to the new rules.

Sections 5–7 of the Act of 1980 deal with 'works contracts' under which one authority may carry out work on behalf of another. Such contracts must not exceed a value prescribed by the Secretary of State unless in consequence of accepting a tender made by an authority in competition with at least three other organisations, and must in other cases comply with regulations made by the Secretary of State. Works contracts in the form of long-running maintenance agreements had to end within 12 months of these provisions coming into effect if in conflict with them; and this counts as 'frustration' for the purposes of the law of contract.

Sections 8–9 deal with 'functional work'. This is construction or maintenance work going beyond that covered by the definition of 'works contracts' in s 5 which is undertaken directly (ie not by placing any contract elsewhere) by any local authority for their own functions or, by delegation, for those of some other public body. Authorities must not undertake such work without first preparing a written estimate (or equivalent details) and also, if the work comes within descriptions laid down by the Secretary of State, without the acceptance of a tender made by them in similar circumstances to those prescribed for 'works contracts'.

Sections 10–14 lay down rules for accounting procedures, notably that there must be a separate 'DLO revenue account', and other accounts as well if the Secretary of State so requires. These must distinguish between general highway works, new construction works respectively exceeding and not exceeding £50,000, and maintenance works within the meaning of the Local Authorities (Goods and Services) Act 1970—which empowers local authorities to provide goods and services and carry out maintenance (but not construction) works for one another—namely of land or buildings within the authority's care. The remaining provisions (ss 15–23) are supplementary. It may be noted that s 15 entitles any authority doing 'functional work' by delegation under s 8 to be paid the appropriate amount required to be credited to the DLO revenue account had they done the work for their own benefit, irrespective of any provision or agreement to the contrary. Section 16 requires authorities to secure a sufficient rate of return, as specified by the Secretary of State, on the capital cost of work undertaken.

5. CAPITAL EXPENDITURE AND RECEIPTS

Local authority expenditure in general can be divided into capital expenditure and maintenance expenditure. The former has attracted

9 S 21.

recent legislation in the shape of the Local Government, Planning and Land Act 1980, Part VIII.[10] This has introduced a system of block approvals to control the amount of capital expenditure of local authorities from year to year. The Secretary of State (or the Minister of Transport) thereby authorises the amount of capital expenditure and arrives at separate block figures for different kinds of function (education, housing, and so on) as an indication of central government priorities; though the authorities themselves can in general use their total allocation as they think fit. Section 72 provides that the basic amount so authorised in any year may be exceeded by a margin of up to 10%, or such other amount as the Secretary of State may substitute, plus any additional amount he may specify for any authority, plus all or a prescribed proportion of the authorities' net capital receipts—money received on disposal of property, or as repayment of grants or other capital sums—plus profit from trading undertakings. Overspending in any one year will lead to a corresponding reduction in the next year's basic amount; but that reduction will be offset by any underspending the year before, up to the extent of the 10% (or amended) margin referred to above.

Section 77 permits agreements for the transfer of part of an allocation from one authority to another. Section 73 empowers the Secretary of State (or Minister of Transport) to impose further control by earmarking a specified portion of a year's aggregate permitted total of capital expenditure for any project of 'national or regional importance', or part of such a project, or conversely by specifying some project for which *none* of the permitted total is to be used. If the Secretary of State decides that an authority have exceeded, or will exceed, the limit in any year, s 78 empowers him to direct that a specified amount shall not be exceeded, and he may also direct that they are not to make any contract for expenditure above a specified amount. Action by an authority which contravenes a direction under s 73 or s 78 is ultra vires, though this does not render a contract void.[11] Special provision is made for transport undertakings, the London Transport Executive being dealt with in detail in Sch 13.

Schedule 12 of the Act prescribes the kinds of capital expenditure covered by these provisions. These include: the acquisition, reclamation, improvement or laying out of land; the acquisition, construction, preparation, conversion, improvement, renewal or replacement of buildings or other structures; the repair or maintenance of council housing; the acquisition, renewal, replacement or installation of vehicles, vessels, plant, machinery, etc; and capital grants and loans which are not made to other local authorities and various transport undertakings.

Capital expenditure and borrowing are closely connected. Capital expenditure is of course the converse of capital receipts, which are taken

10 Ss 71–85.
11 S 79.

into account under s 72 of the Local Government, Planning and Land Act 1980, as discussed above, for the purposes of central government control of such expenditure. Money held by local authorities as a result of capital receipts by them is in a general sense 'capital money', and what constitutes this is fundamentally a question of fact and degree in every case. In principle, of course, it comprises lump sums as distinct from rent. The Local Government Act 1972, s 153, states that capital money received by any local authority from disposal of property in land under Part VII[12] of the Act, ie s 123 in respect of 'principal councils' and s 127 in respect of parish and community authorites, 'shall be applied towards the discharge of any debt of the local authority or otherwise for any purpose for which capital money may properly be applied'. The application of capital money is subject of course to the ultra vires doctrine, and therefore depends on statutory authorisation covering each case; in addition s 153 lays down a general rule requiring the Secretary of State's consent.

Capital receipts, as distinct from 'income' or 'revenue', of local authorities are not on the whole likely to match the level of their capital expenditure as intended by themselves, or for that matter as approved by the central government or even (perhaps) the general public and the electorate. Their resources are chiefly derived from income of the kinds to be described below, which must be capitalised by way of expenditure on long-term projects undertaken by statutory authority in accordance with the ultra vires doctrine.

Local authorities may also acquire resources by way of gift, in accordance with s 139 of the Local Government Act 1972. Under this provision they may accept and use 'gifts of property, whether real or personal' made to them 'for the purpose of discharging any of their functions', as well as gifts made to them 'for the benefit of the inhabitants of their area or of some part of it'. Use of these gifts may be supplemented by the execution of works 'incidental to or consequential on' such use, including maintenance or improvement. But such works if done in connection with a gift for the local inhabitants must be paid for within the limits of the 2p rate as prescribed for the purposes of s 137, described earlier in this chapter.[13]

6. BORROWING AND 'LOAN SANCTION'

Partly because of the inevitability of large fluctuations in the incidence of spending on capital projects, and partly because of the fact that the benefit of such work will usually be enjoyed in large measure by future generations of local inhabitants, it is proper to spread the cost over the

---

12 Ss 111–146.
13 See p 159.

future by borrowing. Local authorities are therefore given wide borrowing powers, but their exercise is subject to extensive central control. The ultra vires doctrine would in principle require borrowing to be undertaken within reasonable limits and in a reasonable manner; but it is perhaps natural that the central government would not want to leave the detailed operation of local authority fund-raising to chance and the courts.

In general the law on this subject is to be found in the Local Government Act 1972, Sch 13 Part I, which according to s 172 'shall have effect with respect to the powers of local authorities to borrow and lend money and with respect to their funds'. Local authorities may borrow by temporary loan or overdraft without specific permission from central government in order to defray expenses pending receipt of current revenues or expenses to be covered by an authorised loan pending the raising of that loan,[14] and may also borrow without consent to repay money already borrowed on an existing authorised loan.[15] Subject to this, the purposes for which they borrow must come within the following categories: lending to another authority who themselves have power to borrow, and (the main category) spending for a purpose approved by the Secretary of State.[16] In other words borrowing must always be in accordance with such approval obtained either *directly* in the second (ie usual) case or *indirectly* in the first case (since the other authority to whom the money is lent will themselves have had to obtain approval). Borrowing by the GLC is authorised by the Secretary of State for the Environment.[17] Other local authorities may in any case obtain powers to borrow under separate Acts, public or private, but are unlikely to obtain substantially easier conditions by doing so.

The Secretary of State's approval, commonly referred to as 'loan sanction', must be given specifically unless any borrowing proposal is covered by a 'general consent'. Currently in force is a 'general consent' which can be consulted in Department of the Environment Circular no 66/76; it sets out three categories of capital projects for this purpose, termed 'key sector schemes', 'subsidiary sector schemes' and 'locally determined schemes'. Even the 'general consent', however, is conditional on the obtaining of approval by the central government department which is functionally concerned with the project, for example the Department of Education and Science if it involves building a new school. More often, that department will be the Department of the Environment itself. There is in any case an annual allocation of capital

14 Sch 13, para 10.
15 Sch 13, para 8.
16 Sch 13, para 1.
17 Local Government Finance Act 1982, s 5 (except for capital expenditure, or re-lending, for which separate statutory authority is needed).

expenditure for the country as a whole in regard to 'locally determined schemes', fixed after consulting local authority associations.

7. MODES OF BORROWING AND LENDING

The sources of loans, once the requisite 'loan sanctions' have been obtained, are the Public Works Loan Commissioners (under the Public Works Loans Act 1965), the authority's own internal resources, and the open market. As far as the authority's own internal resources are concerned, it should be noted that a local authority may use 'any fund established for the repayment of debt, or as a reserve, or for the maintenance, renewal or repair of property, or for superannuation of staff, or for insurance, or otherwise for meeting future expenditure of a capital or non-recurring nature, or for any like purpose'; but the loan must be repaid out of the authority's 'revenue fund', with interest, in just the same way as a loan from an outside source would be repaid.[18] Local authorities are expressly empowered to set up inter alia a 'loans fund', to pool loans and 'average out' interest rates conveniently for the repayment of debt[19] and also a 'capital fund' and a 'renewal and repairs fund', neither of which can be used for any trading undertaking.[20] The 'capital fund' should receive, as a general rule, sums realised from the disposal of property, any revenue surplus for the current year, and other items at the authority's option, subject to limits imposed by the Secretary of State or as statutorily prescribed, and income arising from the fund itself; and money applied from it is repayable into it as the authority thinks fit from whatever account it has been advanced to.[1] The 'repairs and renewals fund' is to receive sums from the 'revenue fund', subject to limits imposed by the Secretary of State, and income arising from the fund itself.[2] The 'revenue fund' is an authority's principal fund, which they are required to keep in accordance with s 148 of the Local Government Act 1972, as referred to earlier in the chapter: namely the 'general rate fund' for district and London borough councils, the 'county fund' for county councils, and the 'general fund' for the GLC.

As for raising money on the open market, it should be noted that the Trustee Investments Act 1961 authorises trustees to invest with local authorities. Such investments are part of the 'narrower range' as prescribed by the Act, in which trustees must invest at least half of the trust funds at their disposal unless they have been expressly given greater freedom of investment. In a general way this means that investors are encouraged to regard loans to local authorities as a prudent form of

---

18 Local Government Act 1972, Sch 13, para 19.
19 Sch 13, para 15.
20 Sch 13, para 16.
1 Sch 13, para 17.
2 Sch 13, para 18.

investment. The Local Government Act 1972,[3] empowers local authorities to borrow in the open market by mortgage; or by the issue of stock, debentures, annuity certificates, bonds or bills; or by any other method with the approval of the Secretary of State and the Treasury. It also authorises borrowing from the Public Works Loan Commissioners, referred to above. Bills may not be used unless the authority's gross income from rates is at least £3 million for the year (or such other amount as the Treasury may by order prescribe) and the aggregate amount borrowed must not exceed one fifth of that gross income (unless the Treasury by order prescribes otherwise). Bearer bonds may be issued only with the consent of the Treasury. Other forms of borrowing are subject to regulations made by the Secretary of State with the consent of the Treasury. These provisions are contained in the 1972 Act, Sch 13, paras 4–6. Paragraph 7 requires that in respect of any loan there shall be debited to the account from which the expenditure 'would otherwise fall to be defrayed' annual amounts equal to instalments of principal and interest combined such that the relevant loan would thereby be paid off within the period prescribed for it by the Act authorising the raising of the loan or by the Secretary of State when granting 'loan sanction' for the relevant project. Naturally this period varies from project to project, but a period of 60 years is quite usual.

Where borrowing occurs to finance capital spending for an undertaking which is intended to produce revenue, or the carrying out on land of such other operations as the Secretary of State may specify, or acquiring land for these or other purposes specified by him, the local authority can if they wish suspend loan repayments for up to five years and borrow to pay interest in that period, or ten years in the case of land acquired for other purposes specified. The amount so borrowed is repayable within the period of the loan itself.[4]

Lending is the converse of borrowing, and it has been shown above how the making of a loan by one local authority to another is a purpose for which the first authority can borrow under the general provisions to that effect. Local housing authorities can lend to individual borrowers for the acquisition or improvement of dwellings, under the Small Dwelling Acquisition Acts 1899–1923 and the Housing (Financial Provisions) Act 1958;[5] and there are various other statutes which confer lending powers. These are, however, part of the functional side of local government as distinct from the general principles of its administration and it would be out of place here to discuss them further.

8. GENERAL INCOME: PROPERTY AND SERVICES

To complete the survey of general financial management in local government it remains to say that the income necessary to balance the books comes from three sources: property and services, government grants, and rates. Grants

3 Sch 13, para 2.
4 Sch 13, para 9.
5 See below, ch 11, p 290.

and rates are specialised forms of income. The law which governs them is complex and peculiar, and will be separately discussed at more length below. Income from property and services is much the same in principle as anyone else's income. Rents from the residential and other types of properties which local councils own and let to tenants, as local housing authorities or general landlords, are of predominant importance. Charges made to customers in the running of trading undertakings, such as passenger transport services, also bring in much revenue; though it is related chiefly to expenditure on the running of those same services, and is also regarded by some authorities not as a lucrative source of revenue which ought to be exploited but a burden on local inhabitants which ought to be alleviated. This issue is controversial in law and politics; and leading cases which have turned on it, such as *Prescott v ˊBirmingham Corp*,[6] and *Bromley London Borough Council v Greater London Council*,[7] have been discussed in Chapter 3.

Charges for a variety of facilities provided by local councils, recreational or otherwise, such as the use of swimming baths, sports pitches, allotments and the like, are other examples of this kind of income. They generate less controversy; but the main principle applies throughout. This is that local councils, being statutory bodies, are expected to behave not arbitrarily but reasonably, charging for their services in a matter which is neither 'thriftless' nor extortionate. They must manage the properties and undertakings for which they are responsible in much the same way as other persons, individual or corporate, but subject to the requirement of 'reasonableness' within the meaning of the *Wednesbury* case and the ultra vires doctrine generally.[8]

The ultra vires principle must not, however, be pressed too far. In *Peabody Housing Association v Green*,[9] the Court of Appeal took the view that public bodies properly carrying out the function of providing housing accommodation to tenants are entitled and required to exercise the normal functions of landownership; these are not overridden by their statutory nature and origin, even if they operate with the help of public money. In matters of principle and detail the ultra vires doctrine establishes a boundary; it does not intrude within the boundary.

It is true that council house tenants now have security of tenure under the Housing Act 1980, Part I, Chapter II; but rents still are fixed largely at the authorities' discretion, at least in theory. The Housing Act 1957, s 111, authorises councils to make such reasonable charges for a tenancy or occupation as they may determine. The same Act, s 113(1A),[10] says: 'A local authority shall from time to time review rents

6 [1955] Ch 210, [1954] 3 All ER 698.
7 [1982] 1 All ER 129, [1982] 2 WLR 62.
8 Ibid.
9 (1978) 35 P & CR 644.
10 A provision inserted by the Housing Rents and Subsidies Act 1975.

and make such changes, either of rents generally or of particular rents, as circumstances may require'. This is subject to rebates and allowances payable under the Housing Finance Act 1972, Part II. In *Evans v Collins*,[11] a claimant sought to compel a local housing authority to apply a 'differential rents scheme' so that various tenants' rents would have to go up. In *Luby v Newcastle-under-Lyme Corp*,[12] a council tenant asserted the same (in effect) with the aim that his rent would have to come down. The court in each case rejected the claim. The Housing Act 1957, s 111, gives a general discretion to authorities which is not subject to such outside constraints. 'Reasonableness' requires that an 'economic rent' be charged as distinct from arbitrary rents, but not a 'market rent' obliging a council to make 'a profit out of its tenants', nor a rent specially reduced to match a particular tenant's financial resources (though rebates and allowances now largely cover this point).

B. Grants

I. THE GRANT SYSTEM

The system of central government grants has developed from small beginnings in the nineteenth century to a point where now the major proportion of local government revenue comes in this form. Income from rents and services is the most 'natural'; income from rates is the most characteristic of local government; but income from grants is the most substantial. It has been so since the Second World War, and is likely to go on being so.

The history of government grants to local authorities is likely to be of absorbing interest only to specialists. Here it will suffice to deal with the situation as it is now, in law. That situation is extremely volatile. Political antagonisms and economic crises have put the whole question of local government finance under ever-increasing pressure and strain. The central government, changing its political colour from time to time, intervenes to rearrange the grant system again and again in the hope of establishing what it affects to regard as a proper measure of political and economic control. The course of events is made more complicated by a feeling that too much intervention will reduce the vaunted autonomy of English local government to vanishing point. To some minds there appear to be elements of contradiction in all this. One factor that stays constant, however, is the existence of a distinction in principle between two kinds of grants: specific grants and general grants. But the details of these grants and the balance between them constantly change.

11 [1965] 1 QB 580, [1964] 1 All ER 808.
12 [1965] 1 QB 214, [1964] 3 All ER 169.

2. SPECIFIC GRANTS

Of the specific grants not much need be said here. They are 'specific' in regard to various functions performed by local authorities; and their existence is a pointer to the attitude of the central government to those functions. That is, they have been instituted, and are being continued, in order to support those functions and not leave the extent and manner of their financial upkeep purely to the discretion of local authorities.

Once again, housing comes to the fore. The most prominent of the specific grants are the housing subsidies. Each change of political colour in central government tends to produce a new upheaval in the system of granting housing subsidies, which go to local housing authorities—ie district councils, and virtually all authorities in London—and also to new town authorities and housing associations which between them account for the bulk of 'public sector' housing. Housing subsidies for local authorities are currently administered in accordance with the Housing Act 1980, Part VI.[13] There is a 'base amount', derived from a pre-existing annual subsidy, modified by the Secretary of State to take account of a 'housing costs differential' which increases it and a 'local contribution differential' (related to increased income) which reduces it. There are also provisions for withholding or 'recouping' subsidies where the Secretary of State believes that a local authority are not justified in receiving or retaining some amount. He is in fact given a great deal of discretion in the paying of subsidies; and is therefore not subject to legal control so long as the discretion is exercised in a 'reasonable' and not an arbitrary way.

There are other grants. Brief mention may be made here of the existence of a number of specific grants for highway and transportation functions (both general and special), for town and country planning (particularly conservation, land reclamation, historical buildings and so on), for social needs and welfare services of various kinds, for care of children, for coast protection, for civil defence, for police, for administration of justice, for youth employment and student grants, for smallholdings and rural water sewerage, for smoke control, and for rate rebates. Various qualifications are imposed as to the relation of the amount of grant to expenditure and financial factors generally, and also as to the quality of the services provided by each recipient local authority (which may further depend on the views of other government departments or public bodies interested in those functions). Such matters of detail obviously cannot be gone into here. It may be added that the Local Government, Planning and Land Act 1980 has specifically provided grants to cover rate rebates to disabled persons[14] and grants for providing gipsy caravan sites.[15]

13 Ss 96–105.
14 S 69.
15 S 70.

3. GENERAL GRANTS

The general grant system is changed with much the same frequency as the housing subsidies, and for much the same reasons. The theory behind it is that an amount is given to each authority to spend according to that authority's discretion, thus preserving local government autonomy. The reality is that each amount is worked out very carefully in accordance not only with a discretion conferred on the Secretary of State but with some extremely elaborate rules provided by statute. The system, in short, is that the proper spending needs of each recipient local authority are carefully worked out, together with what is considered to be that authority's proper income from other sources (property and services; rates) and a specially tailored amount is granted to balance proper income against proper expenditure. Note that these items are proper not merely in a legal sense—ie intra vires—but in a policy sense—ie desirable in the eyes of central government. This underlines the enduring truth that such independence as English local government enjoys comes to it on sufferance. In a metaphor, the freedom of local government finance under the general grant system is not so much a kaftan, more a strait-jacket.

The Local Government, Planning and Land Act 1980, Part VI[16] is the statute governing the general grant system under the present dispensation. These provisions deal first with the phasing out of the previous general grant system,[17] and next with the structure of the system which replaces it,[18] followed by provisions covering various matters of detail.[19] To understand this legislation it is necessary to consider briefly the system being superseded.

4. ELEMENTS OF GRANT BEFORE 1980

The Local Government Act 1966, Part I, as amended by the Local Government Act 1972, Sch 13, para, 27 and by the Local Government Act 1974, Part I, enacted that every financial year starting in 1967–68 a general grant should be paid to all or most local authorities, known as a 'rate support grant'. The aggregate amount of the rate support grants for any year was worked out by estimating the total revenue-based 'relevant expenditure' of all local authorities in England and Wales (excluding payments between local authorities by precept or otherwise, payments into a trading account or housing revenue account, and any other payments specially indicated), deciding upon an aggregate amount (excluding housing subsidies) of grants to be payable towards that 'rele-

---

16 Ss 48–68.
17 Ss 48–52.
18 Ss 53–56.
19 Ss 57–68.

vant expenditure', and deducting from that aggregate amount the amount needed for specific grants (other than housing subsidies). The grant was intended to augment the revenue raised by each authority from rates, hence its name, but the total amount was a matter for central government policies entrusted to the Minister of Housing and Local Government, predecessor of the Secretary of State for the Environment. Local authorities would levy rates to make up the total of necessary revenue when added to their grant income and their income from property and services. Those central government policies were geared to an objective, namely to increase the proportion of rate-borne expenditure met by grants (envisaged as 54% in 1967–68 and 60% in 1973–74).

The assessment of grants depended on a distinction between three 'elements': the 'needs element', the 'resources element' and the 'domestic element'. The system, as amended after 1974, was as follows. The 'domestic element' was payable to all rating authorities—that is the 'second-tier' district and London borough councils and the City of London Corporation—and was the amount necessary to balance the total reduction in rates payable by domestic ratepayers under the General Rate Act 1967, s 48. The 'resources element' was payable to those same 'second-tier' authorities whenever any such authority would receive a below average revenue from rates, calculated in proportion to population.

The 'needs element' was the residual element, in other words the remainder of the national aggregate of rate support grants after deducting the other items, distributed to local authorities in proportions according to nationally calculated formulae based on various objective factors. These related chiefly to population: the total inhabitants of an authority's area, the young, the elderly, high density of population, high road-mileage per head of population, proportion of school-children, and so on. Adjustments could be made by the Secretary of State to take account of factors such as cases where authorities provided services to benefit authorities other than themselves, or areas other than their own. The 'needs element', thus calculated, was to be paid to non-metropolitan *county* councils but to metropolitan *district* councils and London borough councils and the City Corporation; though the GLC and metropolitan *county* and non-metropolitan *district* councils might receive payments instead in special circumstances to be prescribed under regulations made by the Secretary of State.[20] In other words, the general or 'rate support' grant would not normally be paid to 'upper-tier' authorities in the metropolitan areas or in London.

5. ELEMENTS OF GRANT SINCE 1980

The Local Government, Planning and Land Act 1980, ss 48–52, provided for this system to continue until 31 March 1981 on a transitional

---

20 Local Government Act 1974, s 2.

basis. The Secretary of State could reduce the rate support grant during that time in respect of any authority which exceeded a 'national uniform rate' decided by himself on the basis of what he considered they would need in order to meet expenditure (and precepts, if any). He was also empowered to vary 'resources' and 'needs' elements and supplementary transport grants under the Local Government Act 1974, s 6.

The 'commencing year' for the new system was fixed as the financial year 1981–82, starting on 1 April, 1981, by the Local Government, Planning and Land Act 1980 Commencement (No 2) Order 1980.[1] The 1980 Act s 53, empowers the Secretary of State, 'for the commencing year and each subsequent year', to make 'rate support grants' to first and second-tier local authorities generally—ie county and district councils and all local authorities in London—each such grant being composed of a 'domestic rate relief grant' and a 'block grant'. The system is based on the Secretary of State's 'fixing the aggregate amount of the rate supports grants for any year', under s 54. This first requires the 'relevant expenditure' for the year to be ascertained, which is 'the expenditure for that year falling to be defrayed out of the rate fund of a local authority', excluding amounts to be paid to other authorities, such as precepts, or paid by way of various training grants or rent allowances.

He then, independently, but *in relation to* the 'relevant expenditure' of local authorities as a whole, decides on 'the amount available for grants', excluding grants by way of housing subsidies and certain other specific grants which are dealt with separately. This amount is within his discretion, though he has a duty to consult with 'such associations of local authorities as appear to him to be concerned', as with earlier grant systems, about costs of and need for services. From that amount he must deduct sums required for various other specific grants in order to arrive at 'the aggregate amount of the rate support grants'.

The next step is to determine the 'aggregate amount of the domestic rate relief grant', which is *not* payable to county councils, the GLC or the Inner London Education Authority for the obvious reason that they are not rating authorities.[2] This is essentially the same as the previous 'domestic element', which means that the grant is a reimbursement of the shortfall in rate income that rating authorities incur because of the reduced amounts paid by domestic ratepayers.

The 'block grant', which when added to the 'domestic rate relief grant' makes up the 'rate support grant', is arrived at by another process of deduction, elaborately set out in s 56. First, a figure is arrived at which represents expenditure; then another figure is arrived at which represents rate income; the second figure when deducted from the first

1 SI 1980/1893.
2 S 55 and Sch 9.

leaves a balance which will be the 'block grant'. The figure representing expenditure is termed 'total expenditure'. It is arrived at by taking the amount of 'relevant expenditure' referred to in s 54 (above) and subtracting from that *expenditure* figure the amount of the various specific *grants* which have to be deducted, also under s 54, from the 'amount available for grants' in order to arrive at 'the aggregate amount of the rate support grants'. Thus a *grant* figure is deduced from an *expenditure* figure to produce what is called '*total expenditure*' (subject to any adjustments the Secretary of State sees fit to make).

As for the rate income figure, that is arrived at by multiplying a notional amount called the 'grant related poundage' of a local authority by an actual figure which is the gross rateable value of that authority's area. This notional 'grant related poundage' is the figure of so many pence in the pound as the Secretary of State considers to be appropriate for arriving at the amount of income from rates which a given local authority ought to raise in view of its probable and proper expenditure. What they ought to spend, less what they ought to get in rate-income, equals what the Secretary of State will give them by way of 'block grant' to spend as they wish. This does not of itself prevent an authority raising a different amount in rates, regardless of the 'block grant'. Nevertheless, in a general way, the amount raised in rates is conditioned by the amount given in grant, which in turn is conditioned by the amount *expected* to be raised in rates.

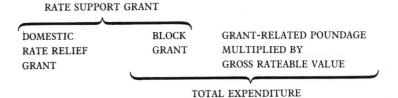

```
          RATE SUPPORT GRANT
         ⌒‾‾‾‾‾‾‾‾‾‾‾‾‾‾‾‾‾⌒
DOMESTIC            BLOCK       GRANT-RELATED POUNDAGE
RATE RELIEF         GRANT       MULTIPLIED BY
GRANT                          GROSS RATEABLE VALUE
                      ⌣‾‾‾‾‾‾‾‾‾‾‾‾‾‾‾‾‾‾‾‾‾‾‾⌣
                        TOTAL EXPENDITURE
```

One or two supplementary points may be noted. First, any county council or the GLC or the Inner London Education Authority can agree to forgo the block grant for any year, in which case it will be distributed among the second-tier authorities for the area. Second, the notional 'grant-related poundage' of any authority may be arrived at by the Secretary of State as being 'related (a) to a given ratio' between the 'total expenditure' as defined above and the 'grant-related expenditure' (which is 'the aggregate for the year of their notional expenditure having regard to their functions') or '(b) to a given difference between their total expenditure divided by their population and their grant-related expenditure so divided'.[3]

---

3 1980 Act, 56(8).

The remaining provisions[4] of Part VI of the Act of 1980 deal with various points of detail. Each year the Secretary of State must, with Treasury consent, lay before the House of Commons a Rate Support Grant Report giving details of the grant 'determinations', and the 'considerations' leading to them; and grants shall not be paid until the House of Commons has by resolution approved the Report.[5] The Secretary of State is given a wide discretion in operating the grant system; but the grant-related poundage and grant-related expenditure must be determined 'in accordance with principles to be applied to all authorities'.[6] There is provision for various adjustments to be made to avoid burdensome grant fluctuations and other difficulties, for presenting supplementary Reports where necessary, for taking account of expenditure on education, for determining grants in the Metropolitan Police District, and procedural matters generally. The Local Government Finance Act 1982[7] provides that adjustments are to be subject to guidance by the Secretary of State to take into account 'general economic conditions'.

C. Rates

I. DIFFERENCE BETWEEN A RATE AND A CHARGE

The characteristic, traditional source of local government revenue is rates. The special fiduciary duty to which in law all local authorities are subject is owed to the ratepayers, as discussed at the beginning of this chapter. Indignant ratepayers are stock figures of fun in Punch cartoons and elsewhere. The word 'rate', which lends itself to easy puns ('London is an over-rated place', etc), simply refers to the level at which this tax is set on any particular occasion: 'a rate of Xp in the £' (hence the expression 'rate poundage').

The fact that a rate, like any other tax, is levied to help pay for what public authorities do for the benefit of the community and its members—to 'defray expenditure'—sometimes leads people to regard it as a sort of price for services rendered in accordance with a contract to provide them. In an underlying sense this is true: the state earns its living by protecting its people in return for being maintained in the style to which it wishes to be accustomed. But no specific reliance can be put on this. The people cannot put the contract for their protection out to tender; they can only—in a constitutional country—elect different state functionaries to replace those who dissatisfy them.

4 Ss 57–68.
5 S 60.
6 S 57.
7 S 8.

This is not to say that public authorities never perform services under contract: their income under this head has been referred to already in this chapter and their contractual powers have been considered in chapter 5. The fact is that local and other authorities raise some income under contract by performing services in return for making an agreed charge, and raise other income by way of tax. This distinction is clear, at least in principle, and the House of Lords has upheld it. The mere fact that there are many contracts which at least one party to the contract has little or no choice but to enter into is not an argument to the contrary and applies much more widely than just in local government. Contracts with monopolists are nothing unusual.

In *Daymond v South West Water Authority*,[8] the House of Lords had to deal with a claim that sewerage charges are not payable by a person whose premises are not connected to a public sewer. Lord Dilhorne observed: 'Sewerage and sewage disposal, prior to the enactment of the Water Act 1973, had been for many, many years the responsibility of local authorities and they recovered the cost by including charges for sewerage, and sewage disposal, in the general rate demand so that for years the occupiers of premises not connected with public sewers paid their share of the cost of sewerage in the local authority's area'. The new Act transferred these functions to newly-created 'water authorities', who were empowered to make a 'charge' rather than a 'rate'. It did not say who must pay these charges; but the authorities concerned took it for granted that they were to be met in the same way as rates; and the Secretary of State for the Environment made the Water Authorities (Collection of Charges) Order 1974[9] instructing water authorities to serve a 'general services notice' on each rating authority to impose a 'general services charge' on 'every person who is liable to pay the general rate in respect of a hereditament . . .'—ie exactly like a rate precept, except that it was not called one. No statutory authority existed for this, unless a general inference could be drawn from the Water Act 1973, s 30.

The House of Lords, by three votes to two, declined to draw it. Clear statutory wording could have ensured that a payment, though called a 'charge', would have the incidence of a 'rate'; but such was not found to be the case here. The 1974 Order was thus ultra vires and the plaintiff was awarded the declaration he sought that the rating authority were not authorised 'lawfully to demand from [him] any sum in respect of sewerage or sewage disposal services on behalf of the [water authority]'. This was a test case affecting thousands of other ratepayers. Parliament did not legislate to reverse its effect but, on the contrary, authorised the necessary repayments or discharges.[10] The distinc-

---

8 [1976] AC 609, [1976] 1 All ER 39.
9 SI 1974/448.
10 Water Charges Act 1976. But see *Anglian Water Authority v Castle* (1983) Times, 23 February.

tion between rates and charges has therefore been endorsed; and it is submitted that this is a most welcome development. A charge is not a tax, but a rate is.

2. ENFORCEMENT OF RATES

Rates are a long-established form of taxation. Though recognised by the common law and taken over by statute, they had an ecclesiastical origin. The lordship exercised in England by the medieval church, with royal support, extended to making local inhabitants of each parish pay for the upkeep of the church buildings and contents whenever income from land, profits from festivities, customary fees and voluntary offerings were insufficient. Church courts had authority to order churchwardens to levy a rate, if they needed any bidding to do so; and magistrates and secular courts generally would enforce these orders by distraining on or imprisoning defaulters: *R v St Mary Lambeth Churchwardens*.[11]

Distress remains the only method of enforcing rates today—except in regard to unoccupied premises (when rateable at all), where there are not likely to be chattels available which can be seized as a distress—though imprisonment is possible if there is a 'default of sufficiency of distress': General Rate Act 1967, Part VI.[12] A distress warrant must be obtained by the local (rating) authority from the magistrates in accordance with the procedure in the 1967 Act; and the 'costs and charges' incurred are payable by the ratepayer. These will be less or greater depending on whether he pays the amount of rates due (i) after a summons has been issued, or (ii) after a distress warrant has been issued pursuant to that summons, or (iii) after goods have actually been seized as authorised by the warrant.

In *Brintons v Wyre Forest District Council*,[13] the plaintiffs withheld £83,000 due from them in payments of rates, in 'protest against the increase in the rates demanded by [the defendants]', as Donaldson J [as he then was] put it. 'The rating authority took out a summons before the local justices, [who] . . . were bound to issue a distress warrant and did so. The plaintiffs' intention was to pay the rates the next day, but the rating authority moved with a speed which is unusual in a local authority. No doubt they had it in mind that the non-payment of these rates was costing the general body of ratepayers £24 a day by way of interest'. A council official and the bailiff went to the plaintiffs' offices that same afternoon; whereupon, to avoid having goods seized, the plaintiffs paid the amount of rates due and also, under protest, £1,255 added on as 'costs and charges'.

They promptly sued to recover the latter sum and succeeded. The

11 (1832) 2 B & Ad 651.
12 Ss 96–107, as amended.
13 [1977] QB 178, [1977] 1 All ER 836.

Secretary of State had, it is true, made the distress for Rates Order 1972[14] under Part VI of the 1967 Act; but in it he had only specified the charges payable in respect of the actual seizure of goods (ie event (iii) referred to above). He had not specified any charges payable merely for *attendance* by a bailiff in consequence of the issue of a warrant, if full payment of rates was made without any seizure taking place (ie event (ii) referred to above, and the situation in this case). Yet the 1967 Act[15] empowers him to specify such charges; and the judge suggested that the Secretary of State might now wish to do this, by order, 'as a matter of urgency', which was shortly afterwards done.

3. DEVELOPMENT OF THE SYSTEM OF RATES AND PRECEPTS

The medieval obligation on parishioners to pay for church upkeep was essentially a burden on them as owner-occupiers of land in the parish. F. W. Maitland[16] discusses how the parishioners, in return for complying with this obligation, would meet to take collective decisions in the church vestry, and succeeded eventually in getting the relevant administration and control put into the hands of two (or more) of their number as 'churchwardens'. These in turn were empowered to spread the cost reasonably and generally among them all. 'Money-voting vestries became as indispensible to the rector as money-voting parliaments are to the king', as Maitland put it. In the sixteenth century this procedure became frequent; and parish landowner-occupiers became accustomed to the burden of having to pay a proportion, assessed rateably according to the value of their property, of such expenditure. Parliament then took a hand; and in the Poor Relief Act 1601, the imposition of a rate to finance poor relief expenditure was imposed statutorily. Other rates were statutorily authorised from time to time to finance expenditure by parish constables and parish highway surveyors; and in this way the parish became the organ of secular local government with a statutorily approved system of local taxation to pay for it.

The ensuing 'chaos of areas . . . chaos of franchises . . . chaos of authorities . . . chaos of rates'[17] led eventually, among other things, to a rationalisation and comparative simplification of the rating system. The statutes which achieved this have been repealed and re-enacted in a consolidating statute, the General Rate Act 1967 (itself subject to certain subsequent modifications); and the provisions of that Act, as modified, will now be considered in order to give a general picture of the modern law of rating in England and Wales. Although rates had been statutorily authorised for various purposes, the system of rates for poor

14 SI 1972/820.
15 S 101, as amended. See now SIs 1979/1038 and 1980/2013.
16 In Pollock and Maitland *History of English Law* Vol 1, Book II, ch III, section 7.
17 According to Rathbone and Pell *Local Administration* (1885).

relief was the primary one, and the modern system is chiefly derived from it. The 1967 Act accordingly took in law from the Poor Relief Acts 1601 and 1743, the Poor Rate Act 1801, and a host of other more recent statutes.

As modified by the Local Government Act 1972, s 149, the General Rate Act 1967, Part I[18] provides that there is only one rate, a 'general rate' levied for each rating area. That area is the one administered by each rating authority, these being the district and London borough councils and the City Corporation. The GLC, county councils, parish authorities and certain other bodies are entitled to a share of the income raised in the general rate, and do so by issuing 'precepts' to the rating authorities for their area, calculated at the appropriate 'rate poundage' producing the amount they require: 1967 Act, Part II.[19] The duty of each rating authority to comply with a valid precept is enforceable by way of judicial review in an order of mandamus as in *R v Poplar Borough Council (No 2)*.[20] County councils must account separately in respect of their 'general expenses', to which the county as a whole must contribute, and of any 'special expenses' for which only part of the county is liable, so that the precepts they issue must be in accordance with this distinction; and district councils may also distinguish 'general' from 'special' expenses: 1972 Act, ss 147–8. Conversely, rate equalisation schemes may be agreed between rating authorities in London (London Government Act 1963, s 66) and in metropolitan counties (1972 Act, s 170). Under the 1967 Act, s 5, a prescribed procedure must be followed for publishing the making of the rate and serving demand notes upon the ratepayers.

The Local Government Finance Act 1982, Part I,[1] imposes additional control by prohibiting the levying of (i) rates or precepts except in respect of a regular financial year and (ii) supplementary rates or precepts. But *substituted* rates or precepts are allowed provided that the sum to be raised is not greater than the original amount.

4. RATEABLE OCCUPATION

The liability for rates rests nowadays on persons as occupiers rather than owners of land, in accordance with 1967 Act, Part III.[2] 'Occupation' of land for rating purposes requires use, duration, benefit and exclusiveness. 'Use' includes readiness for use, as in *Bayliss v Chatters*,[3] where empty bungalows were advertised as available for letting, includ-

---

18 Ss 1–10. And see Local Government, Planning and Land Act 1980, Part V.
19 Ss 11–15. For the origin of precepts see below, ch 10, p 253.
20 [1922] 1 KB 95.
   1 Ss 1–6.
   2 Ss 16–54.
   3 [1940] 1 All ER 620.

ing a 'show house', or *R v Melladew*,[4] where an empty warehouse was advertised as available for storing goods; but a mere intention to use is not included, as in *Bexley Congregational Church Treasurer v Bexley London Borough Council*,[5] where a church manse was vacant pending appointment of a new minister. In *Westminster City Council v Southern Rly Co Railway Assessment Authority and W H Smith & Son Ltd*[6] Lord Russell said: 'The owner of an empty house has the legal possession, but he is not in rateable occupation'. The 1967 Act, s 17 and Sch 1, empowers rating authorities to resolve that unoccupied property may be rated; and the Local Government Act 1974, ss 15–16 makes this system more flexible and adds a progressive surcharge for commercial property. These provisions, however, have been modified in certain respects, by the Local Government Planning and Land Act 1980, ss 41–42.

'Duration' is a question of fact and degree. Enjoyment of occupation for a very fleeting period does not involve liability for rates, but persistence of occupation does. Accordingly, licensees whose occupation of land persists for some time are liable for rates, as were contractors occupying Air Ministry Land in *John Laing & Son v Kingswood Assessment Committee*.[7] 'Benefit' does not depend on commercial profit. In *Jones v Mersey Docks and Harbour Board Trustees*,[8] Lord Cranworth said he could 'discover nothing . . . exempting from liability the occupier of valuable property, merely because the profits of the occupation are not to be enjoyed by him . . . but are to be devoted to the benefit of the public'. This would not, of course, be the case for 'the occupier of a barren rock, neither yielding, nor capable of yielding, any profit from its occupation'.

'Exclusiveness' refers to the occupation and not the occupier. In *Peak v Burley Golf Club*,[9] the defendants were licensees of common land and could exclude neither the public nor the owners of rights of common, and so were not in rateable occupation, unlike the licensee in the *Laing* case or in *LCC v Wilkins*,[10] (huts on a building site). But there can well be co-enjoyment of exclusive occupation by two or more persons as co-owners or co-licensees. In *Paynter v R*,[11] a number of shareholders who had contributed to the building of Putney Bridge, which originally was in private ownership, were all held to be in rateable occupation, the Court of Exchequer Chamber saying that 'any one of several joint occupiers is liable for the whole amount . . and a warrant of dis-

4 [1907] 1 KB 192.
5 [1972] 2 QB 222, [1972] 2 All ER 662.
6 [1936] AC 511, [1936] 2 All ER 322.
7 [1949] 1 KB 344, [1949] 1 All ER 224.
8 (1865) 11 HL Cas 443.
9 [1960] 2 All ER 199, [1960] 1 WLR 568.
10 [1957] AC 362, [1956] 3 All ER 38.
11 (1847) 10 QB 908.

tress against any one alone is good', subject to a right to be recouped by contributions from the other joint occupiers.

This applies no less to dwellings, including matrimonial homes. In *Routhan v Arun District Council*,[12] the rating authority were held to be entitled to treat a wife, who remained in occupation of the matrimonial home after divorce, as rateable occupier even though they had so treated the husband previously. But Brandon LJ (as he then was) said that the departure of a husband does not automatically mean that he himself ceases to be in rateable occupation. This is because he is under a common law duty to maintain his wife and children, and by leaving them in occupation of the dwelling it may be that 'he is discharging, in part at least, his common law duty to maintain them and is thereby turning the use of the home to his own account: see *Cardiff Corp v Robinson*,[13] per Donovan J'.

These cases and others mark out the extent of the concept of rateable occupation. There are, however, a number of exceptions and special cases. For example, the 1967 Act, s 37, provides that premises occupied by or on behalf of the Crown for public purposes are not rateable; but a proper calculation is made nevertheless by the Treasury, which gives a contribution in lieu of rates to the rating authorities concerned. In *Coomber v Berkshire Justices*,[14] Lord Blackburn said: '. . . the administration of justice . . . and . . . police . . . belong to the Crown'; so that courts, police stations and the like, are covered by this rule. Places of public worship are exempt[15] as are agricultural land and buildings other than dwellings.[16] This exemption now includes 'factory farming' structures such as broiler houses.[17]

Premises occupied by charities and similar bodies can be charged no more than half the rate due, under the 1967 Act, s 40, and the Rating (Charity Shops) Act 1976. Various nationalised utility and transport undertakings, and other public bodies such as water authorities and the Post Office, are subject to special arrangements or exemptions, under the 1967 Act, Schs 4–7, as amended, the Local Government Act 1974, s 19, and the Post Office Act 1969, s 52. As mentioned on p 171, rates on premises wholly or partially used as dwellings are reduced;[18] and rate rebates are available for the benefit of domestic ratepayers with low incomes[19] and disabled persons.[20]

---

12 [1981] 3 All ER 752.
13 [1956] 3 All ER 56 at 58.
14 (1883) 9 App Cas 61.
15 1967 Act, s 39.
16 1967 Act, s 26; also s 26A (fish farms).
17 Rating Act 1971, Pt I.
18 1967 Act, s 48; also Local Government, Planning and Land Act 1980, s 33.
19 Local Government Act 1974, ss 11–14, as amended.
20 Rating (Disabled Persons) Act 1978.

5. ASSESSMENT

Premises liable to rates are referred to as 'hereditaments'; and the 1967 Act, s 19, provides that each shall be assessed at a 'net annual value' based on rent paid by what is commonly referred to as a 'hypothetical tenant'. This is 'rent at which it is estimated that the hereditament might reasonably be expected to let from year to year if the tenant undertook to pay all usual tenant's rates and taxes and to bear the cost of the repairs and insurance and other expenses, if any, necessary to maintain the hereditament in a state to command that rent'.[1] For dwellings and certain other non-industrial property, this figure is known as the 'gross value'; and to reach the 'net annual value' in these cases certain deductions have to be made as specified in an order to be made by the Secretary of State. The value of portions of premises provided for disabled persons is disregarded.[2] These 'net annual value' figures, being based on a somewhat Victorian approach to valuation, are artificial by modern standards, and made more so by the fact that they are only arrived at, since 1948, by a national valuation or re-valuation exercise at rather long intervals. New valuation lists based on these exercises have come into force in 1956, 1963 and 1973; an intention to apply a five-year pattern is frustrated by continual postponements, for reasons of economy.

Since the Local Government Act 1948, valuation for rating has been entrusted, on a national basis, to a valuation officer of the Inland Revenue appointed for each of a series of areas and districts.[3] Proposals to amend valuation lists can be made by valuation officers, rating authorities and 'aggrieved' persons. Owners and occupiers must, if they have not instigated any proposal, be notified; and if no agreement is reached on any proposal the matter is referred to arbitration or, failing that, to a local valuation court, appeal from which lies to the Lands Tribunal. These procedures are governed by Part V of the 1967 Act.[4] There is no appeal from any decision of the Lands Tribunal except by way of 'case stated', purely on a point of law and within a six weeks' time-limit, to the Court of Appeal[5] and thence to the House of Lords.

Rating authorities decide each year, according to their own requirements and the precepts served on them, how much money has to be raised by way of rates and what sum must be levied for every pound of rateable value at which the rateable hereditaments in their area are assessed on the valuation list. This is the 'rate poundage'. Thus if the total of the rateable values in a given area is £1 million, and £900,000 must be raised in rates, a rate of 90p in the £ is levied. Grants, rebates,

1 See s 19(3). For the Order in the next sentence, see SI 1973/2139.
2 1967 Act, s 45.
3 1967 Act, ss 67 and 115.
4 Ss 67–95.
5 Lands Tribunal Act 1949.

reductions, and special arrangements will already have been taken into account. Discounts may be allowed: and domestic ratepayers may pay by instalments.[6] Appeals against the rate levied,[7] as distinct from appeals against the valuation of the hereditament, lie to the Crown Court.[8]

The 1967 Act, Part IV[9] provides that in some circumstances persons other than occupiers of rateable hereditaments may be liable to rates. Thus rating authorities may direct that there may be 'compounding' for rates with owners of hereditaments the rateable values of which do not exceed a prescribed limit;[10] and a percentage reduction is allowed to owners of compounded properties who pay in full by half-way through the rating period. 'Compounding' is obviously convenient as a mode of arranging for payment of rates in bulk where one person is the owner of a number of hereditaments separately occupied. Where properties are let at a rent payable more frequently than once every quarter, the owner can agree with the rating authority to collect the rates on the authority's behalf, again with the benefit of an allowance.[11]

D. Audit

1. ACCOUNTS AND AUDITING

The provisions of the Local Government Act 1972 concerning audit of local authorities' accounts,[12] and the replacement provisions of the Local Government Finance Act 1982, Part III,[13] have been referred to earlier in this chapter.[14] The audit system about to be described will eventually, as a consequence of the 1982 Act, be modified to some extent. Supervision by the Secretary of State will, in general terms, be handed over to a national Audit Commission in England and Wales, to be set up on a 'First Appointed Day'. The body will, as from a 'Second Appointed Day,' appoint auditors in place of the 'district' and 'approved' auditors operating under the present system. A Code of Practice for the new system will be drawn up.

The law on this matter requires separate consideration here, not merely because of its intrinsic importance but because auditors' functions lead them in effect to act as a species of tribunal. Audit of any local authority's accounts, as of anyone else's, involves a book-keeping

---

6 1967 Act, ss 50, 51 and 54.
7 See *R v Rochdale MBC ex p Cromer Ring Mill* [1982] 3 All ER 761.
8 1967 Act, s 7, as amended by the Courts Act 1971, Sch 9.
9 Ss 55–56; as amended (see footnote 11).
10 £200 under the Rating of Owners Order 1972; SI 1972/1983.
11 See Local Government, Planning and Land Act 1980, s 36.
12 Ss 154–167.
13 Ss 11–36 and Schs 3 and 4.
14 See above, p 157 (and below, p 187, for the new Audit Commission).

exercise to check that the accounts are efficiently kept and also a regulatory exercise to detect negligence or fraud in the conduct of financial affairs. In addition, audit involves a consideration of the statutory legality of the activities of the authority in so far as these are reflected in the accounts, including the preparation of the accounts themselves, together with a duty to instigate procedures which will reverse or correct such activities as are shown to be ultra vires. The third of these exercises is not part of the duty of an auditor outside the ambit of public authority finance. The first and third exercises are concerned with matters which are open and above board in the accounts which are being audited; whereas the second is concerned with matters which are concealed and need to be brought to light.

Local authorities' accounts must be made up on a yearly basis, each financial year running from 1 April to 31 March unless the Secretary of State prescribes otherwise, in accordance with the Local Government Act 1972, s 155. The 1972 Act, s 159, currently empowers 'any persons interested' to inspect the accounts to be audited 'at each audit', and in addition to inspect 'all books, deeds, contracts, bills, vouchers and receipts relating thereto', which presumably means all independent documentary evidence relating to items in the accounts if that evidence is held by the authority, being evidence which will give further detailed information pertaining to any item in the accounts and help bring to light any hidden irregularities. Such persons may also 'make copies of all or any part of the accounts and those other documents'. It has been held that a ratepayer can appoint a professional expert who is not a ratepayer to inspect for him.[15] A local government elector for the area, as distinct from a 'person interested', is under the present system entitled to an opportunity when he or his representative can question the auditors or, if it is the district auditor, 'attend before the auditor and make objections to any of those accounts'. If it is an approved auditor, any such local government elector can request the Secretary of State for a direction to hold an 'extraordinary audit'. The Secretary of State may under the present system make regulations governing the keeping of accounts and the procedures relating to audit,[16] including deposit of accounts, publication of information regarding them, and the exercise of rights of inspection and objection.

2. SELECTION OF AUDITORS

The choice between having their accounts audited by an 'approved auditor' or the district auditor was given to local authorities by the 1972 Act, s 154. Authorities were to notify the Secretary of State accordingly. They could apply to change again later; but it has been indi-

---

15 *R v Bedwelty UDC, ex p Price* [1934] 1 KB 333.
16 1972 Act, s 166.

cated that he will not consent to any change occurring within a period shorter than five years. This indication is in the present Audit Code of Practice, contained in Circular 79/73 issued by the Secretary of State, which gives guidance as to 'proper accounting practices' to be observed by auditors. This is required under the present system by s 157 of the 1972 Act, along with compliance with regulations under s 166 and all other relevant enactments, and proper consideration as to what should be reported on in the public interest.

'Approved auditors' are chosen by a local authority from a list of auditors approved by the Secretary of State who belong to one of a number of professional bodies listed in s 164 of the 1972 Act. 'District auditors' are appointed by the Secretary of State. Either kind of auditor 'shall have a right of access at all times to all such documents relating to the accounts . . . as appear to him to be necessary for the purpose of auditing the accounts . . . and shall be entitled to require from any officer . . . or any other person holding or accountable for any such document such information and explanation as he thinks necessary . . . and . . . require any such officer or person to attend before him . . .'.[17] Default is an offence punishable by a fine up to £100 and a continuing fine thereafter up to £20 a day. Unjustifiable disclosure of information by an approved auditor is an offence punishable by a fine up to £400 if he is summarily convicted, or by a fine (unspecified) or imprisonment up to two years, or both, if he is convicted on indictment. When an audit is complete, the auditor has a duty to consider, under s 157 (referred to above) whether any matter calls for a report; if so, he must send his report to the local authority within 14 days.[18]

3. SANCTIONS

The most important aspect of audit, in law, is the nature of the sanctions which it entails in the event of irregularities (or worse) being brought to light. The 1982 Act procedures, when brought into effect, will continue in general terms to apply this system of control.

An approved auditor under the present system, however, has no sanctions at his command other than to make a report to the Secretary of State if 'it appears to him that there is reasonable ground for believing—(a) that any item of account is contrary to law, or (b) that any person has failed to bring into account any sum which should have been so included, or (c) that a loss has been incurred or deficiency caused by the wilful misconduct of any person'.[19] The Secretary of State may then decide whether to exercise his power, under s 165, to direct a *district* auditor to hold an 'extraordinary audit'.

17 S 158.
18 S 160.
19 S 162.

A district auditor has, in relation to any audit, a power of direct sanctions which the approved auditor lacks; and these are set out in s 161. The three matters (a), (b) and (c), which concern the approved auditor under s 162 above, concern him also. The first, an item which appears to him to be 'contrary to law', is a matter he can bring before a court to seek a declaration to that effect. This does not apply, however, if the Secretary of State sanctions the item. The court is the High Court, unless the amount comes within the limit of the jurisdiction of the county court for claims in cases founded on contract (currently £5,000[20], in which event the county court has concurrent jurisdiction. If the court does make such a declaration, it may also order any or all of the following: repayment to the local authority of any unauthorised expenditure; rectification of the accounts; and disqualification from membership for a specified period for any person responsible who is a member of the local authority and has made or authorised expenditure of this kind exceeding £2,000. No such order may be made, however, if the person responsible 'acted reasonably', or thought that such expenditure was lawful; and his means and all other relevant circumstances must be taken into consideration.

The other two matters—ie items appearing to the district auditor to involve *either* a failure to bring a sum into account (unless with the sanction of the Secretary of State) *or* a loss or deficiency caused by wilful misconduct—are matters entitling the auditor to certify the amount involved. If he does so, he or the authority can sue for payment on the authority's behalf from the person or persons liable in respect of it, after 14 days.

Any person who is 'aggrieved' by an auditor's decision to certify, and any person who made an objection under s 159 and is 'aggrieved' by a failure of an auditor to certify or to seek a declaration, as the case may be, may within six weeks require the auditor to state his reasons in writing, and may appeal to the court. On such appeal, the court can, in regard to a refusal to seek a declaration, make a decision in the same terms as if the auditor had applied for one; and in regard to a decision or refusal to certify it may confirm, quash or vary the decision and give any certificate the auditor could have given. If a certificate is given by the auditor or the court relating to a loss or deficiency caused by wilful misconduct of a member of the local authority, and the amount thereby due from him exceeds £2,000, he shall be disqualified from membership for five years.

4. AUDIT AND THE 'ULTRA VIRES' DOCTRINE

The provisions in s 161 repeat, with various alterations, the terms of earlier statutes to similar effect. There have been a great many cases,

---

20 As prescribed by the County Courts Jurisdiction Order 1981; SI 1981/1123.

virtually all of which turn on some application of the ultra vires doctrine, rather than on such questions of fraud or negligence as might be uncovered in audit.

Among the most recent of these are two cases arising out of the unanimous refusal of the members of Clay Cross Urban District Council to implement increases in council house rents which were necessary to comply with the Housing Finance Act 1972. They did this regardless of the warnings of the council's officers. The Secretary of State directed the district auditor to hold an extraordinary audit; and the auditor reached the conclusion that there was a shortfall of almost £7,000 because of the refusal—ie that sum should have been credited to the housing revenue account but was not—for which the councillors should be made personally liable. The auditor's decision was challenged in the Queen's Bench Division, but unsuccessfully, the court holding that the 'misconduct' of the councillors had caused a 'loss or deficiency' under the statute then current, namely the Local Government Act 1933. This case was reported as *Asher v Lacey*.[1] The councillors then brought proceedings in the Chancery Division, reported as *Asher v Secretary of State for the Environment*.[2] They sought a declaration that the direction to hold the extraordinary audit was made for an ulterior and punitive purpose and was thus ultra vires; also that rebates might have offset the increased rents so that the liability was only potential (if anything) and not actual. (This last point ignored the fact that the shortfall was a separate feature of the accounts in its own right and legal or illegal as such irrespective of all other items.) Megarry J (as he then was) ordered the claim to be struck out, and the Court of Appeal upheld his decision. Lord Denning MR said: 'Here they are, the 11 councillors of Clay Cross. Each of them deliberately broke the solemn promise which he gave when he accepted office. Each of them has flagrantly defied the law. Each of them is determined to continue to defy it. Yet they come to the court and complain that the Secretary of State has acted unlawfully'.

Local authority decisions of this kind are true policy decisions. The question whether they are ultra vires is not always as easy to answer as it was in the Clay Cross affair. In *Re Magrath*,[3] Durham County Council made a retrospective payment to the county treasurer for additional work which he had carried out some years before without financial recognition. The auditor held this to be an ultra vires payment because no general statutory authority existed for local authorities to make gifts; and the House of Lords agreed that this was so. But special circumstances sometimes justify non contractual payments of this kind.

---

1 [1973] 3 All ER 1008, [1973] 1 WLR 1412.
2 [1974] Ch 208, [1974] 2 All ER 156.
3 [1934] 2 KB 415.

In *Re Hurle-Hobbs*,[4] a payment beyond the amounts contractually agreed was made to a contractor to prevent a service from being discontinued; this was held to be reasonable on the facts of the case.

Many of these cases obviously arise out of political conflicts. Similar in some respects to the Clay Cross dispute was *Taylor v Munrow*,[5] where a local authority resolved to pay a proportion of certain rents due from residential occupiers without considering whether their circumstances justified this, on the ground that such consideration would involve a 'means test'. The court upheld the auditor's decision that this policy was ultra vires. The authority had enjoyed a discretion which they had failed to exercise 'reasonably' if at all. Also similar was *Roberts v Hopwood*,[6] referred to in chapter 3, where the House of Lords upheld an auditor's decision that a local authority had acted ultra vires in raising the wages of their employees well over the level of wages paid to persons in comparable employment locally.

This certainly does not mean that auditors can control the policies of local authorities. In *R v Roberts*[7] the court emphasised that authorities are to decide their own policies without interference by the auditor. His task is restricted in this context to drawing attention, and imposing sanctions, only when local authorities' policies are framed in such a way as to go outside the legal boundaries of their discretion.

It should be noted that the auditor's powers under s 161 are restricted to the authority whose accounts are subject to his audit. Therefore, a reference in the statutory provisions to 'any person', in respect of whose decisions or conduct he can take action, refers only to members, officers and servants of that authority, and he cannot proceed as auditor against anyone else, as was made clear in *Dickson v Hurle-Hobbs*.[8] In addition it should be remembered that only those members, officers and servants who are implicated in the wrongful decision deserve to be saddled with personal liability as a result of his audit findings—ie members who voted for that decision, or officers or servants who advocated it or assisted in it, not those who voted or advised against it.

NOTE—The new Audit Commission was set up on 21 January 1983 by the Accounts and Audit (First Appointed Day) Order 1982.[9]

---

4 [1944] 2 All ER 261. Likewise in *Pickwell v Camden LBC* [1983] 1 All ER 602, an agreement to pay striking employees a cost-of-living increase was upheld.

5 [1960] 1 All ER 455, [1960] 1 WLR 151.

6 [1925] AC 578.

7 [1908] 1 KB 407. Audit is 'verification and not detection'—per Pollock MR in *Re City Equitable Fire Insurance Co* [1925] Ch at 509.

8 [1947] 2 All ER 47.

9 SI 1982/1881 (see above, p 182).

Chapter 8

Composition and working of local authorities

A. Areas and elections

I. BOUNDARIES

The modern pattern of local authorities and areas has been discussed in an earlier chapter. The Local Government Act 1972, Schs 1–3 and 4–5, deals with the areas in England and in Wales respectively; the questions to be considered now are, first, whether those areas can be altered and, second, how they are organised internally. The 1972 Act deals with these matters in Part IV,[1] and for that purpose has set up two Local Government Boundary Commissions, one for England[2] and one for Wales.[3] Sections 20 and 269 of that Act provide that 'Wales' now includes the area of what used to be the county of Monmouthshire, together with the Borough of Newport, to make up the new county of Gwent. What remains is England. Section 62 empowers the two Commissions, acting jointly and with the consent of the county councils affected, to propose alterations in the boundary between England and Wales which the Secretary of State may embody in an order (with or without modifications) that will come into effect if approved by resolution of both Houses of Parliament.

Private bills to promote alterations in any local government areas or their electoral divisions in future are prohibited.[4] The boundary between Surrey and West Sussex was altered by the Charlwood and Horley Act 1974—a public Act.

The Local Government Boundary Commission for England, whose constitution is prescribed in detail in Sch 7, has the duty[5] of reviewing the following at intervals of 'not less than ten or more than fifteen years' as from 1 April 1974: all English counties, metropolitan districts and London boroughs, and the boundaries of Greater London and the City of London. As a second priority they may review parts of those areas and boundaries, and any areas or boundaries referred to them by par-

1 Ss 46–78.
2 S 46.
3 S 53.
4 S 70.
5 S 48.

188

ticular local authorities. They may formulate proposals to the Secretary of State[6] for altering or abolishing areas or creating new ones. The Secretary of State may direct them to conduct particular reviews of areas,[7] generally or specifically, or delay any review. He may direct any council to review the parishes in their area and submit a report thereon to the Commission, who may also hold their own review or be directed by him to do so. The Secretary of State may give directions generally to the Commission[8] and they may submit reports to him, with proposals or recommendations for change which he may embody, subject to modifications and a further review if he wishes, in an order which will take effect if not annulled by resolution of either House of Parliament.[9] Similar provisions apply to the Welsh Commission.[10]

Various attendant procedural matters are provided for, notably a power (not a duty) to hold public local inquiries.[11] In a review it is mandatory to consult all local authorities concerned together with bodies representing staff who ask to be consulted and other persons at discretion, and to give notifications and information to interested persons in respect of draft proposals or recommendations, and to take into account such representations as are made.[12] The conduct of inquiries, consultations and investigations can be delegated to individual Commissioners or specially-appointed assistant Commissioners.[13] Special rules apply to boundaries at the seashore or along watercourses.[14] Transitional arrangements and a limited power to revoke orders are also prescribed;[15] and any sums payable by way of adjustment of financial or property matters may be by way of a lump sum or terminable annuities. An authority may borrow to pay a lump sum.

If a county, district or London borough council should wish to change the name of their area, this can be done provided that there is a two-thirds majority at a specially convened meeting of the council and that certain requirements as to notifications and publicity are complied with.[16] The name of a parish or community can be changed by the district council at the request of the parish or community authority.[17] The name of Greater London, or its council, or the titles of the chairman or the vice-chairman or deputy chairman, can be changed if the Secretary of State consents.[18]

6 S 47.
7 S 49.
8 S 52.
9 S 51.
10 Ss 53–59.
11 S 61.
12 S 60.
13 Ss 65–66.
14 Ss 71–73.
15 Ss 67–69.
16 S 74.
17 Ss 75–76.
18 S 77.

2. ESTABLISHMENT OF CONSTITUENCIES

In addition to these provisions for alterations relating to local authority areas there are provisions for alterations within those areas. This is a matter of what the 1972 Act calls 'electoral arrangements', which s 78 defines as follows:

> '(a) in relation to [the area of a county or district, or any local authority area in London], the number of councillors in the council for that area, the number and boundaries of the electoral areas into which that area is for the time being divided for the purpose of the election of councillors, the number of councillors to be elected for any electoral area in that . . . area, and the name of any electoral area;
> (b) in relation to a parish or community council or a common parish or community council, the number of councillors, the question of whether the parish or community or any parish or community, as the case may be, should or should not be or continue to be divided into wards for the purpose of the election of councillors, the number and boundaries of any such wards, the number of councillors to be elected for any such ward or in the case of a common parish or community council for each parish or community, and the name of any such ward.'

This part of the law is concerned with how local authority areas are divided for the purpose of electing the councillors who make up the membership of each authority, how many councillors are elected for each division, when they are elected, for how long they serve when elected, what persons are eligible to serve as councillors or to elect them. The relevant law is contained in the Act of 1972 and statutory instruments made thereunder, and the Representation of the People Act 1949 as later amended and supplemented, with various decided cases thereon.

The way in which the geographical areas of local authorities are divided for the purpose of electing council *members* is quite different from the way in which they are divided so as to produce smaller—ie second or third 'tier'—*authorities*. In the latter sense, as discussed in an earlier chapter, the area administered by a county council, whether metropolitan or non-metropolitan, is divided up into areas administered by district councils; and Greater London, the area administered by the GLC, is divided up into areas administered by London borough councils and the City Corporation; while some but not all of the areas administered by district councils are divided up into areas of local government parishes, as distinct from ecclesiastical parishes, in England and communities in Wales.

However, it is the former sense which is relevant to the present discussion. In this sense, the area of '(a) every county shall be divided into electoral divisions, each returning . . . one councillor; (b) every metropolitan district shall be divided into wards, each returning a number of councillors which is divisible by three; and (c) every non-metropolitan district shall be divided into wards, each returning such number of councillors as may be provided by an order . . .' In all these cases 'there shall be a separate election for each electoral division or ward'. These provisions apply to Wales as well as to England.[19]

County council elections are held every four years from and after 1973, the entire council membership retiring simultaneously. Metropolitan district council elections are held every year except the year when the county council elections are held; and one third of the councillors in each ward retire in turn, thus serving a four-year term each. Other district councils may choose whether to have the same system either as county councils or as metropolitan district councils, deciding by resolution passed (by a two-thirds majority after 1 April 1974) at a specially convened meeting. Choice of the former (simultaneous re-election of the whole council) involves, as from and after 1979, an election every four years. Choice of the latter—ie 'staggered' elections—empowers the Secretary of State to refer the proposal to the Local Government Boundary Commission to prepare a scheme; but if so the authority can, unlike metropolitan district councils, choose whether any or all of the wards shall have single members or groups of members in multiples of three. However, in 'staggered' elections the councillors must retire in accordance with 'a system of election by thirds, that is to say, the election of one-third, as nearly as may be, of the councillors of the district at the ordinary elections of such councillors in any year', such elections being held each year in turn except the year when the county council elections are held. Once a choice of system is made no resolution to alter it is permissible within ten years. These provisions apply in England and in Wales.[20]

A similar system applies in London. The electoral arrangements for GLC councillors have been brought into line with county councillors, and London borough councillors broadly with certain of the district councillors. The election of these councillors are now held every four years, on and after 1977 for the GLC and 1978 for the London borough councils. These provisions are contained in the 1972 Act, s 8 and Sch 2, amended by the London Councillors Order 1976.[1]

As for parish councils, s 16 of the 1972 Act specifies that for each of them the district council shall fix the number of parish councillors (at

19 1972 Act, ss 6 and 25.
20 1972 Act, ss 7 and 26.
1 SI 1976/213.

least five), who 'shall be elected by the local government electors for the parish' for a term of office of four years (after 1976) 'and the whole number of parish councillors shall retire together'. There must be 'a separate election of parish councillors for each ward' if the parish is divided into wards, but otherwise 'one election of parish councillors for the whole parish'. A similar system applies to the election of community councillors in Wales.[2]

3. ALTERATION OF CONSTITUENCIES

The above provisions represent the original pattern of 'electoral arrangements ' under the Act of 1972, in accordance with the definition in s 78, set out above,[3] and a number of requirements of principle and detail set out in Sch 11. Next to be considered are the subsequent changes in that pattern. First there is the 'initial review of electoral arrangements'. Section 63 and Sch 9 state that 'as soon as practicable' after the first elections the Local Government Boundary Commission for England should review those arrangements for each district 'for the purpose of considering future electoral arrangements for the district' and 'formulate proposals for those arrangements accordingly'. The Secretary of State was empowered to give effect, by order, to any such proposals reported to him. After all districts in any given county have been reviewed in this way, and orders made as necessary, the Commission should then review the arrangements for the county itself, for the same purpose.

Section 64 and Sch 10 provide a similar procedure for Wales; except that, before the initial review was to take place in relation to the districts, the Local Government Boundary Commission for Wales had to conduct a 'special community review for the whole of Wales' for the purpose of making any necessary proposals to the Secretary of State concerning changes in the pattern of communities—by their alteration, abolition, creation, rearrangement, and so on—and of their councils. In this review 'the Welsh Commission shall have regard to the wishes of the inhabitants of the areas in question'. After the completion of this review in regard to any district, but not until then, the 'initial review' can then be conducted for the district itself, as in England. When all districts in a particular county have been reviewed and any proposals formulated, the review can then in turn be conducted for that county, again as in England.

The 1972 Act then looks further ahead. In s 50 it imposes on the English Commission 'not less than ten or more than fifteen years after the completion of the initial review of the electoral arrangements for counties', as described, 'to review the electoral arrangements' for all county, district and London authorities 'for the purpose of considering whether or not to make proposals to the Secretary of State for a substantive change in those electoral arrangements', and to formulate any necessary proposals. They may also carry out such a review ad hoc if asked to do so. District councils must 'keep under review' any parish electoral arrangements in their area, and must 'consider any request' from the parish council, or 30 local government electors, concerning those arrangements. A district council may 'give effect' to any 'substantive changes' they wish to make; or the parish council or electors (as stated) may put their request to the English Commission to formulate proposals to put to the district council or, failing the latter's agreement, the Secretary of State. The Welsh Commission has a parallel function.[4] These reviews are to be repeated at intervals of ten to 15 years, so the Commissions are expected to be in business for a long time to come.

These provisions have received some attention from the House of Lords. In *Enfield London Borough v Local Government Boundary Commission for England*,[5] the plaintiff council brought an action claiming a declaration that proposals produced by the defendants failed to comply in certain important respects with the statutory requirements. The plaintiffs favoured a scheme for having 35 wards and 70 councillors in the borough; the defendants rejected this and adopted a scheme for 33 wards and 66 councillors. The plaintiffs relied on Sch 11 which sets out detailed considerations relating to 'electoral arrangements' as defined in s 78. Paragraph 3(2)(a) of the schedule states that there shall be electoral equality 'as nearly as may be' in the ratio of voters to councillors as between wards. The defendants claimed that this requirement was subordinate to another, stated in s 47, that any review proposals should be made 'for effecting changes appearing to the Commission desirable in the interests of effective and convenient local government'.

Since s 47 deals with the powers of the Commissions on a general and fundamental level, concerning reviews as a whole and not merely those relating to 'electoral arrangements', it is not surprising that the House agreed with the defendants. The attention to be given to 'electoral equality' is to be interpreted in context, namely Sch 11, where para 3(2) says this requirement is to have priority in regard to fixing boundaries. But that, though important, must yield priority in turn to 'the interests of effective and convenient local government' as stated in s 47.

The defendants' priorities were thus in accordance with the Act, and the plaintiff's were not. Lord Dilhorne said: 'Having decided on the appropriate number of councillors required for effective and conve-

4 S 57.
5 [1979] 3 All ER 747.

nient local government, it is then the duty of the commission to give effect so far as is reasonably practicable to the requirements of para 3(2) and then as nearly as may be secure electoral equality; but to say that that must take priority over what is required for such government is, in my view, to misconstrue the Act'.

4. THE FRANCHISE

So much for the electoral areas. The electors in those areas derive their entitlement to vote in local government elections from common law and statute. Common law debars persons who are not of sound mind.[6] This applies to elections generally, whether Parliamentary or local.

The Representation of the People Acts 1949 to 1980 impose various detailed rules. They require a person to be entered on the register of electors for the particular local government area and to be on the 'qualifying date' a British or Irish citizen, not serving a custodial sentence, and a resident or occupier of premises in the area. Peers may vote at local elections. Registers of electors are revised yearly and take effect on 16 February each year; the 'qualifying date' is 10 October in the previous year.[7] Voters must be at least 18 years old when they vote.

'Residence' is to be interpreted in its ordinary sense, but implies some 'degree of permanence'. Temporary absences are disregarded. It is possible to be 'resident' in more than one home, including student accommodation, as the Court of Appeal held in *Fox v Stirk*.[8] This means that an elector may be qualified as a voter on more than one register; but he or she can only cast one valid vote on the occasion of each election held in a given local government area; and to infringe this is a criminal offence. An alternative to 'residence' is 'occupation'—ie the right to occupy premises of any kind by virtue of freehold or leasehold ownership if their yearly value is £10 or more. Members of the armed services and their spouses living with them may be registered in respect of the premises where they would be living but for their service posting. The same applies to other persons in Crown service if posted abroad. Absent voters generally may apply for postal votes; but a service voter also has the option of voting by proxy.

Part III[9] of the 1972 Act deals with elections. A registration officer is appointed by each district or London borough council, and the register in his charge applies to Parliamentary as well as all local elections.[10] Objections to entries in or omission from the register must be formally heard by him, subject to a right of appeal to the County Court by any-

---

6 See, eg, *Bridgwater case (Tucker's Case)* (1803) 1 Peck 101 at 108.
7 Electoral Registers Acts 1949 and 1953.
8 [1970] 2 QB 463, [1970] 3 All ER 7.
9 Ss 39–45.
10 S 39.

one aggrieved.[11] The conduct of the elections is the function of separate returning officers appointed by each county council for county elections, by each district council for district elections, and by each district council for parish or community elections.[12] They may in their turn appoint deputies. Rules are made by the Home Secretary for these purposes,[13] namely the Local Elections (Principal Areas) Rules 1973[14] and the Local Elections (Parishes and Communities) Rules 1973.[15] The Parish and Community Meetings Polls Rules 1973[16] are made similarly, but under the 1972 Act, Sch 12.[17]

5. CHALLENGE PROCEDURES FOR ELECTIONS

These Rules, together with the Election Petition Rules 1960,[18] and the Representation of the People Act 1949 ss 37 and 112–137, govern the limits of the jurisdiction of the returning officer and the role of the court. A person declared elected by the returning officer is duly elected, but the validity of the election is thereafter subject to challenge by an 'election petition' to the High Court, Queen's Bench division, presented by an unsuccessful candidate or by four voters, the successful candidate or the returning officer being the respondent.

A breach of the rules or any other breach of duty will not result in the election being invalid if it was conducted substantially in accordance with the law—ie errors were technical or trivial only—and in addition the breach did not affect the result. In *R v Election Court, ex p Sheppard*[19] the nomination paper omitted the successful candidate's address; the election court's decision that his election was void was upheld. In *Gunn v Sharpe*,[20] 98 ballot papers were inadvertently not stamped and the votes were disallowed; two successful candidates' elections were held void because the result of the election had been affected. In a similar case, *Morgan v Simpson*,[1] only 44 out of 24,000 votes were invalidated by a failure to stamp the ballot papers; again, the successful candidate's election was held void because the error 'affected the result' by turning a majority of seven votes for the unsuccessful candidate into a majority of eleven for the other candidate; it was therefore not material to the case that the conduct of the election was otherwise 'substantially in

---

11 Representation of the People Acts 1949 and 1969.
12 1972 Act, s 41.
13 1972 Act, s 42.
14 SI 1973/9.
15 SI 1973/1910.
16 SI 1973/1911.
17 Part III, para 18(5), and Part V, para 34(5).
18 SI 1960/543.
19 [1975] 2 All ER 723, [1975] 1 WLR 1319. For election courts see below, p 198.
20 [1974] QB 808, [1974] 2 All ER 1058.
 1 [1975] QB 151, [1974] 3 All ER 722. See also *Ruffle v Rogers* [1982] 3 All ER 157, where a voter wrote a candidate's name on the ballot paper; this did not invalidate it.

accordance with the law'. In *Cornwell v Marshall*,[2] a ballot paper was held to have been wrongly accepted because the cross upon it straggled over two names, and another was held rightly rejected because it was marked with figures instead of a cross. In *Greenway-Stanley v Paterson*,[3] an election was declared void on the ground that a candidate's nomination paper had been wrongly rejected; the court said that the returning officer should only have considered whether the paper was valid on its face and should *not* have considered, still less accepted, independent evidence that the name of the candidate was incorrectly stated, this being a point of substance which must be considered, if at all, by the election court itself in proper proceedings giving due opportunity for both sides to be heard. In *James v Davies*,[4] a petition to challenge an election was rejected, because although incorrect notices were displayed yet the election had been conducted 'substantially in accordance with the law' and there was no reason to consider that the result had been affected.

The ground for challenging elections by an election petition in these cases is that the candidate was not 'duly' elected. There are other grounds also, of varying seriousness. One is that the candidate was disqualified. The 1972 Act[5] requires every candidate nominated at local elections to be a British or Irish citizen, aged 21 (not 18), who is a local government elector for the area *or* has occupied land or other premises there (freehold or leasehold) for 12 months *or* has had his or her main place of work there throughout that period *or* has resided there throughout that period *or*, if it is a parish or community election, has resided not further than three miles away throughout that period.

The Act of 1972[6] in addition *disqualifies* from membership of a local authority anyone who holds 'any paid office of employment (other than the office of chairman, vice-chairman or deputy chairman)' within the appointment of that local authority, or of any committee or sub-committee thereof, or of any joint authority representing the local authority, or of any other person so paid. It also disqualifies such a person from membership of any *other* local authority represented on any such committee, sub-committee or joint body. But a teacher or similar employee of the Inner London Education Authority is not disqualified from membership of an inner London borough or from membership of the GLC as a representative of an outer London electoral area, or from being chairman, vice-chairman or deputy chairman of the GLC. Also a teacher employed by one council can be a member of another, even if that other council should nominate members to the education committee of

2 (1977) 75 LGR 676.
3 [1977] 2 All ER 663.
4 (1977) 76 LGR 189.
5 S 79.
6 S 80.

the employing council.[7] In *Lamb v Jeffries*,[8] it was held that confirmation of a schoolmaster's appointment by the local authority disqualified him from membership of the authority; yet in *Boyd v Easington RDC*,[9] a similar appointment did not disqualify because it was neither made nor confirmed by the local authority, or a committee thereof, even though half the members of the appointing body were individual members of the authority.

Also disqualified are persons who have committed corrupt or illegal practices or who, within the past five years, have been sentenced to imprisonment for three months or longer without the option of a fine, and bankrupts.[10] In addition persons may be disqualified for up to five years under the audit system described in the previous chapter,[11] if found to be responsible for a loss or deficiency, or unauthorised expenditure, exceeding £2,000.

In general those disqualifications apply to persons already elected as well as candidates for election; and of course if a sitting councillor is disqualified a vacancy is caused. But a person's conviction before the date of an election of an imprisonable offence can only disqualify that person from being elected, not from continuing as a member if the election is not challenged: *Bishop v Deakin*.[12]

Another ground for challenging elections by petition is the actual occurrence of corrupt or illegal practices, quite apart from disqualifications to which they lead. They are criminal offences under the Representation of the People Acts 1949 and 1969. Corrupt practices involve deliberate dishonesty, such as impersonation, bribery, 'treating' and undue influence, and are triable summarily or on indictment, the penalty being imprisonment or a fine or both. Illegal practices do not depend on dishonest intent, and are punishable by a fine; and relief may be obtained on application to the court if the person concerned shows that the illegal conduct was inadvertent because it arose from mistake, not bad faith. In *Re Berry*,[13] relief was refused because of insufficient good faith on the part of the culprit, not to mention previous offences. Illegal practices include: making payments for canvassing and for hiring transport for voters; broadcasting, during the five weeks before the election, of events in which any candidate actively participates[14] if the candidate does not consent; making any false statement

---

7 S 81.
8 [1956] QB 431, [1956] 1 All ER 317.
9 [1963] 3 All ER 747, [1963] 1 WLR 1281.
10 Until five years after their bankruptcy ends: s 81.
11 See above, p 185.
12 [1936] Ch 409, [1936] 1 All ER 255.
13 [1978] Crim LR 357.
14 This does not apply to a programme in which the candidate is only shown or heard or referred to incidentally: see *Marshall v BBC* [1979] 3 All ER 80 (a parliamentary election). See the Representation of the People Act 1969, s 9.

about a candidate's character without reasonable belief in its truth; causing disorder at meetings; failing to comply with prescribed requirements as to limits on expenditure (or returns and declarations of expenditure) or as to the inclusion of the name and address of the printer on election material. Limits on expenditure are varied officially by statutory instrument from time to time.

Some of these offences are only capable of being committed by candidates or their election agents. However, to found an election petition, as distinct from prosecution, corrupt or illegal practices must have been sufficiently extensive to make it reasonable to regard the result of the election as having been affected by them; or else they must in fact have been committed by a successful candidate or his or her election agent. Alternatively the candidate or election agent in fact engaged as an agent or canvasser someone who it should reasonably have been known had been convicted of a corrupt or illegal practice.

The election petition, whatever the ground of complaint, is presented to the High Court; and the election court which tries that petition is conducted by a barrister of 15 years' standing appointed by the High Court as commissioner. On the merits his decision is final, and it states whether the candidate complained of, or any other person, was in fact elected, and also whether the election was valid or invalid. A case can, however, be stated to the High Court on a point of law; and it may be that judicial review is not excluded either.[15] The Director of Public Prosecutions must be represented, because evidence of corrupt or illegal proceedings may emerge, and if so a report must be prepared for the Attorney-General. He or the election court may order that a prosecution be instituted, or the Director may institute it of his own accord, either in the election court itself or in an ordinary criminal court.

6. RETURNING OFFICERS

The conduct of a local government election, in accordance with the Representation of the People Acts 1949–80, the Local Government Act 1972 and the statutory instruments made under them, is the responsibility first and foremost of the returning officer, referred to earlier in this chapter. The 1972 Act[16] requires local government elections to be held on the first Thursday in May of the year when they are due to take place. This is referred to as 'the ordinary day of election of councillors'; and it can only be changed by an order made before 1 February in the previous year. An exact and detailed timetable is laid down for the events preceding the actual polling of votes on election day, starting with an official notice of the election to be published 25 days before-

---

15 See the remarks of Lord Wigery CJ in *R v Election Court, ex p Sheppard* [1975] 2 All ER 723, [1975] 1 WLR 1319.

16 S 43. Returning officers were referred to on p 195, above.

hand. Candidates' nomination papers have to be handed in not later than 19 days beforehand (the deadline is at noon), in prescribed form signed by a proposer, a seconder and eight other electors of the electoral area as assentors, signing their usual signatures.

In *Re Melton Mowbray (Egerton Ward) UDC Election*,[17] a case was stated to the High Court (Queen's Bench Division) on the question whether the returning officer for a local election had wrongly rejected a nomination paper. Reviewing the facts of the dispute, Paull J said: 'in this case . . . a married woman is entered on the roll by the name of "Nellie". Now we know that her husband entered that name on the roll. He entered it because she is always known at home by the name of Nellie, but her usual signature is . . . "E" standing for Ellen, for her real name is Ellen, but all her life she has been called Nellie'. It was argued that since the returning officer had honestly decided that the signature with 'E' was 'not as required by law' because of the discrepancy with the entry 'Nellie' on the electoral register, his decision could not be questioned. But the judge pointed out that the relevant rule only empowered the returning officer to hold a signature to be insufficient if it was not 'the signature' of the person in question. In this case 'E' was part of the usual signature and 'Nellie', or 'N' was not; therefore the rejection of the nomination paper was wrongful and the election which followed was void. The judge further observed that the returning officer 'has the opportunity to make such enquiries as he may think right (and) . . . at least twenty-four hours in which to do so'. He could easily have telephoned the candidate's agent to settle the matter.

The returning officer must make quick decisions for obvious practical reasons. He must decide whether a nomination paper is valid or not. An election petition may lead later on to his *rejection* of a nomination being declared contrary to law by the election court; but it cannot be questioned at the time. His *acceptance* of a nomination cannot be questioned at all. He can only reject it from what appears or does not appear on its face: *Evans v Thomas*.[18]

Each candidate, having formally submitted a written consent to nomination attested by one witness, stating his or her qualification to be a candidate, must appoint an election agent; but the candidate and the election agent can be the same person. Responsibilities are imposed by the law on the election agent to see that the statutory requirements are complied with, notably in regard to expenditure. The candidate is responsible for the wrongful acts of the election agent done 'within the scope of his authority'—ie as if he were the candidate's servant.

If there are more candidates than vacancies a poll in due form[19] is

---

17 [1969] 1 QB 192, [1968] 3 All ER 761.
18 [1962] 2 QB 350, [1962] 3 All ER 108.
19 1972 Act, s 42.

held on the day of the election. The returning officer's decision on the validity of ballot papers, or the votes indicated on them, is final, subject to an election petition, similarly to his decision on nomination papers. If votes are tied he must resolve the tie by drawing lots. He must declare the result as soon as possible, publish the relevant details as the statutory rules require, and deliver documents into the custody of the local authority in the person of a 'proper officer' appointed for the purpose, together with a formal report. If, however, an election does not take place as it should, or vacancies remain unfilled for some other reason, the returning officer must order another election to be held within 42 days afterwards.[20]

B. Council members, meetings and committees

I. CONDUCT OF MEETINGS

The most important requirement for the council of each local authority, as for any other body of persons, is that they should meet. The 1972 Act,[1] provides that meetings and other proceedings of local authorities must take place in accordance with detailed provisions set out in Sch 12. Paragraph 42 of Sch 12 empowers local authorities to make standing orders 'for the regulation of their proceedings and business'; and these must be complied with until varied or revoked.

There must be an *annual meeting* of every council, on such day in March, April or May, as they may fix, though in a local election year for any council it must be at a date within a specified period shortly after the elections. Parish and community councils are included, but their annual meeting must be in May. Meetings other than the annual meeting may be held as desired. They are in practice unlikely to be held more frequently than monthly and may be two-monthly or quarterly. The chairman can call an extraordinary meeting; and if he does not then such a meeting can be requisitioned within a prescribed time by five members (twenty, for the GLC; two for a parish or community council), three of whom (or the two parish or community councillors) must sign the notice and agenda of the meeting.

Three clear days' notice of all meetings must be given and a summons, with agenda, sent by post to all members. In *R v Herefordshire Justices*,[2] it was stated that in calculating 'clear' days the dates of both the notice and the meeting respectively must be disregarded: ie notice of a meeting on 1 May must be given on 27 April or earlier. Decisions on matters discussed without having been stated on the agenda are ultra

20 1972 Act, s 44.
1 S 99.
2 (1820) 3 B & Ald 581.

vires; in *Longfield Parish Council v Wright*,[3] the dismissal of an employee was held void for this reason. The only exceptions to this rule are items of business which either must, in accordance with statute, in any case be transacted at the annual meeting or are raised under the council's standing orders as a matter of urgency. Yet if a summons to a meeting, though sent, is not in fact served on any particular councillor the meeting is none the less valid. The chairman (or mayor, in a London borough) must preside or, failing him or her, the vice-chairman (or deputy-mayor), and failing him or her in the GLC the deputy chairman. Failing all these the council members present must choose one of their number to preside. The quorum is one quarter of the entire membership: in *Newhaven Local Board v Newhaven School Board*,[4] this was held to mean all the membership inclusive of vacancies. But if by reason of disqualifications the number of members of an authority falls below two-thirds of the full membership, the quorum then falls to one quarter of 'the number of members . . . remaining qualified'.[5]

The rule about decisions is that, in principle but subject to statutory provisions to the contrary in particular cases, 'all questions coming or arising before a local authority shall be decided by a majority of the members of the authority present and voting thereon at a meeting of the authority'.[6] The chairman or other person presiding 'shall have a second or casting vote' if there is 'an equality of votes'.[7] These must be valid votes; and if it is adjudicated later that any of them are not valid this in turn may well affect the validity of a casting vote: *Bland v Buchanan*.[8] The chairman or mayor or appropriate deputy if present must preside; but no-one may preside over a decision affecting himself or herself individually, particularly a decision whether he or she should be elected to some post: *Re Wolverhampton Borough Council's Aldermanic Election*.[9] In such a case that person should stand down and the next appropriate person take charge of the meeting.

A record must be kept of the names of the members present at every meeting. Minutes must be duly kept 'and shall be signed at the same or next following meeting of the authority by the person presiding thereat, and any minute purporting to be so signed shall be received in evidence without further proof'.[10] But evidence *disproving* the authenticity of a minute, or of the meeting itself, or the qualification of the any member, can be adduced independently in appropriate proceedings.

3 (1918) 16 LGR 865.
4 (1885) 30 Ch D 350.
5 1972 Act, Sch 12, para 45.
6 1972 Act, Sch 12, para 39(1).
7 Para 39(2).
8 [1901] 2 KB 75.
9 [1962] 2 QB 460, [1961] 3 All ER 446.
10 1972 Act, Sch 12, para 41.

These provisions for the conduct of meetings also govern committee and sub-committee meetings, including joint committees between authorities.

2. CHAIRMEN AND THEIR DEPUTIES

When councillors (including parish and community councillors) have been elected they come into office at the date on which the councillors whose term of office has come to an end retire, namely four days after the election.[11] The same rule now applies to London.[12] There is no restriction on retiring councillors as such being re-elected.

The council's annual meeting, as already mentioned, follows swiftly thereafter. 'The election of the chairman shall be the first business transacted at the annual meeting';[13] moreover every council chairman 'shall be elected annually by the council from among the councillors'[14] and 'shall, unless he resigns or becomes disqualified, continue in office until his successor becomes entitled to act as chairman', notwithstanding the normal rules as to retirement. If the chairman—whether or not, as in a London borough, termed the 'mayor'—has come to the end of a period as councillor, and did not stand for re-election to the council, or has failed to be re-elected, he or she may not cast any vote in the election of a successor except for a casting vote in the event of there being 'an equality of votes'; and the same is true of the vice-chairman.[15]

Parish and community councils may, and other councils must, appoint a vice-chairman as well as a chairman. The person appointed 'shall, unless he resigns or becomes disqualified, hold office until immediately after the election of a chairman at the next annual meeting of the council' notwithstanding the normal rules as to retirement.[16] The vice-chairman may act in any way in which the chairman can act, unless standing orders provide otherwise.

3. PARISH AUTHORITIES IN ENGLAND

Parishes in England, in the local government sense, existed only in rural districts when the 1972 Act was passed. These continue to exist subject to some modifications under Parts III and IV of Sch 1; and Part V of Sch 1 empowers the Local Government Boundary Commission for England, after consulting local authorities in the area, to recommend to the Secretary of State that towns demoted from borough or district status under the Act should become local government parishes. Section 9

11 1972 Act, ss 7, 16, 26, 35.
12 S 8, and the London Councillors Order 1976 (SI 1976/213).
13 Ss 14, 15, 23, 34.
14 Ss 3, 15, 22, 34.
15 Ss 4, 15, 23, 34.
16 Ss 5, 15, 24, 34.

provides as follows with regard to local government parishes: 'For every parish there shall be a parish meeting for the purpose of discussing parish affairs and exercising any functions conferred on such meetings by any enactment'. It provides also that a parish with an existing parish council should continue to have that council, and empowers the district council for the area to establish a separate parish council for any parish with 200 or more local government electors (150 or more such electors, if the parish meeting so resolves). This power may be exercised if the parish is one of a number currently grouped under a 'common' parish council, and *must* be exercised if it has no council at all. There are also powers for a district council to group or regroup parishes, and dissolve parish councils in parishes with fewer than 150 local government electors.[17]

A parish which was a parish *council* does not on that account cease to have a parish *meeting*, which comprises all the local government electors for the parish.[18] Where however a parish has no parish council, or is merely one of a number of grouped parishes having a 'common' parish council, the parish meeting must elect a chairman 'at their annual assembly'.[19] All parish meetings must hold this assembly at some date not earlier than 1 March or later than 1 June;[20] though where there is no separate parish council the parish meeting must assemble again on at least one other occasion in the year. Procedure for meetings[1] is similar to that for community meetings in Wales discussed below.[2] The chairman for the year elected by a parish meeting under s 15 in accordance with this rule 'shall continue in office until his successor is elected'. Orders by district councils constituting or reconstituting groups of parishes may however make different and particular arrangements about the holding of parish meeting 'assemblies' or the election of a chairman for a parish meeting.

4. COMMUNITY AUTHORITIES IN WALES

A more radical development was put in hand at parish level in Wales. Existing parish councils there were for some reason renamed 'community councils', and existing parishes (in rural districts only, as in England) were correspondingly renamed 'communities'. Under the 1972 Act, s 27, community councils thus came into existence for separate communities, together with new community councils to be established by the Secretary of State for all or part of any town other than Cardiff,

17 Ss 10–12.
18 S 13.
19 S 15.
20 Sch 12, Part III, para 14.
1 Sch 12, Part III.
2 Sch 12, Part V. See p 204.

Merthyr Tydfil, Newport, Port Talbot, Rhondda and Swansea. Some were also established for groups of communities. The special community review to be carried out as a matter of priority by the Local Government Boundary Commission for Wales under Sch 10 of the 1972 Act, referred to above,[3] is calculated to lead to more communities being created in any or all of the rest of Wales. Subject to this review procedure, any community meeting may require the district council for the area to establish a separate community council for that community,[4] whether the community is one of a number grouped under a common community council or has no council at all. District councils may also be required, by all the community meetings concerned, to constitute or reconstitute groups of communities having common community councils.[5] No application under these provisions can be made to alter arrangements less than two years old.[6]

Community councils in Wales meet and conduct business in much the same way as parish councils in England[7] as discussed above.[8] As for community *meetings*, these like parish meetings in England consist of local government electors for their area.[9] There is no 'assembly' as in England; but a 'meeting' can be convened at any time by the chairman of the community council, or any two councillors from the community serving on that community council, if there is one for the area, or 'in any case' by six local government electors for the community.[10] A prescribed procedure is to be followed. The chairman of the community council, if there is one for the area, presides if present at the meeting; otherwise the meeting chooses its own chairman.[11] The chairman of the community council, if any, is entitled to attend but not to vote, except for duly giving a casting vote as chairman, unless he is a local government elector for the community. No poll can be demanded unless by a third of the local government electors present, and by not less than ten persons, or unless the chairman of the meeting consents.[12] Any poll must be by ballot in due form under s 42: see now the Parish and Community Meetings Polls Rules 1973.[13] Otherwise any 'question to be decided by a community meeting shall, in the first instance, be decided by the majority of those present at the meeting and voting thereon'; and 'each local government elector may, at a community meeting or at a poll

3 See p 192.
4 S 28.
5 S 29.
6 S 30.
7 Sch 12, Parts II and IV.
8 See p 200.
9 S 32.
10 Sch 12, Part V, para 30.
11 Para 33.
12 Para 34.
13 SI 1973/1911.

consequent thereon, give one vote and no more on any question'. If at all possible, 'premises licensed for the sale of intoxicating liquor'[14] are to be avoided.

5. ATTENDANCES, VACANCIES AND DISQUALIFICATIONS

Every person elected as a councillor, or as a chairman or a vice- chairman or deputy chairman, must make an official declaration in due form of acceptance of office.[15] Any such person may resign at any time by delivering written notice to that effect in a prescribed manner;[16] resignation is an official and not a merely personal decision and cannot be reconsidered. Failure for six consecutive months to attend any meeting of an authority, or of a related committee, automatically disqualifies a member unless there is a reason approved by that authority within that time, or some other justification such as absence on service in the armed forces.[17] Loss of membership for this reason, or because a member becomes disqualified by ceasing to comply with the requirements laid down for qualification as discussed earlier in this chapter,[18] creates a casual vacancy,[19] which must be publicly declared by notice to take effect as at a prescribed date.[20]

An election to fill a vacant office of chairman shall be held not later than 'the next ordinary meeting of the council' occurring more than 14 days after the date of the vacancy, either at that meeting or at one specially convened.[1] A bye-election to fill a vacancy for a councillor must take place within 42 days of the notification of that vacancy to the returning officer by two local electors or of its declaration by the High Court or the council as the case may be, but not if there are less than six months to go before the departed councillor would have retired normally unless the total of vacancies is brought above one-third of the council's membership.[2] Rules under s 42, referred to earlier in this chapter,[3] deal with vacancies for parish and community councillors. Drawing lots to resolve a tie in a contested election must be done at once by the returning officer. Anyone who fills a casual vacancy retires at the end of the term for which the person replaced would have served.[4] District councils must appoint persons to fill vacancies for parish

14 Para 32.
15 1972 Act, s 83.
16 S 84.
17 S 85.
18 See p 196.
19 S 86.
20 S 87.
 1 S 88.
 2 S 89.
 3 See p 199.
 4 S 90.

and community councillors if 'there are so many vacancies . . . that the parish or community council are unable to act'.[5]

As for disqualification, any member who becomes disqualified should resign. If he or she refuses, and 'has acted as a member of a local authority', any local government elector for the area, but no-one else, can under s 92 institute proceedings in the High Court for a declaration, an injunction, or an order to 'forfeit to Her Majesty' an amount up to £50 'for each occasion for which he so acted while disqualified'. Proceedings may instead be brought in a magistrates' court for a fine equivalent to the penalty, but may be transferred to the High Court. If however he or she denies being unqualified, proceedings may only be brought in the High Court and there is no financial penalty. Disqualification means that the person does not comply with the requirements for qualification referred to earlier, or does not qualify as a member of the authority in question because of resignation, failure duly to attend, or failure duly to make the declaration of acceptance. Disqualification extends to membership of committees of or connected with the authority[6] except for teachers or similar employees of any assisted or maintained educational establishment or local authority committees set up for educational purposes or under the Public Libraries and Museums Act 1964, including joint committees. Members of the GLC may not vote, in council or committee, on any financial matters not affecting their electoral area, except to give a valid casting vote when in the chair.[7]

6. PECUNIARY INTEREST

An important restriction is contained in s 94, to the effect that: 'if a member of a local authority has any pecuniary interest, direct or indirect, in any contract, proposed contract or other matter, and is present at a meeting of the local authority at which the contract or other matter is the subject of consideration, he shall at the meeting and as soon as practicable after its commencement disclose the fact and shall not take part in the consideration or discussion of the contract or other matter or vote on any question with respect to it'. A member who knowingly fails to comply is liable on summary conviction to a fine up to £200 if prosecuted by or on behalf of the Direction of Public Prosecutions.

Lord Esher MR said in *Nutton v Wilson*[8] that this provision 'is intended to prevent the members of local [authorities] . . . from being exposed to temptation, or even to the semblance of temptation'. In

5 S 91.
6 S 104.
7 S 93.
8 (1889) 22 QBD 744.

Rands v Oldroyd,[9] it was suggested that in the words 'contract or other matter' the expression 'other matter' means merely some specific trans-action which can be construed as ejusdem generis with 'contract'. But Lord Parker CJ said: 'Bearing in mind the mischief aimed at by this Act, I do not think those words are to be read in other than a very gen-eral way . . .' As a result it was held that a councillor had a 'pecuniary interest' in a vote relating to the local authority's direct labour force, by reason of the fact that he was himself a local building contractor whose firm, by submitting tenders for council contracts, could well compete with the direct labour force. He had voted for an amendment, which was passed, to reject a proposal to extend the direct labour force. Yet he had also in fact decided that his firm should not, for the time being at least, submit any tenders for council contracts.

A 'pecuniary interest' also exists where a person 'or any nominee of his' is a member of a company which has any such interest; or where a person is the partner or employee of another person who has any such interest; or where a person lives with a spouse who, to his or her know-ledge, has such an interest.[10] But this provision does not apply to mem-bership of a company or other body by any person who has no benefi-cial interest in it, nor to membership of, or employment by, any *public* body including any nationalised industry or educational institution or the National Trust.[11] The right of council members to claim due expen-ses and allowances is not a 'pecuniary interest'.[12]

'Pecuniary interest' is a neutral term which does not restrict disabil-ity to cases in which members vote for decisions which will tend to their financial benefit. In *Brown v DPP*,[13] Lord Goddard CJ put it as fol-lows: 'Parliament has not said that they may vote against their interest and not for their interest: it has said that they must not vote on any mat-ter in which they have a pecuniary interest'. It was therefore held that a council tenant could not participate in a vote on a proposal to increase council house rents, even by voting for the increase.

But supplies and services to the public as a whole, or ratepayers as a whole, as distinct from special groups such as council tenants however numerous, do not involve any such 'pecuniary interest' notwithstand-ing payment by a member as a consumer of these facilities. Section 97, which states this, also enacts a de minimis rule, so that an interest 'which is so remote or insignificant that it cannot reasonably be regarded as likely to influence a member' does not count. Nor does 'a beneficial interest in securities of a company or other body' if 'the total

9 [1959] 1 QB 204, [1958] 3 All ER 344.
10 S 95.
11 S 98.
12 S 94(5).
13 [1956] 2 QB 369, [1956] 2 All ER 189.

nominal value of those securities does not exceed £1,000 or one hundredth of the total nominal value of the issued share capital of the company or body, whichever is the less'; though in this kind of case the member must declare his interest. Section 97 also empowers the Secretary of State to remove the disability arising from a 'pecuniary interest' under s 94, conditionally or unconditionally, 'in any case in which the number of members of the local authority disabled by that section at any one time would be so great a proportion of the whole as to impede the transaction of business', or for any other good reason. This does not apply to parish and community councillors; but a similar power exercisable for their benefit is conferred on district councils. The relieving power may be exercised in relation to such interests and matters as may be specified; and the Secretary of State may exercise it for 'any class or description of member' and not merely for particular individuals. No councillor is precluded 'from taking part in the consideration or discussion of, or voting on', a proposal to apply for this relief.

It is a 'sufficient disclosure' under s 94 for a councillor to give written notice, unless and until it is withdrawn, of any organisation or partnership for which he or she works (or his or her spouse), and the same applies to tenancies of council housing. The authority should have a 'proper officer' to record all disclosures and keep these available for inspection by all the members.[14]

If a councillor disregards the obligation to disclose any 'pecuniary interest' in any matter and to abstain from considering or discussing that matter or voting on it, the question arises whether there are any consequences other than the possibility of prosecution. In *Re Louth Municipal Election, Nell v Longbottom*,[15] a vote cast by a member in a matter in which he had an interest was held to be invalid and therefore not cast at all. In *R v Hendon RDC ex p Chorley*,[16] a councillor who had an interest in certain landed property took part in a vote on whether 'interim development control' should apply to it under the planning legislation of that time. This was held not merely to be wrong as regards the member and his pecuniary interest, but tantamount to bias on the part of the authority, acting 'quasi-judicially', so that their decision was ultra vires and must be quashed by certiorari.

It may be added here that the restrictions arising from 'pecuniary interest' apply not only to council meetings but to committee meetings also, including joint committees.[17]

---

14 S 96.
15 (1894) 63 LJQB 490.
16 [1933] 2 KB 696.
17 S 105.

7. DELEGATION TO COMMITTEES

Parts VI and VII[18] of the 1972 act make general provision for the conduct by local authorities of their business. First and foremost is s 101, which confers a very wide power for any authority to 'arrange for the discharge of any of their functions—(a) by a committee, a sub-committee or an officer of the authority; or (b) by any other local authority.'

This involves considering the concept of 'delegation'. There is a legal maxim: delegatus non potest delegare—ie a person to whom functions are delegated cannot in turn sub-delegate them to someone else. This is applicable to fiduciary responsibilities in the law of trusts, but also to administrative functions. There is an ambiguity in it, as between executive acts and legal responsibilities. The true legal significance is probably that *executive acts* can be sub-delegated to some other person if, but only if, it is reasonable in the circumstances to do so, while legal *responsibility* remains in the person to whom it was originally delegated unless the terms of the delegation clearly authorise its sub-delegation. Section 101 of the 1972 Act does not empower local authorities to transfer responsibilities, merely to 'arrange' how the functions entrusted to them shall be 'discharged'. Where responsibilities lie in law is a separate question.

In any case local authorities are abstractions and therefore cannot themselves carry out physical actions of any kind whatever but must operate through executive agents. Even the group of individual persons to whom collectively the abstract personality of incorporation is attached can only carry out one physical activity in their corporate capacity, which is to take policy decisions by passing resolutions at meetings. All other 'actions' of corporate bodies are carried out physically by agents in furtherance, or purportedly in furtherance, of those decisions. But the responsibility of the abstract person which is the corporation need not be affected by this. As *principal* it is answerable for those things which are done by its *agents* in its name, or for their failure to do those things which should have been done.

A consequence of those realities is that, subject to any rule about a quorum,[19] it is immaterial how many individual members of the incorporated group are present at meetings, or for that matter how many of those who are present actually participate in any real sense. A formal meeting could in strictly practical terms take decisions if only one individual attended it. There is therefore no *practical* obstacle in the way of a full meeting taking a *formal* decision that a fraction of its members should be entrusted with some or all of its decision-making, ie that such matters should be *committed* to the smaller group. *Committees* means in

18 Ss 101–110 and 111–146.
19 See above, p 201.

law the person or persons to whom some responsibility is committed, on a formal basis. If only a small number of persons out of a larger group is involved in decision-making it saves time and effort in arranging and conducting the meetings involved. It is often convenient to give formal recognition to this.

8. GROWTH OF THE COMMITTEE SYSTEM

Parliament long ago recognised the convenience of the committee system. So did local authorities: it has a great attraction for the oligarchically-minded. This is especially true of the counties; and it is probably right to say that the committee system obtained its strong hold on local government as a result of its development before 1888 by the county magistrates in quarter sessions. Their body as a whole consisted of a great many magistrates who though meeting in a formal but unwieldly group every three months, were much more interested for the rest of the time in the affairs of their local parishes, or at any rate in their petty sessional divisions broadly comparable in area with modern districts.

In the eighteenth century it became increasingly common for quarter sessions in various counties to delegate functions to committees comprising some of their number in small groups. The process was slowest in the remotest counties. In their English Local Government volume *The Parish and the County*, the Webbs say:[20] 'We did not notice in the manuscript Minutes of Quarter Sessions, Breconshire, that the word "committee" was ever used until 1814'. But they show[1] that standing committees were already being appointed in Middlesex in George I's time. In 1723 it was recommended there that the county accounts should annually be 'examined and a state thereof drawn up by a committee to be appointed and approved by the Sessions'. The Webbs add[2] that, by the early nineteenth century: 'In the admirably organised County of Gloucester the system of committees, standing and special, was extended to all the county services—a General Audit Committee, a Vagrant Committee, various Bridge Committees, as well as specialist committees on the prison dietary, on the county archives, and on the actuarial bases of friendly societies . . . In 1834 it is even ordered that no account be submitted to Quarter Sessions for payment unless it has 'first submitted to a standing Committee of Accounts'.

This 'admirably organised' use of committees passed over from the nineteenth century local government system of county magistrates and municipal borough corporations into the twentieth century local government system of county and district councils. The 1972 Act[3]

20 P 529.
 1 P 531.
 2 P 532.
 3 S 101.

makes this committee system as flexible and adaptable as possible. Local authorities can 'arrange' for committees, sub-committees or officers to 'discharge any of their functions'. They can also arrange for other local authorities to discharge functions; and those authorities in turn can delegate to committees, sub-committees and officers. Committees can delegate to sub-committees and officers. Sub-committees can delegate to officers. But delegation of functions does not prevent the delegating council, committee or sub-committee from continuing to administer them as well. In addition, two or more authorities can delegate jointly on such basis as they choose[4] 'subject to all necessary modifications' to relevant enactments. Parish councils can delegate to parish meetings,[5] and parish meetings can delegate to committees of their members.[6]

9. RESTRICTIONS ON DELEGATION

There are, however, some exceptions to the application of this libertarian principle. Borrowing money, or levying (or precepting for) a rate, must not be delegated by the responsible authority.[7] Functions under the Diseases of Animals Act 1950 cannot be delegated to another authority.[8] Requirements in particular Acts for specified committees to be set up are expressly retained in the following cases:[9] education committees of local education committes;[10] the special education committee of the GLC;[11] police committees;[12] any committee under the Sea Fisheries Regulation Act 1966, s 1; children's regional planning committees;[13] social services committees;[14] any committee on local government superannuation, etc;[15] and joint and special boards and committees dealing with planning and countryside administration in National Parks.[16] In these special cases local authorities can delegate functions to their officers but not to any committee or sub-committee, nor to any other authority.[17] Special committee requirements in other pre-1972 statutes were repealed.[18] But s 101(11) authorises the GLC to delegate functions

4 Including financial: s 103.
5 S 109.
6 S 108.
7 S 101(6).
8 S 101(7).
9 S 101(9).
10 Education Act 1944, Sch 1 Part II, paras 1, 3–11.
11 London Government Act 1963, s 30(2).
12 Police Act 1964, ss 2, 3.
13 Children and Young Persons Act 1969, s 35(3).
14 Local Authority Social Services Act 1970, s 2.
15 Superannuation Act 1972, s 7.
16 Sch 17, Part I of the 1972 Act itself.
17 S 101(10).
18 S 101(9).

to the Inner London Education Authority or a committee thereof set up under the Education Act 1944, Sch 1, Part II; and the London Government Act 1963, s 5, still empowers the GLC to delegate various functions to London borough councils and the City Corporation and authorises agency arrangements among local authorities within or contiguous to Greater London.[19] Similarly, the Local Authorities (Goods and Services) Act 1970 still empowers local authorities to contract to furnish one another with goods, materials, provision of administrative or professional or technical services, the use of plant or the performance of works of maintenance as distinct from construction.

Further details are contained in s 102. The general power to delegate by appointment of committees, sub-committees and joint committees must be exercised subject to a clear specification of size of membership, term of office and scope of authority in each case. Outside members may be co-opted, except to a finance committee, up to a maximum of one-third of the committee membership, provided that they are not persons who are disqualified from standing for election as councillors should they so wish.[20] Anyone who retires as a councillor without being immediately re-elected ceases to be a committee member. The rule that statutory authority to carry out local government functions extends to 'the doing of anything which is calculated to facilitate, or is conducive or incidental to, the discharge of any of those functions' applies also to the performance of delegated functions under these provisions.[1]

These provisions as to delegation by local authorities also apply in general terms to police authorities (other than the Home Secretary), with some exceptions; for example one police authority cannot delegate to another and power to delegate to officers is extremely limited.

10. COUNCILLORS' RIGHTS AND CONFIDENTIALITY

The decisions taken by local authorities, and the steps taken to prepare for and to implement those decisions, are the work of individuals at the practical level but are not done for any individual's benefit, even individual council members. It is true that an individual member cannot be compelled to serve on a committee: *R v Sunderland Corp*;[2] but it is even truer that the authority cannot be compelled to allow a member to serve on a committee, since it cannot be compelled (in the absence of special statutory provisions) even to set up the committee or to retain it in existence. In *Manton v Brighton Corp*[3] the plaintiff was a councillor who claimed that the defendant council had no right to revoke his member-

---

19 S 101(14).
20 S 104.
 1 S 101(12).
 2 [1911] 2 KB 458.
 3 [1951] 2 KB 393, [1951] 2 All ER 101.

ship of a committee; he failed because the council could revoke the authority of the entire committee at any time, let alone the authority of any individual member of it. But while a committee functions its decisions bind the authority which set it up. In *Battelley v Finsbury Borough Council*,[4] the plaintiff succeeded in a claim that the offer of employment to him by a committee could not be disregarded by the local authority whose committee it was.

There is often a question of 'the consideration of the public interests involved', as Lord Denning MR said in *R v City of Birmingham District Council, ex p O*.[5] In that case the applicants were foster parents of a child placed in the care of the local authority. Their application to adopt gave rise to long discussions, in the light of their particular circumstances. A councillor who was familiar with these (for official reasons) asked to see certain confidential files of the social services committee on the applicants; but, not being on that committee she was refused access to the files. The requirement in the Local Authority Social Services Act 1970, s 2, for the appropriate authorities to have these committees was referred to above.[6] Lord Denning said that the nature of files of this kind is so confidential 'that in general the courts will not allow or require them to be disclosed: not in wardship proceedings or custody proceedings (see *Official Solicitor v K*,[7] *Re D (infants)*;[8] nor in actions by parents or foster parents (see *D v National Society for the Prevention of Cruelty to Children*;[9] nor in an action by the child himself (see *Gaskin v Liverpool City Council*);[10] nor in adoptive proceedings (see reg 10 of the Adoption Agencies Regulations 1976);[11] but it might do so if the interests of justice were so great as to outweigh the interest in preserving confidentiality (see *Re P A (an infant)*[12] . . .'

The local authority's solicitor advised that the files should be shown to the councillor to enable her to carry out her duties as a council member; whereupon the foster parents sought a prerogative order of prohibition. This was refused by the Queen's Bench Divisional Court, but granted by a majority of the Court of Appeal on the following ground. Delegation to the committee meant that, subject to any subsequent decision to the contrary by the full council, it was for the committee to decide how far the information in its files was confidential and how it should be used. On balance, in the circumstances of this case, the pub-

---

4 (1958) 56 LGR 165.
5 [1982] 2 All ER 356, [1982] 1 WLR 679. But now see below, p 220.
6 See p 211.
7 [1965] AC 201, [1963] 3 All ER 191.
8 [1970] 1 All ER 1088, [1970] 1 WLR 599.
9 [1978] AC 171, [1977] 1 All ER 598.
10 [1980] 1 WLR 1549.
11 SI 1976/1796.
12 [1971] 3 All ER 522, [1971] 1 WLR 1530.

lic interest in council members as a whole being fully informed so as to
enable them to carry out their duties properly, though a very important
legal principle, was overridden by the public interest in maintaining the
confidentiality of the files, which is equally an important legal principle, being narrower but more intense. But the House of Lords decided
otherwise (see below, p 220) and reversed the decision.

In *R v Lancashire County Council Police Authority, ex p Hook*,[13] a
newly elected councillor was refused permission to inspect a report of
an official inquiry into certain complaints about the local police. The
report was regarded as containing statements inherently capable of
founding one or more actions for libel; and any qualified privilege
which applied to it might well be lost if there was too wide a publication. In all the circumstances it was not reasonably necessary to the performance of the applicant's functions as a council member for the
report to be disclosed to him; and the majority of the Court of Appeal
rejected the claim for a prerogative order of mandamus to compel such
disclosure. In this application of the principle that an individual councillor can only compel disclosure of documents to him 'if it is reasonably necessary to enable him properly to perform his duties as a member of the council', the court was following *R v Barnes Borough Council,
ex p Conlan*.[14] In that case a councillor who objected to certain legal proceedings being conducted by his local authority[15] failed in his claim to
obtain access to the documents relevant to their case. 'Perhaps he
wanted to tell the other side about it. That was going too far.'[16]

A case which went the other way is *Campbell v Tameside Metropolitan
Borough Council*.[17] The plaintiff schoolteacher was severely injured by a
violent pupil, but before deciding whether to bring an action for negligence against the employing authority sought 'preliminary discovery' of
relevant documents which, as Lord Denning MR commented, 'is now
permitted by statute and by the rules'. The defendants claimed that the
documents, being confidential, should not be disclosed because staff
whose duty involved making such reports would be inhibited from committing themselves frankly in future. The Court of Appeal refused to
believe that there was a real likelihood of a general feeling of inhibition
descending upon local authority staff if such disclosure was ordered, and
said that it is necessary to weigh in the balance the public interest in the
maintenance of proper confidentiality against the public interest in
achieving justice with the help of the production of documents for the
pursuance of rightful claims. The plaintiff's application succeeded.

---

13 [1980] QB 603, [1980] 2 All ER 353.
14 [1938] 3 All ER 226.
15 They were defending an action brought against them.
16 Per Lord Denning MR, in [1980] QB 603 at 618, [1980] 2 All ER 353 at 359.
17 [1982] 2 All ER 791, [1982] 3 WLR 74.

The public interest that individual councillors should be sufficiently well informed about council business is therefore, though important in law, limited by the consideration that it applies only to their functioning ex officio in furtherance of their council's work. If a councillor demands to know something he will be met by the question, *not*: 'is it in your interests to know that, Councillor X?', but: 'is it in the council's interests that you should know that, Councillor X?' It may be limited even further by counter-considerations of public interest in matters such as preserving confidentiality and furthering the cause of justice. What an individual can do under the law is one thing; what that individual can do in the capacity of a councillor is quite another, and the distinction must in the public interest be rigorously observed.

11. DEFAMATION AND PRIVILEGE

Councillors enjoy the benefit as distinct from the burden of this distinction. As councillors their essential role is to lend their voice at council and committee meetings to the deliberations which culminate in decision-making and the evolution of policies for government at local level. Therefore frank speaking on relevant matters, but not irrelevant ones, should never be inhibited by fears of defamation actions.

Here, as elsewhere in the public interest, there is 'privilege'. Whereas in the proceedings of Parliament and the Supreme Court this privilege of the freedom of speech is absolute, in local council meetings it is qualified. The difference is, however, fairly narrow. Qualified, as against absolute, privilege does not cover statements actuated by malice. This means *deliberate* utterance in violation of the law; and what the law requires is that untruths shall not be said to the detriment of people's reputations. An untrue statement is *deliberately* uttered if the speaker does not believe it to be true, irrespective of what every other person, or every reasonable person may think. The test, therefore, is subjective. In *Horrocks v Lowe*,[18] the defendant made a defamatory statement about the plaintiff at a meeting of the council to which they both belonged. The trial judge found as a fact that the statement, though untrue, was believed by the defendant, even if by no-one else, to be true. The House of Lords held that this exonerated the defendant from liability for slander, because honest belief brought him within the scope of qualified privilege. This was so even if his state of mind displayed 'gross and unreasoning prejudices'.

Qualified privilege covers those who report statements as well as those who make them. The Defamation Act 1952, s 7, extends it to copies, and fair and accurate reports and summaries, of what is said at council or committee meetings, or of statements issued by local author-

18 [1975] AC 135, [1974] 1 All ER 662.

ities to the public—notices, press releases and the like—provided that, when asked, those publishing the allegedly defamatory statements publish reasonable counter-statements of denial or explanation.

But this privilege does not cover reports of meetings not open to the press and the public. A general right of public admission to meetings is given by the Public Bodies (Admission to Meetings) Act 1960, including local authorities, joint bodies, parish meetings and the like. The press must be supplied, on request, with the agenda and other details. The 1972 Act,[19] extends this to local authority committees generally, including occasions when an authority resolves to go into a committee of its entire membership for the purpose of relaxing formal rules of debate. Yet authorities can expressly resolve to exclude the press and the public if the particular circumstances on any occasion demand it in the public interest, for 'special reasons' which the resolution must state. There are for example occasions when, in fairness to individuals (including the authority's own officers), confidentiality must be preserved; and where the circumstances reasonably indicate this an authority can act accordingly. The Act of 1960 requires three clear days' notice of meetings to be displayed publicly, to make it easier for the public to be able to attend.

Publication of any defamatory statement goes outside the boundaries of qualified privilege where it is extended to hearers or readers who have no sufficient interest to receive it. Obviously this cannot apply to the extent that public reporting is lawful, but it will apply on these occasions where confidentiality is necessary. In *De Buse v McCarthy and Stepney Borough Council*,[20] damaging statements about persons who were believed to have helped themselves to the council's petrol were made in an official report to the council. What should have been a confidential consideration of this report was carelessly made available to press and public as part of a routine distribution locally of news of the council's proceedings. Such publication in the circumstances was much too extensive to be covered by qualified privilege; and the individuals responsible, together with the local authority corporately, were liable.

C. Staff, management and ceremonial

1. OFFICERS

The appointment of staff, particularly the chief officers of the various council departments, is very much at the discretion of each local authority, within the bounds of reasonableness. The 1972 Act,[1] lays

---

19 S 100.
20 [1942] 1 KB 156, [1942] 1 All ER 19.
 1 S 112.

down in general terms that they 'shall appoint such officers as they think necessary for the proper discharge' by them of their functions, or any other authority's functions which they are lawfully carrying out. Officers 'shall hold office on such reasonable terms and conditions, including conditions as to remuneration', as the authority think fit.[2] Freedom of appointment does not, however, extend to certain officers who under other statutes must be appointed.[3] These are: GLC district surveyors and deputies, under the London Building Acts Amendment Act 1939;[4] chief education officers, under the Education Act 1944;[5] chief officers and other staff required to be appointed under the Fire Services Act 1947; inspectors of weights and measures, under the Weights and Measures Act 1963; the chief education officer of the Inner London Education Authority, under the London Government Act 1963;[6] agricultural analysts and deputies, under the Agriculture Act 1970;[7] and directors of social services, under the Local Authority Social Services Act 1970.[8] In addition there continues to be a duty to appoint public analysts under the Food and Drugs Act 1955,[9] and any other particular person required to carry out some specified function. But council members must not be appointed as officers.[10]

One such specified function of a local authority is responsibility for 'the proper administration of their financial affairs', which they must entrust to one of their officers in accordance with the 1972 Act, s 151, whether they choose to call him their 'treasurer', 'comptroller', 'director of finance' or any other title. But all officers to whose charge the local authority's money is in any way entrusted are, under s 115, strictly accountable for it at all times during their tenure of office, and remain so for three months afterwards, and must duly make all such payments as they are directed to make. Officers have under s 117 a duty to disclose pecuniary interests similar to the duty of council members under ss 94–98. Financial staff are discussed above, on p 157.

2. STAFFING ARRANGEMENTS

Local authorities may second their officers, provided that they consult them first, to other local authorities.[11] For superannuation purposes their service during secondment is regarded as service with the author-

2 S 112(2).
3 S 112(4).
4 SS 75, 80.
5 S 88.
6 S 30(4).
7 S 67(3).
8 S 6.
9 S 89.
10 1972 Act, s 116.
11 S 113.

ity seconding them, though for the purpose of discharge of functions they are in the service of the authority to whom they are seconded.

Connected with service and superannuation is compensation for loss of office. Under s 259, regulations have been made to compensate for 'loss or diminution of emoluments which is attributable to' the 1972 Act or 'any instrument' made under it. The Local Government (Compensation) Regulations 1974[12] were made under this provision, and were in issue in *Mallet v Restormel Borough Council*.[13] Shortly after the reorganisation under the 1972 Act, in which Newquay Urban District Council in Cornwall disappeared and was replaced by the defendant authority, the plaintiff, who had been manager of the local authority's airport under both councils, became redundant when the defendants decided to place it under the management of a company. He claimed resettlement and long-term compensation under these regulations, arguing that the loss of his employment was 'attributable' to the 1972 Act, as stated in s 259, because the continuance of the old council would have meant the continuance of his post as airport manager. The defendants argued that 'attributable' referred solely to direct consequences of local government reorganisation, not indirect ones; but Griffiths J held that this was 'an unnaturally restricted meaning' and not consistent with provisions in the regulations keeping compensation rights open for ten years. He therefore remitted the case to the industrial tribunal, which had heard the claim and rejected it in reliance on the defendant's legal arguments. If a newly-constituted tribunal found on the facts that the old council would have continued the direct management of the airport, then the claim would be justified; but he stressed that the burden of proof lay on the plaintiff and would not be easy to satisfy.[14]

Other provisions dealt with staff adjustments under the reorganisation of local government; but as far as continuing importance goes it is sufficient here to note the setting up of a staff commission for England[15] and one for Wales,[16] to promote fairness and efficiency in local government service in regard to staff recruitment, appointment and transfers, and advise the Secretary of State thereon.

3. MANAGEMENT

As far as general questions of management are concerned, ss 132–4 of the 1972 Act empower local authorities including parishes and communities

12 SI 1974/463.
13 [1978] 1 All ER 503.
14 A change of policy, in itself, cannot be said to be attributable to the 1972 Act: see *Walsh v Rother District Council* [1978] 3 All ER 881.
15 S 257.
16 S 258.

to acquire and provide 'halls, offices and other buildings', in their area or elsewhere, for public meetings and assemblies, including the hire of local school premises where parishes and communities lack a suitable hall for such use. Sections 120–131 deal with land transactions. On the whole these involve questions of acquisition by compulsion or agreement which are dealt with elsewhere in works on compulsory purchase and related matters.[17] It may be noted that in s 122 there is a general power to appropriate land from use for one purpose to use for another, but not normally within ten years of compulsory acquisition unless the minister concerned with approving its acquisition consents, and not in the case of open spaces and allotments exceeding 250 square yards. Disposals of land are also a matter for the discretion of the authorities which own it (s 123), but not land exceeding 250 square yards if 'held as public walks or pleasure grounds or in accordance with s 10 of the Open Spaces Act 1906 (public open spaces)'. Ministerial consent is needed for disposals at less than full market value, and in circumstances similar to those in s 122. Parish and community councils needing to acquire land compulsorily must apply to the district council to do so on their behalf;[18] but their acquisitions by agreement,[19] appropriations[20] and disposals[1] are treated in much the same way as those of larger authorities. In general these provisions operate without prejudice to more specific requirements in other Acts dealing with various particular functions.[2]

As for contracts, a local authority's standing orders may contain rules governing how they are made, and *must* do so in respect of contracts relating to supply of goods and carrying out works—notably provisions for tendering, except in respect of values below a specified level, or where special circumstances justify exemption.[3]

4. POMP AND CIRCUMSTANCE

The traditional decorative side of local goverment was not altogether overlooked in the 1972 Act. The style, ceremonial and dignities of historic cities and boroughs were generally preserved.[4] Authorities newly

---

17 Note, however, the Local Government (Miscellaneous Provisions) Act 1976, s 13, and Sch 1, under which local authorities, but not other public bodies, may compulsorily acquire 'new rights' in land as distinct from existing ones.

18 S 125.

19 S 124.

20 S 126.

1 S 127.

2 S 131.

3 S 135. As regards the general question of local authority management, see the Local Government (Miscellaneous Provisions) Act 1976, Part I, and the Local Government (Miscellanous Provisions) Act 1982, Part XII, which deal with an assortment of matters such as computers, insurance, legal liability, etc.

4 S 246.

set up under the Act are given power to petition for a charter conferring similar privileges and dignities, if a specially convened meeting so resolves by a two-thirds majority;[5] and parishes and communities can become 'towns' and have a 'town mayor' and deputy. The inherited office of 'freeman' was preserved in historic cities and towns, together with the right in future to claim the status of 'freeman'[6] subject to the rule that 'his claim for admission shall be examined by the chairman of the relevant district council'. Any London borough, and any district which has the status of a borough or city[7] whether new or historical, can confer the rank of *honorary* freeman on persons who are thought deserving;[8] and counties, districts and London authorities can confer the rank of 'honorary alderman' on former members of the council, or of a predecessor council, in recognition of their services. Her Majesty by Order in Council may transfer armorial bearings of pre-1972 authorities to new authorities,[9] provided that they are first 'exemplified according to the laws of arms and recorded in the College of Arms'.

NOTE—The decision of the Court of Appeal in *R v City of Birmingham District Council v O* (above, p 213) has been reversed by the House of Lords, thus making it clear that councillors are entitled to see documents, notwithstanding confidentiality, if this is reasonably necessary to enable them properly to perform their duties as members of the council.[10] Lord Brightman said that, unlike a councillor who is a member of a particular committee to which confidential documents relate, a councillor who is not such a member 'has no automatic right of access to documentary material . . . a "need to know" must be demonstrated' before he can claim to see such documents. This calls for a delicate 'screening process'. The decision 'is ultimately one to be taken by the councillors themselves sitting in council'. But it can be expressly or impliedly delegated, possibly to the relevant chief officer (or deputy). Like any other exercise of discretion, it is subject to the ultra vires doctrine and therefore to the *Wednesbury* principle discussed in Chapter 3 (p 63).

5 S 245.
6 S 248.
7 Under ss 245–6.
8 S 249.
9 S 247. See *Manchester Corp v Manchester Palace of Varieties* [1955] P 133, [1955] 1 All ER 387 (above, p 53).
10 *City of Birmingham District Council v O* [1983] 1 All ER 497.

Chapter 9

Governmental control of local authorities

A. Legislative procedures

I. PRIVATE LEGISLATION

The intervention of the Secretary of State for the Environment and other ministers has been noted at a great many points during the survey of various aspects of the law in the foregoing chapters. A general intervention process which should be mentioned at this point occurs in local legislation. Local authorities as corporations have always shared in the power enjoyed by all persons, natural and artificial, subject to existing statutes, to petition Parliament for conferment of special powers and rights by private Acts.

The Local Government Act 1972, s 239, now replaces all existing private legislative provisions governing local authorities' rights to petition for private Acts by a standardised provision. All local authorities including parish and community councils can, if they think it 'expedient', oppose any private Bill; and local authorities with the exception of parish and community councils can promote a private Bill. The procedure which must first be followed is that a meeting shall be held, after 'requisite' advance notice in the local press over and above the ordinary notice of meetings, at which a resolution to promote or oppose a private Bill, as the case may be, is 'passed by a majority of the whole number of the members of the authority'. As stated previously,[1] 'whole number' means the number of the entire membership of councillors, vacancies included: *Newhaven Local Board v Newhaven School Board*.[2] 'Requisite notice is 30 'clear days' for promoting Bills and 10 'clear days' for opposing them; and, as stated previously,[3] 'clear days' are calculated by excluding both the date of service of the notice and the date of the meeting: *R v Herefordshire Justices*.[4] A resolution to promote a Bill must also be 'confirmed by a like majority at a further such meeting' convened similarly and 'held as soon as may be after the expiration of fourteen days after the Bill has been deposited in Parliament' failing which 'the

---

1 See ch 8, p 201.
2 (1885) 30 Ch D 350.
3 See ch 8, p 200.
4 (1820) 3 B & Ald 581.

local authority shall take all necessary steps to withdraw the Bill'. The authority must not pay any of its members for acting as counsel or agent. It will however be remembered that local authorities cannot, since the 1972 Act, promote a Bill to change any local government area or 'electoral arrangements'[5] because changes of that kind must be done in accordance with the procedures in Part IV of the Act.

Countless private Acts have been passed over the years conferring powers and duties, rights and obligations, on local authorities up and down the land. The 1972 Act, s 262, enacts a procedure for rationalising pre-existing local legislation. Subject to a power in s 254 for the Secretary of State to make any necessary modifications to administrative arrangements, by statutory instrument, and to a general provision in s 262 itself that local Act provisions were normally to continue to apply for the time being in the same areas in which they were effective previously, despite amalgamations of areas and boundary changes, he or any 'appropriate minister' may nevertheless modify such provisions to ensure as far as possible that they 'operate harmoniously'. There is also in s 262 a general rule that local Act provisions should have ended by the end of 1979 in metropolitan counties and by the end of 1984 'elsewhere'; but this was subject to such exemptions and postponements as the Secretary of State or 'appropriate minister' might think desirable. A minister is 'appropriate' in accordance with the governmental functions referred to in the relevant local Act: for example if it deals with schools he will be the Secretary of State for Education and Science. Any existing local Act provision for the Secretary of State to adjust the charging of tolls was repealed outright.

Apart from these rules, s 251 and Sch 29 provide for various consequential amendments of existing statutes, s 252 authorises the making of any further such amendments as are necessary by Order in Council, and s 253 empowers the Secretary of State by order to make such transfers of functions as are desirable from one authority to another, provided that they consent.

2. NATURE OF MINISTERIAL SUPERVISION

Within existing statutory rules, central governmental control takes many forms. Under the original common law the Crown was the source of all authority: legislative, executive and judicial. Any public authority or personage was subject to royal control. In essence this royal prerogative still survives in law; but for most practical purposes it has been superseded by statute because the common law, at least since 1688, recognises that the Crown in Parliament is superior to the Crown alone. For the purposes of local government virtually everything is statutory,

---

5 S 70. See ch 8, p 188.

apart from royal charters and their contents which are virtually concerned merely with ceremonial. What local authorities may do, and what ministers may tell them to do, are dependent on statute.

The surprising thing is that this system does not impose, at any rate on the surface, a coherent pattern of control. The guiding spirit is one of pragmatism. The need for ministerial supervision, and its nature, we are all expected to regard as self-evident, in reality perhaps as a convention of the constitution. Detailed statutory provisions exist in plenty; but the principle is inferred from these details by legal recognition founded on long use. Occasionally an Act gives an express formulation of central control in principle, but only for some particular aspect of administration.

The Minister of Town and Country Planning Act 1943,[6] created the post of minister of that name 'charged with the duty of securing consistency and continuity in the framing and execution of a national policy with respect to the use and development of land throughout England and Wales'. The minister on whom this duty was laid subsequently became transformed into the Minister of Local Government and Planning; later in the same year (1951) the name was changed to the more ideologically respectable one of Minister of Housing and Local Government. During these years English planning law evolved through a series of statutes into something very like what it is today, as regards the detailed functions of local planning authorities as well as the generalised functions of the central government. All of a sudden, in 1970, s 1 of the Act of 1943 was repealed by the Secretary of State for the Environment Order 1970[7] which was made under the Ministers of the Crown Act 1964, s 4. The wording in s 1 of the 1943 Act thus ceased to be part of the law. It was not re-enacted or replaced in any way. But the functions of the central government in regard to planning administration were not in the slightest affected by this change and have continued to be exercised to this day in exactly the same way. Only the particular details change, not the principles.

Other statutes also impose general duties. The Local Authority Social Services Act 1970,[8] requires local authorities 'in the exercise of their social services functions' to act 'under the general guidance of the Secretary of State'. The Housing (Homeless Persons) Act 1977,[9] requires local authorities to 'have regard in the exercise of their functions to such guidance as may from time to time be given by the Secretary of State'. 'Guidance' is a vague but comforting word. Any such provision can hardly be treated as directly enforceable in legal proceedings

6 S 1.
7 SI 1970/1681.
8 S 7. The Secretary of State for Social Services is meant.
9 S 12. The Secretary of State for the Environment is meant.

of any kind whatever; but it must obviously have an indirect legal effect. If a dispute arises over whether the policy of a local authority or a Minister in any of these fields of administration should be legally upheld as being intra vires or quashed as ultra vires, one of the tests which should be applied to it is whether it conforms with the stated duty or not.

Even this, however, is a statement of theory rather than practice. Those provisions are much too broad to be the subject of any likely dispute between authorities, or between an aggrieved person and an authority. In effect they enact truisms which give expression to the general expectations in governmental circles of how a given system of administration should work.

3. LIMITS OF MINISTERIAL SUPERVISION

One such provision which has in fact received judicial consideration is s 1 of the Education Act 1944. This concerns (now) the Secretary of State for Education and Science, 'whose duty it shall be to promote the education of the people of England and Wales and the progressive development of institutions devoted to that purpose, and to secure the effective execution by local authorities, under his control and direction, of the national policy for providing a varied and comprehensive educational service in every area'.

In *Secretary of State for Education and Science v Tameside Metropolitan Borough Council*,[10] Lord Diplock expressed his judgement of the effect of s 1 of the 1944 Act as follows, in regard to a dispute between central and local government over the introduction of certain comprehensive schools in the area of a particular local education authority. He said:

'The Act does not leave the national policy for education to be determined from time to time by successive Secretaries of State. The Act itself says what the policy is. In s 1 its purpose is described as being for providing a varied and comprehensive educational service in every area. In this context comprehensive bears its dictionary meaning . . . What is to be provided by way of secondary education in accordance with the national policy is expanded in s 8 . . . I pause here to draw attention to the underlying assumptions, as disclosed by the 1944 Act read as a whole, and in particular by ss 1, 7, 8 and 36: (a) that the contribution to be made by education towards "the spiritual, moral, mental and physical development of the community" (see s 7) is by developing the particular abilities and aptitudes of the individual pupil; (b) that individual pupils differ from one another in ability and aptitude; and

10 [1976] 3 All ER 665 at 694.

(c) that these differences will call for different methods of teaching for pupils of differing ability or aptitude if the statutory policy for education is to be carried out. The 1944 Act leaves to local education authorities a broad discretion to choose what in their judgement are the means best suited to their areas for providing the variety of instruction called for by those provisions which I have mentioned.'

On this view the discretion of the central government under s 1 of the 1944 Act to 'promote the education of the people of England and Wales' is certainly not unrestricted. That being so, the 'broad discretion to choose' enjoyed by local education authorities is a robust power which must encourage those who look for as many signs as possible of genuine local democratic autonomy. This the case even though in practice it can normally only find expression in terms of party political conflict, and even though it is open to Parliament at any time to change the rules of the game.

The upshot in the *Tameside* case was that, because of the 'broad discretion', conferred by the 1944 Act, the local authority could not be said to be, by implementing a policy to which the central government then objected, acting 'unreasonably', in the absence of any other relevant and significant factors, in the objective sense of that word under the *Wednesbury*[11] principle—ie that *no* reasonable authority could have acted in that way. It was not unreasonable (objectively) for the central government to regard as unreasonable (subjectively) a policy which the local education authority (equally subjectively) did not regard in that light. But the 'broad discretion' under the Act left the decision-making in the hands of the local authority, so long as they acted intra vires. Only objective 'unreasonableness' on their part would have made their policy ultra vires, and this was not demonstrated. Therefore the local authority were entitled to succeed. This involved no encroachment upon the legitimate exercise of the function conferred by s 1 of the 1944 Act on the Secretary of State.

4. MINISTERIAL CONTROL OVER STATUTORY INSTRUMENTS

Of the multitudinous statutory provisions giving to central government departments control over local authorities in points of detail, probably the most important in a legal sense are those which are legislative in character. There can be few if any ministers who do not have conferred upon them by some Act the power to make subordinate legislation of some kind affecting local government. Town and country planning is one area in which this abounds; and perhaps the most prominent exam-

---

11 See ch 3, p 63.

ple is the 'GDO' or Town and Country Planning General Development Order 1977,[12] made by the Secretary of State for the Environment in accordance with the Town and Country Planning Act 1971, s 24.[13] This prescribes the detailed procedure to be followed by persons applying for planning permission to carry out 'development' of land as defined in s 22 of the 1971 Act. It also prescribes various clauses of 'development' for which the 'GDO' itself automatically gives permission, so that in those cases no separate application need be made. Section 22 itself has authorised the making of another piece of subordinate legislation, the Town and Country Planning (Use Classes) Order 1972,[14] in which various classes of use of land and buildings are specified for the purpose of providing that any change from one use to another within the same 'use class' is not 'development', with the consequence that the question of planning permission for such a change does not arise at all.

Public land use control has produced subordinate legislation in great quantities in regard to planning, compulsory purchase, housing, highways and public health, most of it relevant to local authorities. All subordinate legislation (or 'delegated legislation') enacts law. The detailed provisions are interpreted by the courts in decided cases in exactly the same way as the provisions of Acts of Parliament, with one important exception, as follows. No Act can be impugned for being ultra vires, or for any other reason;[15] but subordinate legislation can be impugned on the ground that it is ultra vires the Act under which the relevant minister purported to make it. In *Chester v Bateson*,[16] an Act gave a minister power to make regulations for war-time emergency conditions, and under it a regulation was made forbidding the bringing of legal proceedings to recover possession of certain premises. This was held to be ultra vires the authorising Act because it took away from the owners of those premises their normal right as citizens to have recourse to the courts, which was something neither expressly nor, in the view of the courts, impliedly authorised by the Act.

In *Daymond v South West Water Authority*,[17] the subordinate legislation in question consisted of Part III of the Water Authorities (Collection of Charges) Order 1974[18] made by the Secretary of State for the Environment under the Water Act 1973, s 34(1). The dispute in this case, which has been referred to already in an earlier chapter,[19] turned on the interpretation of the Water Act 1973, s 30, over the question

12 SI 1977/289, as amended by SI 1980/1946.
13 See ch 11, p 292.
14 SI 1972/1385.
15 See ch 6, p 139.
16 [1920] 1 KB 829.
17 [1976] AC 609, [1976] 1 All ER 39.
18 SI 1974/448.
19 Ch 7, see p 175.

whether sewerage charges could be imposed on persons whose premises were not connected to the public sewer. Before the Act of 1973 came into force public sewers were provided and maintained by local authorities and financed by rates instead of charges. Rates, being a form of tax, are payable by occupiers of rateable property regardless of what benefit, if any, they get from the services for which those rates help to pay. Charges, however, are inherently contractual payments in return for benefits provided, not a tax; and although the Act of 1973 could have stated that the 'charges' were to be payable on the same basis as if they were 'rates', it did not do so. The House of Lords, by a majority of 3 to 2, held that s 30 of that Act therefore did not authorise the imposition of charges on the plaintiff and others whose premises were not connected to the public sewer, notwithstanding that he and they had previously had to pay rates on the same basis as those ratepayers whose premises were connected.

It followed from this that the Water Authorities (Collection of Charges) Order 1974 was ultra vires the 1973 Act under which it purported to have been made by the Secretary of State. The water authority attempted to argue that, as the Local Government Act 1972, s 254, referred to earlier in this chapter,[20] empowers the Secretary of State to modify enactments by making 'such incidental, consequential, transitional or supplementary provision' as he thinks necessary 'for giving full effect thereto', this would cure any defect in the Order. The argument was rejected. Lord Edmund-Davies said:[1]

'If . . . s 30(1) does not empower a "sewerage etc charge" to be made against the ratepayer, then in my judgment no order, whether "transitional" or otherwise, can do so . . . If an Act confers *no* power . . . to charge certain persons . . . an order which declares that they *can* be charged is not "incidental" or "consequential" or "supplementary" to the Act, and the mere fact that it may be "transitional" cannot, of itself, make it intra vires if, were it intended to operate permanently, it would be ultra vires. Such is, in my judgment, the case here.'

The 1974 Order was temporary because it applied for one year, beginning on 1 April 1974. It was not stated to be transitional; but it was later amended;[2] and another Order followed it in 1975.[3]

5. MINISTERIAL CONTROL OVER ORDERS AND SCHEMES

Also legislative in character, but less obviously so, are ministerial confirmations of orders and schemes made by local authorities. If statutory instru-

---

20 See above, p 222.
1 [1976] AC 609 at 657, 658, [1976] 1 All ER 39 at 64.
2 By SI 1974/1081.
3 SI 1975/396.

ments are the subordinate legislative equivalent of public Acts, orders and schemes subject to ministerial confirmation are the subordinate legislative equivalent of private Acts. The historical process which produced them seems to have begun with the inclosure movement. Inclosures of medieval common fields in the eighteenth century were achieved by countless numbers of private acts promoted by groups of individual landowners in their respective parishes, who obtained statutory powers under those Acts to make and give effect to inclosure awards. The constant enactment of repetitive detail in the clauses of inclosure Bills was eventually superseded, in the Inclosure Act 1801, by a public statute enacting a standard-form code of clauses which were incorporated by reference into streamlined private Bills, thus saving much time and money. The next stage, in the Inclosure Act 1845, was to supplant private inclosure Bills altogether by inclosure schemes approved in a standard-form procedure by a permanent statutory body of inclosure commissioners, after the holding of public inquiries into draft schemes prepared and published by the local bodies of promoters now freed from the burden of preparing private Bills. An assistant commissioner conducted each of these public local inquiries into objections resulting from publication, and reported to the commissioners themselves, who were a central government authority subsequently taken over by the Board (now the Ministry) of Agriculture. They made the decision, under the public statute of 1845 (amended) as authorising Act, whether or not to confirm each scheme, with or without amendments.[4]

This procedure therefore amounted to compulsory purchase (or redistribution) of property rights in agricultural land, with compensation in the form of money or of new rights in land under the redistribution, the values being assessed by a competent valuation surveyor. It was in turn adapted to a general procedure for compulsory purchase. Numberless private Bills authorising compulsory purchase of land by promoters of canal undertakings, railway undertakings, gas supply undertakings, water supply undertakings, electricity supply undertakings, and other projects were at first being drafted with the same constant enactment of repetitive detail. The Lands Clauses Consolidation Act 1845 was a public statute enacting a standard form code of clauses for incorporation by reference into streamlined private Bills thereafter, as had been done for inclosures by the Inclosure Act 1801. Then, once more following the example of inclosures, the private Bills were largely- —thought not wholly, because of the much greater variety of projects involving compulsory purchase—superseded by ministerial orders. At first these were 'provisional orders', an interim stage of evolution still requiring Parliamentary confirmation by 'provisional order confirma-

4 See *Cooke's Inclosure Acts* (4th edn).

tion Bills' composed by ministers and containing groups of orders rather than single ones. This procedure was used for example under the Public Health Act 1875. Then, from about 1909, public authorising Acts began to make it possible to dispense with Parliamentary confirmation altogether by using 'compulsory purchase orders'. These, like inclosure schemes after the Inclosure Act 1845, involved preparation in draft by promoters, including local authorities, in regard to individual schemes involving specific land. Then followed publication, submission to an appropriate minister in accordance with the authorising Act in each case, and examination at a public local inquiry into objections conducted by a ministerial inspector in a procedure modelled (in general) on the inquiries conducted by assistant inclosure commissioners. In the light of his report a ministerial decision was reached whether or not to confirm the draft order with or without modifications.

Compulsory purchase orders when confirmed, like inclosure schemes when confirmed, are legislative in nature because they change the law in relation to a particular project. They empower the promoting body to purchase compulsorily the specified properties required for each scheme. They do not transfer or 'convey' those properties; and it is open to each promoting body to decide whether or not to take advantage of the power thus conferred by going on to acquire under a 'notice to treat', normally within a standard time-limit of three years after which the power lapses if it has not been used. Without the legislative conferment of that power by compulsory purchase order, compulsory purchase is unlawful; though there may be an independent statutory power to purchase by agreement by means of an ordinary open-market transaction. Until the Compulsory Purchase Act 1965 a compulsory purchase order together with the authorising Act (public or private) under which it was made, was compendiously referred to as 'the special Act' in recognition of the pedigree of this procedure in succession to the separate private Acts of earlier days.

The procedure evolved for confirming compulsory purchase orders was in turn applied to 'orders' and 'schemes' setting out in detail various functional projects to be undertaken by local authorities, and other bodies, for which the compulsory purchase of land might or might not be required. Where this is the case the authority do not simply draw up the project in detail, obtain any necessary ministerial loan sanction to cover the capital cost, and then (if necessary and if authorised) embark on the procedure for obtaining powers of compulsory purchase of the particular rights in land they need to acquire. They must first prepare in draft an official 'scheme' setting out the details of the project; and that 'scheme' must be published and submitted to the appropriate minister in the now familiar manner for him to hold a public local inquiry, conducted by an inspector, to hear objections and report on the 'scheme' so that, once again, a ministerial decision can be made whether or not to confirm it, with or without modifications. If it is not confirmed its implementation will be ultra vires. If it is confirmed, and rights in the land required for the purposes of the 'scheme' need to be compulsorily acquired, then the procedure for making a compulsory purchase order must be set in train.

Examples of 'schemes' can be seen in the provisions of the Coast Protection Act 1949 and the Highways Act 1980.[5] In the latter Act, under s 16 and Sch 1, Part II, local highway authorities can make 'schemes' for 'special roads'; and the detailed procedure for submission and confirmation is set out following the pattern first described. In the same Act, ss 14 and 18 and Sch 1, Part I, set out a similar procedure for 'orders' to be made by local highway authorities for the purpose of altering or improving 'special', 'trunk' and 'classified' roads. In the Act of 1949 a similar procedure is laid down for use by coast protection authorities—ie district councils whose area borders the sea—proposing to undertake 'works schemes' for coast protection works (sea-walls and the like) which appear to them to be necessary to prevent flooding from the sea.

The latter procedure was examined by the Court of Appeal in *Webb v Minister of Housing and Local Government*.[6] In that case, Bognor Regis Urban District Council in 1961 prepared a 'works scheme' under the 1949 Act. After introducing some controversial changes to the details of their original proposals, they submitted the draft scheme as amended to the minister who, after holding the necessary public local inquiry, confirmed the scheme with modifications in 1963. The legal validity of the scheme, like such schemes and orders generally and compulsory purchase orders as well, cannot be challenged after ministerial confirmation, by judicial review or in legal proceedings of any other kind, except by application within a strict six weeks' time-limit to the High Court to quash (or suspend) it on certain specified legal grounds, in the way described in an earlier chapter.[7] The 'works scheme' in this case was not challenged. The council then moved on to the next stage, which was to prepare a draft compulsory purchase order in relation to the land of certain property owners which the council need for constructing the proposed sea-wall. Some of these owners now decided that the proposed sea-wall was too wide for their taste—being not so much a sea-wall as a seaside promenade—and objected to having an excessive quantity of their land taken for building a new promenade, as they saw it, under cover of building a new sea-wall. They were within the six weeks' time-limit for challenging the legality of the compulsory purchase

---

5 See ch 11.
6 [1965] 2 All ER 193, [1965] 1 WLR 755. For the existence of powers rather than duties under the Coast Protection Act 1949, see *Fellowes v Rother DC* [1983] 1 All ER 513.
7 See ch 4, pp 98–99. See also below, p 234.

order, yet the substance of their objections related to the details of the project set out in the preceding 'works-scheme'. The Court of Appeal, by a majority, held that the *compulsory purchase order* was invalidated by the defects—which on the evidence they held to be clearly established—in the *works scheme*, and that consequently it was right to quash the order, since it was challenged in due time, even though the works scheme, which was the cause of the trouble, had *not* been challenged in due time (or indeed challenged at all, in formal terms).

6. MINISTERIAL CONTROL OVER BYELAWS

The remaining area subject to ministerial control which is legislative in character is that of local authority byelaws. These have been discussed in an earlier chapter.[8] All that need be touched on here is the point that, like the orders and schemes just considered, byelaws are clearly legislative because they change the law, and count as subordinate legislation because Parliamentary sanction for them is given in a general public authorising Act under which a specified minister—more often than not the Secretary of State for the Environment—is empowered to decide whether to confirm, or not to confirm, particular sets of byelaws. These authorising Acts, for example the Local Government Act 1972,[9] commonly require the intended byelaws to be submitted to the minister in draft and publicised; though the holding of public inquiries and confirmation subject to modifications are not provided for, at any rate under the 1972 Act. The relevant minister may of course let it be known, probably by reference to the model byelaws, if any, which are available in his department, that the byelaws will only be confirmed in an amended form and specify the amendments.

Unlike local authorities' schemes and orders, however, their byelaws are general and not particular in scope and are in force for indefinite periods instead of for single projects. They are procedurally part of the criminal law rather than administrative law. Their legal validity may be challenged in the courts without the standard-form six weeks' time limit and other restrictions commonly applied to schemes and orders.

At common law there was one type of byelaw which could be made without ministerial approval: those made by churchwardens for the good rule and governance of their parish, as recognised by the common law since early times; but in practice this common law power is obsolete and has been replaced by the statutory provisions of the 1972 Act already mentioned. The one kind of subordinate legislation which local authorities can in practice make without submission for ministerial confirmation consists of their own standing orders, and this power is itself conferred by statute, namely the 1972 Act, Sch 12.[10] Standing orders

8 Ch 6. See p 141.
9 Ss 235–238.
10 Part VI, para 42.

do not directly affect anyone other than council members and staff; but, as shown in an earlier chapter,[11] in spite of being intended for internal regulation only they can have a definite indirect effect on other persons: *R v Hereford Corp, ex p Harrower.*[12]

B. Executive procedures

I. CONSENTS AND DIRECTIONS

In addition to control of subordinate legislation by local authorities, there is much ministerial control of an executive kind which the law authorises, notably in the form of statutory provisions which subordinate local to central decision-making. In planning, for example, a planning permission may be revoked or modified, or an order made for an established use of building to be terminated or demolished,[13] and apart from revocations and modifications which are uncontested the consent of the Secretary of State for the Environment must be obtained. If he consents he will then confirm the relevant revocation, modification or discontinuance order.

Consents or approvals of this kind are frequently met with in financial matters. 'Loan sanction', which means consent by the Secretary of State, is normally necessary when local authorities borrow, and is often necessary also in relation to their choice of the method they use when borrowing, as discussed in an earlier chapter.[14] A particular example is the issue of housing bonds by district councils acting as local housing authorities under the Housing Act 1957, s 138. Under the Town Development Act 1952, his approval is required for the making of financial contributions to the councils of 'receiving districts' by 'exporting' councils when the former provide new 'overspill' housing for the benefit of people transferred from the area of the latter. As for land use, a general power has been referred to earlier[15] under which local authorities can appropriate to a different use, provided it is used for a function they are empowered to carry out, land already acquired and held by them for some other such use, provided that the appropriate minister concerned with the function for which the land has hitherto been held consents to the appropriation.[16] There are exceptions, for example if the land has been so held for more than 10 years. A somewhat similar need for ministerial consent applies[17] to disposals of land at less than market value. These are just a few of many examples.

11 Ch 6. See p 145.
12 [1970] 3 All ER 460, [1970] 1 WLR 1424.
13 Town and Country Planning Act 1971, ss 45, 51. See ch 11.
14 See ch 7, p 163.
15 In Ch 8. See p 219.
16 Local Government Act 1972, s 12.
17 Under s 123 of that Act.

Somewhat similar are provisions that a minister may give directions to local authorities under which they must take action or with which they must otherwise comply. Under the Town and Country Planning Act 1971 the Secretary of State for the Environment may direct that a planning application before a local planning authority be referred to him for decision instead of them.[18] Under s 38 of that Act he may direct that planning permission be granted to a person applying for compensation, so as to remove the need or justification for payment of that compensation. Under s 15 of the Town and Country Planning Act 1947 a direction was issued on 12 December 1952, by the Minister of Housing and Local Government, with long-standing effect, that if a local planning authority should receive a planning application to change the use of premises from use as a dwelling to some other use, they must first consult the local housing authority if different from themselves.[19]

The Education Act 1944, s 68, empowers the Secretary of State for Education and Science, if he is 'satisfied' that any local education authority 'have acted or are proposing to act unreasonably . . . to give such directions . . . as appear to him to be expedient' to that authority, 'as to the exercise of the power or the performance of the duty' about which he feels concern. However, in a case discussed earlier, *Secretary of State for Education and Science v Tameside Metropolitan Borough Council*,[20] the House of Lords held that the Secretary of State is only empowered so to act if he is 'satisfied' in circumstances in which it is objectively reasonable on his part to be satisfied. It is not enough for him genuinely to disagree with an authority on the grounds that in his subjective view their policy is misguided or wrong. He can only be thus 'satisfied' if the authority's policy is such that viewed objectively, *no* reasonable authority could have resolved to apply it—ie the *Wednesbury*[1] principle must be applied as the test to discover if the power to give any directions under s 68 has arisen. The right of any minister to give directions inevitably restricts the freedom of action of local authorities. The House of Lords in this case clearly thought that this restrictive effect itself needs to be kept within the bounds of an objective test of reasonableness, at any rate where 'reasonableness' is itself imported into the express definition of the power to give the directions. But it may well be that the courts will go on to apply the 'reasonableness' test to all exercises of discretion.

2. REVIEW OF DECISIONS: APPEALS

Closely related to these procedures are administrative proceedings which bear a superficial resemblance to judicial ones: appeals and inquiries. Under

18 S 35.
19 Town and Country Planning (Housing Accommodation) Direction 1952, set out in that Minister's Circular No 94/52.
20 [1977] AC 104, [1976] 3 All ER 665. See above, p 224.
1 See ch 3, p 63.

the Superannuation Act 1972, ss 7 and 11, the Secretary of State for the Environment may make regulations about payment of pensions to Local Government staff. Part II of the Local Government Superannuation Regulations 1974[2] made thereunder allow any person dissatisfied with a decision by the local authority as his employer to appeal against it to the Secretary of State, whose decision on the merits of the case is final.

Under the Town and Country Planning Act 1971,[3] an applicant for planning permission who receives an adverse decision—a refusal, or a permission subject to unwelcome conditions—may appeal to the Secretary of State. There are in fact several provisions for such appeals under that Act: against refusals of listed building consents, or conditional consents;[4] against enforcement notices;[5] against listed building enforcement notices;[6] against decisions requiring replacement trees to be planted when protected trees have been felled;[7] and against determinations of development.[8] But if a local authority should object to a purchase notice, that notice is to be automatically referred to the Secretary of State without need for a decision to appeal.[9] Under the Land Compensation Act 1961, Part III, an applicant for a certificate of appropriate alternative development (claiming an assumption of planning permission which may enable an expropriated landowner to include development value in his compensations for compulsory purchase) can, in the event of an unfavourable decision by the local planning authority, appeal to the Secretary of State.[10] The statutory provisions in these cases normally provide that the Secretary of State's decision can only be challenged by an application within six weeks to the High Court to quash (or suspend) on certain specified legal grounds, and in no other proceedings whatever. For enforcement notices there is instead a more general right of appeal on a point of law to the High Court under the Town and Country Planning Act 1971:[11] but the Rules of the Supreme Court[12] provide a mere 28-day period for bringing such appeals. The Superannuation Act 1972, referred to above, empowers the Secretary of State to state a case for the High Court on a point of law.[13]

In considering these and many other similar rights of appeal to the

2 SI 1974/520, as amended.
3 S 36.
4 Sch 11, para 8.
5 S 88, as amended.
6 S 97, as amended.
7 S 103, as amended.
8 S 53, applying s 36.
9 S 181.
10 S 18.
11 S 246.
12 Order 55, r 4.
13 S 12.

Secretary of State for the Environment, or other ministers, it is important not to be misled by the word 'appeal'. A judicial appeal lies from a court of first instance to an appeal court, and the party appealing from the one to the other does so because he has been partly or wholly unsuccessful at first instance. Thus in a normal case the parties to the proceedings at first instance are the same as the parties to the appeal even if the roles are reversed by the defendant (if he was the unsuccessful party) becoming the appellant. If the appeal is a full rehearing, then issues of fact as well as law will be dealt with; but the emphasis will usually tend to be on issues of law, and if the appeal is only on issues of law then of course the facts cease to be in dispute at all.

An administrative dispute is very different because the issues of this kind of proceeding lie between the appellant and the local planning authority. There is thus no respondent to an administrative appeal; or perhaps it is truer to say that the tribunal at first instance and the respondent are one and the same, which is something which would make no sense in a judicial appeal. The nearest thing to this in judicial terms occurs in judicial review if the body being subjected to the supervisory jurisdiction of the High Court is itself an inferior court. In such a case, of course, the proceedings do not involve a full rehearing or 'appeal' in the ordinary judicial sense, but a challenge to the inferior body's view of the law when arriving at the decision being complained of.

No less important is the fact that an administrative appeal is not substantially concerned with the same kind of issues as a judicial appeal. Whereas the latter is mainly concerned with issues of law, and to a lesser extent with issues of fact, an administrative appeal is chiefly concerned with something quite different—issues of policy. These form the 'merits' of an administrative appeal. Thus the Secretary of State dealing with a planning appeal should be accurate in his application of the relevant law and in his assessment of the relevant facts; but his chief concern is with policy. The question in such cases is: should the development for which the appellant seeks to be granted planning permission be allowed or not allowed, ie is it good or bad planning policy to decide in favour of that development in all the circumstances of the case? Judges are the experts on the law; but they are not the experts on administrative policy. Ministers may be empowered to substitute their own discretion for that of a local authority without a formal appeal.[14]

There can accordingly be no further *administrative* appeal on the merits of the case. Apart from extraneous pressure, the only way of challenging the ministerial decision is to attack its legality, on which High Court judges will of course be the experts. What was a peripheral issue then becomes the substantial—indeed the sole—issue. If the challenge succeeds, the ministerial decision will be quashed as invalid. The

14 *Norwich City Council v Secretary of State for the Environment* [1982] 1 All ER 737.

minister, though conscientiously considering the legal position with the help of his officials, must be prepared to accept that his reading of the law is wrong if the High Court, Court of Appeal or House of Lords so decides.

But an adverse legal decision does not inherently change the policy factors; and so long as the law is complied with, the decision of the minister may be repeated on the same view of policy as before. As Sachs J pointed out at first instance in *Hartnell v Minister of Housing and Local Government*,[15] the success of the appellant in that case (later upheld by the Court of Appeal and the House of Lords) in obtaining a judgment to quash an unfavourable appeal decision made by the minister under what is now s 36 of the 1971 Act merely had the effect of remitting the decision to the minister. All the minister then needed to do—if he was so minded, after all the litigation—was to repeat his conditional grant of planning permission—which was for use of land as a caravan site— provided only that this time the conditions imposed did not unlawfully cut down the owner's existing use rights in the field. To do that lawfully would have necessitated paying him compensation, and using a different procedure, namely a discontinuance order under what is now s 51 of the 1971 Act.

3. REVIEW OF DECISIONS: INQUIRIES

Equally deceptive is the procedure in a public local inquiry; though here the deception is more purely practical or even visual. The radical difference between judicial appeals and administrative appeals is obscured verbally by the use of the word 'appeal' for both. The radical difference between an inquiry and a trial is obscured practically, because in both there is a contested hearing, between what in substance appear in most cases to be two sides, with a person presiding over the proceedings in a manner very reminiscent of a judge, though without robes and other ceremonial trappings. In addition to that, the proceedings usually take the form of examination and cross-examination of witnesses, both ordinary and expert, conducted at least in the more prestigious inquiries by barristers appearing for each 'side' who will in addition not hesitate to raise legal arguments as well where it seems appropriate.

But appearances are deceptive. In *Wednesbury Corp v Ministry of Housing and Local Government*,[16] Lord Denning MR speaking of an inquiry, said 'it cannot be regarded as if it were a lawsuit'. Lord Loreburn LC dealt most authoritatively with the whole matter in *Board of Education v Rice*,[17] in which he described inquiries as arising from: 'the practice of imposing on departments or officers of State the duty of

15 [1963] 3 All ER 130, [1963] 1 WLR 1141.
16 [1965] 1 All ER 186, [1965] 1 WLR 261.
17 [1911] AC 179.

deciding or determining questions of various kinds . . . what comes for determination is a matter to be settled by discretion'—ie policy—'but sometimes it will involve matter of law as well as matter of fact . . . In such cases the [minister or department] will have to ascertain the law and . . . the facts, I need not add that . . . they must act in good faith and listen fairly to both sides . . . But I do not think they are bound to treat such a question as though it were a trial . . .'

Public local inquiries are fundamentally administrative fact-finding exercises, undertaken by ministers in order to ensure for their own benefit, and thus ultimately the public's, that they are as well informed as possible on the factual and other issues relating to a local policy matter in which the decision rests with them. It may have reached them by way of an administrative 'appeal', or on some other footing which could be essentially an executive policy matter or possibly a procedure involving subordinate legislation such as the confirmation of a compulsory purchase order or a local authority's 'scheme' as in *Webb v Minister of Housing and Local Government*, discussed above.[18] It will almost certainly be required by virtue of some statutory provision.

As earlier discussed in chapter 3, the fundamental legal principle, not quite but almost referred to in so many words by Lord Loreburn LC above, is 'natural justice', which arises from the 'quasi-judicial' nature of an inquiry even though it serves the purposes of an administrative policy decision-making process. The subsequent decision may be quashed as ultra vires, either on an appeal specifically to the High Court as prescribed by statute or by judicial review; but in this type of situation the reason for the quashing is the prior mismanagement of the inquiry, including the procedures immediately before and after it, by committing a breach of natural justice. All that need be added here is a reminder that in planning and compulsory purchase 'natural justice' is reinforced by statutory 'inquiries procedure rules' which must be complied with as well.

But none of this alters the fact that an inquiry is not a trial. Legality is satisfied by giving objectors what the law regards as a fair hearing, not what they regard as a fair decision. Indeed an inquiry does not end in a decision. It ends in a report. The decision is made, after due consideration of that report, with in many cases the rejection of its recommendations on policy grounds, by the minister concerned, or in certain lesser planning disputes by the inspector himself. Acting through the inspector, though without impairing the latter's independent status, the minister ultimately controls the inquiry, in particular as far as its costs are concerned. Unless otherwise stated, all parties bear their own costs.

A general statutory provision governing public local inquiries as they affect local authorities is contained in the Local Government Act 1972,

18 See p 230.

s 250. It provides that 'the person appointed to hold the inquiry'—ie the Secretary of State's inspector—'may by summons require any person to attend, at a time and place stated in the summons, to give evidence or to produce any documents in his custody or under his control which relate to any matter in question at the enquiry, and may take evidence on oath, and for that purpose administer oaths, or may, instead of administering an oath, require the person examined to make a solemn affirmation' except that title deeds of private owners may not be demanded, and the expenses of attending must be paid. The conduct of an inquiry is, at the inspector's discretion, within reasonable limits and subject to 'natural justice' and where applicable the 'inquiries procedure rules'. He does not need to use the powers in s 250 in so far as they are not mandatory. But the more use he makes of them the more likely the public are to regard his inquiry as if it were a trial.

Disobedience of the inspector's summons is an offence punishable summarily by a fine up to £100 or up to six months' imprisonment, or both. There is a general rule that the ministerial costs, including a fee for the inspector's services, are to be paid by the local authority involved; and the minister may certify any amount, as appropriate, as costs which then becomes 'recoverable . . . summarily as a civil debt'. But liability for payment of costs involved in holding the inquiry may be imposed on any person, as may seem appropriate in the circumstances. Any party entitled as a result to recover his costs against any other may apply to have the order made a rule of the High Court for enforcement purposes. Similar provisions may be found in other Acts, such as the Housing Act 1957,[19] the Town and Country Planning Act 1971,[20] the Highways Act 1980,[1] and others. But they usually incorporate the substance of the procedure under s 250 of the 1972 Act, as just described.

4. INSPECTIONS AND DEFAULT POWERS

More in the nature of routine are central government powers relating to inspections and the control of officers of local authorities. The Education Act 1944,[2] requires the Secretary of State for Education and Science to ensure that there are regular inspections of schools and other educational establishments. The Home Secretary has a duty, under the Police Act 1964,[3] to appoint inspectors of constabulary to ensure that all police forces are regularly and properly inspected, and under the Fire Services Act 1947,[4] to appoint inspectors of local authority fire bri-

19 S 181.
20 S 282.
 1 S 302.
 2 S 77.
 3 S 38.
 4 S 24.

gades. The same Act[5] empowers the Home Secretary to make regulations governing the appointment of chief fire officers; and the Police Act 1964[6] provides that the appointment of chief constables is to be subject to his approval.

At the opposite end of the scale are ministerial default powers, which are anything but routine in function and indeed are only called into use with extreme rarity. One of these rare occasions occurred in regard to Clay Cross Urban District Council in Derbyshire. The refusal of this local authority to comply with the Housing Finance Act 1972 in regard to raising council house rents has been discussed in an earlier chapter;[7] but what is relevant here is the action taken by the Secretary of State for the Environment under ss 95–99 of the Act in the course of the affair. Those sections empowered him to appoint a 'housing commissioner' to carry out specified functions taken out of the hands of the local housing authority and entrusted to him. Acting under s 95(1) he made a 'default order', the Clay Cross Urban District Council (Housing Default) Order 1972;[8] and on their disregard of the instructions in the order to put into effect the increases they were required by the Act to make he went on under s 95(7) to appoint a housing commissioner by making the Clay Cross Urban District Council (Housing Commissioner) Order 1973[9] to that effect.

The appointment of the housing commissioner could have been made immediately after the expiry of the time given for compliance with the 'default order', which was 16 days, if that order had not been complied with by them. But the Secretary of State did not appoint the housing commissioner until nearly a year later. The reasons given for this were that there would be a loss of democratic control exercisable through locally elected representatives—which must be so whenever default powers are exercised; though who should be held blameworthy for that is obviously a separate question—and that there would be a delay in so doing which would aggravate the council's financial loss. Instead the Secretary of State directed the holding of an extraordinary audit, as discussed in a previous chapter,[10] which would open the way to having the council's financial loss, if duly confirmed by that audit, made good by the individuals responsible, namely the councillors, since the responsible officers had advised them not to defy the Act and had warned them of the possible consequences. In *Asher v Lacey*,[11] the councillors challenged the extraordinary audit, it having resulted in a

---

5 S 18.
6 S 4.
7 Ch 7, see p 186.
8 SI 1972/1713.
9 SI 1973/1675.
10 Ch 7, see p 184.
11 [1973] 3 All ER 1008, [1973] 1 WLR 1412.

decision by the auditor that they be made personally liable by a 'surcharge' under Part X of the Local Government Act 1933, which was the statutory procedure then still in force. They did so on the ground that the holding of it was inappropriate, and thus ultra vires the 1933 Act, because the appropriate course would have been to appoint a housing commissioner instead. The Queen's Bench Divisional Court rejected the challenge, the auditor being the respondent, holding that the Secretary of State was entitled to make a choice between the courses of action open to him (there were others) and had on the facts made his choice *bona fide*.

Shortly after that decision the housing commissioner was at last appointed. Rather than appeal against the Divisional Court's judgment the councillors began fresh proceedings to challenge the holding of the audit by claiming a declaration against the Secretary of State that his decision to hold the audit was ultra vires the 1933 Act because it was punitive and thus not bona fide but made for an ulterior motive. Although the housing commissioner had been appointed, the appointment was said for these reasons to be faulty because it should have occurred sooner, in place of the audit. Megarry J made an order striking out the claim as disclosing no reasonable cause of action; and the Court of Appeal upheld his decision. The proceedings were an unjustified attempt to relitigate the previous case, and the reasons for rejecting the plaintiffs' claim remained the same. The fact that the Secretary of State for Wales had promptly appointed housing commissioners for two other defaulting authorities without first holding an extraordinary audit did not mean that the course of action chosen in this case was wrong, merely that in exercising bona fide a choice among the same range of possibilities one minister had decided on one course and the other minister had decided on a different course, and this difference of choice was inherently quite proper.

In the words of Orr LJ,[12] 'the Secretary of State was . . . entitled to take into account that the plaintiffs might yet repent of their defiance of the law, as other councillors elsewhere apparently did', when delaying his decision to appoint a housing commissioner, bearing in mind that the exercise of default powers is 'a negation of local government, or at least an acceptance of its failure.' Lawton LJ[13] said: 'Balancing the advantages and disadvantages of one possible course of action against another and making a decision is what Secretaries of State have to do: it is the very stuff of government and the courts should not interfere save for good reason and disagreeing with the decision is not in itself a good reason.'

The fact that ss 95–99 were repealed by the Housing Rents and Sub-

---

12 *Asher v Secretary of State for the Environment* [1974] 2 All ER 156 at 166.
13 Ibid at 168.

sidies Act 1975 does not affect the fundamental significance of the way default powers were operated under them. Default powers can still be found in the Town and Country Planning Act 1971, s 276, which (as amended) enables the Secretary of State for the Environment to make any of certain orders or notices under that Act, if he thinks that any such order should be made but the appropriate county or district planning authority have not done so. He must consult the authority before exercising this default power which, it should be noted, does not require the appointment of a 'commissioner' or any other such special functionary. The orders or notices in question are revocation and modification orders wholly or partly withdrawing planning permission already given; discontinuance orders terminating some established use of land; tree preservation orders or amendments or revocations of such orders; and completion notices, stop notices and enforcement notices. He can exercise a similar default power in respect of decisions that local authorities shall acquire land for 'proper planning' purposes, enforceable by an order of mandamus.

The same Act, s 17, confers default powers on the Secretary of State in respect of the making, repeal or amendment of development plans (whether 'structure' or 'local') and of the carrying out of surveys on which they are based. A local inquiry or hearing must be held, and the Secretary of State may either carry out the relevant function or give it to another authority, at the defaulting authority's expense. The Local Government Act 1972, Sch 16,[14] also empowers him to order a district planning authority to arrange with another local planning authority for the proper discharge of functions relating to listed building control or conservation areas which need specialist advice, which may go so far as to transfer the discharge of functions to the other authority.

Another default power which may be mentioned here is the power given to the Secretary of State for Education and Science under the Education Act 1944, s 99, to issue instructions to any local education authority which he considers to be in default by failing currently to carry out any of their proper statutory functions.[15] This default power is enforceable by an order of mandamus.

It is also possible, though rare, for one local authority to exercise a default power over another. The Local Government Act 1972, s 194, empowers county councils to provide local authority housing in default of any district council, which is the local housing authority in normal circumstances, if the latter should appear not to be doing so. But this 'reserve power' requires the consent of the Secretary of State for its exercise.

14 Paras 58–59.
15 This is to be distinguished from the question of policy disagreements under s 68; see above, p 233.

5. CONSULTATIONS AND CIRCULARS

For purposes of day-to-day routine, however, the normal mode of control exercised by central over local government is administrative guidance rather than legal power. The Department of the Environment and other central government departments exercise this control at an informal level by frequent discussions and consultations. At a more formal level there are circulars. These, unlike statutory instruments, have no inherent legislative force; though they sometimes contain 'directions' which some legislative provision may empower a minister to give to local authorities and which must be obeyed, as discussed earlier in this chapter.[16]

But normally of course local authorities comply with recommendations in circulars, for a combination of reasons. In the first place, statutory duties are so multitudinous that it makes life easier for local authorities to be told what they should do rather than having to work it out laboriously for themselves. In the second place, the central departments are in a sense the experts on the administrative subject-matter of the circulars, in that they normally have much closer contact with the policy-making decisions which lie behind the circulars and determine the functions which the local authorities have the power, and often the duty, to carry out. That is to say the powers and the duties emanate from the central government in legislative form which in detail, even if not in essence, is shaped in Whitehall. Acts may be conceived by politicians but are largely worded with the help of, or by, the Parliamentary draftsmen's office; while subordinate legislation in the form of statutory instruments will normally be drafted inside the relevant central department. Thus the Department of the Environment will be consulted over, but will not actually draft, a planning or housing Bill; but it will actually draft a Use Classes or a General Development Order or Compulsory Purchase of Land Regulations. No local authority therefore will lightly disregard what a Circular recommends, especially as the Circular will almost inevitably be framed in general terms (which is why it is so called) for circulation to local authorities all over the country. To depart without good cause from what a Circular generally prescribes is to be odd man out. It would be rather like navigating a reef-strewn sea and throwing the charts or the radar overboard.

Even consultations are to a great extent formalised, and do not consist solely of ad hoc letters and queries. Advisory councils and committees abound, including ones expressly called for by statute, such as the consultative bodies relating to the grant system under the Local Government, Planning and Land Act 1980, Part IV, referred to in an earlier chapter.[17] National associations of local authorities have been in

16 See p 233.
17 Ch 7, see p 172.

existence for many years, whose special expertise, based on long experience, matches that of the central government departments themselves. Nor do the messages only flow one way, from the centre outwards. There is a constant movement of information inwards to the centre, without which the central government would scarcely be able to make any decisions relating to local authorities. This is quite separate from the ad hoc reports submitted by the inspectors who have been sent out to conduct public local inquiries.

Regular returns of information are called for under various statutes, such as the Education Act 1944,[18] which requires returns from local education authorities, and the Local Government Act 1972,[19] which requires financial information. The same Act,[20] states that the local authorities 'shall send the Secretary of State such reports and returns, and give him such information with respect to their functions, as he may require, or as may be required by either House or Parliament'.

C. Maladministration

I. NEED TO COMBAT MALADMINISTRATION

Local authorities like other legal persons both natural and artificial are answerable judicially before the courts for any actionable wrongdoing; and they are answerable administratively to superior governmental bodies in the various ways already discussed in this and earlier chapters. In general terms there is a profound distinction between judicial and administrative control; though certain functionaries, notably auditors (as has been seen), can exercise both, so long as they do not confuse them.

The ordinary citizen can therefore bring a local authority to book by pursuing a judicial cause of action in the courts if it arises, or by using administrative appeal procedures (for example in planning) in circumstances where they are prescribed. Until recently he has not been able to pursue grievances in any other way, except by private or public complaints or the ballot-box. The latter may only produce changes among the local politicians, often not even that. The former may not produce anything at all except soothing words or rebuffs (and may not deserve to); but on the other hand justifiable complaints may lead to redress, especially if taken up by a local councillor on the complainant's behalf.

The real difficulty is that if officers or servants of a local authority are truly at fault, and a legal cause of action cannot be shown, they will have a strong incentive to deflect efforts to bring it to light—in order

18 S 92.
19 S 168.
20 S 230.

not so much to prevent redress as to avoid discovery. The more capable and upright they are, the less likely it is that they will either give cause for complaint or prevent matters from being put right; but unfortunately the converse is equally likely to be true. The word to describe the default of officers and servants which cannot be translated into a cause of action at law is 'maladministration'. This is not the implementation of policies of which someone may disapprove. It is the performance of duties in a manner of which, if it is found out, *no* reasonable person can approve.

2. LOCAL COMMISSIONERS ('OMBUDSMEN')

The new-found saviour of the citizen afflicted by maladministration is popularly known as the 'ombudsman', who sounds like a character out of Hans Andersen (not surprisingly since the word is Scandinavian). In British dress this personage is a 'commissioner' for 'administration'. He appeared first on the national scene as the Parliamentary Commissioner for Administration under the Parliamentary Commissioner Act 1967, and was given the task of uncovering maladministration in the civil service. The Local Government Act 1974, Part III,[1] extended the idea to local government by creating what are popularly known as 'local ombudsmen'. The Act[2] set up a Commission for Local Administration for England and another for Wales, both consisting of the Parliamentary Commissioner and one, or more Local Commissioners. Each actual 'local ombudsman' is a local Commissioner. One has been appointed for Wales and three for England on the basis of one for each of three areas: (1) Greater London together with Kent, Surrey and Sussex, (2) the Midlands and the rest of Southern England, and (3) northern and eastern England. Each one reports annually to his Commission.[3]

The British principle of fair play naturally requires facilities to be provided enabling the poachers to keep abreast of the gamekeeper. Therefore a 'representative body' was set up to match each Commission,[4] being composed of representatives of local authorities and related bodies such as water authorities appointed through their appropriate national associations. Yearly 'general' reports made by the Commissions[5] go to these 'representative bodies' to be officially received and published. Estimates of the expenditure involved go to them also; and if they object to these the dispute is if necessary resolved by the Secretary of State, the expenditure itself being met by county councils and the GLC in proportion to rate income.[6]

---

1 Ss 23–34, Schs 4–5.
2 S 23.
3 S 23(11).
4 S 24.
5 S 24(4).
6 Sch 4, paras 6–11.

It is important to realise that, however judicially they appear to operate, the Commissioners, like inspectors, are not judges. They are investigators sent among local authorities by the central government. They investigate complaints relating to local authorities (including joint bodies), local police authorities, water authorities, and such other bodies as may if entitled to levy or precept for rates be specified by an Order in Council.[7] Investigations are[8] to be started by 'a written complaint made by or on behalf of a member of the public who claims to have sustained injustice in consequence of maladministration in connection with . . . action taken in the exercise of administrative functions' performed by any of those authorities since 1 April 1974.

3. INVESTIGATIONS BY LOCAL COMMISSIONERS

This wording contains the crucial point of the procedure. The term 'maladministration' is itself not defined. But the following matters are in general *not* to be investigated:[9] the taking of civil or criminal legal proceedings; the investigation or prevention of crime; commercial transactions *other than* those relating *either* to land *or* to the exercise of functions (except necessary procurement of goods and services) under any public General Act; and matters relating to an authority's staff or to the running of educational establishments. Nor must there be an investigation of any matter in which the 'person aggrieved' has a right of recourse to a court, tribunal or minister[10] unless the Local Commissioner 'is satisfied that in the particular circumstances it is not reasonable to expect the person aggrieved' to exercise that right. A Local Commissioner must also refrain from investigating 'any action which in his opinion affects all or most of the inhabitants of the area of the authority concerned'.[11]

In *R v Local Commissioner for Administration for the North and East Area of England, ex p Bradford Metropolitan City Council*,[12] it was held that a complainant need only specify the acts which are alleged to give rise to injustice suffered, and need not specify the 'maladministration'. Thus the Local Commissioner, bearing in mind the above matters which he is excluded from investigating, has a discretion reasonably to arrive at his own decision as to whether 'maladministration' can be said to have occurred, provided merely that events are specified in the complaint such that he can direct his investigation to them, and further that there is an allegation of injustice in respect of those events. In this par-

7 S 25.
8 S 26.
9 Sch 5.
10 S 26(6).
11 S 26(7).
12 [1979] QB 287, [1979] 2 All ER 881.

ticular case an unmarried mother had left her two young children in the care of a neighbour in Bradford when summoned by their father to join him in London. Bradford Metropolitan City Council then took the children away from the neighbour and into their care in accordance with the Children Act 1948, s 1, as having been abandoned by the parents. On the mother's return she was refused information as to their whereabouts; but eventually she was allowed to see them once a month at a children's home, not the homes of the foster-parents to whom they had been separately entrusted. The council then successfully applied to the magistrates for an order formally authorising the placing of the children in care, since it is illegal to deprive their mother of them against her will without such an order.[13] When the matter was put before the Local Commissioner and he decided to investigate, the council applied for judicial review in the form of a prerogative order of prohibition on the ground that he was acting ultra vires because maladministration had not been specified. The Court of Appeal refused to restrain the Local Commissioner and held that he was acting intra vires.

Lord Denning MR said:

'In the nature of things a complainant only knows or feels that he has suffered injustice. He cannot know what was the cause of the injustice. It may have been due to an erroneous decision on the merits or it may have been due to maladministration somewhere along the line leading to the decision. If the commissioner looking at the case, with all his experience, can say: "It looks to me as if there was maladministration somewhere along the line, and not merely an erroneous decision", then he is entitled to investigate it. It would be putting too heavy a burden on the complainant to make him specify the maladministration: since he has no knowledge of what took place behind the closed doors of the administrator's offices.'

An 'erroneous decision' is presumably one which the local ombudsman (or anyone else) may well disagree with, perhaps strongly, on policy grounds; but maladministration is not established by demonstrating that. Wrongfully handling some question, not wrongfully deciding it, is the essence of the matter. In regard to the Parliamentary Commissioner the then Lord President of the Council (the Rt Hon Richard Crossman MP) gave his views on what should be considered in arriving at a decision whether maladministration has occurred: this was during the debate on the Bill which became the Parliamentary Commissioner Act 1967. He said that the concept would cover: 'bias, neglect, inattention, delay, incompetence, inaptitude, perversity, turpitude,

13 On this, see ch 12, below, p 307.

arbitrariness, and so on'; but any 'discretionary decision, properly exercised, which the complainant dislikes but cannot fault the manner in which it was taken, is excluded'.[14] Despite some differences in the statutory wording this applies to maladministration in local as well as central government.

A complaint must be 'made in writing to a member of the authority, or of any other authority concerned, specifying the action alleged to constitute maladministration', but not, of course, necessarily specifying the maladministration itself, and passed on by him to the Local Commissioner for the area.[15] But the Local Commissioner can deal with the matter even if it has not been passed on to him 'if he thinks fit'. This in fact happened in the *Bradford* case, where the councillor who received the complaint made his own enquiries and as a result decided not to proceed further. As to time-limits, the complaint 'shall not be entertained unless it was made to a member of any authority concerned within twelve months from the day on which the person aggrieved first had notice of the matters alleged in the complaint', except when the 'Local Commissioner . . . considers that there are special circumstances which make it proper to do so'. He must in any case first 'satisfy himself that the complaint has been brought, by or on behalf of the person aggrieved, to the notice of the authority to which the complaint relates and that that authority has been afforded a reasonable opportunity to investigate, and reply to, the complaint'. The hope, though not the certainty, is always that the relevant authority will set matters right. The Local Government Act 1978 empowers them to make payments to the victims of maladministration.

Individuals (singly or in groups) and corporations can make complaints; but other local authorities and public bodies generally are excluded.[16] An individual's personal representative if he has died, or some 'member of his family or . . . body or individual suitable to represent him' if he 'is for any reason unable to act for himself', may act for him. The Local Commissioner must give authorities or persons complained of the chance to comment on the allegations.[17] He must investigate in private, but may go about it in such manner as he thinks fit. How he decides to obtain information and whether he allows anyone to be represented, legally or otherwise, are matters within his reasonable discretion. He can require members and officers of the authority concerned, and other persons as appropriate, to appear before him or produce documents, including correspondence with government departments;[18] and failure to comply 'without lawful excuse' may be treated as con-

14 734 HC Official Report (5th series) col 51.
15 1974 Act, s 26.
16 Ibid, s 27.
17 Ibid, s 28.
18 Ibid, s 29.

tempt of court and reported to the High Court to be dealt with there on that basis.

But disclosure of information given by the Parliamentary Commissioner or a Health Service Commissioner[19] is restricted; and no-one can be compelled to give evidence or produce documents if he could not be so compelled in civil proceedings in the High Court. Crown privilege does not apply;[20] but a minister, or any local authority or other body subject to investigation by a Local Commissioner, may give him written notice that it would be contrary to the public interest to disclose specified documents or information.[1]

In *Re Complaint against Liverpool City Council*[2] it was held that since such a notice expressly rules out disclosure to 'any other person', this must mean that even the Local Commissioner himself is excluded. Accordingly, a subpoena issued by the Local Commissioner concerned to Liverpool City Council to produce confidential records, relating to a child in the council's care, was set aside by the Queen's Bench Divisional Court. Lord Widgery CJ spoke of 'a tug of war conflict between . . . the public interest in the city's records which requires them to be confidential and the public interest in making the Commissioner's duties work which requires the records to be published at all events to him'. On a careful interpretation of the relevant wording the court held that total confidentiality would have to prevail. But the Local Government, Planning and Land Act 1980,[3] now enables Local Commissioners to see such documents. The allegation of maladministration in this case concerned an unexplained decision to transfer the child from one pair of foster-parents to another. The court pointed out that any such notice preventing disclosure as being contrary to the public interest could[4] have been discharged by the Secretary of State but was not.

4. REPORTS AND CONSULTATIONS

A Local Commissioner must report on his findings after having conducted an investigation, or on his reasons for declining to investigate, to the complainant, to the member (if any) who passed on the complaint, and to the relevant authority and any persons particularly implicated. Individuals must not normally be named; but the report must normally be made available for public inspection.[5] If he reports that injustice has in fact been caused by maladministration, then the authority concerned

---

19 Under the National Health Service Reorganisation Act 1973.
20 1974 Act, s 29(4).
1 Ibid, s 32(3).
2 [1977] 2 All ER 650, [1977] 1 WLR 995.
3 S 184.
4 Under a proviso in s 32(3) of the 1974 Act.
5 1974 Act, s 30.

are required to notify him, after considering the report, of the action to be taken by them as a result of it; he may if he thinks fit report further after they have either notified him or failed to notify him in accordance with this provision.[6] Consultations must take place with the Parliamentary Commissioner or a Health Service Commissioner if either appears to be involved.[7] Reports and communications properly concerned with a Local Commissioner's functions are absolutely privileged from liability in defamation;[8] but information obtained in an investigation must not be disclosed for extraneous purposes, apart from any proceedings for perjury or breach of the Official Secrets Acts 1911 to 1939.[9]

6 S 31.
7 S 33.
8 S 32(1).
9 S 32(2).

Chapter 10

Local government functions I— law and order

A. Police

1. COMMON LAW ORIGINS OF THE POLICE

Unlike most modern local government functions, which are of statutory origin, that of the police derives from the common law. Maintaining order, together with raising revenue, was the earliest concern of government. Indeed there would be no government of any kind without such elementary control. It was one and indivisible throughout the realm, local government being in early times not local autonomy but central control exercised in every locality. The King's chief adherents and officers were entrusted with the task of controlling each part of his kingdom on his behalf, and of resisting threats to that control whether of external origin, by invasion, or internal origin, by revolt or disorder of any kind prejudicial to the 'king's peace'. Any real local 'autonomy' then meant effective revolt, or at least ineffective central control.

Sometimes this was accepted and as far as possible regularised in the medieval period, at any rate in the north and west where the Bishops of Durham and the Earls of Chester or Dukes of Lancaster had to be allowed an autonomous 'palatine' (ie vice-regal) authority in controlling the Scots or Welsh 'Marches'. These political and military jurisdictions eventually produced the palatine Chancery Courts of Durham and Lancaster which survived until the Courts Act 1971.[1]

Elsewhere the King's central government, increasingly dependent on a permanent base in London, preferred to retain a surer grip on the localities through the regular shire organisation. The sheriff survives to this day as a symbol of central power—some of which is still actually exercised by his subordinates, the 'sheriff's officers' who where necessary compel recalcitrant defendants to submit to court judgments (and who also 'double' in the role of certificated bailiffs levying distress). He was the officer on whom the King relied on to repress disorder in each shire, as well as to account yearly for royal revenues payable into the King's Exchequer; though from the reign of Edward VI[2] onwards the local militia of the county was entrusted instead to a 'lord lieutenant'. A

---

1 S 41, which merged them in the High Court.
2 3 and 4 Edw 6, c 1 (1550).

sheriff had to be powerful enough to enforce and sustain the control essential for the King's government to be a reality, though not powerful enough to be tempted to become a law unto himself. Even the achievement of the right balance had its drawbacks for the local population, because the weight of his authority was heavy and not usually exercised with undue consideration for the governed.

Of lesser importance were the subordinate units of government in the localities. The weight of power bore down on the actual units of habitation, the villages and towns, of which only the most prominent achieved any effective autonomy by charters granting 'borough' status. Here were the taxpayers, the general run of prosperous subjects of the Crown, together with their various dependants. It was always taken for granted that the more prominent local inhabitants would have a sufficient patrimony to make it possible for the government to place unpaid burdens on them in addition to taxes, and so for the purposes of law and order they were subjected, in the tenth century if not earlier, to group liability under the 'frankpledge' system, the earliest form of local police administration. This, according to Sir Edward Coke's *Institutes*,[3] 'consisted most commonly of ten households . . . the masters of nine families (who were bound) . . . and the master of the tenth household [who was] chief pledge and those ten masters of families were bound one for another's family [to] answer for the injury or offences by him committed'. That is to say the actual wrongdoers, if caught and found guilty, would themselves be subjected to the appropriate punishment, capital or otherwise; but the 'masters of families' bound in 'frankpledge' were separately liable for bringing the wrongdoers to justice if members of their households, under penalty of being 'amerced' (ie fined) in the event of failure. Each group of ten households in 'frankpledge' was called a 'tithing'. In practice a 'tithing' was usually equated with a village, and so there was a rough, though by no means universal, equation of 'tithings', villages and parishes. In course of time, as the parish came more and more to be treated as the general basic unit of English local administration, the 'tithing' came accordingly to be the parish as local police authority.

A pledge is a formal legal obligation, often imposed on oath. The Anglo-Saxon word for it is 'borh': a word easily confused with 'burh'—ie 'borough'. In the local government context it is not surprising that 'burh' and 'borh' overlapped. The Anglo-Saxon words for the 'chief pledge' under the frankpledge system was 'head borh', which became 'headborough'. The best-known 'headborough' is a fictional character: Verges, in Shakespeare's *Much Ado About Nothing*.

Just as villages or parishes were for police purposes officially regarded as 'tithings', groups of ten households of local inhabitants,

3 Second Institute, p 72.

there were also larger administrative units known as 'hundreds'. Whether this meant groups of a hundred households is uncertain; but for practical purposes a 'hundred' was roughly the equivalent of the modern 'district', and thus a sub-division of the shire, not the equivalent of any settlement such as a village or town. Twice every year the 'chief pledge' of each 'tithing' had to attend the court of the hundred in which the 'tithing' (or village) lay, for the sheriff to check that the 'frankpledge' system was being properly maintained, and for wrongdoers to be 'presented' for trial either in the 'hundred' court itself for lesser offences or, subject to being imprisoned in the meantime, eventually in the shire court for greater offences. The sheriffs' 'tourns'—ie circuits—through the various 'hundred' courts in their shires were parallelled by the circuits of royal judges of 'assize' through the shire courts themselves. Later on, the justices of the peace displaced the sheriffs for most purposes as far as criminal justice was concerned, and were authorised by various statutes to try criminal cases of medium seriousness in 'quarter sessions' for each shire, in between the 'assizes' held by the visiting royal judges. They were also empowered to try an increasing number of minor criminal cases summarily, ie without a jury, in 'petty sessions' in the various 'hundreds' (renamed 'petty sessional divisions').

2. THE OFFICE OF CONSTABLE

The 'chief pledges' long continued to be required to carry out the police function of presenting suspected or detected wrongdoers for trial in these courts. From the fourteenth century they were increasingly reinforced by officers known as 'constables'.[4] Various prominent local landowners—noblemen and gentry—were allowed by the Crown to hold their own manorial courts as the equivalent of, and to the exclusion of, the sheriff's 'tourns' in the 'hundred' courts, and these manorial criminal courts were known as 'courts leet'. It was in these courts that constables were appointed. Although in theory 'courts leet' existed on the same level as 'hundred' (ie district) courts, in practice the manors in which they were held were more likely than not to coincide with villages and parishes. Consequently the 'constable' would be recruited from the same class of prominent local inhabitants—prosperous farmers and craftsmen—as the 'chief pledges' or 'headboroughs'. The two offices became interchangeable, but on the whole the 'constable' soon tended to be regarded as more important, perhaps because his office seemed less archaic. In *Much Ado* the constable, Dogberry, has precedence over the 'headborough', with the result that the latter is deferential

---

4 S and B Webb *The Parish and the County* p 26, note 1, say that the office of constable is first mentioned in literature in Langland's *Piers Ploughman* (c 1362).

to him (though Dogberry is stupider and much funnier). When 'courts leet' declined with the decay of the manorial system it became customary for the justices of the peace to appoint the constables, and to do so for the parish as the unit of local administration. These retained the medieval and manorial title of 'petty constable'; while a parallel practice had developed of appointing a 'high constable' in each 'hundred' to superintend their activities.

Social realities being what they were, and are, the 'high constable' would be appointed—originally by the sheriff, later by the county magistrates in quarter sessions—from among 'the most respectable farmers and yeomen of the Hundred',[5] ie well-to-do leasehold and freehold landowners below the ranks of the gentry; whereas 'petty constables' would be persons prominent only in their own parishes. Yet both types of personage would enjoy established incomes and properties and would be selected because they could afford to serve without pay. Obligatory voluntary service in public office was thus the price of enjoying local social prominence combined with economic independence. With the burden of the office went its authority. A constable could by virtue of this not only arrest wrongdoers and 'present' them for trial before the appropriate criminal court but also compel other individuals to 'keep watch and ward' for such wrongdoers, equally without payment. Again Shakespeare in *Much Ado* illustrates this system, with a sardonic eye not only to the quality of the unpaid constable and his deputy but also to that of the unpaid men of the 'watch' compelled to assist them.

In addition to preserving law and order on their own initiative the constables had to execute the warrants issued by the magistrates and obey their orders generally. Their most surprising duty was financial. When the magistrates in quarter sessions—ie the county authority —needed money they would levy it by a county rate. This was to be raised, the procedure being the origin of the modern precept system,[6] on the parish rating assessments already in existence for the poor law and other purposes, through the instrumentality of the 'high' constable for each hundred who in turn collected it from the 'petty' constable of each parish in accordance with the appropriate parish quotas. Being unpaid, these officials not surprisingly tended to increase the amounts demanded so as to reimburse themselves for their trouble. In addition the 'petty' constables were sometimes authorised to levy rates parochially on their own account to recoup the cost of rounding up vagrants as part of the general system of poor-law administration.[7]

This antiquated system of police was radically altered in the nine-

5 S and B Webb, *The Parish and the County* p 491, note 2.
6 See ch 7, p 178.
7 See ch 12, p 302.

teenth century, when county and borough police forces were created in the wake of the Metropolitan Police set up under Sir Robert Peel's Metropolitan Police Act 1829. These new forces consisted of paid constables directed by officers of higher rank. But no change was made in the basic legal status of 'constable', which in essence remained, and remains, an independent public office. As Lord Denning MR said in *R v Metropolitan Police Comr, ex p Blackburn*[8] '. . . every constable in the land . . . is independent of the executive'. The far-reaching changes since 1829 have not abolished the common law principle that a constable, by virtue of his office and not of powers delegated to him by any superior, is still empowered to arrest (after reasonable enquiries: *Dumbell v Roberts*)[9] suspected wrongdoers and required to execute warrants issued by magistrates. He may arrest without warrant only in respect of the more serious of 'arrestable' offences defined in the Criminal Law Act 1967, s 2. The Constables Protection Act 1750 exempts him from liability arising from any warrant being ultra vires. In *Fisher v Oldham Corp*,[10] it was held that he is not the 'servant' of the local police authority which pays his salary. The Police Act 1964,[11] provides however that if a constable or other police officer commits a tort in the scope of his duty the chief officer of police of the particular force to which he belongs will also be liable for it ex officio.

3. POLICE AUTHORITIES TODAY

Nevertheless all police officers belong to a disciplined force by virtue of their terms of service as well as being individual office-holders at common law. In addition a great many statutory powers and duties are conferred upon them to regulate in detail, according to modern requirements, the performance of their basic common law function of preserving the peace. Except for the Metropolitan Police, whose area is similar to but does not coincide exactly with Greater London, under the London Government Act 1963,[12] and who constitute a police force for whom the statutory 'police authority' is the Home Secretary, 'police authorities' remain local authorities. Even the Metropolitan Police can be regarded as a local authority as far as finance goes, because that force like the other police forces, and like local authorities generally, is financed partly by the central government and partly by rates. These are levied, by precept, on the rating authorities in the Metropolitan Police

---

8 [1968] 1 All ER 763 at 769.
9 [1944] 1 All ER 326. See also the Local Government (Miscellaneous Provisions) Act 1982, s 12, in regard to a constable's power to enforce byelaws.
10 [1930] 2 KB 364. Parish constables had neither salary nor uniforms.
11 S 48.
12 S 76. The Metropolitan Police District includes a few border areas of the administrative counties of Essex, Surrey and Hertfordshire where they adjoin Greater London.

District under the Local Government Act 1948,[13] and the London Government Act 1963,[14] by the Receiver for the Metropolitan Police District, who is a separate corporate body (a 'corporation sole') in his own right, in accordance with the Metropolitan Police (Receiver) Act 1861. At the head of the Metropolitan Police is a Commissioner, appointed by the Crown, plus five assistant commissioners.

The function of the police generally is regulated today by the Police Act 1964, which swept away the previous system of county and borough police forces. London includes, in addition to the Metropolitan Police, the City of London Police, for whom the City Corporation are the police authority,[15] and who are headed by their own Commissioner. Elsewhere in England and Wales there are county police forces and combined police forces. In a county force the 'police authority' is a committee of the county council, two-thirds of which are county councillors and one-third magistrates from the county, under the 1964 Act,[16] and the Local Government Act 1972.[17] In a combined force the 'police authority' is, by virtue of the 'amalgamation scheme' under which any combined force is set up, either a committee of one of the county councils or a separate 'combined police authority'. The latter is an independent corporate body two-thirds of which are councillors drawn from the county areas concerned and one-third are magistrates from those areas.[18] County councils include police expenditure in their rate precepts, subject to their entitlement to grants as referred to below.

The chief constable is responsible for the operational effectiveness of the police force, and appoints all members of it under the rank of assistant chief constable.[19] But it is the 'police authority' which is responsible for the general administrative efficiency of the force: it must appoint the chief and deputy chief constable, and may appoint assistant chief constables, subject to the Home Secretary's approval.[20] The authority must manage the finances by a separate 'police fund',[1] out of which are met not only the due expenses of the force but also, under the Riot (Damages) Act 1886[2] compensation payable to 'any person who has sustained loss' because 'a house, shop or building in any police district has been injured or destroyed, or the property therein has been injured, stolen or destroyed, by any persons riotously and tumultuously

13 S 121.
14 Sch 18.
15 Police Act 1964, s 31.
16 S 2.
17 Sch 30.
18 1964 Act, ss 3, 21.
19 1964 Act, ss 7, 16.
20 1964 Act, ss 4–6.
 1 1964 Act, s8.
 2 S 2.

assembled together . . .' In *Dwyer v Receiver for the Metropolitan Police District*,[3] a claimant failed to obtain compensation for loss caused by criminals who were only 'riotous' not 'tumultuous'.

A member of each council must be appointed to answer questions asked in council about police administration.[4] The chief constable must render reports to the authority; but he can resist giving information contrary (in his view) to the public interest unless the Home Secretary so orders.[5]

The Home Secretary is the minister responsible for national supervision. He is authorised to make detailed regulations for police forces and authorities under the 1964 Act,[6] and the Police Regulations 1971,[7] together with various other subordinate legislative provisions on specialised matters such as promotion and discipline. He may call for reports from chief constables, beyond the scope of any particular 'police authority'; and he may order inquiries and appoint, in the name of the Crown, inspectors of constabulary.[8] He may require an authority to call for a chief constable's retirement, subject to a proper inquiry,[9] and may with Treasury approval pay grants to authorities. Grants currently cover 50% of approved expenditure of each authority, provided that he is satisfied with the efficiency of its police force, under the Police (Grant) Order 1966.[10] He has a 'general duty' to exercise his powers as appears to him best calculated to promote the efficiency of the police.[11]

The reorganisation of 'police authorities' in 1964 largely anticipated the general pattern of county organisation produced by the Local Government Act 1972. The latter Act accordingly needed to do very little in regard to local police administration except to bring the 1964 Act into line with its procedures over one or two matters such as audit and the acquisition of land, in accordance with the 1972 Act,[12] which also modifies various 1964 Act provisions relating to schemes of amalgamation and the powers of special constables. The police, therefore, continue broadly to operate as a local government function at county level, even though in London the 'police authority' lacks the element of elected local councillors it possesses elsewhere.

---

3 [1967] 2 All ER 1051.
4 1964 Act, s 11.
5 1964 Act, s 12.
6 1964 Act, ss 33–36.
7 SI 1971/156, as amended.
8 1964, Act, ss 30, 32, 38.
9 S 29.
10 SI 1966/223, as amended.
11 1964 Act, s 28.
12 S 196. Parish constables lasted (in theory) until the 1964 Act, Sch 10, repealed the Parish Constables Acts 1843 and 1872. G. K. Chesterton wrote of his consternation when appointed parish constable for Beaconsfield ('The Comic Constable,' *Daily News*, 2 April 1910, repub 1964: 'The Spice of Life').

B. Fire-fighting and civil defence

1. FIRE SERVICES

The fire services, of which fire brigades are the operational part, are the local authority function which is most similar to that of the police. Like the general run of local functions, however, it is of statutory origin, and relatively recent. In the nineteenth century permissive powers were granted by various statutes to local authorities, but there was no duty upon a national pattern of authorities before the Fire Brigades Act 1938. This imposed the task of maintaining a fire brigade on 'second-tier' authorities, but it was short-lived. In the Second World War fire brigades were combined into a National Fire Service (not surprisingly in view of the constant fire risk from air-raids). After the war the duty was returned to local authorities but this time at 'first tier' level. The Fire Services Act 1947 established a pattern of fire authorities which, as updated by the London Government Act 1963,[13] and the Local Government Act 1972,[14] consist of the Greater London Council and county councils; though, as with police forces, there can be a combination scheme involving two or more authorities as a result of agreement or imposition by the Home Secretary. He is given a general power to make detailed regulations, particularly in regard to staffing.

The general duty resting on each local fire authority is to provide and maintain an efficient fire brigade. This involves having suitably trained and equipped staff, and a reasonably arranged water supply by way of fire-hydrants or otherwise. Drastic and peremptory intrusion on property is obviously often essential, but damage should be mitigated as far as reasonably possible.[15]

In *Buckoke v Greater London Council*[16] it was held that an order to disregard red traffic lights at the fire-engine-driver's discretion, and subject to proper care, was reasonable and therefore intra vires; disciplinary action for disobeying the order was therefore lawful. But Lord Denning MR condemned the proposition, derived from the decision of the Queen's Bench Divisional Court in *Ex p Fry*,[17] 'that the rules of natural justice do not apply to disciplinary bodies. They must act fairly just the same as anyone else: and are just as subject to control by the courts'. The disciplinary action taken in both those cases was, however, reasonable and thus lawful.

As for the legal liability of fire authorities, it was held in *Atkinson v Newcastle and Gateshead Waterworks Co*[18] that the duty to provide suffi-

---

13 S 48.
14 S 197.
15 1947 Act, ss 1–30.
16 [1971] 1 Ch 655, [1971] 2 All ER 254.
17 [1954] 2 All ER 118, [1954] 1 WLR 730.
18 (1877) 2 Ex D 441.

cient water pressure for effective fire-fighting use was owed only to the public as a whole, and could not give rise to liability in tort to a plaintiff whose property suffered more severely than necessary from a fire which could not for that reason be properly fought. The court was strengthened in this view by a special statutory sanction being expressly provided in such cases; but since all that this sanction involved was a complaint to a minister, it could not give much comfort to the plaintiff. In recent times the courts have shown themselves more ready—as in *Cutler v Wandsworth Stadium*,[19] and *Thornton v Kirklees Metropolitan Borough Council*[20]—to recognise a liability in tort to individuals based on breach of statutory duty, which depends on interpreting the relevant statutes, in the light of the function to be performed and the persons likely to benefit from its proper performance and suffer from lack of proper performance. It seems more likely than not that inefficiency of the kind shown in the *Atkinson* case would now produce a favourable reaction by the courts to an allegation that there was a privately action-able breach of statutory duty. Already in *Dawson v Bingley UDC*,[1] the court was prepared to hold that the mis-siting of an indication of a fire-hydrant gave rise to an action for breach of statutory duty at the suit of a plaintiff whose premises suffered more severely than necessary in a fire by the consequent delay in fighting the fire: though to do so it was felt necessary to hold that the defendants were guilty of a *misfeas-ance*—ie a positive wrongful act in the mis-siting of the indication of the hydrant—as distinct from mere *non-feasance* by omitting to do some-thing which should have been done.

Fire authorities must notify the Home Secretary yearly of their 'fire brigade establishment schemes', giving details from which he can judge whether their provision of fire services is adequate and efficient.[2] He may make such a scheme himself, if necessary, and must approve any reduction in services provided. He must also maintain a system of inspectors;[3] and where necessary he should approve or initiate schemes for authorities to arrange for the carrying out of their functions by other authorities on their behalf.[4] Similarly, there should be reinforcement schemes for authorities to aid one another, and he must intervene to secure these where necessary.[5]

The Fire Precautions Act 1971 provides that various kinds of pre-mises must not be used without a 'fire-certificate', which will be sup-plied by the local fire authority after the building in question has been

19 [1949] AC 398, [1949] 1 All ER 544.
20 [1979] QB 626, [1979] 2 All ER 349. But now see ch 5, above, p 128.
 1 [1911] 2 KB 149.
 2 1947 Act, s 19.
 3 S 24.
 4 S 12.
 5 S 2.

inspected to see if there are adequate fire precautions and fire escapes having regard to the use of the premises. The Home Secretary is empowered to designate various classes of premises to which this system of control is to apply. A leading case which bears on this area of law is *A–G v Chaudry*, discussed in an earlier chapter.[6] But the whole question of fire precautions is logically related to building control, which is discussed in the next chapter.

2. CIVIL DEFENCE MEASURES

Closely allied to fire services is the question of civil defence. The Civil Defence Act 1948 empowers the Home Secretary, or such other ministers as may be designated from time to time by Order in Council, to take such measures as appear expedient or necessary for civil defence. Police authorities and other local authorities may be given any such functions as a 'designated Minister' may specify in regulations.

The Civil Defence (Planning) Regulations 1974[7] have been made under the 1948 Act, ss 2 and 8. These give to the Greater London Council and county councils the duty of making plans to deal with the effect of hostile attacks so as to preserve as far as possible all essential local services and look after the victims. 'Second-tier' authorities must be consulted. But steps to implement these plans must only be taken if a 'designated Minister' authorises them. The cost is reimbursed by the central government, totally in respect of some matters and up to 75% in others under the Civil Defence (Grants) Regulations 1953.[8]

C. Legal functions

1. LOCAL AUTHORITIES AND THE ADMINISTRATION OF JUSTICE

Local government areas in England and Wales have since the earliest times had judicial as well as administrative significance, and local authorities have had judicial functions. Mayors of boroughs were normally magistrates ex officio; and the counties were until 1888 actually administered by the magistrates in quarter sessions. As for civil cases, chartered boroughs up and down the land almost invariably had their own borough court, as had some other areas also. Most of these became obsolete by recent times; but the Liverpool Court of Passage, the Salford Hundred Court, the Norwich Guildhall Court and the Bristol Pie Powder and Tolzey Courts, survived with a local jurisdiction somewhere between the High Court and the county courts until abolished by

---

6 Ch 6; see p 152.
7 SI 1974/70.
8 SI 1953/1777.

the Courts Act 1971.[9] The Local Government Act 1972[10] has now abolished all the rest. Part X of the 1972 Act[11] brings other aspects of the legal system into line with the new local government system, parallel with the changes in local authorities even though the legal system is no longer an integral part of local government. The essential principle is that the local judicial institutions are all related to the new counties,[12] in place of the old counties and boroughs which existed before the 1972 Act. The new counties are also the areas for which rent officers are appointed under the Rent Acts.[13]

Thus under s 217 there are 'commissions of the peace', to which the magistrates are appointed, for all the metropolitan and non-metropolitan counties; though magistrates' courts committees are prescribed for the districts in the metropolitan counties, not the counties themselves. A lord-lieutenant is appointed for every new county (and Greater London), and additional lieutenants may be appointed.[14] The sheriffs appointed for the 1972 counties (and Greater London) are officially renamed high sheriffs.[15] As for coroners, these are appointed by county councils, the Greater London Council and the City of London Corporation.[16] All these functionaries, except lords-lieutenant, have a remote origin in the early medieval common law, although their functions have been regulated by a great many statutes over the years. They continue to serve for their respective local government areas but as part of the judicial or ceremonial side of public affairs and not the governmental side.

But it should be noted that the expenses of the magistrates' courts are paid by local authorities: namely by non-metropolitan *county* councils, out of the county fund, and metropolitan *district* councils, out of the general rate fund. The Home Secretary pays grants of up to eighty per cent of this expenditure, but receives the money taken in fines. County and district councils are empowered to petition to Crown, via the Home Secretary, for the appointment of a stipendiary (ie salaried professional) magistrate in their area in place of the lay magistrates. These provisions are contained in the Justices of the Peace Act 1979.[17]

2. LOCAL LAND CHARGES

One other legal aspect of local government should be mentioned. This is a regular administrative function undertaken by local councils, though it

---

9 S 43.
10 S 221 and Sch 28.
11 Ss 216–221.
12 S 216.
13 1972 Act, s 205.
14 S 218.
15 S 219.
16 S 220.
17 Ss 13–16, 55–61.

is done for the benefit of the legal system and of the legal rights of citizens. The function is the maintenance of local land charges registries in accordance with the Local Land Charges Act 1975 and rules made under it by the Lord Chancellor.[18] The local authorities responsible are the 'second-tier' bodies: district and London borough councils and the City of London Corporation. Local land charges are burdens or restrictions on landowners imposed on their land, normally by a public body, in accordance with some statute, notably in connection with planning control, street works, coast protection, land compensation, new towns, and the prevention of acquisition of rights of light (this type of charge being created for a private instead of a public purpose, though the existence of public planning control has made it necessary).

The purpose of this system of registration is to make it practicable to do two things at the same time: to enforce the restrictions on land use which the charges record, these being necessarily either directly or indirectly in the public interest; and to warn prospective purchasers or tenants of the land in question, or other persons intending to acquire rights in that land in return for payment, of those restrictions. The system operates by means of an administratively maintained public register, the contents of which are discoverable on proper enquiry by means of a 'search'.

The important question is what happens if any local land charge is not duly registered, or if registered it is not disclosed by due search in response to a proper enquiry. In *Ministry of Housing and Local Government v Sharp*,[19] a charge embodying a ministerial right to recover a planning compensation payment was duly registered, but negligently it was not disclosed on a search by a purchaser, who therefore refused to make the required repayment, as was his right. The minister recouped his loss by recovering damages for negligence from the local authority responsible for the register. The Local Land Charges Act 1975,[20] now provides that a failure to register or to disclose will no longer prevent a charge from being enforceable but that compensation is to be paid instead. Generally speaking, a purchaser can only obtain this compensation if his search occurs before he makes his contract. The registering authority must pay the compensation, but may recover in turn from the authority creating the charge if they are at fault.

D. Licensing

The registration and licensing powers of local authorities appear in the

---

18 Local Land Charges Rules 1977, SI 1977/985, as amended. See also the Local Government (Miscellaneous Provisions) Act 1982, s 34.
19 [1970] 2 QB 223, [1970] 1 All ER 1009.
20 S 10.

context of various different functions. For the sake of a general review certain of their powers may be briefly mentioned here. The Betting, Gaming and Lotteries Act 1963, the Gaming Act 1968 and the Lotteries and Amusements Act 1976 empower district and London borough councils to grant permits to use premises for 'amusements' with prizes or gaming machines. The 1976 Act empowers local authorities themselves to promote local lotteries. The Theatres Act 1968 makes district councils and the GLC local licensing authorities for theatres (not for purposes of censorship, however). The London Government Act 1963, Sch 12, makes the GLC the licensing authority for other entertainments in Greater London, and various other statutes make provision elsewhere. The Cinematograph Acts 1909–52 and the Cinematograph (Amendment) Act 1982 similarly make district councils and the GLC licensing authorities for films and the premises which show them: the purpose includes safety and also censorship, as can be seen from *R v Greater London Council, ex p Blackburn*.[1]

Taxicabs and other vehicles for hire are licensed by district councils under the Local Government (Miscellaneous Provisions) Act 1976, Part II, and earlier statutes; in the Metropolitan Police District the relevant statute is the Metropolitan Public Carriage Act 1869, which vests control in the Home Secretary, who exercises it through an Assistant Police Commissioner. The operation of this licensing system can be studied from (for example) the reports of the decision in *R v Liverpool City Council, ex p Liverpool Taxi Fleet Operators' Association*.[2]

Local authorities also have licensing functions which are little other than taxation. The Local Government Act 1972, s 213, gives such functions to district councils in respect of moneylenders, pawnbrokers, dog owners, game-dealers and game-killers.

The most recent statute dealing with licensing and controls by local authorities is the Local Government (Miscellaneous Provisions) Act 1982. This covers licensing of public entertainments (s 1 and Schs 1 and 2); control of 'sex establishments' (s 2 and Sch 3); control of take-away food shops, late-night refreshment houses and the sale of food by hawkers (ss 4–7 and 18–19); and control of acupuncture, tattooing, ear-piercing and electrolysis (ss 13–17).

---

1 [1976] 3 All ER 184, [1976] 1 WLR 550. See above, ch 4, p 92.
2 [1975] 1 All ER 379, [1975] 1 WLR 701. See above, ch 3, p 66.

Chapter 11

Local government functions II— land use

A. Highways

1. PUBLIC RIGHTS OF WAY

Local highway administration, like the police, has a very remote origin. Whereas most local government functions were first imposed by statute, the care of highways was first imposed at common law. No government, however feeble, can afford not to have a care of highways, if for no other reason than the need for direct rapid and unobstructed passage of its messengers, its supplies and its armies. A sophisticated government such as that of imperial Rome constructed artificially surfaced roads on efficiently surveyed lines to provide a network of communications on which the control of its territory depended—for general use by all people no doubt, but chiefly official functionaries and above all its soldiers. Post-Roman rulers were not equal to this task, in view of their lesser resources; but they could at least ensure that the roadways they needed were kept clear, and the speed and range of their military campaigns are a sign of this. Ordinary paved road surfaces might not matter greatly to them, but bridges and causeways did. In Anglo-Saxon charters there are frequent references to liability for the upkeep of bridges (*brycg-bot*) which was an obligation—along with upkeep of fortresses and performance of military service—from which the Kings excused few if any of the lords to whom they granted land.[1] Whether there ever ceased to be a London Bridge after Roman times is an interesting question; the structure there in the time of Kings Ethelred and Cnut was an important factor in hampering military attacks on the city.[2]

But in the English common law the essence of the law of highways was (and is) not concerned with physical structures, however primitive, but an abstraction, a right pure and simple. 'Highway' is a concept, and means a public right of way across land just as an easement of way means a private right of way across land. The right benefits all members of the general public, or for that matter the entirety of mankind. This is of course a general principle, and for that reason it can be qualified with exceptions: but 'exceptions prove the rule'.

---

1 See Sir Frank Stenton *Anglo-Saxon England* pp 287–288.
2 Stenton, op cit, p 385.

The law of highways regulates the relation between the general public and the owner of the land where a public right of way is asserted. What it does is to show when rights of landownership have their usefulness lessened by rights of passage enjoyed by other persons, but it does not detract from the rights themselves. Very often the ownership of land on which there is a highway is vested in a public body; and very often that body is a 'highway authority'; but the ownership is never vested in the general public in whom the public right of way subsists. This is not a modern sophistication: it has been the rule since English common law began. An early legal textbook[3] defines a highway in these words: 'The king has nothing but the passage for himself and his people'.

It follows that a member of the public can be liable in trespass to the landowner if while present on land constituting a highway he does something beyond exercising his common law right of 'passage'. In *Hadwell v Righton*[4] Phillimore J said: 'Members of the public, in addition to using the highway *eundo et redeundo*, are also entitled to use it *morando* for a short time'. So it is not necessary for the public to keep moving incessantly. In *Rodgers v Ministry of Transport*,[5] it was held that lorry drivers were within their rights as highway users in stopping at the side of the road for refreshments. But in *Hickman v Maisey*[6] it was held that a 'racing tout' who kept a landowner's race-horses under observation from a public road on the landowner's property was committing a trespass.

This right of passage exists within boundaries, which may or may not co-incide with boundaries of landownership. In the absence of evidence otherwise, the boundary between two separate properties lying on either side of a highway lies in the centre of the highway: *Beckett v Leeds Corp*.[7] This is often expressly stated in conveyances; but it is also common for property boundaries to be shown at the highway boundary, so that the landownership of the highway coincides with the extent of the highway and may represent the vestigial ownership of an original owner-developer who sold off adjoining plots.

The highway boundaries, as distinct from the ownership boundaries, are to be reasonably inferred from the material features of the strip in use (again subject to particular evidence otherwise). In *R v United Kingdom Electric Telegraph Co*,[8] the Court of Queen's Bench approved the following statement of the law by Martin B: 'In the case of an ordinary highway, although it may of a varying and unequal width, running

3 Rolle's Abridgement 1, 392.
4 [1907] 2 KB 345.
5 [1952] 1 All ER 634.
6 [1900] 1 QB 752.
7 (1872) 7 Ch App 421.
8 (1862) 31 LJMC 166 (an early case where photographs were used).

between fences one on each side, the right of passage or way, prima facie, and unless there be evidence to the contrary, extends to the whole space between the fences, and the public are entitled to the use of the entire of it as a highway, and are not confined to the part which may be metalled or kept in order for the more convenient use of carriages and foot passengers'. In *Neeld v Hendon UDC*[9] Vaughan Williams LJ said '. . . the fences may, prima facie, be taken to have been originally put up for the purpose of separating land dedicated as a highway from land not so dedicated'. Thus in *Rodgers v Ministry of Transport* (above) the lorry drivers were legitimately making use of the public right of way by parking for refreshment not on the metalled carriageway but on the 'roadside waste'.

A cul-de-sac may be a highway: *William-Ellis v Cobb*.[10] Any landowner whose land immediately adjoins the highway, without there being any intervening strip of land, however narrow, in someone else's ownership, is at common law allowed unrestricted access from his land on to the highway regardless of whether or not his ownership includes any part of the highway land at whatever level: *Marshall v Blackpool Corp*.[11] This rule, like any other, is subject to statutory modification; and the Town and Country Planning Act 1971, s 22, now provides that the making of a new access to a highway is an 'engineering operation' and thus a project of 'development' for which planning permission is required. Also, a local highway authority can make a 'carriage crossing' over a verge or footway where any vehicle is habitually driven between the metalled part of the highway and the adjoining 'frontage' property, and the 'frontager' in question, as occupier, must pay for it.[12]

The public right of way constituting a highway is exercisable without distinction of person. But there are restrictions according to the type of use. A 'carriageway' is in law[13] a highway available for use by members of the public in vehicles or on horseback or on foot. A 'bridleway' is one available for use by members of the public on horseback or on foot. A 'footpath' is one available for use by members of the public on foot. Thus, according to Lord Holt, in *R v Saintiff*:[14] 'Highway' is the genus of all public ways, as well cart, horse and foot ways'.

Recent statutes have introduced other kinds of restriction embodied in the term 'special road' by which the use of a highway may be restricted to prescribed classes of persons in accordance with an official scheme made or confirmed by the Minister of Transport.[15] In practice

9 (1899) 81 LT 405.
10 [1935] 1 KB 310.
11 [1935] AC 16.
12 Highways Act 1980, s 184.
13 Highways Act 1980, s 329.
14 (1704) 6 Mod Rep 255.
15 Highways Act 1980, s 16. See also s 329 (cycle tracks), and the Countryside Act 1968, s 30 (public right to use pedal-cycles on bridleways).

the 'special roads' made under this power are the 'motorways' made by the minister. The standard classes of members of the public prohibited from using the 'special roads' which are 'motorways' commonly include pedestrians, pedal cyclists, learner-drivers, and persons using invalid carriages or riding or leading animals. Apart from these restrictions, the extent or mode of use of any highway is not limitless but should be reasonable. A 'footway' (technically not a 'footpath') may be constructed in a highway comprising 'carriageway' alongside the metalled 'carriageway' itself in accordance with the Highways Act 1980,[16] and generally speaking drivers of vehicles are not exercising their right of way reasonably unless they keep off the 'footways'. Road 'islands' or 'refuges', subways and the like may also be constructed[17] as may cycle-tracks,[18] footbridges,[19] dual carriageways and roundabouts,[20] and margins for horses and livestock.[1] All these 'improvements' are made under the 1980 Act, Part V, which authorises a variety of improvements, and segregates the lawful users of highways in some manner. Failure to provide such items may sometimes cause disadvantage to certain classes of lawful highway user de facto even if not de jure.

2. DEDICATION AND STOPPING UP

The creation of highways depends on the common law concept of 'dedication'. This, in essence, is a policy decision by the freeholder of the land on which the highway is situated. No other person in principle can impose the burden on that land; although there are circumstances in which by statute dedication occurs virtually automatically—in effect it is deemed to occur, notably where 'private street works' have been carried out at the bidding of a local highway authority, as will be explained below.[2] Often in modern law a public authority will acquire land and then, as freeholder, will dedicate a highway as a matter of public policy, for example when the Ministry of Transport constructs a motorway or a new 'trunk road'.

Dedication requires an animus dedicandi—ie an intention by the landowner—together with the 'acceptance' by the public if they choose to avail themselves of it. Any indication to the contrary will carry great weight, because a landowner cannot reverse the decision once taken. 'Once a highway always a highway' is the long-established common law expression, as used by Lord Parker CJ in *Redbridge London Borough v*

16 S 66.
17 Ss 68–9.
18 S 65.
19 S 70.
20 S 64.
 1 S 71.
 2 See p 274.

Jacques,[3] following Byles J in *Dawes v Hawkins*.[4] Only an obsolete common law writ ad quod damnum, and now certain statutory procedures, could or can terminate any highway. The Highways Act 1980,[5] empowers a highway authority to apply to the magistrates for an order to 'stop up' a highway, on the grounds that it is unnecessary, or to stop it up as part of a process of diversion to make it 'nearer or more commodious to the public'. If a landowner asks for this to be done and it is agreed he may be required to bear the cost.

A local authority may also apply to the Secretary of State for the Environment to make a 'public path extinguishment order' or a 'public path diversion order' on a similar basis.[6] But the more normal context for stopping up a highway is to obtain an order from the Secretary of State under the Town and Country Planning Act 1971, ss 209–210, to enable re-development of land to take place when permitted under Part III of that Act, or under s 211 if a new highway is to cross the line of an old one, or under s 212 if it is desired to reduce a highway from a public carriageway to a public bridleway or footpath.[7] The Housing Act 1957, s 64, allows a local housing authority to extinguish any highway as part of a slum clearance project.

If a landowner is willing to allow the public to cross his land on a purely permissive basis and not 'as of right' he can indicate this by barring the way at intervals as was done in *Merstham Manor Ltd v Coulsdon and Purley UDC*.[8] Alternatively he can put up notices or, in case these should be torn down, give notice to the local authority that no dedication is intended. But failing these steps a highway will be regarded as having impliedly been dedicated after the public have used it 'as of right'—ie openly, without force and without permission—for 20 years without interruption: Highways Act 1980, ss 31–32. Implied dedication at common law, however, is independent of this and does not require proof of 20 years' use, merely such unimpeded use as the courts recognise as sufficient to prove dedication and acceptance on the facts of a particular case. Any public authority, as freeholder, is in the same position as any private owner so long as dedication is compatible with its statutory functions. In *British Transport Commission v Westmorland County Council*,[9] there was implied dedication where a private bridge across a railway line had been used by the public for a number of years.

Implied dedication by long use thus still operates, although its main

3 [1971] 1 All ER 260.
4 (1860) 8 CBNS 848. See above, ch 4, p 77.
5 Ss 116–117.
6 1980 Act, ss 119–20.
7 This is often done in order to create a 'pedestrian precinct'.
8 [1937] 2 KB 77, [1936] 2 All ER 422.
9 [1958] AC 126, [1957] 2 All ER 353.

effect is to account retrospectively for the old-established highways (some of them on the line of Roman roads, or even older ways) which have been used as such for centuries. Express dedication results from any clear demonstration of intent by the landowner. Public authorities which are highway authorities create new highways in this fashion on land they acquire for the purpose. Housing authorities do so when they lay out highways on their local authority housing estates under the Housing Act 1957, Part V. Private owners may do so in public-spirited fashion as regards public footpaths or bridleways; but they are unlikely to do it in regard to public carriageways, unless these are included in a project of development as being necessary to give access to new buildings. In such a case the developer will normally take the precaution of making an agreement with the local highway authority under the Act of 1980,[10] that the authority will 'adopt' the highway if it is 'made up' to a required standard and dedicated. The developer will then know that his new buildings will sell—except in circumstances where an 'exclusive' housing estate, for example, is intended to attract purchasers who want private access only. The authority will know that additional rate-producing properties will come into existence, so that the new rate revenue will offset the permanent expense of upkeep thereafter.

It will be apparent from this that to speak of the 'creation' of a highway generally means two quite separate things: the 'dedication' of the public right of way, and the material construction (if any) of a suitable hard surface 'made up' to the standard required for the purposes of development or 'adoption' or probably both. 'Making up' without 'dedication' will only produce a private road.

A footpath or bridleway is perhaps less likely to be 'made up' than a carriageway, especially in the countryside. The National Parks and Access to the Countryside Act 1949,[11] requires county councils to make and periodically review a 'definitive' map and statement showing 'public paths'—ie footpaths and bridleways—in their area, subject to publication first in draft followed by the settlement of any disputes by the Crown Court. Since the Act defines a footpath as a right of way *on foot only*, the House of Lords in *Suffolk County Council v Mason*,[12] declared that a definitive map is conclusive as to public footpaths. In that case there was strong evidence that a country lane, though designated under the Act as a public footpath, had been a public carriageway at one time. Yet the principle 'once a highway, always a highway' was nevertheless impliedly overruled by this interpretation of the Act of 1949, at any rate to the extent of demoting the lane from public carriageway to public footpath.

---

10 S 38.
11 Ss 27–38.
12 [1979] AC 705, [1979] 2 All ER 369.

3. HIGHWAY MAINTENANCE

The original function of local authorities at common law was not to create or improve highways, merely to maintain them. The Statute of Winchester 1285 ambitiously provided that all main roads between towns were to be cleared of brushwood for two hundred feet on either side to reduce the danger from robbers lurking in ambush. But in practice little was done to ensure that highways were properly maintained. A temporary Statute of Highways 1555, repeated and made permanent in 1563, imposed a liability for upkeep on each parish. An official called the 'surveyor of the highways', chosen by the parish, was required to impose compulsory unpaid labour on all occupiers of land in the parish for six days in the year. Under the Highways Act 1691 the surveyor was appointed by the magistrates and made subject to their directions, and in addition he was empowered to levy a sixpenny rate on the occupiers of land in the parish for additional expenditure over and above their compulsory labour. But like other parish officers he was unpaid and untrained—normally in fact a local farmer. The standard of maintenance was, not surprisingly, very low.

Nevertheless 'the inhabitants at large' were liable at law for proper upkeep, and could be 'presented'—ie prosecuted—at quarter sessions for the county if they failed to reach even the current low standard of highway maintenance. The sanction was a fine, though the proceedings were in truth administrative rather than criminal. In *Russell v Men of Devon*,[13] it was held that there was no civil liability to match the criminal burden, so that no traveller injured by reason of a failure to maintain a highway could have any redress by an action for damages founded on the negligence of the parish.

The Highway Act 1835 ushered in (tentatively) the modern era of local highway administration. It created parish highway authorities, who took over the magistrates' role of giving directions to the surveyor and could levy a rate. The compulsory unpaid labour burden hitherto resting on the parish disappeared. The 1835 Act also provided that, while pre-existing highways must continue to be publicly maintained, no subsequently dedicated public carriageways should give rise to this liability until 'adopted' by the highway surveyor. He need only agree to this if the way had first been 'made up' to his satisfaction.

No change was made to the rule that civil liability could not be imposed for failure to maintain ('non-feasance'); but civil liability did come to be recognised for positive acts of negligence ('mis-feasance'). Thus in *Thompson v Brighton Corp*,[14] an action failed in respect of injury caused by neglect to repair a highway surface which had crum-

---

13 (1788) 2 Term Rep 667.
14 [1894] 1 QB 332.

bled round a metal grating which itself had been properly fixed. But in *Skilton v Epsom and Ewell UDC*[15] one succeeded in respect of injury caused by a defective metal stud inefficiently placed on the road-surface. Eventually the immunity of highway authorities for negligent upkeep confined to 'non-feasance' was abolished by the Highways (Miscellaneous Provisions) Act 1961.[16] But the liability is none the less founded on negligence and is not absolute; and it involves a question of fact and degree in the circumstances of each case: *Rider v Rider*.[17] But the possibility of there being any civil liability at all depends on the fact that highway authorities as such were created under the 1835 Act. The old criminal liability of the parish ('inhabitants at large') was obsolete thereafter, and finally abolished by the Highways Act 1959.[18]

This liability to maintain (and clear) which the Acts impose on highway authorities applies only to those highways—virtually all the important ones and most of the unimportant ones—which are 'maintainable at public expense'.[19] This, by virtue of the 1835 Act,[20] means all highways existing in 1835 and all public carriageways 'adopted' by the local highway authorities since 1835. By virtue of the National Parks and Access to the Countryside Act 1949,[1] it also means all public footpaths and bridleways already existing in 1949 and any created thereafter if 'adopted'. The Act of 1980,[2] contains the modern procedure for adoption of highways dedicated by private landowners. The making and dedication of a highway on a public authority's own land makes the minister or local highway authority liable for its maintenance automatically[3] without 'adoption'.

All highways 'maintainable at public expense', automatically or by 'adoption', are said to 'vest' in the authority responsible for them, by s 263 of the Act of 1980. In *Tunbridge Wells Corp v Baird*,[4] Lord Herschell said that this 'vests in the . . . authority . . . such property only as is necessary for the control, protection and maintenance of the [way] as a highway for public use', ie the highway surface and immediate sub-surface and drains, and enough air-space above the surface for the persons and vehicles using the highway and for posts, lights, signs and other equipment. The rest of the space above and below the surface belongs to whoever is the landowner, in that capacity, subject to

15 [1937] 1 KB 112, [1936] 2 All ER 50.
16 S 1, now replaced by the Highways Act 1980, s 58.
17 [1973] QB 505, [1973] 1 All ER 294. See also *Levine v Morris* [1970] 1 All ER 144, where the negligent siting of a road sign was in issue.
18 S 38.
19 Highways Act 1980, ss 36, 41.
20 S 23.
 1 Ss 47–49.
 2 S 37.
 3 S 36.
 4 [1896] AC 434 at 442.

various provisions in the Act of 1980,[5] for the prevention of wrongful interference with the highway.

The duty of modern highway authorities is therefore to maintain the substance of the highways 'vested' in them.[6] This carries a public liability to the community as a whole and a private liability to persons injured by the default of the authority. It does not, of course, apply to highways not 'maintainable at public expense'. Occasionally these are subject to surviving forms of ancient private liability to maintain; but normally there is no private liability at all. In *Greenhalgh v British Railways Board*,[7] the Court of Appeal held that anyone present on land 'as of right', such as a member of the public when using a highway, has no right of action in negligence against the occupying landowner *as such* for damage or loss caused by failure to repair. Liability for highway maintenance is thus independent of ordinary 'occupier's liability': they are in fact two quite different varieties of the same species of liability. An authority declining to 'adopt' will therefore avoid two perpetual burdens: the administrative burden of paying to maintain, and the legal burden of liability in negligence.

It should however be noted that, under the Act of 1980,[8] although any authority can resist a landowner's proposal that a highway dedicated on his land should be 'adopted', yet a magistrates' court has power to decide this issue against them, according to whether or not the highway will 'be of sufficient utility to the public'. Part IV[9] of the Act contains a variety of other more specialised provisions relating to maintenance.

4. HIGHWAY AUTHORITIES AND CLASSIFICATION OF HIGHWAYS

Local highway authorities today, under the Act of 1980, no longer include parishes; though parish and community councils have a limited role to play, notably by exercising a right to complain of obstructions and encroachments and to require their local highway authority to 'take proper proceedings accordingly'.[10] The question of what bodies are highway authorities depends largely on a statutory classification of highways which cuts across the common law classification described earlier. Highways which constitute the network of principal national routes for through traffic are 'trunk-roads'; and under the Act of 1980,[11] these can be created by new construction works or by the designation

5 Pt IX.
6 In *Reigate Corpn v Surrey County Council* [1928] Ch 359, this included two walls and roof of a tunnel through which a highway passed.
7 [1969] 2 QB 286, [1969] 2 All ER 114. See above, ch 5, p 120.
8 S 37.
9 Ss 36–61.
10 S 130(6). See below, p 277.
11 Ss 10, 24.

of existing roads. Motorways are 'special roads',[12] as mentioned above,[13] which are part of this network of 'trunk roads'.

There are also 'classified' and 'principal' roads.[14] The former are Class 'A' and 'B' main roads designated as such under the Ministry of Transport Act 1919, and Class 'C' roads designated subsequently. The Local Government Act 1966 created 'principal' roads, being largely the same as the Class 'A' roads other than trunk roads; and grants may be made in respect of them. But the Act of 1980,[15] has for practical purposes largely absorbed grants into a general power of the Minister of Transport to 'advance' money, by either loans or grants, to local highway authorities in accordance with formulae approved by the Treasury which are made known in ministerial circulars. Central government financial assistance to local highway authorities is, however, largely encompassed by the general or 'rate support' grant, discussed in an earlier chapter,[16] which supplements their general rate revenue. In Greater London the 'principal' roads, and others designated by the minister, are termed 'metropolitan roads'.[17] These rank next in importance to trunk roads.

The Act of 1980, Part I, specifies the 'highway authorities' today. The Minister of Transport or the Secretary of State for Wales is the highway authority for 'trunk roads'.[18] The Greater London Council are the highway authorities for 'metropolitan roads', and the London boroughs and the City corporation are highway authorities for other highways in Greater London. Elsewhere county councils are, subject to any special provisions to the contrary, the highway authorities for highways other than 'trunk roads'. But it should be noted that under ss 4–9, county councils act as agents for the minister in regard to much of the detailed work involved in regard to trunk roads. Various other agreements to delegate or transfer executive functions are also authorised between authorities; so that for example district councils may carry out highway works in their areas, and sometimes do so as of right.[19] Local highway authorities are also 'street lighting authorities';[20] but district, parish and community councils may make themselves responsible for lighting footways.

5. NEW HIGHWAYS AND STREETS

The creation, as distinct from the maintenance, of highways was not a local government function until recent times. In the eighteenth century a great

---

12 S 16.
13 See p 266.
14 Under the 1980 Act, ss 12–13.
15 S 272.
16 Ch 7, see p 172.
17 1980 Act, s 15.
18 S 1.
19 S 42 and Sch 7.
20 S 97.

many 'turnpike trusts' were set up by private Acts. Local landowners could at any time dedicate new highways at common law; but those Acts empowered them to finance the construction and upkeep of new public roads by charging tolls. Groups of landowners and other notables were authorised to act together in their localities as 'turnpike trustees'; and by the early nineteenth century most main roads were managed in this way. 'Turnpike roads' were largely the 'trunk roads' of those days.

The advent of the railways, plus the inefficient finances of many turnpike trusts, resulted in the turnpike system coming to an end by 1895; but the arrival of motor transport on the roads led to a new government initiative for the creation and administration of an improved national road system in the twentieth century.[1] This has brought about the modernisation of the system of highway authorities as described above, the Ministry of Transport being entrusted with national administration generally and the upkeep and improvement of the network of 'trunk' and 'special' roads in particular. The Act of 1980[2] empowers the minister and the local highway authorities to create new highways (and road ferries); and Part XII[3] contains various authorising powers for the acquisition of the necessary land, or rights over land, by agreement or compulsion, including any to be used for works to mitigate the adverse effects of highways on land nearby. County and district councils, London authorities and national parks joint planning boards may agree with landowners for the dedication and upkeep of new public footpaths and bridleways, by 'public path agreements', or may create these compulsorily by 'public path orders' confirmed by the Secretary of State for the Environment.[4]

The most elaborate works of construction normally relate to 'trunk' and 'special' roads, under Part II of the Act of 1980.[5] The minister may make orders under which roads become, or cease to be, 'trunk' roads,[6] and he (and in theory other highway authorities) may make schemes for providing 'special' roads.[7] Bridges and tunnels may be constructed and maintained as part of a highway; but a distinction must be made between bridges which carry highways over natural obstacles such as rivers and those which carry them over, or under, artificial obstacles such as railways and canals. Normally such structures have been built by railway, canal, dock, harbour or similar undertakings, under separate statutory powers, subject to a liability to maintain the highway

1 Development and Road Improvement Funds Act 1909.
2 S 24.
3 Ss 238–271.
4 Ss 25, 26.
5 Ss 10–23.
6 S 10.
7 Ss 16–18.

they cross; much the same is true of level-crossings. The Highways Act 1980,[8] and the Transport Act 1968,[9] provide for the transfer of responsibility for these from the relevant undertaking to the appropriate highway authority. This may be done either by agreement or (with ministerial approval) compulsorily, with reconstruction where necessary; for there may be a transfer of the highway but not the bridge.

Special procedures have been enacted for 'streets', which the Act of 1980 now contains in Parts X and XI. 'Street' has been defined in leading cases as meaning any way with an appreciable number of buildings along it: 'a highway with houses on each side' according to Lord Blackburn in *Robinson v Barton-Eccles Local Board*.[10] But the Act of 1980[11] adds that the term 'includes any highway and any road, lane, footpath, square, court, alley or passage, whether a thoroughfare or not, and includes any part of a street', without expressly stating whether this is subordinate to the above judicial definition. Reason suggests that it is.

Part X[12] empowers county councils, and London borough councils and the City Corporation, to make byelaws regulating the construction and dimensions of new streets. In practice, this control is largely covered by planning legislation today, as also are ss 73–74 which empower highway authorities to impose 'improvement' and 'building' lines regulating development adjoining highways. In *Westminster Bank Ltd v Minister of Housing and Local Government*[13] the House of Lords held that the local planning authority could tacitly apply an 'improvement line', de facto with an eye to subsequent road-widening, by simply refusing to grant planning permission, instead of prescribing the line formally and so making themselves liable to pay compensation to the landowners. Lord Reid observed that the Ministry of Transport, in its Circular 696 dated 27 August 1954, threatened withdrawal of grant money from any authority formally making an 'improvement line' when planning control could be relied on instead. Thus a statutory provision under which compensation would be payable to landowners was in effect cancelled by ministerial policy.

6. PRIVATE STREET WORKS

Part XI of the 1980 Act,[14] enacts a procedure for 'private street works'. Under this code a 'street works authority',[15] which will be the same as

---

8 Ss 93–94.
9 Ss 116–122.
10 (1883) 8 App Cas 798.
11 S 329.
12 Ss 186–202.
13 [1970] 1 All ER 734, [1970] 2 WLR 645.
14 Ss 203–237.
15 S 203.

the authority empowered to make 'new street byelaws' under Pt X, above, is entitled to enforce the 'making up' of any 'private street', that is to say a 'street' which is either not a highway at all or not one 'maintainable at public expense', provided that it has not been 'made up' already 'to the satisfaction of the . . . authority'.[16]

The essence of the procedure is that the burden of cost should fall proportionately on the various 'frontagers', but that in return the authority shall adopt the street as a highway maintainable at public expense and thus be liable for its upkeep in perpetuity thereafter.[17] The frontagers must accept this bargain whether they like it or not, so long as the procedure is duly followed. In *Alsager UDC*[18] *v Barrett*, Widgery J (as he then was) said that 'the onus of proof . . . undoubtedly rests on the local authority' if there is a dispute whether a way is or is not a 'private street'; therefore if the street in this case had existed before 1835 it would (if dedicated) already have been 'maintainable at public expense', but the evidence showed that it had not then existed and even if it had become impliedly dedicated it had never been 'adopted'. An authority must 'adopt' the street in its current condition.[19]

The authority must pass a resolution to apply this procedure in respect of a particular private street. Their surveyor then prepares a specification of the works, an estimate of cost, and a 'provisional apportionment' (registrable as a local land charge) among the frontages. The authority must then, in order to proceed, pass a 'resolution of approval', and publish it. The 'provisional apportionment', as approved, must in general terms be made in proportion to the frontages. But 'the greater or less degree of benefit to be derived by any premises' may be taken into account to justify an adjustment, at the authority's option,[20] and so may any 'degree of benefit' to 'premises which do not front the street but have access to it through a court, passage or otherwise.[1] In *Buckinghamshire County Council v Trigg*,[2] it was held that the authority could have applied the latter principle[3] to a first-floor maisonette, the access to which lay across the front garden belonging to the ground-floor maisonette of the particular house fronting on to the private street which was being 'made up'. But churches and some other types of property are exempt.[4]

16 S 205(1).
17 S 228.
18 [1965] 2 QB 343, [1965] 1 All ER 889.
19 *Urban Housing Co v Oxford Corp* [1940] Ch 70, [1939] 4 All ER 211. In this case the local highway authority unlawfully used their steam-roller to knock down a wall to which they objected.
20 S 207(2).
1 S 207(3).
2 [1963] 1 All ER 403, [1963] 1 WLR 155.
3 S 207(3).
4 S 215.

A frontager may resist a provisional apportionment on any of six grounds specifically listed;[5] and if he and the authority cannot agree the dispute must be decided by the magistrates. The next step is for the authority to perform the work, and then make a final apportionment;[6] this too can be resisted on any of three specified grounds, and any unresolved disputes settled as before. Within three weeks of the authority's demand for payment he may appeal to the Minister of Transport, and raise any relevant issue other than those referred to as grounds for resisting an apportionment.[7] The amount assessed to each frontager is a charge on the frontage premises,[8] and the authority can enforce the charge in the manner of a mortgage, or as an ordinary creditor suing in the court. If the frontager conveys the frontage of his property to a nominee without assets, the court can be asked to make the transferring owner liable regardless.[9] An alternative mode of ensuring payment is for an authority to apply what is termed the 'advance payments code'[10] requiring frontagers to pay, or give security for, the cost of prospective street works before permission is given for development of sites fronting any private street. The frontagers subjected to this code, to which there are numerous exceptions, have a corresponding right to call for the street works to be carried out at an appropriate stage.

7. LAWFUL AND UNLAWFUL INTERFERENCE WITH HIGHWAYS

Interference with highways is sometimes lawful, sometimes not; and the Act of 1980, Part IX,[11] deals with these, together with the Public Utilities Street Works Act 1950. The latter Act prescribes procedures whereby works to place or repair or move utility apparatus in a highway (such as pipes and cables) and works to repair or improve the highway itself, can be arranged with the minimum of disruption by proper consultation between the various highway authorities and public utility undertakers concerned.

Damage to and obstruction of highways is a public nuisance, as described in an earlier chapter.[12] In addition there are several specific provisions in Part IX of the Act of 1980 which impose safeguards, restrictions or criminal penalties. It was held in *Arrowsmith v Jenkins*,[13] that

---

5 S 208.
6 S 211.
7 S 233.
8 S 212.
9 S 235.
10 Ss 219–225.
11 Ss 130–185.
12 Ch 5. See *Harper v Maden* [1933] 1 Ch 298 and also *Potter v Mole Valley District Council and Surrey County Council* (1982) Times 22 October, in which the highway authority themselves were liable.
13 [1963] 2 QB 561, [1963] 2 All ER 210.

criminal liability is strict in these cases. There is also a general provision[14] which imposes on the relevant highway authority a 'duty . . . to assert and protect the rights of the public to the use and enjoyment of any highway . . .'; and it confers on any other council in the area or power (but not a duty) to do the same. As under the Local Government Act 1972, s 222, described earlier, in chapter 6, authorities can also under s 130 'institute legal proceedings in their own name, defend any legal proceedings, and generally take such steps as they deem expedient.

Local highway authorities must remember that they have a duty under s 130, not a mere power. In *R v Surrey County Council, ex p Send Parish Council,*[15] some house-owners extended their gardens so as to encroach unlawfully on a public footpath. The local parish council successfully sought judicial review to compel the local highway authority to take legal proceedings to end the abuse. The Queen's Bench Divisional Court said that a legal duty must be viewed in reasonable terms; and it was unreasonable in law for the highway authority in this case not to take appropriate proceeding when it was undisputed that a highway existed and was being unlawfully interferred with. On the other hand, in *Re Guyer's Application,*[16] an assertion by a local resident that a path was subject to a public right of way was truly in dispute, being denied by the landowner and genuinely doubted by the authority; the court held that in consequence there was no duty on the authority to bring proceedings.

B. Public or environmental health

I. ENVIRONMENTAL HEALTH AUTHORITIES

The modern era of constant functional legislation began with the alarm over sanitation during the cholera epidemics of the 1830s. Public health statutes, designed to ensure that proper sanitation be provided in the public interest and to make landowners comply with the necessary requirements, were passed from time to time, culminating in the Public Health Acts 1872 and 1875. The modern pattern of district councils is derived from the local boards of health and other sanitary authorities set up under this legislation, and the Department of the Environment derives much of its responsibility from the central government department set up to supervise those authorities, the Local Government Board.[17]

---

14 S 130. See also the Local Government (Miscellaneous Provisions) Act 1982, Part X (ss 20–23).
15 (1979) 40 P & CR 390.
16 [1980] 2 All ER 520, [1980] 1 WLR 1024.
17 See ch 2, p 34.

Modern local administration in the field of public (or 'environmental') health has changed much in detail from those origins but little in essence. The principal statute is the Public Health Act 1936, but several other important Acts must also be considered. The Local Government Act 1972,[18] provided that for 'public health' functions the 'local authority and sanitary authority', should be the district of London borough council for each area, and the City Corporation. There are however some functions which county councils and the GLC exercise, and a few are given to parish and community councils.

2. WATER AUTHORITIES: WATER AND SEWERAGE

The most important transfer of responsibility, however, concerns water supply and sewerage, both of which for obvious reasons were of primary importance in public health administration from the beginning. The Water Act 1973[19] set up regional 'water authorities' to take over those functions from the district councils and other bodies which exercised them before. The Secretary of State, aided by a National Water Council,[20] continues to exercise general control. The new authorities are much fewer and larger than their predecessors; but many of the latter (notably water companies set up under Private Acts) remain for the purpose of carrying out functions as the water authorities' agents. The Water Act 1945[1] empowers private residential developers to require water mains to be provided, so far as practicable; and water authorities must maintain the supply therein in a proper manner, including pressure.

All water publicly supplied for domestic use must be 'wholesome';[2] and as described earlier, in chapter 5 the water authorities will be privately liable in tort for failure to comply with this duty. The water supply must also be suitable for fire-fighting purposes.[3] The mode of charging for water supplies has been discussed in an earlier chapter.[4] Safe construction and upkeep of reservoirs is governed by the Reservoirs Act 1975; shortages in dry weather are to be dealt with by the Secretary of State under the Drought Act 1976; and a system of general national conservation of water resources under his direction is prescribed under the Water Resources Act 1963.

Although they are 'regional' bodies, specialised in functions and not democratically elected, water authorities have to be considered here because their administrative functions are still closely analogous to

18 S 180.
19 S 2.
20 Ibid, s 4.
 1 S 37.
 2 Water Act 1973, s 11.
 3 Water Act 1945, Sch 3.
 4 Chapter 7, see p 175. See also the Water Charges Equalisation Act 1977.

those of local authorities. This is substantially so for water supply because even though some of their predecessors in this were water companies (others were borough and district councils) the system was operated in close connection with local government and, like it, was subject only in a general way to central government control.

As for sewerage, this was previously carried out as a straighforward local government function under the Public Health Acts, which still apply in essence to the sewerage administration of the water authorities. The Public Health Act 1936,[5] defines a 'drain' as a pipe used for drainage from a single 'curtilage' or set of premises, and a 'sewer' as a pipe used for drainage from more than one. 'Private sewers' are within the control of private owners; 'public sewers' are those which belong to the mains sewerage networks provided and maintained by the sewerage authorities themselves. These are the water authorities set up under the Water Act 1973; but that Act[6] requires them to enter into agency arrangements with district and London borough councils for the routine performance of their sewerage functions, at the water authorities' cost. The public sewers, pumping stations and sewage disposal works are vested in the water authorities. The local authorities must be consulted about plans to make, close or alter public sewers, and must keep a map of them.[7] Sewage must be suitably purified before it is discharged into rivers or the sea; otherwise the discharge is illegal and subject to actions for public or private nuisance—referred to in an earlier chapter—or prosecution under the Control of Pollution Act 1974.[8]

Distinct from 'sewage' is 'trade effluent'—ie liquid, whether or not containing matter in suspension, produced in the course of trade or industry—which must only be discharged into sewers or elsewhere in compliance with the requirements of the water authority for the area under the Control of Pollution Act 1974.[9] Discharge in contravention of these restrictions is an offence, proof of which requires merely the knowledge that the discharge has occurred and not that the manner of it amounts to an offence: *Alphacell Ltd v Woodward*.[10]

In this connection it should be noted that water authorities have general responsibility for prevention of pollution of inland and coastal waters, under the Control of Pollution Act 1974, Part II,[11] and also for land drainage under the Land Drainage Act 1976. The latter function is concerned with keeping rivers and main watercourses in an efficient state to prevent flooding, by carrying out works of cleansing, repair,

5 S 343.
6 S 15.
7 Public Health Act 1936, s 32.
8 Ss 31–32. See ch 5, pp 119, 122.
9 S 43.
10 [1972] AC 824, [1972] 2 All ER 475.
11 Ss 31–56.

improvement and new construction, subject to general supervision by the Minister of Agriculture, Fisheries and Food. Administration is carried out through a specialised regional land drainage committee; and routine work is carried out by internal drainage boards administering internal drainage districts. The expenses of the latter are defrayable by drainage rates. The expenses of water authorities outside those districts are defrayable by drainage charges, and their expenses for land drainage generally are defrayable by 'precepting' on local rating authorities as described in chapter 7. County and district councils can also carry out minor functions. Private civil liability may be incurred for failure to carry out land drainage functions properly; but compensation for damage is statutorily payable where negligence is not proved, under the Land Drainage Act 1976.[12]

3. CONTROL OF BUILDINGS

Another major public health function is building control. This has been retained by district and London borough councils and the City of London Corporation. Inner London boroughs are governed by a separate code of control in the London Building Acts; but in the rest of the country the code is contained in the Building Regulations which the Secretary of State makes by statutory instrument[13] under the Public Health Act 1961.[14] The Health and Safety at Work etc Act 1974, Part III[15] authorises additional regulations to be made in respect of working premises, and these are applicable also to Inner London boroughs. Before the 1961 Act came into effect (1 February 1966, in this connection) public health authorities made their own building byelaws for the purposes of building control. Although modern byelaws are always subject to ministerial approval, it was thought that this earlier system was too haphazard to be allowed to continue.

The Building Regulations govern, in principle and in exhaustive detail, the specification of new building construction works, including alterations and additions to existing buildings, from the standpoint of safety and health. They cover choice of materials, modes of construction, sanitation, fire-precautions, and various related matters. New building work must not be carried out until plans have been submitted to the local authority for approval. This is not a policy matter as planning control is. If building plans as submitted comply with the Building Regulations and are not defective for any other significant reason, the authority must approve the plans;[16] if not the plans must be rejected. It is an offence to build in contravention of these requirements;

---

12 S 17.
13 Currently SI 1976/1676, with later amendments.
14 Ss 4–11. See also ch 6, p 141.
15 Ss 61–76.
16 Public Health Act 1936, s 64.

and in addition the authority may give orders for remedial works or demolition to take place, or do such works in default at the owner's cost. Appeals lie to the Secretary of State, with a further appeal to the High Court on a point of law.[17] Heat insulation of factories is regulated separately under the Thermal Insulation (Industrial Buildings) Act 1957.

The Health and Safety at Work etc Act 1974 was passed to impose on local authorities, subject to inspection and general supervision by the new Health and Safety Executive set up by the Act, the duty of enforcing new regulations governing working conditions in non-domestic premises. Districts and London borough councils and the City of London are given these functions by the Health and Safety (Enforcing Authority) Regulations 1977[18] made under the Act by the Secretary of State for the Environment. The intention is to supersede earlier provisions under the Offices, Shops and Railways Premises Act 1963, the Factories Act 1961, and other statutes. Fire precautions are separately covered by the Fire Precautions Act 1971, under which various premises need a fire certificate, from the 'fire authority' referred to in the last chapter,[19] before they can be lawfully used. This function is parallel to the requirement of adequate fire-precautions in new buildings under the Building Regulations, and also to the requirement under the Public Health Act 1936[20] that fire-escapes must be provided in various buildings of public resort such as theatres and hotels.

Control of building use in the interests of health and safety is also dealt with by certain other statutory provisions, enforced by the same local public health authorities. These can order the owners of dangerous structures to carry out remedial works, and carry them out in default at the owner's cost.[1] A criminal penalty may also be imposed, and in cases of urgency authorities may do the work themselves at once. Demolition works need advance notification to the local authority, which may impose necessary requirements as to safety precautions.[2] Other powers relate to derelict buildings, rubbish tips and similar land. The Prevention of Damage by Pests Act 1949 empowers local authorities to deal with property infested by rodents; and authorities are also empowered to cleanse verminous houses.[3]

4. STATUTORY NUISANCES, OFFENSIVE TRADES, REFUSE AND POLLUTION

An allied code of control of land use relates to 'statutory nuisances'. In *National Coal Board v Thorne*,[4] the Queen's Bench Divisional Court held

17 1936 Act, ss 64–67, subject to later amendments.
18 SI 1977/746.
19 See p 258. See also the Local Government (Miscellaneous Provisions) Act 1982, ss 8–10.
20 S 59.
1 Public Health Act 1936, s 58 and Public Health Act 1961, ss 24–25.
2 1961 Act, s 29.
3 1936 Act, ss 83–84.
4 [1976] 1 WLR at 546.

that a 'statutory nuisance' is not a separate concept but 'must be either a private or public nuisance as understood by common law'. This means that conditions which only affect an occupier, as against other persons coming to the premises, cannot be a 'nuisance'. The Act of 1936,[5] speaks of 'premises in such a state as to be prejudicial to health or a nuisance' constituting a statutory nuisance, and it goes on to refer to animals, accumulations or deposits, dust or effluvia, or insufficiently ventilated workplaces. Mere 'inert matter', even if potentially injurious such as broken or scrap metal, is not 'prejudicial to health', according to the Divisional Court in *Coventry City Council v Cartwright*;[6] there has to be something actively threatening public health whether animal, vegetable or mineral.

The procedure for remedying statutory nuisances is for the local authority to serve an 'abatement notice' on the owner or occupier of the premises. If the remedial works specified in it are not complied with a 'complaint' should be laid before the magistrates asking them to grant a 'nuisance order' ordering compliance with the abatement notice. A fine may also be imposed. If there is default, the authority can do the work at the offender's cost. Persons other than the authority can bring proceedings for a 'nuisance order', notably if the alleged offender is in fact the local authority as in *Salford City Council v McNally*.[7] If there is or may be a recurrence of a statutory nuisance a 'prohibition notice' may be served alternatively to an 'abatement notice': Public Health (Recurring Nuisances) Act 1969. In cases of urgency the authority may do the work on nine days' notice in accordance with the Public Health Act 1961.[8]

Offensive trades, such as bone-grinding, tripe-boiling or glue-making, may not be carried on without the local authority's consent, with a right of appeal to the magistrates, under the Act of 1936.[9]

The Control of Pollution Act 1974,[10] now deals with the removal of refuse. 'Collection authorities' are the public health authorities, which must remove household waste from premises in their area, and commercial waste as well on request and at a reasonable cost. 'Disposal authorities' are county councils and the GLC, whose functions is to provide sites where refuse can be incinerated or otherwise destroyed, and also to collect industrial waste on request at a reasonable cost. These authorities control the deposit of waste on other premises by a

---

5 S 92, as amended by the Local Government (Miscellaneous Provisions) Act 1982, s 26. See also the Local Government (Miscellaneous Provisions) Act 1976, ss 23–26, in regard to dangerous trees and excavations.
6 [1975] 2 All ER 99, [1975] 1 WLR 845.
7 [1976] AC 379, [1975] 2 All ER 860.
8 S 26.
9 S 107; *Epping Forest DC v Essex Renderings* [1983] 1 All ER 359.
10 Ss 12–21.

system of control licences,[11] and provide sites for depositing refuse in accordance with the Refuse Disposal (Amenity) Act 1978.

The Act of 1974 also controls noise-levels by empowering district and London borough councils and the City of London Corporation to serve abatement notices, subject to appeal to the magistrates, and to designate 'noise abatement zones'; and together with the Clean Air Acts 1956 and 1968 it empowers public health authorities to enforce a system of smoke control and atmospheric pollution generally. Yet other statutes empower these same authorities to control common lodging houses,[12] premises where upholstery materials are used,[13] sites used for caravans and other moveable dwellings,[14] and canal boats.[15]

5. ENTRY ON PREMISES

Authorities carrying out duties under the Public Health Acts can authorise their officers to enter any premises in furtherance of those duties, at any reasonable time of day on 24 hours' notice.[16] But if due notice is not given or any other requirement is not reasonably met, such forcible entry is a trespass: *Stroud v Bradbury*.[17]

C. Housing

1. HOUSING AUTHORITIES AND HOUSING STANDARDS

Arising out of public health administration in Victorian times, there was also legislation on housing. The dangers of disease from insanitary premises were (and are) specially obvious in regard to dwellings, particularly in industrial towns with their large concentrations of buildings on congested sites. Partly on medical and partly on moral grounds a succession of Acts have been passed during the last hundred years for the purpose of improving the general stock of housing accommodation. These statutes have conferred a body of administrative functions on local authorities, subject to central government supervision, in the familiar pattern.

Since the Local Government Act 1972,[18] the pattern, as with public health, has consisted of local housing authorities which are district and London borough councils and the City of London Corporation; and the supervision by central government is carried out by the Department of

---

11 1974 Act, ss 3–5.
12 1936 Act, ss 235–248.
13 Rag Flock and Other Filling Materials Act 1951.
14 Caravan Sites Acts 1960 and 1968; and the 1936 Act, ss 268–9.
15 1936 Act, ss 249–258.
16 1936 Act, s 287.
17 [1952] 2 All ER 76.
18 Ss 193–4 and Sch 22.

the Environment. The 1972 Act,[19] confers reserve housing powers on county councils, which are for use only when local housing authorities prove insufficient and when the Secretary of State for the Environment approves. The principal statute is the Housing Act 1957; but a great many changes and new provisions have since been enacted.

The ever-changing mass of housing enactments, chaotic at first sight, are variations on a single theme. This is the principle that substandard housing ought to be replaced by adequate housing. The yardstick provided is the concept of fitness for habitation: adequate housing is 'fit' and substandard housing is not. The Housing Act 1957, s 4 (as amended), expresses the definition of 'fitness' in negative wording: 'unfit for human habitation'. A house is 'unfit' if it is defective in regard to one or more of certain specified factors: repair, stability, freedom from damp, internal arrangement, natural lighting, ventilation, water-supply, drainage and sanitary conveniences, and facilities for preparing and cooking food and disposing of waste water. But it is only unfit if so far defective as not to be reasonably suitable for occupation in that condition. The specified factors in s 4 show the close connection between housing law and public health, since most of them are the subject-matter of public health legislation as described above, including the Building Regulations.[20] Not only that, but the procedures for dealing with 'unfit' houses under the Act of 1957 are normally initiated by the local housing authority's medical officer.[1]

Later statutes have added a second yardstick, which is the presence or absence of what are called the 'standard amenities'. Certain procedures are to be applied for the purpose of making good any deficiencies in these, so that houses are required to be fully equipped with them as a result of these procedures and 'fit for habitation' as well. The seven standard amenities are: a fixed bath or shower, a wash-basin, a sink, a hot and cold water supply to each of those three items, and a water-closet.[2] The standard of adequacy applied to houses by these twin yardsticks is pretty modest, depending on how it is applied in practice. The various statutory procedures envisage the local housing authorities applying the appropriate test; but their decisions can be challenged and will, if objectively unreasonable, be ultra vires on the *Wednesbury* principle referred to earlier in this book.[3]

Local housing authorities are empowered to achieve the aims of this legislation, first, by following procedures designed to get rid of substandard housing. The issue lies, for most purposes, between the housing

---

19 S 194.
20 See p 280.
1 S 157.
2 Housing Act 1974, s 58 and Sch 6.
3 See ch 3, p 63.

authority on the one hand and the 'person having control' on the other. The expression means the person who has a property interest in the house such that he receives the 'rack-rent'—ie the full market rent, subject to statutory controls—or would do if the house were let at a rack-rent.[4] This definition, by and large, includes owner-occupiers and most landlords, but it excludes tenants at a market rent and 'ground landlords' receiving a low rent. It coincides with the definition of 'owner' in planning and other legislation; whereas 'owner' under the Housing Acts means instead a freeholder or a leaseholder with three or more years to run.[5]

2. CLEARANCE OF SLUMS

In aiming to get rid of substandard housing, authorities have a choice between tackling houses singly or in groups, and also a choice between demolition and renovation. Part II[6] of the Act of 1957 enables them to serve on the 'person having control' of an 'unfit' house a notice to carry out repairs,[7] or a demolition order.[8] The former, usually known as a 'repair notice', is only justifiable if the unfit house can be made fit at reasonable expense ie expense not disproportionately high in relation to the improvement in capital value: *Hillbank Properties v Hackney London Borough Council*.[9] If it cannot be made fit at reasonable cost a demolition order is the appropriate step; but the 'person having control' should first be given a chance to propose works of repair on his own account if he so wishes. If a demolition order would be appropriate but for the fact that the house or dwelling is part of a larger structure (eg it is a terrace house or a basement flat) a closing order should be made instead, under which the premises may be used for some other purposes (if suitable) which is non-residential.[10]

Appeal lies in all those cases to the county court, which may uphold, quash or vary the authority's decision which is being challenged. The county court's decision is final on the merits, but is subject to appeal on legal grounds. In *Pocklington v Melksham UDC*,[11] a demolition order made with the shortest time-limit allowed by the Act (vacation of the premises in four weeks and demolition within six further weeks) was varied on appeal by substitution of a period of seven years; the Court of Appeal held that this was an unreasonable exercise of the county court's

4 1957 Act, s 39.
5 1957 Act, s 189.
6 Ss 4–41.
7 S 9, as amended (it may be in bad repair but not 'unfit').
8 S 16.
9 [1978] QB 998, [1978] 3 All ER 343.
10 Ss 17–18.
11 [1964] 2 QB 673, [1964] 2 All ER 862.

discretion, and restored the order to its original terms. In lieu of demolition an authority may adhere to a repair notice by acquiring the house compulsorily and carrying out the works specified;[12] or the house may be 'patched up' and retained for temporary use without making it fit.[13]

Unfit houses in groups can be dealt with by way of 'slum clearance' under Part III[14] of the 1957 Act. The authority declares a 'clearance area' by resolution[15] if satisfied that the houses in it are unfit, or else dangerous or injurious to the health of the inhabitants (even if not unfit) because of bad arrangement, and that other buildings are similarly dangerous or injurious to health, and if satisfied in addition that the best solution is to demolish them. Procedure is by way of compulsory purchase, unlike demolition orders which require the 'person having control' himself to demolish.

But equivalence is maintained (at least in theory) because when an unfit house is acquired the market value purchase price compensation payable is limited to 'cleared site value',[16] which requires the existence of the house to be disregarded. However, the existence of an unfit house on land may well be a liability and not an asset, if it represents merely an obligation to pay demolition costs; if so, the value of site-plus-house, being lower than 'cleared site value', must instead be paid.[17] If an unfit house has been 'well maintained' a special 'well maintained' payment must be made[18] provided that the value of site-plus-house is not exceeded. If an unfit house has been owner-occupied for two years the 'cleared site value' must be brought up to the value of site-plus-house by an 'owner-occupier payment'.[19] It may be added that 'cleared site value' is not expressed to be confined to existing use value to the exclusion of development value; however, many individual properties are in fact too small to command any development value to speak of. Apart from the 'cleared site value' requirement, compulsory purchase compensation does not depart from the general compensation rules.

Property in a clearance area, or adjoining it, is to be acquired and cleared of buildings under this procedure, and then used for redevelopment either by the housing authority or by some other public body or private developer. This is similar to comprehensive development or 'urban renewal' under Part VI of the Town and Country Planning Act

---

12 S 12.
13 S 17(2).
14 Ss 42–75.
15 S 42.
16 S 59.
17 Land Compensation Act 1961, s 10 and Sch 2 (which also prescribes gross value for rating as the minimum compensation for owner-occupied dwellings).
18 Ss 30, 60.
19 1957 Act, ss 31, 61, amended by the Housing Act 1969, Part V.

1971, except that the latter procedure will not normally be confined wholly or mainly to houses. Slum clearance sites are often, in fact, used for new local authority housing.

3. HOUSING IMPROVEMENTS AND GRANTS

The Act of 1957 makes no provision for renovation of houses in groups, but this omission has been made good by later statutes which provide for 'housing action areas' and 'general improvement areas'. The Housing Act 1969, Part II,[20] modified by the Housing Act 1974, Part V,[1] and Housing Act 1980,[2] provides that local housing authorities can declare 'general improvement areas' where living standards ought to be improved and authorities can help to bring this about. The means used are not modes of compulsion, as under Parts II and III of the Act of 1957, but encouragement in the shape of grants; though compulsory purchase may also be used. Part IV of the Act of 1974[3] empowers authorities in similar terms to declare 'housing action areas' where the needs are more urgent and deserve greater priority, the assumption being that such areas can be dealt with quickly in a period of five to seven years.

These procedures apply the 'carrot' treatment rather than the 'stick' treatment of the 1957 Act; but the 'stick' is also available because Part III[4] of the Act of 1974 allows authorities to use a procedure involving 'improvement notices'. Such a notice orders the 'person having control' who is a landlord (or in some special cases an owner-occupier) to carry out works to instal 'standard amenities', referred to above, in which the house is deficient. The recipient must first be allowed to offer to do works of his own; but if he defaults the authority then proceed. There is a right of appeal to the county court, as there is under the 1957 Act. The procedure only applies to houses which date back before 3 October 1961.

Whether or not an 'improvement notice' has to be served, any owner or tenant of a house deficient in 'standard amenities' is entitled to apply for an 'intermediate grant' under the Act of 1974, Part VII,[5] as amended by the Housing Act 1980.[6] An applicant must obtain approval in advance for his proposed works; and if they are suitable and not excessive, a grant is payable of one half of the cost up to a 'ceiling' for each 'standard amenity' to be installed and any necessary additional works.

20 Ss 28–42.
1 Ss 50, 51.
2 S 109.
3 Ss 36–49.
4 Ss 85–104.
5 Ss 56–84.
6 Ss 106–7.

But higher proportions are payable in 'housing action areas' and 'general improvement areas', variable at the discretion of the Secretary of State. Applicants must certify that the improved houses will be retained for their own family or for letting for five years; if this is disregarded the grant money will become repayable. In addition there are 'improvement grants', payable at the housing authority's discretion for works which go beyond the mere installation of 'standard amenities' (though these must where necessary be included) and which comply with higher standards specified administratively by the Secretary of State. The house grant-aided in this way must be given a life expectancy of 10 to 30 years at least. Applicants must certify retention of use of the premises as they do for 'intermediate grants' and similarly must apply in advance for approval. There are rateable value limits for applicants who are owner-occupiers, except in 'housing action areas'; and amounts of grant are variable in much the same way as for 'intermediate grants'.

There are also 'special grants' for houses in 'multiple occupation' and 'repairs grants' for works of repair only.

4. MULTIPLE OCCUPATION AND OVERCROWDING

The 1957 Act, Part IV,[7] empowers local housing authorities to deal with overcrowded houses by a system of criminal sanctions; but continual housing shortages have meant that these powers are little used, except for s 90 (amended by the Housing Act 1969, s 58) which empowers authorities to impose restrictions to prevent overcrowding of houses occupied by 'persons who do not form a single household'. These 'houses in multiple occupation' have been subjected to further controls under the Housing Acts 1961 and 1964. The Act of 1961, Part II,[8] has empowered the Secretary of State to prescribe a code of management for such houses, which can be applied by a local housing authority to a particular 'house in multiple occupation' by a 'management order'. The code prescribes various requirements relating to fitness for habitation and for safety (eg fire-escapes); and in addition authorities may serve orders specifying remedial works which must be carried out, subject to appeals to the magistrates or the county court. Directions limiting the maximum number of 'individuals or households or both' may also be made, infringement of which is an offence. The Act of 1964, Part IV,[9] further strengthens these controls by empowering local housing authorities to make 'control orders' taking over the management altogether, but not the ownership, in such houses.

7 Ss 76–90.
8 Ss 12–28.
9 Ss 64–91.

5. PROVISION OF COUNCIL HOUSING

A positive policy of supplying adequate housing accommodation is authorised by Part V[10] of the Act of 1957, which empowers local housing authorities to build council houses and flats and acquire land for the purpose if 'slum clearance' land is not available for use. The policies which authorities may choose to follow in fixing the rents they charge have been discussed in chapter 7.[11] Rate revenue helps to finance council housing, and also the rate-support grant; but there are in addition specific grants payable to local housing authorities in the form of 'housing subsidies', at present governed by Part VI[12] of the Housing Act 1980.

Part I, Chapter II,[13] of the 1980 Act gives council house tenants security of tenure on similar lines to that enjoyed by private residential tenants under the Rent Act 1977. Part I, Chapter I,[14] of the 1980 Act, however, gives council tenants the right to buy the freehold of their houses, or long leases of their flats, with the help of a mortgage from the authority, at a discounted market value purchase price. This varies from a 33% discount for a tenant who has occupied for the minimum period of three years to qualify, up to a maximum discount of 50% for a tenant who has occupied for 20 years, by stages of one percentage point up for each year of occupation. If the purchasing tenant resells within five years the discount will have to be repaid, less 20% for each complete year that has elapsed since his purchase.

Council houses are much in demand, with considerable waiting lists. In spite of this, special priority may have to be given to applicants who are homeless, under the Housing (Homeless Persons) Act 1977. This requires local housing authorities to make 'appropriate enquiries' on the following lines. First, actual 'homelessness' must be shown which means that the applicant and his or her household has no living accommodation available under any property interest, licence or statutory right. Such a person may have a 'priority need' if he or she is accompanied by any dependent child or incapacitated adult, or is (or is accompanied by) a pregnant woman. It must also be discovered if the homelessness is *not* the applicant's own fault and if in addition he or she has a 'priority need'. If only the latter factor applies temporary accommodation only is to be provided. Unless both factors apply the duty is merely 'to furnish . . . advice and appropriate assistance'. But if an applicant comes from the area of another local housing authority, he or she can in any case be transferred to that authority.

10 Ss 91–134.
11 See p 167.
12 Ss 96–105.
13 Ss 28–50.
14 Ss 1–27.

6. HOME LOANS

Finally mention should be made of certain financial provisions. Under the Housing (Financial Provisions) Act 1958, ss 43–45, and also the Small Dwellings Acquisition Acts 1899 to 1923, local housing authorities, and also county councils, are empowered to make 'home loans' for the purchase, construction, conversion or improvement of dwellings, on reasonable terms taking into account the market value of the premises.[15]

There is in addition under Part II of the Housing Subsidies Act 1967, as amended, the 'option mortgage scheme', whereby a 'qualifying lender', which includes local housing authorities and county councils, as well as certain other bodies, lends money up to a specified maximum on mortgage for the acquisition, construction, conversion or improvement of a dwelling subject to that mortgage (whether owned freehold or leasehold), and the borrower opts to give up income tax relief and deductions in return for having his mortgage repayment instalments reduced by the amount of a subsidy payable by the Secretary of State to the 'qualifying lender'. This subsidy is a sum calculated on the differential between the rate of interest contractually payable on the outstanding capital debt and a prescribed lower interest rate. Residence conditions and other particular requirements are specified.

D. Planning

1. PLANNING AUTHORITIES AND DEVELOPMENT PLANS

Just as the impetus of housing legislation was derived from early public health legislation, so in turn the impetus of planning legislation was derived from early housing legislation. The widening outlook of reformers led to the view that the general pattern of national life and land use would have to be improved as well as housing and sanitation. Private planning control by restrictive covenants had already produced results, but only in new well-to-do residential areas. Private planning on a more ambitious scale produced model suburbs, and also garden cities, such as Bourneville and Port Sunlight, or Letchworth.

But Parliament introduced planning into the public sector with the passing of the Housing, Town Planning etc Act 1909 and in the now familiar pattern conferred planning functions on local authorities subject to general ministerial supervision by the Local Government Board. That body, after many intervening changes, is now transformed into the Department of the Environment; and the local planning authorities

---

15 See also the Home Purchase Assistance and Housing Corporation Guarantee Act 1978.

today are county and district councils. These are 'county planning authorities' and 'district planning authorities' as prescribed by the Local Government Act 1972.[16] County councils are responsible for certain 'strategic' matters, but district councils handle most routine planning administration. A similar pattern applies in Greater London where the GLC handles the 'strategic' matters and the London borough councils and the City of London Corporation handle most routine administration.[17] Planning administration in National Parks, however, is largely in the hands of joint or special planning boards or county national park committees.[18]

Three major concepts predominate in planning—'planning' itself, 'development' and 'amenity' (which will be discussed later). 'Development' is statutorily defined, as will be seen, so as to refer to projects carried out on particular sites. 'Planning' is not defined, but in practical terms it can be said to mean harmonising generally the 'development' of the many sites within the areas administered by the various planning authorities in accordance with settled policies. 'Planning' is general and 'development' is particular.

In the light of this it is first necessary to consider the system of 'development plans'. Part II[19] of the Act of 1971, as amended by the Act of 1972, s 183, and other provisions, requires county planning authorities to prepare and regularly revise 'structure plans', dealing with broad 'strategic' planning policies, and district planning authorities to prepare and regularly revise 'local plans' within their areas to implement those broad policies in more detail. All these authorities collaborate to produce a 'development plan scheme' to harmonise the various plans which, together, constitute a complete development plan. A 'plan' is essentially composed of written policy statements, with maps and diagrams to illustrate them. Elaborate legal rules govern the preparation and approval of plans; though as a rule only the structure plans need to be approved by the Secretary of State. But the legal consequences of a plan after it is approved are mostly indirect, the main purpose of the plan being administrative, namely to harmonise the individual planning decisions.

2. DEVELOPMENT CONTROL

Routine planning functions carried out in general by district planning authorities are contained in Part III[20] of the Act of 1971. This begins by defining 'development' in s 22 in terms of building, engineering, mining and other operations on land or 'material' changes in its use.

16 Ss 182–3 and Sch 16.
17 Town and Country Planning Act 1971, Schs 3–4.
18 Local Government Act 1972, s 184 and Sch 17.
19 Ss 6–21.
20 Ss 22–53.

Subject to certain specialised exceptions, for development to be law-fully carried out a planning permission is 'required'.[1] The Secretary of State has made the Town and Country Planning (Use Classes) Order 1972[2] specifying certain changes of use which are not 'material', and the Town and Country Planning General Development Order 1977,[3] or 'GDO', which specifies various classes of development which are auto-matically permitted. The GDO, and various 'special development orders' in special cases, are made under s 24; and the GDO also sets out the procedure for applying to the local planning authority specifically for planning permission in other cases not covered by the automatic grant of permission. 'Outline' permission can be sought for buildings granting permission in principle but leaving the details ('reserved mat-ters') to be dealt with separately.

The local planning authority can, under s 29, refuse permission, or grant it either with or without conditions attached according to their planning policies for the area and the particular land. Authorities may impose such conditions 'as they think fit', but the House of Lords has held that these must 'fairly and reasonably relate to the permitted development': *Pyx Granite Co v Ministry of Housing and Local Govern-ment.*[4] Permissions normally lapse after five years[5] unless development has been started in that time; and to ensure that development is not left unfinished for an indefinite time authorities can serve a 'completion notice', if the Secretary of State approves, requiring completion of the project within a year or longer period, as specified.[6] The GDO provides that decisions should be given within eight weeks.

The Act of 1971 empowers the Secretary of State, to 'call in' planning applications and deal with them himself at first instance,[7] and appli-cants can appeal to him against an adverse decision.[8] He substitutes his own decision, according to his views on planning policy, but must com-ply with all legal requirements including 'reasonableness' (the '*Wednes-bury* principle') and 'natural justice', as discussed in chapter 3,[9] Plan-ning decisions can be challenged on legal grounds in the High Court; but in regard to decisions of the Secretary of State this is restricted to issues of ultra vires considerations, or procedural defaults, and subjected to a strict six weeks' time limit.[10] He must afford a hearing or public

---

1 S 23.
2 SI 1972/1385.
3 SI 1977/289, as amended by SI 1980/1946.
4 [1958] 1 QB 554, [1958] 1 All ER 625.
5 1971 Act, ss 41–2.
6 Ibid, s 44.
7 S 35.
8 S 36.
9 See pp 63–71.
10 Ss 242, 245.

inquiry and comply with Inquiries Procedure Rules in the way in which inquiries are conducted. He has been empowered to delegate to inspectors conducting inquiries the authority to take the final decision instead of reporting back to him in the Town and Country Planning (Determination of Appeals by Appointed Persons) (Prescribed Classes) Regulations 1972.[11]

Special procedures apply to development by planning authorities themselves and by the Crown; and development by public bodies which requires the consent of a government department is deemed to receive planning permission along with that consent.[12] If a project comprises industrial development the applicant must first obtain an industrial development certificate from the Department of Industry, except in cases where a specified minimum amount of floor space will not be exceeded.[13] In deciding any application, authorities must 'seek the achievement of the general objectives of the structure plan';[14] but although regard should be had to the relevant development plans it is not necessary that authorities should 'slavishly adhere' to them, as was stated judicially in *Enfield London Borough Council v Secretary of State for the Environment*.[15] This is especially stressed in view of the fact that the time involved in getting development plans formally approved may well mean that in points of detail they are no longer up-to-date.

Fees are chargeable for planning applications,[16] which must in addition be recorded in a public register for free inspection[17] and in many cases publicised as well.[18] A prospective developer may enter into a planning agreement with the local planning authority as an alternative to applying for permission;[19] or he may apply for a 'determination' whether an intended project does or does not amount to development anyway.[20]

3. REDRESS FOR PLANNING RESTRICTIONS

In principle, compensation is not payable for the loss of development value in land caused by a refusal, or a merely conditional grant, of planning permission. If the land in question was once the subject of an 'established' claim for compensation under Part VI of the Town and Country Planning Act 1947 it may currently enjoy what is called an

11 SI 1972/1652, amended by SI 1977/477, SI 1977/1939.
12 S 40.
13 Ss 66–73.
14 Local Government, Planning and Land Act 1980, s 86(3).
15 (1974) 233 Estates Gazette 53.
16 Local Government, Planning and Land Act 1980, s 87.
17 1971 Act, s 34.
18 Ibid, s 26.
19 S 52.
20 S 53.

unexpended balance of established development value' (or 'UXB') and under Part VII[1] of the Act of 1971 compensation will be payable by the Secretary of State up to the amount of any such balance, or the amount of development value not realised, whichever is the less (but these amounts now are usually insignificant).

This principle applies to most varieties of development, known as 'new development' to distinguish them from certain categories specified in Sch 8 of the Act of 1971. These categories are of little significance on the whole, since the development in them normally does not depart greatly from the 'existing use' of the land, but they include the rebuilding of existing or destroyed buildings within certain limits, and the alteration of buildings, also within limits, and the prospect of this sometimes commands considerable development value. Provisions in Part VIII[2] of the 1971 Act allow compensation to be claimed 'as of right'—from local planning authorities, not the Secretary of State—and by s 169 some of the categories of development in Sch 8 carry an entitlement to such compensation in the event of an adverse decision. Excluded from this right to compensation, however, are two of the categories of Sch 8 development: rebuilding, and conversion of houses into flats. But development value attributable to the prospect of *all* Sch 8 categories is payable as of right in the event of a compulsory purchase of the land in question.

Compulsory purchase is not normally something which a landowner can bring about; but two planning procedures in fact enable him to do so. These are purchase notices and blight notices, both dealt with by Part IX[3] of the 1971 Act. A purchase notice[4] can be served by any 'owner' of land, a term which is defined in the same way as 'person having control' under the Housing Acts, described above.[5] He can do so provided that as the result of an adverse planning decision his land is 'incapable of reasonably beneficial use'. This means that the land is deprived of development value, while its existing use value is negligible and not merely less than development value: *R v Minister of Housing and Local Government, ex p Chichester RDC.*[6] In such a case the owner serves his purchase notice on the district or London borough council (or the City of London Corporation); and it will take effect unless, within nine months at the outside, it has been accepted, or else has been referred to the Secretary of State for decision. The latter may, however, substitute a permission for some other development in lieu of upholding the notice. If it is accepted or upheld the land is transferred on the footing of a compulsory purchase, which automatically means that

---

1 Ss 134–163.
2 Ss 164–179. See also s 278 and Sch 8 and 18.
3 Ss 180–208.
4 Ss 180–191.
5 See p 285.
6 [1960] 2 All ER 407, [1960] 1 WLR 587.

the vendor will receive in his compensation (for what it is worth) the value of the prospect of all categories of Sch 8 development at least. If he has been refused permission to rebuild on a derelict site this will be an effective mode of redress for him.

Blight notices, on the other hand,[7] are served where the market value of land (particularly existing use value) is appreciably depressed by public authority proposals which foreshadow the possibility of eventual compulsory purchase so that all other prospective buyers fight shy of the property except at a substantially reduced price. Three requirements have to be satisfied. First, the land itself (not neighbouring land) must come within one of a long list of 'specified description' of public authority proposals, which include various kinds of highway projects, slum clearance, and public authority schemes indicated in development plans. Second, the claimant must have an interest 'qualifying for protection', which means a freehold or a leasehold with three or more years to run in respect of which he is the resident owner-occupier of a dwelling, or the owner-occupier of a farm, or the owner-occupier of any other property provided that it has a rateable value not exceeding a specified limit;[8] and a minimum period of actual occupation is prescribed. Third, there must have been genuine, but unavailing, attempts to sell at a reasonable price. The blight notice is served on the 'appropriate authority' likely to acquire the land. If within two months the authority should object by serving a counter-notice the claimant may within a further two months refer the blight notice to the Lands Tribunal to decide whether it is, or is not, 'well-founded'. The burden of proof lies on him to establish the three above requirements, if challenged, but lies on the authority if the objection is that the land is not in fact to be acquired.

Compensation 'as of right' under Part VIII of the Act of 1971 is also payable, by the local planning authority in certain other cases. Planning permission once given may be revoked or modified (normally with the Secretary of State's consent) under s 45 of the Act. If so full compensation must be paid to cover loss of development value (other than any within Sch 8), and any abortive expenditure incurred.[9] If any permission automatically given by the GDO is withdrawn, as it can be by a planning authority, and a specific planning application for that development is then turned down, this is compensated similarly.[10] Also, an existing lawful use of land can be terminated by a discontinuance order under s 51 of the Act; this too is compensated in full as of right to cover the cost of compliance and the loss of value of the land.

---

7 1971 Act, ss 192–208, as extended by the Land Compensation Act 1973, ss 68–81.
8 £2,250 at present, under the Town and Country Planning (Limit of Annual Value) Order 1973, SI 1973/425.
9 1971 Act, s 164.
10 S 165.

4. ENFORCEMENT

A major problem in planning control is enforcement, covered by Part V[11] of the 1971 Act as amended by various provisions including the Local Government and Planning (Amendment) Act 1981. It arises if anyone carries out development without the requisite planning permission, which is referred to as a 'breach of planning control'. The local planning authority (normally the district council) may, if it is 'expedient' to do so—ie not merely vindictive, because permission if sought would have been given—issue an 'enforcement notice' and serve a copy of it on the owner and occupier and anyone else appropriate.[12] This must specify the breach, state clearly the steps to be taken to remedy it, specify the time allowed for compliance, and state when the notice takes effect. This must not be less than four weeks ahead. Before (but not after) the notice takes effect the recipient can appeal in writing on any or all of eight specified grounds to the Secretary of State,[13] who must afford a hearing or a public inquiry if requested, before deciding whether to quash, vary or confirm the notice. Although a notice may be challenged in the High Court on any other legal ground,[14] it cannot be challenged on any of the eight specified grounds other than by appeal to the Secretary of State. His decision, however, is in turn subject to appeal on a point of law to the High Court.[15] A 'stop notice'[16] can also be served, during these appeal periods, to prevent further unauthorised development, though the local planning authority may have to compensate a developer for consequent losses if the enforcement notice is eventually quashed. If an enforcement notice is defied, instead of being quashed on appeal, the person responsible is liable to prosecution[17] and the local planning authority may in default of compliance enter and carry out the works specified in the notice at the wrongdoer's cost.

There is, in effect, a limitation period for breaches of planning control. Any unauthorised operation (building or otherwise) or a change to use of a building as a single dwelling is immune from enforcement after a lapse of four years; but no other unauthorised material changes of use are immune unless they took place before 1964.[18] Any mistakes in an enforcement notice can be corrected by the Secretary of State provided that no injustice is caused thereby: *Miller-Mead v Minister of Housing and Local Government.*[19] An enforcement notice will lapse on the grant

---

11 Ss 87–111.
12 S 87, as amended.
13 S 88, as amended.
14 Those listed in s 88 are founded partly on policy, but mostly on law and fact.
15 S 246; but the Rules of the Supreme Court impose a strict time limit of 28 days.
16 S 90, as amended.
17 S 89, as amended.
18 S 87(4).
19 [1963] 2 QB 196, [1963] 1 All ER 459.

of a subsequent planning permission for the unauthorised development, but not merely upon compliance with the notice in case the offender then repeats the breach of planning control.[20]

5. AMENITY

The other main area of planning control relates to the protection of amenity. This is not defined, but its meaning emerges from various statutory provisions in Part IV[1] of the 1971 Act, dealing with trees, special buildings, advertisements and waste land. There is also the Caravan Sites and Control of Development Act 1960, Part I, which imposes a system of control by means of 'site licences' for land (with certain exceptions) used for stationing caravans. Use of land in this way requires planning permission to authorise the material change (if any) from its previous use; but detailed requirements must be dealt with in the site licence. This was stressed by Lord Denning MR in *Esdell Caravan Parks v Hemel Hempstead RDC*;[2] though he added: 'Many considerations relate both to planning and to site . . . there is a large overlap . . .' The precise number and distribution of caravans is purely a site licence matter, being relevant to public health as much as to amenity, along with sanitation, water-supply and fire-prevention.

Tree are often protected by planning conditions requiring that they be preserved or replaced during development;[3] but the main method of control is a tree preservation order.[4] This may be made by a local planning authority, but unless it is uncontested the Secretary of State must confirm it. It will prohibit any felling or lopping of the tree or trees specified in it without a consent first being obtained from the local planning authority, normally the district council. The procedure for making application for consents, appeals, enforcement procedures, and other matters, forms a code of control contained in the order, which can be expected to follow closely the terms of the 'model' order devised by the Secretary of State. This code is very similar to the general planning procedures described above.[5] Interference with protected trees is also a criminal offence.

Buildings (apart from places of worship) if considered by the Secretary of State (subject to expert advice, but not necessarily consultation with the owners) to be of 'special architectural or historic interest', may be protected by being 'listed'.[6] A copy of this 'list' for their area is to be

20 Ss 92–3.
1 Ss 54–86.
2 [1966] 1 QB 895, [1965] 3 All ER 737.
3 1971 Act, s 59.
4 S 60.
5 See p 292.
6 1971 Act, s 54.

held by each local planning authority and owners are notified. The result of the Secretary of State causing a building to be 'listed' in this way is that planning authorities must have regard to its special 'character'. Not only is it subject to general planning control but any unauthorised interference with it which, even if not amounting to development, spoils that 'character' is also a contravention of planning control. Painting in unsuitable colours is one possibility; but the most serious is of course demolition. Criminal penalties are imposed for unauthorised interference; and as far as may be appropriate the local planning authority may take enforcement proceedings similar to those in general planning control as described above.[7] Interference is lawful if authorised by a listed building consent given by the district planning authority. It may be subject to conditions requiring works to preserve, restore or reconstruct the listed building to be carried out as far as practicable.[8] A planning authority may compulsorily purchase a listed building which has not been properly preserved, so that its 'character' is at risk; but a 'repairs notice' must first be served on the owner, who can resist the acquisition if he complies with the notice.[9] Also, local authorities can preserve a listable but unlisted building by serving a 'building preservation notice', which protects it for six months while they apply to have it listed.[10]

Any 'area of special architectural or historic interest the character . . . of which it is desirable to preserve or enhance' may be designated by a local authority as a 'conservation area'.[11] 'Special attention' must then be given to it, by concentrating on preserving trees or special buildings within it, and by giving careful attention to all planning applications (which must be publicised unless in the view of the local planning authority this is unnecessary).

Advertisement control is dealt with in substance by regulations.[12] These currently are the Town and Country Planning (Control of Advertisements) Regulations 1969.[13] They are prescribed in the interests of safety and amenity though not of morals. Consent is 'deemed' to be given for the use of any site to display advertisements in most routine cases; subject to this, consent must be specifically obtained on application to the local planning authority, normally for a five-year period. Appeal lies to the Secretary of State against a refusal of consent or against a 'discontinuance notice'. Authorities can declare 'areas of special control' where, in order to preserve rural surroundings or for

7 See p 296.
8 Ss 55–6, as amended, and Sch 11.
9 Ss 114–7, as amended.
10 S 58.
11 S 277, as amended.
12 Ss 63–4, as amended.
13 SI 1969/1532.

some other good reason, rather more stringent restrictions are thought necessary. Contravention of control is a criminal offence.

Waste land, neglected sites and similar areas may be dealt with by the local planning authority serving a notice on the owner and occupier 'of any garden, vacant site or other open land' which is in a 'condition' injurious to local amenity. The notice must specify the steps to be taken for remedying that condition.[14] A procedure roughly similar to enforcement notices is involved; but appeal lies to the magistrates instead of to the Secretary of State.[15] Failure to comply is a criminal offence.[16] The 'condition' of land is not to be regarded in isolation from its use (eg as a scrap dump): *Britt v Buckinghamshire County Council*.[17]

6. POSITIVE PLANNING, NEW TOWNS, ETC

All these planning control provisions tend to be regarded as 'negative' planning, by which local planning authorities attend to development by other people rather than carrying out development of their own. Part VI[18] of the 1971 Act, however, confers 'positive' planning powers on them. These effectively turn on acquisition of land for redevelopment, usually in practice in old town and city areas where 'urban renewal' schemes are carried out in much the same way as 'slum clearance'[19] except that properties of all kinds are involved and not merely or chiefly houses. What is usually needed is for the authority to acquire land and redistribute it to private developers or to other public authorities, or retain it, for replanning and redevelopment in line with current development plans and other policies for future land use. Acquisition is thus authorised 'in connection with development', and also 'for other planning purposes'.[20] The latter phrase means 'to secure the treatment as a whole, by development, redevelopment or improvement, or partly by one and partly by another method'. Areas may be designated in development plans for treatment of this kind under the name of 'action areas'.[1] Proposals devised for each area as a whole thus govern the development of all its parts.

Procedures for large-scale development or redevelopment appear also in other forms. New town corporations, currently operating under the New Towns Act 1981, acquire land for making or extending new towns; and although the corporations themselves are not local author-

---

14 1971 Act, s 65, as amended. See also the Derelict Land Act 1982.
15 S 105.
16 S 104, as amended.
17 [1964] 1 QB 77, [1963] 2 All ER 175.
18 Ss 112–133.
19 See above, p 285.
20 S 112, as amended.
 1 S 7(5).

ities yet they act on a comparable scale and need to collaborate with them constantly, to say nothing of the fact that eventually the land may be transferred to them. Also, local authorities have achieved similar results more directly under the Town Development Act 1952, whereby one district council may carry out new development in order to receive and accommodate inhabitants and businesses from another ('overspill'). The same approach is now being applied to an increasing extent in town centres by local authorities under the Inner Urban Areas Act 1978, and also by 'urban development corporations' set up under Part XVI of the Local Government, Planning and Land Act 1980, these latter bodies being concentrated in metropolitan districts and London boroughs. Various government grants of a specific nature are available for such purposes, notably under the Act of 1971,[2] the Inner Urban Areas Act 1978, and the Local Government Grants (Social Need) Act 1969.

E. Recreation, coast and countryside, and general land use

Local authorities have a number of functions in relation to use of open land which are closely related to their planning functions. Parks and open spaces have often been acquired under private Acts, many in the nineteenth century; but a general power is enjoyed by local authorities under the Open Spaces Act 1906 and the Physical Training and Recreation Act 1937. The National Parks and Access to the Countryside Act 1949, which has been mentioned earlier in relation to public rights of way,[3] empowers local planning authorities to provide various recreational facilities in national parks and to make 'access' agreements and orders for the public to go on to private land in the countryside. There is no recognised common law right for the public at large to use land for recreation, though local communities have often been acknowledged to have customary rights of this kind, over village greens and the like, which will bind the owners including local authorities if they acquire such land: *New Windsor Corp v Mellor*.[4] Access agreements require the Secretary of State's approval; access orders do so a fortiori since they involve compulsion. Under the Countryside Act 1968 local authorities can acquire land to create 'country parks' and provide recreational facilities. The Wildlife and Countryside Act 1981 extends local authorities' powers in certain miscellaneous respects, including public rights of way.

2 Ss 250–4.
3 See p 268.
4 [1975] Ch 380, [1975] 3 All ER 44.

It may be noted here that the Commons Registration Act 1965 requires county councils and the GLC to maintain a register of commons and town or village greens, and the rights over them, which may be 'rights of common' which are private property rights, or may be customary rights of recreation and access. Rights not duly registered have now statutorily lapsed. The workings of this system may be studied in cases such as *Thorne RDC v Bunting*[5] and *Re Tillmire Common Heslington*.[6]

Functions not concerned with recreation include coast protection and also the provision of smallholdings and allotments. The Coast Protection Act 1949 empowers district councils whose areas border on the seashore to carry out protection works, such as the provision of sea-walls, and to acquire land for the purpose, compulsorily if necessary.[7] The Allotments Acts 1908 to 1950 empower district and London borough councils, and also parish and community councils, to provide 'allotments' and 'allotment-gardens' for rent; while under the Agriculture Act 1970, Part III, county councils and the GLC are empowered to provide smallholdings for tenants at fair market rents, subject to approval by the Minister of Agriculture, Fisheries and Food.

General land use provisions which may be noted include the Local Authorities (Land) Act 1963, which enables local authorities to carry out building and other works on land they have acquired under their various powers, and duly to maintain and manage such buildings and works, so as to benefit or improve their areas. Other assorted powers and duties are contained in the Local Government (Miscellaneous Provisions) Acts 1976 and 1982.

5 [1972] Ch 470, [1972] 1 All ER 439.
6 [1982] 2 All ER 615.
7 See ch 9, p 230.

Chapter 12

Local government functions III— personal services

A. Social services

1. THE POOR LAW

In *A–G v St Ives RDC*,[1] Salmon J (as he then was) said: 'There were only four parish officers: the clerk, the constable, the overseer and the surveyor'. By 'officer', it will be remembered, is meant a prominent landowner or other man of substance in a parish who paid the price for his local eminence and independent means by being compelled to exercise authority without being paid for doing so. Although forms of election might be observed for churchwardens, on the whole the county magistrates, on the Crown's behalf, saw to it that the leading local farmers and others did not escape their share of these burdens and that suitable people as far as possible were entrusted with them by being appointed to these offices. If they were lucky their out-of-pocket expenses and the general costs incurred in performing their duties might be reimbursed by rates and charges, but to a large extent these matters were left to private enterprise. The lesser functionaries: parish clerks, beadles, criers, haywards and so forth, were parish 'servants' rather than 'officers'—the paid subordinates of the latter.

Three of the four 'officers' have been discussed in preceding chapters; there remains the fourth: the overseer of the poor. The office of overseer may have come from the task of collecting parish rates or other money on behalf of the medieval churchwardens for distribution of alms to the needy, according to the Webbs in *The Parish and County*.[2] These 'collectors of the Poor's Rate' are mentioned in various Tudor statutes and also in a leading law book: Christopher St Germain's *Doctor and Student*.[3] In 1572 an Act of Elizabeth I[4] authorised the county magistrates to appoint parish overseers to take charge of work which the unemployed were set to do. The Poor Relief Act 1597[5] instituted the office of 'overseer of the poor' which combined the work of the ear-

---

1 [1961] 1 QB 366, [1961] 1 All ER 265. For 'clerk', read 'churchwarden(s)'.
2 Pp 30–31.
3 The Parish, p 178.
4 14 Eliz I, c 5 (1572).
5 39 Eliz I, c 3 (1597).

lier 'overseer' with that of the 'collectors'. Each 'overseer of the poor' was appointed by the magistrates; but a practice developed that they tended to be nominated by their predecessors because of a lack of enthusiasm for the work, so that 'poor labouring men, temporary inhabitants, and women (sic), were held to be eligible if no more suitable persons were available'.[6]

It can be seen that poor relief, in the form of doles of money, or the 'workhouse', is one of the oldest local government functions. The modern welfare state represents the views of those who wished to get away from the defects of this 'poor law' system because though worthy in principle, it was grudging, amateurish and degrading in operation. Alongside this system of public administration there also developed the law of charities, whereby various public purposes including poor relief were pursued on private initiative under the forms of property law in equity, referred to as charitable 'uses' or trusts. The preamble to the Charitable Uses Act 1601,[7] though since repealed, continues to govern the case law of charities today, and one of the four categories of charity within the 'spirit of intendment' of the Act of 1601 is the relief of poverty. Modern statutes, as will be seen, try to link and harmonise the workings of local authorities with those of voluntary or charitable organisations as far as possible. Both the public and the private sides have a past to live down, a depressing combined heritage of social attitudes which makes the word 'charity' almost as repellent as the word 'workhouse'.

One notable aspect of the Elizabethan new poor law is its finance. The medieval power to raise a Church rate, exercised by the churchwardens, was not founded on statute. It was thus governed by the much more lax common law ultra vires principle than the strict statutory one. Since the churchwardens were often elected, the Church rate could be regarded as being levied under parochial democratic control, potentially at least, right down to the nineteenth century. It was available for parish purposes generally, by extension of reasoning from church purposes in the strict sense; and relief of poverty or 'almsgiving' was a natural and proper reason for raising money by a Church rate.

But the Poor Relief Act 1597 gave separate and permanent statutory authority to levy a specific Poor rate, the assessments for which could be and were used easily for other statutorily approved rates thereafter, for instance Highway rates. The pattern of increasing statutory intervention thereafter, together with the applicability of the strict statutory version of the ultra vires principle and the substitution of the magistrates' control for that of the parson, meant that there were now two rating systems of which the Poor rate was statutory and in tune with the

---

6 The Webbs, op cit, p 31, note 1.
7 43 Eliz I, c 4 (1601).

post-Reformation style of government while the Church rate was a pre-statutory thing, surviving on sufferance. 'If the Justices, or any other critic, objected to any payment being charged against the Poor rate or the Highway rate, as being unauthorised by law, all parties would agree to transfer the item to the Church rate, which needed no magisterial allowance and had never been limited or restricted by any statute', as the Webbs say in *The Parish and the County*.[8]

The decade of radical change in public affairs, 1829–39, that saw the Representation of the People Act 1832 which reformed the House of Commons, the Municipal Corporations Act 1835 which reformed the boroughs, the Highway Act 1835 which reformed highway administration, and the Metropolitan Police Act 1829 and the county Police Act 1839 which reformed police administration, also saw the Poor Law Amendment Act 1834 which reformed the administration of poor relief. This Act introduced a system of central control which, although it did not itself last long in its original and draconian form of the three Poor Law Commissioners (1834–47)—the 'Pinch-Pauper Triumvirate'—was nevertheless the pace-maker generally for new developments in central control. In 1847 Poor Law administration was put under regular ministerial supervision in the form of the Poor Law Board. Public health was first put under a General Board of Health (1848–58) and then split between the Privy Council and the Home Office. Finally in 1871 the Local Government Board was set up to embrace poor relief, public health, and general supervision of local authority powers under private legislation, all in one central government department.[9]

This drastic change in 1834 was paralleled at local level by removing poor relief from the parish. Larger new units were created from 'unions' of parishes and given elected 'boards of guardians' which, with similarly conceived local boards of health and highway boards under subsequent legislation, created a new pattern of 'district' authorities intermediate in standing between parishes and counties. These 'boards of guardians' employed their own paid staff of workhouse masters and others, though the unpaid parish 'overseers' continued to exist until the Local Government Act 1894 abolished them. The power to levy the Poor rate was transferred to the guardians, and was eventually used as the basis of the modern general rate for local government. The immemorial Church rate, which might have survived to give a sound financial basis at common law for a modernised independent parish democracy, in fact perished for a quite independent reason. Nonconformist hostility, according to the Webbs in *The Parish and the County*, was its undoing.[10]

The Local Government Act 1929 transferred poor relief to local

8 P 115.
9 See ch 2, p 34.
10 Pp 171–172.

authorities and abolished the boards of guardians. The Poor Law Act 1930 abolished the phrase 'poor law' as an official expression and replaced it by 'public assistance'. The introduction of employment exchanges and unemployment benefit—the 'dole'—together with statutory 'national insurance' and pensions widened the scope of 'poor relief' but did so through the medium of central government, administered after 1916 by the Ministry of Labour and Pensions. A separate Unemployment Assistance Board was set up in 1934 and transformed into the National Assistance Board in 1948. The Ministry of Social Security Act 1966 replaced this by the Supplementary Benefits Commission. These developments should be considered with the reorganisation of hospitals and medical care—previously run by private practitioners, charitable institutions and local authorities—on a national rather than local basis by the National Health Service Act 1946. The result of them was that comparatively little in the field of health and social welfare remained for local authorities to administer.

2. MEDICAL HEALTH ADMINISTRATION AND SOCIAL SERVICES AUTHORITIES

The National Health Service Reorganisation Act 1973 carried out a yet further rearrangement which transferred personal health and school health services previously run by local authorities, to the reorganised National Health Service Administration. The National Health Service Act 1977, amended by the Health Services Act 1980, provides that under the general guidance and 'central strategic planning' of the Department of Health and Social Security, the minister for which is the Secretary of State for Social Services by virtue of the Secretary of State for Social Services Order 1968,[11] a nationally conceived hierarchy of regional, area and district health authorities is responsible for medical health care generally, including the functions transferred from local authorities by the 1973 Act. What remains to be considered in this field as far as local government is concerned is the representation of local authorities on the various bodies in that hierarchy, which in the Act of 1977 are described as 'local administration', and the interconnection between their services and those still administered by local authorities.

Thus at least four members of an area health authority must be appointed by local authorities for that area, which must also appoint members to family practitioner committees and to the community health councils which uphold the public interest in the running of the health service.[12] Health authorities and local authorities are required to set up joint consultative committees to further their general duty of

11 SI 1968/1699.
12 1977 Act, ss 8, 10, 15, 20.

cooperation in the public interest,[13] covering such matters as control of communicable diseases, sanitation and safety in buildings, food hygiene, and the physical and mental health and welfare of the young. Under Part IV of the Mental Health Act 1959 local authorities may be 'guardians' of mental patients, and their mental welfare officers are responsible for the arrangements for this.

Social services continue to be administered by local authorities under the general supervision of the Secretary of State for Social Services. The principal statute delimiting their scope is the Local Authority Social Services Act 1970. The Local Government Act 1972,[14] provides that the administering local authorities are the county councils in non-metropolitan counties, and the 'second-tier' authorities in other areas. Each of these must appoint a social services committee to administer the functions conferred by the Act of 1970.[15] Related questions which generally affect other aspects of the authority's functions may be allotted to other committees, subject to the social services committee's first considering the matter and reporting on it. The committee may, if the council approve, delegate to sub-committees.

In addition to this committee structure there are certain regional bodies, known as children's regional planning committees, appointed for a pattern of regions specified by the Secretary of State for Social Services for the purposes of the Children and Young Persons Act 1969 s 35.[16] The social services local authorities for each region are represented on the committee, the duty of which is to submit a 'regional plan' to the Secretary of State for the running of 'community homes' provided for children 'in care' both by the local authorities themselves and by voluntary bodies. The Secretary of State may order an inquiry into any aspect of a social services committee's work relating to children.[17]

3. GENERAL WELFARE SERVICES

The work of these local authorities and their social services committees is concerned largely with the welfare of children; but they have some more general welfare responsibilities. The latter derive chiefly from the National Assistance Act 1948. Successors to the old-style workhouses are new-style residential institutions provided and maintained in accordance with the 1948 Act[18] for the old, the infirm, the mentally disordered, and anyone else in need of care and attention.

Authorities may arrange with other bodies, whether public or volun-

---

13 S 22.
14 S 195.
15 Ss 2–5 of that Act.
16 Now replaced by the Child Care Act 1980, s 76.
17 Child Care Act 1980, s 31.
18 Ss 21–27, as amended and updated by various later Acts.

tary, for the provision of these homes; and subject to their means those accommodated must pay charges approved by the Secretary of State. They must be accommodated in their own area unless there are urgent reasons to the contrary. In addition, authorities must provide facilities to help the permanently handicapped or mentally disordered,[19] including training and recreation. The Secretary of State may give directions in respect of these matters; and his approval must be obtained for facilities to be provided for old people's welfare such as home-help services.[20] If voluntary organisations are used for this, the relevant local authority may agree to contribute to the cost, and must in any case keep a register of homes run by such bodies and carry out inspections under the Residential Homes Act 1980.[1] The same Act[2] authorises local authorities to provide meals for old people or contribute to voluntary bodies' costs in doing so. The Chronically Sick and Disabled Persons Act 1970[3] imposes a duty on authorities to find out the number of disabled people in their area, provide a range of special facilities to cater for their needs in their homes or elsewhere and bring these to their attention. Authorities may seek an order from the magistrates that old or disabled persons in need of care and living in unsuitable conditions be taken to a hospital or a special home, and may also do this in respect of chronically diseased persons; and they must look after the belongings of anyone taken to a hospital or a special home if there is no-one else to do it.[4]

4. CHILD CARE

Authorities' functions in regard to the care of children are now mostly, though not entirely, re-enacted in the Child Care Act 1980. First to be considered is their duty under s 2 of that Act to take into their care children who are not looked after properly or at all, whenever the welfare of such children requires it, though normally not after they reach the age of 18. Wherever possible, of course, any such child ought to be entrusted to a parent or other suitable person; and a parent or guardian can in principle insist on this. But the Act of 1980[5] provides that after authorities have had care of children for six months a parent or guardian claiming a child must give 28 days' notice, during which time the authority in question can pass a resolution 'vesting' in themselves the parental rights and duties regarding that child;[6] and they can pass such

---

19 1948 Act, ss 29–32 as up-dated by the Mental Health Act 1959, s 8, and other statutes.
20 National Health Service Act 1977, Sch 9.
 1 Ss 1–7.
 2 S 8.
 3 Ss 1, 2.
 4 1948 Act, ss 47–8, as amended.
 5 S 13.
 6 S 3.

a resolution in other specified circumstances. If within one month a counter-notice is served, the authority must decide whether to make a complaint to the juvenile court, because their resolution will not have any further validity unless the magistrates in that court uphold it. Appeal lies to the High Court.[7]

Provided that these procedures are properly followed a child cannot be made a ward of court: *Lewisham London Borough Council v Lewisham Juvenile Court Justices.*[8] The prerogative power of the Crown to take wardship of a minor has been abrogated to the extent that these enactments provide otherwise. Nevertheless the ultra vires principle applies to confine authorities' jurisdiction to the reasonable exercise of the powers conferred on them by those enactments: *Re M. (an infant).*[9] Wardship is part of the jurisdiction of the High Court, and any interested party can invoke it including the local authority: *M v Humberside County Council.*[10] But if parents or guardians effectively claim children because authorities do not make use of the power to 'vest' parental rights and duties in themselves, there would not normally seem to be any justification for an authority to have recourse to wardship proceedings, at any rate in the absence of other factors. The mere taking 'into care' of a child under s 2 of the 1980 Act is 'transient' according to Lord Denning MR in *Re S (an infant).*[11]

A court exercising domestic jurisdiction may commit a child to the care of a local authority if to entrust that child to a parent or other person would be undesirable and the child is under 17 years of age. In future such a court may be able to make a 'custodianship' order in favour of someone other than a natural parent. The local authority will first have to be notified for the purpose of making a report on the child in question, and the court will be able, if it wishes, to order that care or supervision by the authority be later substituted for that 'custodianship'. This is enacted in the Children Act 1975.[12] Criminal cases are discussed below.[13]

While children are in the care of a local authority they are to be looked after in accordance with the Child Care Act 1980, Parts III–VI, in the homes to be provided and maintained by each authority for that purpose—'community homes' referred to above[14]—or similar homes run by voluntary bodies. Alternatively they may be provided for in any

---

7 S 6.
8 [1980] AC 273, [1979] 2 All ER 297.
9 [1961] Ch 328, [1961] 1 All ER 788.
10 [1979] Fam 114, [1979] 2 All ER 744.
11 [1965] 1 All ER 865, [1965] 1 WLR 483.
12 Ss 33–46. These provisions have not been brought into force yet. The courts in question are the High Court, county courts and magistrates' courts.
13 See p 309.
14 See p 306.

other suitable way such as boarding them out or even returning them de facto to their parents' custody,[15] subject to regulations made by the Secretary of State as to community homes and boarding out. An authority may even pass a resolution 'vesting' parental rights and duties in a suitable voluntary body; though such rights and duties may be resumed by the authority on due notice to all concerned.[16] Contributions to the cost of children in care are to be charged to parents who are able to meet them, or to the children themselves if over 16 and earning.[17] Children may continue to be accommodated, or financially helped, up to the age of 21, where appropriate.[18]

The converse of these powers and duties conferred on local authorities is the question of liability. In *Leeds City Council v West Yorkshire Metropolitan Police*,[19] the appellant council resisted a claim that they were liable to pay compensation under the Children and Young Persons Act 1933, s 55, to the victim of a robbery committed by a boy placed in their care. The House of Lords held that the liability imposed by that section on the 'guardian' of any child does not apply to authorities, only to natural persons, and the council's appeal succeeded. Lord Scarman said that the section 'is unnecessary and inappropriate as a remedy or sanction against a local authority which has received a child into care'. Reviewing the legal position generally, he said: 'The local authority is both accountable to its electorate and liable in law for breach of its statutory duty. It is also liable at common law, if it should fail to take such care as was reasonable in all the circumstances to prevent a child in its care from causing damage to others: see *Home Office v Dorset Yacht Co Ltd*.'[20] But 'the definition of guardian in the criminal proceedings legislation', of which the section under consideration forms part, 'was not intended to include a public authority receiving a child into care as a matter of statutory obligation . . .' Similarly the term 'fit person', under s 76(1) of the 1933 Act, which concerns the power of a court to commit children 'involved in criminal proceedings' into the care of some other person in order to get them away from the influence of a delinquent parent or guardian, although it expressly provides that in such a case the local authority shall be 'deemed' a 'fit person' to be entrusted with care of the child, is apart from that 'not apt and . . . not intended, to include any but an individual human person . . .'

Criminal proceedings which may lead to children being committed to

15 1980 Act, s 21.
16 Ss 64–66.
17 Ss 45–49.
18 Ss 27, 72.
19 [1982] 1 All ER 274, [1982] 2 WLR 186.
20 [1970] AC 1004, [1970] 2 All ER 294.

the care of a local authority are governed by the Children and Young Persons Act 1969, Part I.[1] and the Criminal Justice Act 1972.[2] In the *Leeds* case Lord Scarman spoke of 'proceedings in a criminal court which involve a child either as the victim of offences against him by his parent or other person in charge or control of him or was himself the offender against the criminal law'. The questions to which these cases give rise 'under the modern law . . . have been answered by requiring the courts to shield the child (in almost all cases) from the impact of the criminal law: the court's ultimate power has become, in almost all cases, to make a care order'.

It follows that a local authority will almost certainly be involved in respect of social services. If the juvenile court makes a 'supervision order'[3] the local authority (or the probation service) must help the child or young person to whom it relates, who may well be subjected to conditions imposing various requirements to co-operate with the supervisors. If a 'care order' is made, the child will actually be committed to the local authority; this may also be done temporarily by an interim order.[4] A child or young person comes within the scope of these procedures if 'in need of care or control' for the reasons given by Lord Scarman or for related reasons such as truancy or exposure to moral danger. Apart from the National Society for Prevention of Cruelty to Children and the police (either of whom must first notify the local authority) only the local authority can institute juvenile court proceedings; and only the police or the local authority can do so if the child is himself charged with an offence. Normally the authority should not act without a prior inquiry. A child can be charged with an offence unless aged under ten years.[5] Where a criminal charge is brought care proceedings are in fact unusual, though a remand in custody may be made to the local authority.

Children suffering from mental disorder may be placed in a local authority's 'community home' if this will not be prejudicial to the other children there, under the Mental Health Act 1959.[6] The same Act[7] provides that, if parental powers and duties in respect of such children have become 'vested' in the local authority by the authority's own resolution or by a 'care order' of the juvenile court,[8] the local authority must arrange to make visits and give other attentions to them when in hospital as reasonable parents would do. The 1959 Act empowers a juve-

1 Ss 1–24.
2 Sch 5.
3 Under s 11 of the 1969 Act.
4 1969 Act, s 20.
5 Children and Young Persons Act 1933, s 50.
6 S 9 (as amended).
7 S 10.
8 Under the Child Care Act 1980, ss 3 or 10–11.

nile court in lieu of a 'care order' to commit such children to hospital under a hospital order, or to a local authority under a guardianship order;[9] and in the latter case parental powers and duties are 'vested' in the authority, as they also are if under the 1959 Act[10] the functions of the nearest relatives of such children are formally transferred to the authority. When children in these cases are in hospital the above duty to visit them rests on the local authority.

5. ADOPTION, FOSTERING, ETC

Local authorities also have duties in regard to adoption under the Adoption Act 1976. An application to a court for an adoption order requires the appointment of a 'guardian ad litem' for the duration of the proceedings, and local authorities may consent to their officers being so appointed. They may authorise their social services committees to arrange for children to be adopted. They must register and control adoption societies. They must supervise applicants who wish to adopt by ensuring that the children to be adopted—'protected' children— are in the applicants' custody and properly cared for during a continuous period of at least three months before the court makes an adoption order, having been duly notified in advance by the applicants. The term 'protected children' also applies to children that someone other than a parent or guardian arranges to place in the care of another person who is not a parent, guardian or relative, without using the adoption procedure; and local authorities must ensure that these children too are properly looked after. In addition, local authorities have a duty under the Nurseries and Child-Minders Regulation Act 1948 to register and control nurseries and child-minders (with some exceptions).

Finally there is the question of local authorities' responsibility for foster children, under various statutory provisions now re-enacted in the Foster Children Act 1980. A 'foster child' is one still within the age-limit for compulsory schooling who is cared for and maintained by some person who is not a parent or relative, for payment or free of charge, leaving aside care by institutions and temporary care arrangements. Foster parents must notify the local authority when they have become, or ceased to be, foster parents, and when they change their permanent address, and when a fostered child dies or (with some exceptions) leaves their care. The duty of the local authority is to be satisfied as to the welfare of the foster children in the authority's area, visiting and advising when necessary. The homes of foster children are to be inspected as well as visited; and authorities may require conditions to

9 S 33.
10 S 52.

be complied with in regard to what the accommodation shall consist of, how many foster children may be accommodated, who may look after them, medical arrangements, fire precautions, keeping records, and giving information. If premises are thought unsuitable for particular children, the fostering of those children there can be specifically prohibited. Appeal in respect of these matters lies to the juvenile court, which can substitute its own conditions. Conversely, the local authority can also by complaint to the juvenile court apply for an order that a foster child be removed—if necessary into the authority's own care. This sytem of control extends to children who remain at independent boarding schools in the school holidays.

It may be noted that the Children's Homes Act 1982 introduces a system of registration and inspection of institutions for accommodating children in local authorities' care. Such children are not to be accommodated in unregistered homes.

B. Education

I. EDUCATION AUTHORITIES

The provision of education, like the relief of poverty, has since early times been a function of religion and a recognised branch of the law of charitable trusts. But except for the chartered boroughs it was not a function of public administration, as the relief of poverty was, until the reforming decade of 1829–39 saw the first government grants in the field of education in 1833 and the introduction of government inspection in 1839. Even then the grants and the inspection were introduced in regard to schools run by church organisations. It was not until Gladstone's first government passed the Elementary Education Act 1870 that public authorities were authorised and required to provide schools. The authorities then set up, like those concerned with poor relief, public health and highways, were ad hoc bodies, the school boards. Eventually Balfour's Education Act 1902 transferred elementary schools to the authorities created for general local government purposes under the Local Government Act 1888: the county and county borough councils, which had already had higher technical functions conferred upon them.[11]

Subsequent legislative changes led eventually to the passing of the Education Act 1944, which is still the principal statute governing the provision of education by local authorities, commonly referred to as 'the state system'. This expression reflects the fact that, as with other

11 See ch 2, p 37.

public administrative functions, the work of the local authorities is subject to national control by the central government. Since 1964 the central authority has been the Department of Education and Science under the Secretary of State for Education and Science in accordance with the Secretary of State for Education and Science Order 1964.[12] Subject to a power for the Secretary of State to set up 'joint education boards', the local education authorities today are those set up under the 1944 Act as amended by the London Government Act 1963 and also by the Local Government Act 1972.[13] These are county councils in the non-metropolitan counties and district councils in the metropolitan counties. In Greater London they are the councils of the outer London boroughs themselves but for inner London boroughs there is a single Inner London Education Authority. Each must have a chief education officer.[14]

The duty of the Secretary of State, inherited from the Minister of Education is 'to promote the education of the people of England and Wales and the progressive development of institutions devoted to that purpose, and to secure the effective execution by local authorities, under his control and direction, of the national policy for providing a varied and comprehensive educational service . . .', as stated in the 1944 Act.[15] He must report to Parliament annually.[16] This is the foundation for an administrative system of the familiar type: routine detailed execution by the local authorities, subject to central government supervision by directions, regulations, circulars, consultations and inspections. The power given by s 68 of the Act to substitute the Secretary of State's decision for any local policy decision which is 'unreasonable', and its interpretation in the *Tameside* case, has been discussed in an earlier chapter, in the general context of how legal powers are interpreted.[17] There is also a power, in s 99, for the Secretary of State to make an order where a local body is in default giving directions as to how their duties are to be duly performed, and by whom: this would seem to be concerned with executive performance whereas s 68 is concerned with policy-making.

The Secretary of State's power to make regulations, rules and orders has been widely used. Examples include the Standards for School Premises Regulations 1972,[18] the Handicapped Pupils and Special Schools Regulations 1959,[19] the Raising of the School Leaving Age Order

12 SI 1964/490.
13 S 192.
14 1944 Act, s 88.
15 S 1.
16 S 5.
17 Ch 9, see p 224 (note how Lord Diplock construes 'comprehensive').
18 SI 1972/2051.
19 SI 1959/365, later amended on a number of occasions.

1972[20]—which fixed the upper age-limit at 16—and the Education (Provision of Clothing) Regulations 1980.[1] He must hold regular inspections[2] and settle disputes between authorities and appeals against their decisions.[3] His approval is needed for the way in which local education authorities each set up their education committee,[4] which must include persons experienced in education and persons acquainted with education conditions in the area, though councillors must predominate on it. The authority may delegate to the committee any function except levying rates or borrowing, and except in emergencies must not act in education matters without first obtaining a report from the committee. With his approval also they may compulsorily purchase land needed for educational purposes; though land must not be purchased (compulsorily or by agreement) so as to save a voluntary body from having to meet the cost of discharging its own responsibilities.[5]

The general duty of local education authorities is to 'meet the needs of the population of their area' by 'securing that efficient education' is provided (by themselves or others) for primary, secondary and further education.[6]

2. FURTHER EDUCATION

As for further education, authorities must each produce for the Secretary of State's approval a scheme for full-time and part-time education facilities (including cultural and recreational activities) to be made available in their area for persons beyond compulsory school age, under Part II of the 1944 Act as amended. In line with such schemes the authorities themselves normally run polytechnics, technical and specialist colleges, and colleges of further education; but the schemes must have regard to the existence in their area of universities and other seats of learning.

Local education authorities have a duty (or in some cases a mere power) to grant awards to meet fees and maintenance costs of persons resident in their area who attend courses at universities and various other further education establishments. This is done under regulations made by the Secretary of State, in accordance with the Education Act 1962, s 1, and the Education Act 1980, s 19. In *Shah v Barnet London Borough Council*,[7] the House of Lords, imposing judicial review by

20 SI 1972/444.
 1 SI 1980/545.
 2 1944 Act, s 77.
 3 Ss 37, 67.
 4 Sch 1, Part II, as amended.
 5 S 90, as amended.
 6 1944 Act, s 7.
 7 [1982] QB 688, [1982] 1 All ER 698.

orders of certiorari and mandamus, held that foreign nationals may be entitled to a grant if they are 'ordinarily resident' in this country, from choice and for a settled purpose, which may be confined to the specific and limited purpose of study. Moreover an authority must consider making a discretionary award to somebody who cannot claim one as of right.

3. PRIMARY AND SECONDARY EDUCATION

The primary and secondary education in a local education authority's area must be supplied by a sufficient number of schools providing a variety of education and training suitable for the various 'ages, abilities and aptitudes' of the children there. Local education authorities must themselves provide enough schools of the various kinds necessary to ensure this, including special schools for physically or mentally disabled children, and boarding facilities, under the 1944 Act,[8] amended and supplemented by the Education (Miscellaneous Provisions) Acts 1948 and 1953, the Education (Handicapped Children) Act 1970, and the Education Act 1980.[9] 'Middle schools' which partly overlap primary and secondary schooling are authorised by the Education Act 1964. Nursery schools and day nurseries, for children below the compulsory school age of five, may be provided or supported under the Act of 1980.[10]

Whether secondary (or other) education shall be provided on a basis of selection or by means of comprehensive schools is a policy question to be decided by each local education authority, in the light of any guidance the Secretary of State wishes to give.[11] In *Smith v Inner London Education Authority*[12] the Court of Appeal rejected a claim that to create comprehensive schools is ultra vires the Act of 1944.

4. COUNTY SCHOOLS AND VOLUNTARY SCHOOLS

Primary and secondary schools which local education authorities themselves provide and run are officially termed 'county schools', and other schools which they run or help to run but do not themselves provide are 'voluntary schools'.[13] The Education Act 1980, ss 12, 13 and 15, currently provides that a local education authority must publish any proposals to establish, significantly alter, or maintain or cease to maintain, a 'county school', or to maintain or cease to maintain a 'voluntary school'. These proposals must also be submitted to the Secretary of State; and his approval is necessary if there are objections, or he gives

8 Ss 8, 33–34.
9 Sch 7.
10 Ss 24–6.
11 See the Tameside case, discussed in ch 9, above, p 224.
12 [1978] 1 All ER 411.
13 1944 Act, s 9.

notice within two months that his approval will be required, or in any case involving a 'voluntary' school. Alterations which may be significant include any which relate to ability, age, aptitude or sex of pupils, as well as alterations to the premises. If a 'voluntary' school is to be discontinued, two years' notice of the proposal must be given.[14]

'Voluntary' schools are of three kinds: 'controlled', 'aided' and 'special agreement' schools. Local education authorities meet all expenditure in respect of 'controlled' schools. But they only meet expenditure on internal repairs, repairs of playgrounds and provisions of playing fields in respect of 'aided' schools and 'special agreement' schools, the latter being schools provided or extended by specific agreement with the Secretary of State in each case.[15] The governors of 'aided' and 'special agreement' schools are entitled to payment from the Secretary of State covering 85% of the cost of alterations and repairs.[16] He may also if he thinks fit meet 85% of the capital cost of providing, resiting or altering such schools or of providing new secondary schools for pupils coming from primary schools which are 'aided' or 'special agreement' schools.

The Act of 1944[17] and the Act of 1980,[18] provide that primary and secondary schools must have a body of 'governors' (formerly called 'managers' in primary schools), appointed either for a school or for a group of schools in accordance with an 'instrument of government' drawn up by order of the local education authority for 'county' schools and of the Secretary of State for 'voluntary' schools. For the latter there must be 'foundation' members appointed by the independent body which originally provided the school, commonly a church organisation; these are to constitute at least one-fifth of the 'governors' in 'controlled' schools, the others being appointed by the authority, and in 'aided' or 'special agreement' schools they are to outnumber the authority's appointees by three if there are more than 18 governors and by two if there are not. Both 'county' and 'voluntary' schools with more than 300 pupils must include two governors who are teachers, and the smaller schools must include one. 'County' schools, and 'voluntary' schools also if they are 'controlled', must include two governors who are parents of pupils at the school.

In addition there must be 'articles of government'. These are made by the local education authority for 'county' schools, and for 'voluntary' schools as well if they are primary schools. For 'voluntary' secondary schools they are made by the Secretary of State, who must also

14 1944 Act, s 14.
15 1944 Act, s 15.
16 Ibid, ss 102–5, as amended.
17 Ss 17–22.
18 Ss 1–5.

approve those made for 'county' secondary schools. The 'articles' de-limit the functions of the head teacher, the governors and the local authority respectively for each school.

5. TEACHING, PARENTAL CHOICE AND SCHOOL ATTENDANCE

The Act of 1944,[19] empowers the governors to control the secular education syllabus in 'aided' secondary schools; in other schools it empowers the local authority to do so. In 'county' schools there must be an agreed religious education syllabus, produced by a conference representing the various churches and educational bodies (or by a group appointed by the Secretary of State, in default). The same applies in 'controlled' schools, but particular parents can insist on religious instruction according to the religious denomination of the school. Conversely in 'aided' and 'special agreement' schools the governors must provide instruction according to the religious denomination of the school; but particular parents can insist on instruction according to the agreed syllabus (at the school if it cannot conveniently be given elsewhere). Teachers are appointed by the local authority, unless the articles of government stipulate otherwise, and can only be dismissed by the authority. But this does not apply to 'aided' schools, where the governors perform these functions and there is no contract between the teachers and the local authority, as the Court of Appeal held in *Hannam v Bradford City Council*;[20] though the local authority must have control of the number of teachers and decide whether or not they are dismissed. Teachers' salaries are nationally determined under the Act of 1944[1] and the Remuneration of Teachers Act 1965.

The Act of 1944[2] states that local education authorities must 'have regard to the general principles that, so far as is compatible with the provision of efficient instruction and training and the avoidance of unreasonable public expenditure, pupils are to be educated in accordance with the wishes of their parents'. The Act of 1980[3] restates this, in regard to applications for admission to schools, as a duty resting on the local authority and the governors, but not when this would prejudice efficient education or use of resources nor when it would be incompatible with proper admission or selection arrangements then in force. Parents are, however, given a right of appeal to a special committee under the Act of 1980.[4]

Compulsory school age being currently from five to sixteen, parents

19 Ss 24–30.
20 [1970] 2 All ER 690.
 1 S 89.
 2 S 76.
 3 S 6.
 4 S 7.

and guardians of children between these ages have a duty to ensure their regular attendance at school, under the Act of 1944,[5] as amended by the Act of 1980.[6] Where any question arises over this the authority serves a notice on the parent or guardian, who may accept a school named in that notice or apply within fourteen days for admission of the child in question to another school, which will be dealt with as any other application for admission under the principles expressed in s 6 of the Act of 1980 just referred to. Failure to ensure attendance thereafter leads to the local authority making a school attendance order; though the parent or guardian has another right at this stage to choose a school subject to the local authority's right to apply to the Secretary of State to substitute a different school if the one chosen is unsuitable or would involve them in unreasonable expenditure.

Breach of the order is a criminal offence; but it is a defence in such a case to show that efficient full-time education is in fact being obtained by the child despite non-attendance at school. Other defences to a charge of failure to ensure a child's regular attendance at school include sickness or other unavoidable causes, or religious observance, or the fact that the child's home is not within walking distance of the school and suitable transport or boarding arrangements have not been made. Disagreement with reasonable school discipline is not a defence. Only the local education authority may prosecute.[7] They may also bring the child before the juvenile court, in the manner described in this chapter,[8] as being in need of care and control, because the receipt of a proper education is relevant to a child's physical and moral welfare, as stated by the Court of Appeal in *Re DJMS (a minor)*.[9]

6. OTHER EDUCATIONAL FACILITIES, LIBRARIES AND MUSEUMS

In addition to the general duty of providing education, local education authorities must provide adequate facilities for recreational, social and physical training[10] and such transport facilities as the Secretary of State directs.[11] They may provide clothing, milk and meals under the Education (Miscellaneous Provisions) Act 1948[12] and the Act of 1980.[13] They must give guidance on careers, under the Employment and Training Act 1973,[14] and they may prohibit or restrict the employment of any

5 Ss 35–40.
6 Ss 10–11.
7 1944 Act, s 40.
8 See above, p 310.
9 [1977] 3 All ER 582.
10 1944 Act, s 53.
11 S 55. See *Rootkin v Kent CC* [1981] 2 All ER 227.
12 S 5.
13 S 22.
14 Ss 8–10.

particular child in cases where his health or education will be pre-judiced.[15] Where the Secretary of State so directs they must establish, maintain or assist any 'college of education' or other institution in the provision of facilities for training teachers.[16] School medical and dental services must be provided for local education authorities by the Secretary of State for Social Services, under the National Health Service Act 1977, s 5.

The local education authorities are, in addition, library authorities under the Public Libraries and Museums Act 1964 as amended by the Local Government Act 1972,[17] though Welsh district councils can also be so constituted. They have a duty to provide an efficient and comprehensive library service, and must lend books free of charge to people who live or work in their area or study there full-time. Other facilities may be provided, and charges for them imposed, at the authority's option and this includes hiring out library premises for meetings, concerts and exhibitions. The Secretary of State has a duty to supervise public library services and see that the local authorities perform them properly, including giving him information and submitting to inspections.

In addition, library authorities together with non-metropolitan district councils, metropolitan county councils and the GLC, and also parish and community authorities, may provide or help to provide art galleries and museums, under ss 12 and 25 of the 1964 Act as amended by the Local Government Act 1972.[18]

C. Consumer protection

1. WEIGHTS AND MEASURES

A governmental activity which goes back to the earliest times, along with law and order, and taxation, is economic regulation. In Anglo-Saxon times an ordinance of King Edgar, in the mid-tenth century (about 960) says: 'And let one money pass throughout the King's dominion; and that let no man refuse; and let one measure and one weight pass, such as is observed at Winchester . . .' In Magna Carta (1215), when the capital of England had for all practical purposes become London, there is a provision imposing a standard measure throughout the kingdom for wine, beer, and corn—'the "quarter" in

---

15 1944 Act, s 59.
16 1944 Act, s 62.
17 Ss 206–8. See also the Public Lending Right Act 1979.
18 S 208.

use in London'—and also a standard width for cloth, 'and it is to be the same for weights as it is for measures'.[19]

These laws are national in scope; but national policies have to a large extent to be administered locally, and the amount of latitude enjoyed by the official personages appointed to administer locally is the essence of local government. F. W. Maitland, in *Domesday Book and Beyond*[20] puts it this way:

> 'Taxation is the great force that makes for standard land measures. Then a King declares how many thumbs there ought to be in the cloth-ell or cloth-yard. At a later time he actually makes cloth-ells or cloth-yards and distributes them, keeping an ultimate standard in his own place. Thenceforward all other units tend to become mere fractions or multiples of this royal stick . . . In Richard I's day guardians of weights and measures are to be appointed in every county, city and borough; they are to keep iron *ulnae*. At this time or a little later these *ulnae*, ells or cloth yards were being delivered out by a royal officer to all who might require them, and that officer had the custody of the ultimate standards.

About the same time 'assizes of bread and beer' were being enforced by the courts to maintain a form of price-control over these two staples of diet. Price regulation is important because its legal enforcement percolated down through the shire and hundred courts to the boroughs and also to the 'courts leet' or manorial courts of the feudal barons, knights and squires. The 'franchises' secured by these lords in respect of criminal law enforcement, as referred to in an earlier chapter in regard to police functions,[1] gave rise to the office of constable. The enforcement of these so-called 'assizes' together with law enforcement by the constable, passed from the manor to the parish, when the manorial system of 'courts leet' decayed and was supplanted by the parish vestry and the system of local government founded thereon, subject to the administrative and judicial control of the county magistrates. Constant fines imposed in the enforcement of these laws were a prominent source of official revenue in medieval times and no doubt later. Maitland says: 'out of beer the lords made some considerable profit. It is common to find manorial jurors "presenting" as a matter of course that all the brewers, or rather ale-wives, of the village have "brewed against the assize" (ie overcharged the customers); whereupon all of them are amerced (ie fined) . . .'.[2] From Tudor times onwards the increasing

19 See *Stubbs' Select Charters* (9th edn, ed HWC Davis) pp 83, 297.
20 Pp 429–30.
 1 Ch 10.
 2 Pollock and Maitland *History of English Law* vol 1, p 582.

reliance placed on the magistrates by the central government led to a system of licensing 'ale-houses' which became important as the enforcement of the 'assizes of bread and beer' gradually declined. This licensing system for public houses was an administrative function which, by accident, was not transferred to the newly-established county councils in 1888.[3]

The inspection and enforcement of weights and measures was another of the administrative functions which devolved on magistrates. The Webbs, in *The Parish and the County*,[4] show how in the eighteenth century they exercised it, at any rate in Essex, by appointing 'Public Weighers, whose business it is go go to the several parts of the county and examine the weights of all millers and shopkeepers, and make returns of those in whose possession any light weight is found . . . and whenever complaint of this sort is made the suspected dealer is summoned to appear at the following (quarter) sessions, where . . . he is sure to be exposed and otherwise punished, in proportion to his demerits'. The Weights and Measures Act 1797 transferred this function from the magistrates in quarter sessions to their 'special' or 'petty' sessions—which means from county to district level. Some at least of the more efficient parish vestries are known to have provided themselves with standard sets of weights and measures.[5]

It will be apparent from this that the administration of weights and measures has changed little in its essentials in the last two centuries, whatever technical advances and changes in detail may have occurred. Weights and Measures authorities in local government are now, under the Local Government Act 1972,[6] county councils together with London borough councils and the City of London Corporation; although Welsh district councils may be so designated by the Secretary of State for Trade, who exercises central government supervision. The Weights and Measures Acts 1963 and 1979 contain most of the statutory provisions which give these local authorities their duties. As in times past they must provide standard weights and measures against which all those used in their areas are to be checked. They must appoint a chief inspector and other inspectors as necessary, possessing qualification certificates from the Department of Trade, which is the central government department regulating this administration. Their job is to enforce compliance with the proper standards by verifying and stamping weights and measures, the responsibility vesting in them as individual officials and not in the councils which employ them.

Use of unauthorised weights and measures is a criminal offence. Sub-

3 See ch 2.
4 P 524.
5 S and B Webb, op cit, p 58.
6 S 201.

ject to their obtaining written authority (general or specific) from a
magistrate the inspectors can enter premises to carry out their essential
duty of testing and checking. Selling food or other goods by short
weight or measure is also an offence; and liability is strict, subject to a
defence that there was a mistake or accident and all due care was taken.
Misplaced trust in employees is not a defence, as in *Hall v Farmer*,[7]
when there was a failure to count sacks of coal accurately. An offence
also occurs when importers or packers fail to ensure that goods are
packed in the right amounts. In *Bibby-Cheshire v Golden Wonder Ltd*,[8]
there was a mechanical failure of packing machinery which could not
have been anticipated: a defence of due diligence succeeded. These prosecutions may be brought only by a weights and measures authority or
chief of police.

2.   TRADING STANDARDS

The departments of the above mentioned local authorities administering these weights and measures functions today usually have 'consumer
protection' or 'trading standards' in their titles. In co-operation with
the Director-General of Fair Trading at the national level they give
advice to consumers and the public generally; and with him they are
empowered to enforce controls imposed by the Consumer Credit Act
1974. These include the licensing by the Director-General of hire or
credit businesses. He will be expected to prosecute for offences under
that Act in cases other than those of purely local significance in which
the local authorities should prosecute (notifying him in advance,
though failure does not make such a prosecution invalid). As with the
offences already mentioned, it will normally be necessary to show that
all reasonable diligence was exercised in order to establish a defence.
The various offences stem from infringements of the rules imposed as a
check on the operations of the various hire or credit businesses in the
interests of upholding fair and desirable practices in their mode of
operation.

In addition there is a system of controls, imposed by the Trade Descriptions Acts 1968 and 1972 and enforceable by the local authorities,
to prohibit the use of false trade descriptions of goods, false indications
of their price, and other related false statements. Once again, liability is
strict in much the same way as the offences described above.
Enforcement procedures of a comparable kind are also conferred on the
local authorities by the Consumer Safety Act 1978, the Hallmarking
Act 1973 and the Fair Trading Act 1973.

---

7 [1970] 1 All ER 729, [1970] 1 WLR 366.
8 [1972] 3 All ER 738, [1972] 1 WLR 1487.

3. FOOD AND DRUGS

The same local authorities—county councils, together with London borough councils and the City of London Corporation—also administer the system for controlling food and drugs, as provided in the Local Government Act 1972.[9] The legislation in this field began in the nineteenth century, but its origins lie further in the past. Among the paid parish servants referred to earlier,[10] as distinct from the unpaid parish officers to whom they were subordinate, there was in many parishes an 'ale-conner' and also a 'flesh-taster' (sometimes referred to alternatively as a 'carnival', which presents that word to us in an unexpected light) who seem to be of medieval origin and to have been appointed by the manorial 'courts leet'. These public-spirited people tasted food and drink in their village to see if it was wholesome, and no doubt some of them survived. Their latter-day successors are public analysts, who benefit from a scientific training which they presumably lacked.

The principal statute today is the Food and Drugs Act 1955, s 89 of which places a duty on all local food and drugs authorities to appoint a public analyst. Appointees must be qualified in accordance with the requirements of the Minister of Agriculture, Fisheries and Food, whose department is the central government authority exercising supervision over this branch of local administration. The minister has default powers which enable him to send one of his officers to see to the proper enforcement of duties not being duly performed by one of the local authorities, at the cost of that authority, if he makes an order to that effect.[11] There is also a Food Hygiene Advisory Council representing the authorities, the public and the food industry, which is appointed by the minister in collaboration with the Secretaries of State involved in this area for the purpose of advice and consultation.

The task of local food and drugs authorities is to make investigations and enforce a proper control to prevent the marketing of unwholesome food or of inferior or adulterated food or drugs or the use of misleading statements relating to food or drug sales. These undesirable practices are criminal offences for which the local authorities in question should prosecute; though the power to do so is not restricted to them since it was held in *Snodgrass v Topping*,[12] that any person may bring proceedings. The local authorities concerned are to appoint 'authorised officers' duly qualified to carry out the necessary functions; their powers include entry on to premises, forcibly if a magistrate so authorises.[13]

They may take samples for the public analyst, and private purchasers

9 S 198.
10 See p 302. And see S and B Webb, op cit, pp 34, 224.
11 1955 Act, s 127.
12 (1952) 116 JP 332.
13 1955 Act, ss 86, 100. And see the Food and Drugs (Amendment) Act 1982.

may submit samples for analysis on payment of a fee. One-third of any sample is to be given to the seller, one-third is to be submitted to analysis, and one-third is to be kept in reserve for production in court if necessary so that the court may where appropriate order it to be sent for further analysis by the Government Chemist. The evidence in a public analyst's certificate can only be challenged by requiring his attendance in court.[14] 'Food' includes drink.[15]

Prosecutions for false or misleading labels, descriptions and advertisements relating to food or drugs for sale are obviously akin to prosecutions for false trade descriptions. As in those cases, all reasonable diligence must be shown in order to establish a defence, in addition of course to lack of knowledge.[16] The other offences relate to the condition of the items which are for sale. Adulteration of food or drugs for sale which renders them injurious to health is an offence, as is the advertising or offering for sale of adulterated food or drugs; and the cumulative as well as the direct effect of consumption will be considered.[17]

Three other related offences[18] consist of selling food or drugs to the prejudice of the buyer, by causing him to get something 'inferior to that which he demands and pays for', as it was put by Mellor J., in *Hoyle v Hitchman*[19], in respect of (i) its nature, or (ii) its substance, or (iii) its quality. If by chance he has independent information of the true character of what he has bought this is no defence: *Pearks, Gunston and Tee v Ward*.[20] Nor is it a defence that all reasonable care was taken to exclude extraneous matter as the House of Lords held in *Smedleys v Breed*;[1] though if such matter is present unavoidably that is a defence.[2] A further offence consists of offering or sending for sale food 'unfit for human consumption';[3] though a sender will have a defence if he gave due notification or has used all reasonable diligence. To be 'unfit' the food must be rotten or otherwise unwholesome. An extraneous substance will only have this effect if it is insanitary or unwholesome on its own account as was a used bandage found in a loaf in *Chibnalls Bakeries v Cope Brown*.[4] A local authority's 'authorised officer' may examine and seize food that he suspects is 'unfit', and if he does he must apply for it to be

---

14 1955 Act, ss 91–3, 110–2.
15 S 135.
16 1955 Act, ss 6–7.
17 1955 Act, s 1, as amended by the Medicines Act 1968.
18 Under s 2 of the 1955 Act.
19 (1879) 4 QBD 233 at 237.
20 [1902] 2 KB 1.
 1 [1974] 2 All ER 21.
 2 1955 Act, s 3.
 3 Ibid, s 8.
 4 [1956] Crim LR 263.

condemned by a magistrate.[5] The magistrate must deal with the application with fairness to both sides even though there is no appeal on the merits: *R v Birmingham City Justice, ex p Chris Foreign Foods (Wholesalers)*.[6] Food may also be dealt with as 'unfit' if it is suspected of causing food poisoning; though, if suspicion is unfounded compensation may be payable.[7]

4. FOOD HYGIENE

An important aspect of this branch of administration is food hygiene. The Act of 1955,[8] empowers the Minister of Agriculture jointly with the Secretary of State for Social Services to make regulations for observance of proper hygiene in selling food for human consumption and in activities related to this, namely importing, preparing, transporting, storing, packing, wrapping, displaying, serving and delivering such food and generally safeguarding public health. Under this provision the Food Hygiene (General) Regulations 1970[9] are currently in force, imposing detailed control on persons and premises involved in these activities. Infringement is a criminal offence if, but only if, public health is endangered thereby. Thus in *Macfisheries v Coventry Corp*,[10] food was exposed for sale in a shop in a way which created a risk that it would be contaminated by people in the shop. But it was held that this did not constitute an offence, in the absence of suitable evidence that this was injurious to health.

Prosecutions of this kind are made the responsibility of district councils by the Local Government Act 1972.[11] Where there is a conviction because of the state of the premises, a caterer can be disqualified from continuing to use them for catering.[12] The local authority may also apply to a court for a closure order to prohibit further use of the premises in connection with any food business until the defective conditions there are certified as having been put right, under the Food and Drugs (Control of Food Premises) Act 1976. Such an order can only be made if there is a danger to public health. If there is an urgent danger the order can be applied for without any prior conviction, subject to payment of compensation if a court subsequently finds that the emergency order was unjustified and has caused loss.

There are also the Milk and Dairies Regulations 1959,[13] under which

5 1955 Act, s 9.
6 [1970] 3 All ER 945, [1970] 1 WLR 1428.
7 1955 Act, ss 26–7.
8 S 13.
9 SI 1970/1172.
10 [1957] 3 All ER 299, [1957] 1 WLR 1066.
11 S 199(5).
12 1955 Act, s 14.
13 SI 1959/277, as later amended on various occasions.

the minister has a duty to maintain a register of dairy farms and district councils have a duty to maintain a register of other dairy premises which distribute dairy produce; and there are detailed regulations as to the condition of the premises and how they are run. Sale of unwholesome or adulterated milk is a criminal offence; and liability may be incurred through an employee or sub-contractor, as held in *Quality Dairies (York) v Pedley*.[14] The Act of 1955,[15] and the European Communities Act 1972 under which EEC rules are enforceable, authorise these and other sets of regulations concerning milk and dairy products. The Act of 1955,[16] also imposes on district councils a duty to maintain a register of premises used for making, storing or selling ice-cream, or for making or preparing preserved foods and sausages; persons whose businesses are affected are entitled to a hearing before the authority, with an appeal to the magistrates.

5. SLAUGHTERHOUSES AND DISEASES OF ANIMALS

Another related system of control, entrusted in accordance with the Local Government Act 1972,[17] to district and London borough councils and the City of London Corporation, consists of the licensing of the slaughterhouses and knackers' yards. Use of premises in this way is unlawful without a licence, but the grant of one must only be withheld if there will not be sufficient compliance with regulations or byelaws made under the Slaughterhouses Act 1974. Refusal of a licence must be accompanied by reasons, and an appeal lies to the magistrates. The local authorities are also required to license slaughterhouse operators and enforce proper methods of slaughtering, by entry on to the premises if necessary. They are empowered to provide their own public slaughterhouses, cold stores and refrigerators.

Local authority functions under the Diseases of Animals Act 1950 are entrusted to county councils, though the authorities in Greater London are the London borough councils and the City of London Corporation. But the latter body administers the whole of Greater London as far as imported animals are concerned, and the Minister of Agriculture may make special arrangements as regards imported animals at seaports and airports. There are general powers to provide wharves, sheds and other premises, by compulsory purchase if necessary, for accommodating animals dead or alive.

The public duties performed under these provisions have a longer history than might be supposed. The Webbs, in *The Parish and the*

14 [1952] 1 KB 275, [1952] 1 All ER 380.
15 Ss 28–46.
16 Ss 16–20.
17 S 199(5).

County[18] mention the appointment, by the Essex magistrates in quarter sessions, of inspectors 'who in 1749–50 vainly sought to ward off "the infection now raging among the horned cattle"'. Under the Act of 1950 the minister prescribes regulations to deal with animal diseases, and the local authorities' task is to enforce them, appointing inspectors and other staff as necessary for the purpose.

6. SHOPS

The district councils together with London borough councils and the City of London Corporation are also the local authorities required to enforce the provisions of the Shops Acts 1950 to 1965, this time under central government supervision exercised by the Home Secretary. The essence of control is that shop workers must have the prescribed meal breaks and weekly days and half-days free from work, and that shop closing must be observed at prescribed times including early closing days and Sundays, as laid down in the Acts.

There are various special categories, exemptions and alternative arrangements. One which deserves special mention is that Jewish traders' shops may open on Sunday and close on Saturdays, and thus avoid double closing on both the Jewish and the Christian sabbath. They must make a statutory declaration that they require this on religious grounds and apply to be registered with the authority, under s 53 of the Shops Act 1950. There is a general rule that a temporary stall in a market or street or other open place is not regarded as a 'shop', but if there is sufficient continuity of trading it may well be a 'place' which is treated under the legislation for many purposes as if it were a shop. For various purposes of control the Shops Act 1950 extends the meaning of 'shop' to 'place'; and in particular s 58 does so for the purposes of Jewish trading as regulated by s 53. In *Thanet District Council v Ninedrive*[19] Walton J in the Chancery Division of the High Court said: 'Section 53 was intended to relieve people of the Jewish faith from the double closing, not to give them a loophole through which they could allow others to escape from even a single day's closure'. He granted an injunction to prevent the defendant firm, which had Jewish directors, from getting the best of both worlds when attempting to use a piece of open land at Manston in Kent for a retail market on Sundays. He rejected their claim that they were entitled to the benefit of special arrangements for Jewish traders when in fact most of the actual Sunday traders with stalls on that land were Gentiles.

---

18 P 524.
19 [1978] 1 All ER 703. But see *Wolverhampton Borough Council v B & Q (Retail)*, (1983 Times, 19 January.

D. Trading undertakings

I. MARKETS

Trading at stalls in street markets or on other open land may in this way
be controlled under the legislation dealing with shops. But the markets
themselves are to be viewed in a different light: they are revenue-
producing property assets. The essence of a market is not an open site,
because it may be conducted permanently in a building such as a
market-hall or intermittently in a street or field, but the 'franchise' or
right to hold it. In medieval times this was a matter of lucrative local
monopoly. A franchise-holder made payments to the King or some
other great lord in return for being allowed to prevent persons trading
in a given locality elsewhere than in his market; he in turn recouped
himself at a profit out of the dues which the traders in the market were
compelled to pay him as rent. A 'market' was thus a revenue-producing
arrangement nurtured monopolistically by restrictive legal protection,
in essence rather like a patent in modern law.

But a market today is either a private trading arrangement on suitable premises governed by the Shops Acts, by planning legislation, and
by various other statutory controls; or else it is a similar arrangement
conducted by a public body which has statutory authority to do so.
Absence of such authority would of course render the operation ultra
vires. Such authority has been secured by many councils and other
bodies under private Acts; but public statutory authorisation in general
terms to hold markets is conferred on district and London borough
councils by the Food and Drugs Act 1955.[20] The Secretary of State for
the Environment excercises central government control in respect of
market tolls and charges generally, enforceable by distraining on livestock as well as by actions for debt. The monopoly effect of a medieval
'franchise' can be achieved additionally, to some extent, by excluding
sales in adjoining streets.

2. PUBLIC TRANSPORT

Various other trading undertakings are conducted by local authorities
under public or private Acts. A prominent example is transport. Many
local councils are empowered by private Acts to run bus services. The
Secretary of State for the Environment may, under Part II of the Transport Act 1968, designate 'passenger transport areas', each with a 'passenger transport authority' and a 'passenger transport executive'. The
aim is to ensure an efficient and integrated system of public transport
in each area. The Secretary of State and local authorities in the area

---

20 Ss 49–61. See also the Markets and Fairs Clauses Act 1847, and the Local Government (Miscellaneous Provisions) Act 1982, s 3 and Sch 4 (control of street trading).

appoint the members of the 'authority' which in turn appoints the members of the 'executive' which manages the transport undertaking.

All the metropolitan counties are, by virtue of the Local Government Act 1972,[1] passenger transport areas. London Transport is the 'executive' for the London area, subject to the GLC as the 'authority', by virtue of the Transport (London) Act 1969. As for non-metropolitan counties, the Transport Act 1978 requires their councils to prepare plans to co-ordinate passenger transport undertakings in consultation with district councils and the operators of existing undertakings; and the county and district councils are empowered to pay grants to the operators. Authorities have a fiduciary duty to manage their finances responsibly and fairly, in regard to the fares they charge, and otherwise, as discussed in chapter 3.[2]

3. BATHS, CEMETERIES AND OTHER FACILITIES

Finally certain permissive powers may be briefly noted. The Public Health Act 1936, s 221, and the Local Government Act 1972, Sch 14, para 18 empower district and London borough councils and the City of London Corporation, and also parish and community councils, to provide public baths and wash-houses and also swimming baths. The Local Government (Miscellaneous Powers) Act 1976, ss 11–12, empowers local authorities generally to produce their own heat or electricity, though not to sell it without the Secretary of State's permission. The same Act, s 19, confers on them a wide power of providing various kinds of indoor and outdoor recreational facilities.

The Cremation Acts 1902–52 and the 1972 Act, s 214, and Sch 26, empower the same authorities to provide cemeteries and crematoria. The Secretary of State for the Environment exercises general central government supervision, and has made the Local Authorities Cemeteries Order 1977[3] which provides a 'code of management' for cemeteries. The Public Health Act 1936, s 198 empowers the same authorities to provide mortuaries and premises for conducting post-mortem examinations (and the Secretary of State may direct them to do so); but the National Assistance Act 1948, s 50, *requires* district councils to see to the burial of bodies in their area whenever no other arrangements can be made—the modern equivalent of what they used to call, in the olden days of parish government, a pauper's grave.

---

1 S 202.
2 See p 72, and the cases discussed there. See also *R v Merseyside County Council, ex p Great Universal Stores* (1982) Times, 18 February, a case under the Transport Act 1968 in which Woolf J refused to quosh a decision to issue an additional precept for rates to cover the cost of reducing fares on local public transport.
3 SI 1977/204.

Appendix

Counties in England and Wales

This map shows the pattern of administrative counties of England and Wales after the Local Government Act 1972, including the six Metropolitan Counties and Greater London. District boundaries cannot be

331

reproduced here, but published maps showing these are readily obtainable. Below is a list of the counties and the districts which fall within them.

ENGLAND Counties and Districts

AVON
1 Northavon
2 Bristol
3 Kingswood
4 Woodspring
5 Wansdyke
6 Bath

BEDFORDSHIRE
1 North Bedfordshire
2 Mid Bedfordshire
3 South Bedfordshire
4 Luton

BERKSHIRE
1 Newbury
2 Reading
3 Wokingham
4 Bracknell
5 Windsor & Maidenhead
6 Slough

BUCKINGHAMSHIRE
1 Milton Keynes
2 Aylesbury Vale
3 Wycombe
4 Chiltern
5 South Buckinghamshire

CAMBRIDGESHIRE
1 Peterborough
2 Fenland
3 Huntingdon
4 East Cambridgeshire
5 South Cambridgeshire
6 Cambridge

CHESHIRE
1 Warrington
2 Halton
3 Ellesmere Port & Neston
4 Vale Royal
5 Macclesfield
6 Chester
7 Crewe & Nantwich
8 Congleton

CLEVELAND
1 Hartlepool
2 Stockton-on-Tees
3 Middlesbrough
4 Langbaurgh

CORNWALL
1 North Cornwall
2 Caradon
3 Restormel
4 Carrick
5 Kerrier
6 Penwith

CUMBRIA
1 Carlisle
2 Allerdale
3 Eden
4 Copeland
5 South Lakeland
6 Barrow-in-Furness

DERBYSHIRE
1 High Peak
2 West Derbyshire
3 North East Derbyshire
4 Chesterfield
5 Bolsover
6 Amber Valley
7 Erewash
8 Derby
9 South Derbyshire

DEVON
1 North Devon
2 Torridge
3 Mid Devon
4 East Devon
5 Exeter
6 Teignbridge
7 West Devon
8 Plymouth
9 South Hams
10 Torbay

DORSET
1 North Dorset
2 Wimborne
3 Christchurch
4 Bournemouth
5 Poole
6 Purbeck
7 West Dorset
8 Weymouth & Portland

DURHAM
1 Chester-le-Street
2 Derwentside
3 Durham
4 Easington
5 Sedgefield
6 Wear Valley

DURHAM—*contd*
7 Teesdale
8 Darlington

ESSEX
1 Uttlesford
2 Braintree
3 Colchester
4 Tendring
5 Maldon
6 Chelmsford
7 Epping Forest
8 Harlow
9 Brentwood
10 Basildon
11 Rochford
12 Southend-on-Sea
13 Castle Point
14 Thurrock

GLOUCESTERSHIRE
1 Forest of Dean
2 Gloucester
3 Tewkesbury
4 Cheltenham
5 Cotswold
6 Stroud

HAMPSHIRE
1 Basingstoke & Deane
2 Hart
3 Rushmoor
4 Test Valley
5 Winchester
6 East Hampshire
7 New Forest
8 Southampton
9 Eastleigh
10 Fareham
11 Gosport
12 Portsmouth
13 Havant

HEREFORD & WORCESTER
1 Wyre Forest
2 Bromsgrove
3 Redditch
4 Wychavon
5 Worcester
6 Malvern Hills
7 Leominster
8 Hereford
9 South Herefordshire

HERTFORDSHIRE
1 North Hertfordshire
2 Stevenage
3 East Hertfordshire
4 Broxbourne
5 Welwyn Hatfield
6 St. Albans
7 Dacorum
8 Three Rivers
9 Watford
10 Hertsmere

HUMBERSIDE
1 East Yorkshire
2 Holderness
3 Kingston upon Hull
4 Beverley
5 Boothferry
6 Scunthorpe
7 Glanford
8 Great Grimsby
9 Cleethorpes

ISLE OF MAN

ISLE OF WIGHT
1 Medina
2 South Wight

ISLES OF SCILLY

KENT
1 Dartford
2 Gravesham
3 Rochester upon Medway
4 Gillingham
5 Swale
6 Canterbury
7 Thanet
8 Dover
9 Shepway
10 Ashford
11 Maidstone
12 Tonbridge & Malling
13 Sevenoaks
14 Tunbridge Wells

LANCASHIRE
1 Lancaster
2 Wyre
3 Blackpool
4 Fylde
5 Preston
6 Ribble Valley
7 Pendle
8 Burnley
9 Rossendale
10 Hyndburn
11 Blackburn
12 Chorley
13 South Ribble
14 West Lancashire

LEICESTERSHIRE
1 North West Leicestershire
2 Charnwood
3 Melton
4 Rutland
5 Harborough
6 Oadby & Wigston
7 Leicester
8 Blaby
9 Hinckley & Bosworth

LINCOLNSHIRE
1 West Lindsey
2 Lincoln
3 East Lindsey
4 North Kesteven
5 Boston
6 South Kesteven
7 South Holland

MANCHESTER GREATER
(Metropolitan County)
1 Wigan
2 Bolton
3 Bury
4 Rochdale
5 Oldham
6 Tameside
7 Stockport
8 Manchester
9 Salford
10 Trafford

MERSEYSIDE
(Metropolitan County)
1 Wirral
2 Sefton
3 Liverpool
4 Knowsley
5 St. Helens

MIDLANDS, WEST
(Metropolitan County)
1 Walsall
2 Wolverhampton
3 Dudley
4 Sandwell
5 Birmingham
6 Solihull
7 Coventry

NORFOLK
1 King's Lynn & West
    Norfolk
2 North Norfolk
3 Great Yarmouth
4 Broadland
5 Norwich
6 South Norfolk
7 Breckland

NORTHAMPTONSHIRE
1 East Northamptonshire
2 Corby

NORTHAMPTONSHIRE—*contd*
3 Kettering
4 Daventry
5 Wellingborough
6 Northampton
7 South Northamptonshire

NORTHUMBERLAND
1 Berwick-upon-Tweed
2 Alnwick
3 Castle Morpeth
4 Wansbeck
5 Blyth Valley
6 Tynedale

NOTTINGHAMSHIRE
1 Bassetlaw
2 Mansfield
3 Newark
4 Ashfield
5 Gedling
6 Broxtowe
7 Nottingham
8 Rushcliffe

OXFORDSHIRE
1 Cherwell
2 West Oxfordshire
3 Oxford
4 Vale of White Horse
5 South Oxfordshire

SHROPSHIRE
1 Oswestry
2 North Shropshire
3 Shrewsbury & Atcham
4 The Wrekin
5 South Shropshire
6 Bridgnorth

SOMERSET
1 West Somerset
2 Taunton Deane
3 Sedgemoor
4 Mendip
5 Yeovil

STAFFORDSHIRE
1 Newcastle-under-Lyme
2 Stoke-on-Trent
3 Staffordshire Moorlands
4 Stafford
5 East Staffordshire
6 South Staffordshire
7 Cannock Chase
8 Lichfield
9 Tamworth

SUFFOLK
1 Forest Heath
2 St. Edmundsbury
3 Mid Suffolk
4 Waveney
5 Suffolk Coastal

ENGLAND COUNTIES AND DISTRICTS—*contd*

SUFFOLK—*contd*
6 Ipswich
7 Babergh

SURREY
1 Spelthorne
2 Runnymede
3 Surrey Heath
4 Woking
5 Elmbridge
6 Epsom & Ewell
7 Reigate & Banstead
8 Tandridge
9 Mole Valley
10 Guildford
11 Waverley

SUSSEX, EAST
1 Hove
2 Brighton
3 Lewes
4 Wealden
5 Eastbourne
6 Rother
7 Hastings

SUSSEX, WEST
1 Chichester
2 Horsham
3 Crawley

SUSSEX, WEST—*contd*
4 Mid Sussex
5 Adur
6 Worthing
7 Arun

TYNE & WEAR
(Metropolitan County)
1 Newcastle upon Tyne
2 North Tyneside
3 South Tyneside
4 Gateshead
5 Sunderland

WARWICKSHIRE
1 North Warwickshire
2 Nuneaton & Bedworth
3 Rugby
4 Warwick
5 Stratford-on-Avon

WILTSHIRE
1 Thamesdown
2 North Wiltshire
3 Kennet

WILTSHIRE—*contd*
4 West Wiltshire
5 Salisbury

YORKSHIRE, NORTH
1 Scarborough
2 Ryedale
3 Hambleton
4 Richmondshire
5 Craven
6 Harrogate
7 York
8 Selby

YORKSHIRE, SOUTH
(Metropolitan County)
1 Barnsley
2 Doncaster
3 Rotherham
4 Sheffield

YORKSHIRE, WEST
(Metropolitan County)
1 Calderdale
2 Bradford
3 Leeds
4 Wakefield
5 Kirklees

WALES Counties and Districts

CLWYD
1 Colwyn
2 Rhuddlan
3 Delyn
4 Alyn & Deeside
5 Wrexham-Maelor
6 Glyndwr

DYFED
1 Ceredigion
2 Preseli
3 South Pembrokeshire
4 Carmarthen
5 Llanelli
6 Dinefwr

GLAMORGAN, MID
1 Ogwr
2 Rhondda
3 Cynon Valley
4 Merthyr Tydfil
5 Rhymney Valley
6 Taff-Ely

GLAMORGAN, SOUTH
1 Vale of Glamorgan
2 Cardiff

GLAMORGAN, WEST
1 Swansea
2 Lliw Valley
3 Neath
4 Afan

GWENT
1 Blaenau Gwent
2 Islwyn
3 Torfaen
4 Monmouth
5 Newport

GWYNEDD
1 Ynys Môn- Isle of Anglesey
2 Arfon
3 Dwyfor
4 Aberconwy
5 Meirionnydd

POWYS
1 Montgomery
2 Radnor
3 Brecknock

GREATER LONDON BOROUGHS († denotes outer London boroughs)

1 City of London
2 Barking & Dagenham†
3 Barnet†
4 Bexley†
5 Brent†
6 Bromley†
7 Camden
8 Croydon†
9 Ealing†
10 Enfield†
11 Greenwich
12 Hackney

GREATER LONDON BOROUGHS († denotes outer London boroughs) —*contd*

13 Hammersmith & Fulham
14 Haringey†
15 Harrow†
16 Havering†
17 Hillingdon†
18 Hounslow†
19 Islington

20 Kensington & Chelsea
21 Kingston-upon-Thames†
22 Lambeth
23 Lewisham
24 Merton†
25 Newham†
26 Redbridge†

27 Richmond-upon-Thames†
28 Southwark
29 Sutton†
30 Tower Hamlets
31 Waltham Forest†
32 Wandsworth
33 Westminster (City)

Index